Women and the Media

The media have played a significant role in the contested and changing social position of women in Britain since the 1900s. They have facilitated feminism by both providing discourses and images from which women can construct their identities, and offering spaces where hegemonic ideas of femininity can be reworked. This volume is intended to provide an overview of work on Broadcasting, Film and Print Media from 1900, while appealing to scholars of History and Media, Film and Cultural Studies.

This edited collection features tightly focused and historically contextualised case studies which showcase current research on women and media in Britain since the 1900s. The case studies explore media directed at a particularly female audience such as *Woman's Hour*, and magazines such as *Vogue*, *Woman* and *Marie Claire*. Women who work in the media, issues of production, and regulation are discussed alongside the representation of women across a broad range of media from early 20th-century motorcycling magazines, Page 3 and regional television news.

Maggie Andrews is Professor of Cultural History at the University of Worcester.

Sallie McNamara is a Senior Lecturer in Cultural Theory at Southampton Solent University.

Routledge Research in Gender and History

Women and the Media

Feminism and Femininity in
Britain, 1900 to the Present

Edited by

Maggie Andrews and Sallie McNamara

Routledge
Taylor & Francis Group

NEW YORK   LONDON

First published 2014
by Routledge
711 Third Avenue, New York, NY 10017

and by Routledge
2 Park Square, Milton Park, Abingdon, Oxon OX14 4RN

*Routledge is an imprint of the Taylor & Francis Group,
an informa business*

Library of Congress Cataloging-in-Publication Data
 Women and the media : feminism and femininity in Britain, 1900 to the
present / edited by Maggie Andrews and Sallie McNamara.
    pages cm. — (Routledge research in gender and history ; 18)
Includes bibliographical references and index.
 1. Feminism and mass media—Great Britain—History. 2. Women in
mass media—History. 3. Women—Great Britain—History.
 4. Feminism—Great Britain—History. I. Andrews, Maggie.
 II. McNamara, Sallie.
 P96.F462G796 2014
 302.23082—dc23
 2013042203

ISBN13: 978-0-415-66036-5 (hbk)
ISBN13: 978-0-203-07412-1 (ebk)

Typeset in Sabon
by IBT Global.

SUSTAINABLE FORESTRY INITIATIVE
Certified Sourcing
www.sfiprogram.org
SFI-01234
SFI label applies to the text stock

Printed and bound in the United States of America
by IBT Global.

Contents

Figures

Acknowledgments

The editors would like to acknowledge the role played by the Women's History Network which has, since it was formed in 1991, encouraged the study of Women's History in Britain. A number of the chapters in this collection were initially presented at Women's History Network Conferences, either the national conference or Midlands Regional Conferences, which have been held in recent years at the University of Staffordshire, The National Memorial Arboretum or the University of Worcester. The Women's History Network aims to promote women's history and encourage anyone with a passion for women's history, be they working historians, researchers, independent scholars, teachers, librarians or other individuals both within academia and beyond. The Midlands Regional Conferences in particular have provided a supportive environment which has encouraged many of the contributors when first presenting their research.

The completion of this book has been eased by the co-operation and support of the academic institutions at which we both work. For example: Southampton Solent University provided funding to facilitate Sallie McNamara's research on Lady Eleanor Smith. The Institute of Humanities and Creative Arts at University of Worcester has facilitated dialogue across disciplines, as this volume demonstrates. The University kindly hosted a symposium on Women and Media in April 2012 which brought together many of the contributors to this volume to exchange ideas about their research.

A number of archives and helpful archivists have assisted many of those who have written chapters in this volume when undertaking their research; special thanks go to the BBC Written Archives at Caversham, the British Film Institute and the Media Archive for Central England.

Sallie McNamara would also like to thank Lady Juliet Townsend for her continued help and support, including access to family archives that aided research into the life and work of her aunt, Lady Eleanor Smith.

Finally the biggest thanks have to go to Neil and Ron whose lives have at times been somewhat inconvenienced by the writing of this book but who have shared our enthusiasm for it and supported us through the project. This book is dedicated to them and to our many students, past, present and future, who shared our interest in either women's or media history, and sometimes both.

Introduction

Maggie Andrews and Sallie McNamara

This volume seeks to encourage interdisciplinary work across the boundaries of History and Media, Film and Cultural Studies. Its aim is to encourage those studying Women's History to pay greater attention to considering the role media has played in the contested and changing social position of women in Britain since the Edwardian era. There is a range of academic work on women and contemporary media (Byerly 2005; Thornham 2007; Bell and Williams 2009; Waters 2011) to which we hope to provide a greater awareness of the historical precedents of media and film texts and their production and consumption practices. The volume does not seek to write a history of the British media, as these already exist (see, for example, Williams 2009), but rather to encourage study of the media to become an integral part of the study of women in the twentieth century. In so doing it builds upon the greater interest in Cultural History within Women's History in the last 20 years (see, for example: Noakes 1997; Langhamer 2000; Andrews and Talbot 2000; Rappaport, 2001; Oram 2007). Similarly, we want to acknowledge the historical work that has been done analysing particular media genres, and how they may reflect, shape and articulate culturally constructed gender discourses. For example, Margaret Beetham's research on women's magazines in the long nineteenth century (1996) used magazines to explore shifting notions of class, education and employment in the period. Alternatively, Sue Harper's analysis of women in British cinema (2000) explored not only the representation of women in cinema since the 1930s, but also the influences of those working in the film industry on these representations and discussed the agency of women who were employed in film production. Building upon such foundations this volume brings together a range of work which works across the disciplines of Women's History and Media Studies.

This volume seeks to embrace, with varying degrees of success, the very real problems that interdisciplinary work involves; that is, dealing with twin axes of uncertainty. When the contested terrain of historical analysis meets the multiple readings that media and film texts offer, a complex process of analysis is required. There is a tendency when historians utilise media as a source for research for them to ignore the innate polysemia of popular texts, the multiple layers and contradictory meanings that a magazine article, newspaper front page or film present; instead, they may misinterpret 'a' reading of the text for 'the' reading of the text's meaning. Similarly, those with a background in Media, Film and Cultural Studies may slip into an assumption that there is one history of an era, that it is possible to gain a tangible understanding of, for example, the Second World War, which can contextualise a particular media text, production process or audience engagement. Interdisciplinary work requires scholars to engage with both the multiple histories of an era, to acknowledge that history involves competing explanations of fragments of evidence, and that 'a' history is rarely everybody's history.

The twentieth century witnessed a wide range of changes to the political, economic, social and cultural lives of women in Britain (see, for example, Alexander 1994; Bruley 1999; Zweiniger-Bargielowska 2001; Rowbotham 2012). Many facets of the everyday life of women in the twenty-first century would have seemed unattainable dreams to most of our great-grand-mothers: state funded nursery places, opportunities to attend universities, National Health Service-funded abortions, automatic washing machines or sexual discrimination legislation, for example. There is much historical debate over what is responsible for such changes, their relative importance and even how widespread women's access to them is. For example, it is open to debate how significant the political enfranchisement of women has been (Thane 2010) compared to changes in employment or educational opportunities. Some historians suggest the introduction of birth control in the post-war world has resulted in sexual liberation (Cook 2005), while some of us are less convinced. More recently, some women have begun to question whether greater involvement in paid work outside the home, albeit frequently on far from equal terms with men, whilst offering greater economic independence, has perhaps increased the challenges and pressures in the everyday lives of women. Interdisciplinary research needs to utilise new source material and different theoretical and analytical frameworks to engage with these debates.

If there has been change in twentieth century women's lives, there has also been a high degree of continuity; women retain many of their domestic and caring responsibilities, and on average they earn less than men, own less property, and hold fewer positions of power. Those changes which have occurred in the lives of women have been fragmented, inconsistent, and sometimes temporary in nature. Arguably, women's experiences in the twentieth and early twenty-first century have been framed by shifting and competing discourses of both feminisms and femininities; discourses which are marked by both changes and continuities. Discursive constructions of femininity have been constantly contested, reworked, dislodged, stretched and re-interpreted; this contestation and reworking of discursive formations has to a significant degree taken place within popular culture (Hall 1981). Analysis of the production, consumption and textual construction of media and film texts has the potential to shed light on the twin pulls of change and continuity.

The greater involvement of women in the public sphere in the twentieth century perhaps precipitated an increase in media texts which were produced by women, featured representations of women or were aimed at a female audience. The media became in the twentieth century a significant area of women's leisure, its consumption offering spaces and places in which women could gain education and information, grab a little time for themselves, interact with others and feel part of a community. Furthermore, media texts have provided the lexicon of images and ideas from which women construct their sense of themselves, who they are, and their identity, offering spaces where hegemonic ideas of femininity are reworked and feminism is facilitated. Those campaigning for changes in the social, economic and political position of women in society have always found spaces and places in which to articulate their views in the media; the Edwardian Suffragettes were exceptionally media-savvy. Their campaigns, marches, protests and militant activities were always designed to gain maximum coverage in the daily newspapers. When Emily Wilding Davies stepped out onto the racecourse during the Epsom Derby on June 4, 1913, she did so at Tattenham corner in full view of the plethora of press and film cameras. She created a media event as her carefully managed funeral did 10 days later (Andrews 2011). The suffragettes took advantage of the widespread mass newspaper readership established at the turn of the century by the introduction of mass-circulation dailies for the working class—*The People* (1881), *Daily Mail* (1896), *Daily Express* (1900) and *Daily Mirror* (1903). The media has played a significant role in the contested and changing social position of women in Britain since the Edwardian era and yet has arguably tended to be side-lined within many areas of Women's History, despite Maria DiCenzo and Lucy Delap's interesting study of the suffrage periodicals (2010).

Where Historians have used media texts as source material, their emphasis has been on broadsheet newspapers. The longevity of *The Times* (first published in 1785 as *The Daily Universal Register*) and the speed with which its archives were first placed on microfiche and then digitised has perhaps led to an over-reliance by historians on a newspaper which spoke on behalf of and to only a small percentage of the population. For the historian of women, magazines and popular newspapers may be of greater interest; it is perhaps these 'mental chocolate boxes' (Winship 1987) which gave an insight into the anxieties and dreams which shape women's consciousness. Margaret Beetham's work on women's magazines draws attention to the ways magazines at the *fin de siècle* located the new femininity of consumption within the dominant ideology of the domestic (Beetham 1996). The popularity of the address to middle-class women readers is attested to as the first edition of the new monthly, *Woman at Home* (1893–1920), sold 100,000 copies; the publishers had anticipated 30,000 would make it viable (Beetham 1996, 158–159).

Twentieth century historians have the benefit of a plethora of visual and aural sources to complement print media unavailable to those who studied earlier periods. Since the Lumière brothers first exhibited at the Polytechnic Hall in London's Regent Street in 1896, a wide range of film texts have been produced and preserved and enabled work such as that of Christine Gledhill to illuminate the portrayal of the changing role of women in early twentieth century film (2003). The emergence of radio broadcasting in the 1920s and television in the 1930s has left a further range of material to be studied, including scripts and programme files from the early days, and an increasing number of snippets or complete programmes in later years. These have provided key sources utilised for example by Sian Nicholas in her exploration of Home Front broadcasting in wartime (1996) and Andrews's recent work on domesticity and broadcasting (2012).

Faced with this plethora of material, and a growing awareness that it is untenable to suggest that a particular film, radio programme or magazine is a reflection of either 'reality' or women's experiences at particular point in time, historians may well be stymied as to how to use media texts as a historical source. In an academic milieu shaped by a post-modernist turn at the end of the twentieth century (Morgan 2006; Morgan, Jenkins, and Muslow 2007), there is a tendency to focus on discourse analysis and this extends to media and film texts. There are a number of chapters which are informed by this approach within this volume. Indeed, analysis of language and discourses has been shaped by Cultural Studies and can be identified in a range of women's and gender history written at the end of the twentieth century and in the new millennium. It is an approach which owes much to those who have undertaken interdisciplinary work across the boundaries of literature and history (Beauman 1983; Humble 2001; Light 1991; Showalter 1987, 2009) and prioritises analysis of the text. Privileging the text is perhaps problematic when looking at film, television and radio. Magazines and newspapers are in many respects social media, part of everyday life, enjoyed in the discussion and debate they stimulate with friends, the communities they offer symbolic entry to, as well as via the pleasures of the text. For Women's History an analysis of media which looks beyond the text is important to maintain its relationship with some of its antecedents, for example the social history movement, adult education and public history.

The academic analysis of media texts in Britain came to the fore in the 1970s, influenced by the development of Cultural Studies and in particular the Birmingham Centre for Contemporary Cultural Studies (CCCS) which, founded in 1964, developed analysis of culture in relation to political structures and social hierarchies. It paid significant attention to the study of the media. Early work at CCCS, such as Dorothy Hobson's seminal study of the audience of the popular daytime soap opera *Crossroads* (1964–1988), explored the use of media texts in women's everyday lives (1982). It was perhaps overshadowed by other academic approaches, particularly in Film

Studies, which placed a strong emphasis on representation and its effects, which followed the publication of Laura Mulvey's influential work 'Visual Pleasure and Narrative Cinema' (1975). Mulvey argued that within the institutional framework of mainstream Hollywood cinema in the 1930s and 1940s women were objectified by the male gaze. This argument has been over-simplified and somewhat over-utilised ever since, to the detriment of many other areas of analysis.

By the end of the 1990s, the initial focus on representation in examining women's complex relationship to the media had been replaced by a range of more theoretically nuanced approaches. Richard Johnson's development of the Cultural Circuit (Johnson 1986) as analytical tool was taken up by the Sociology department at the Open University (duGay 1996) and later by Penny Summerfield as a historian looking at wartime film (2008). This approach suggests that to understand how media and cultural artefacts create meaning it is necessary to consider how meaning is shaped by practices of: production, consumption, identity, regulation and representation. Arguably, however, much analytical work tends to slip towards greater emphasis on one or more of these factors as can be seen in this volume.

In recent years, analysis of media texts has leant more towards the use of a communication studies model which emphasises the inter-relationship of production, text and audience (Evans and Hesmondhalgh 2005). The questions and approaches needed for consideration of each of these diffuse and contradictory areas needs to be considered by historians. For example, what is the significance of individual and institutional influences on the production of a media or film text? How have they framed its content, meaning, reception and visual style? Examples of this can be seen in this volume. Consideration of audiences and their processes of consuming texts also requires attention to which identity groups, when, where and how texts were consumed. Historians looking at print media tend to analyse it as a whole, examining the content methodically, sometimes focussing on a particular area such as the letters page, but the reader would not necessarily have done so. Readers may engage with the headlines, the front page and back page or particular features which address them only, yet how such issues can be brought into the analytical framework by historians analysing the text remains complex. The audience research, for example, that the BBC undertook with listeners of early radio talks in the inter-war years or *Woman's Hour* in the post-war era emphasises the very varied responses that media texts have evoked. The multiplicity of interpretations and engagements that women had towards media texts in the past is a reminder that national histories are not individual women's histories. Indeed, the 1990s working class women, lesbian and bisexual women, women of colour or those from a range of marginalised communities emphasised how problematic it can be to generalise femininity and the category of 'woman'. However, although the overarching certainties of feminist scholarship in the seventies and eighties may have now gone, this volume suggests that the category of 'women' continues to be an analytical tool utilised in both History and in Media and Film analysis.

To avoid generalisation when either analysing either diverse media texts or the multiple and varied experiences of women when they engage with, produce or consume these texts, this volume is made up of a number of tightly focussed and historically contextualised case studies exploring British media. With contributions from established academics and young researchers, this edited collection provides 16 case studies, which showcase historically contextualised research on women and media in Britain since the 1900s. The case studies explore media directed at a particularly female audience such as *Woman's Hour* (1948–) and women's magazines such as *Vogue* (1916–), *Woman* (1937–) and *Marie Claire* (1937–), and the spaces carved out for women's interests in, for example, personal columns in popular newspapers. Women who work in the media, issues of production and regulation are explored alongside the representation of women across a broad range of media from early twentieth century motorcycling magazines, Page 3 and regional television news. The range of research aims to present a snapshot of the diversity of approaches and topics that the history of women and the media involves.

The volume begins with an example of how media can provide a useful source for historians of women and ends with an example of how history is now utilised by media industries as an inspiration and source in constructing media texts. Rosey Whorlow and Sallie McNamara's exploration of what some might consider an unlikely source for women's history—Edwardian motorcycling magazines—sheds light on debates about the social construction of femininity and discourses of feminism in the Edwardian Media. Maggie Andrews's final chapter seeks to remind readers that history now has a symbiotic relationship with the media. Heritage productions, whether television series such as *The Village* (2013), *Downton Abbey* (2101–) or the range of factions such as *The Young Victoria* (2009) are a profitable area of contemporary media. Indeed, film and television, alongside popular fiction, are where many people now indulge their interest in women's history and gain their sense of women's lives in the past.

There has been a significant emphasis within media history on the institutions and individuals which produce the media, despite the on-going academic debate over the degree to which individuals can shape the form, structure, discursive content and values of individual media texts. Women's under-representation in media industries is held by some as responsible for the problematic portrayal of women in media texts. Yet Kate Murphy's exploration of the women involved in the production of BBC Talks for Women between1923 and 1939 suggests a more complex perception of the past may be needed. Some women found spaces and places within institutions such as the BBC to produce programmes which explored feminine interests. These women and their programming laid the foundations of post-war television and radio programming aimed at women in Britain, including *Women's Hour* (1948–) analysed by Kristin Skoog and *For The Housewife* (1948) and *Women's Viewpoint* (1951) discussed by Mary Irwin. The specificity of the production processes which framed these texts, a national public service broadcaster and the number of women involved in their production, created spaces in the programmes for discussion and debate and scope for these to be framed by discourses of both femininity and feminism. The unique resources of the BBC's written archive at Caversham are in part responsible for the over-representation of the BBC in broadcasting history, and Gillian Murray's chapter, which examines the portrayal of women bus workers in ATV's regional television news from 1963 to 1979, is a welcome exception to this. It demonstrates what rich sources for the historian some of the smaller regional archives such as the Media Archive for Central England can be.

Given the 1970s' slogan 'the personal is political', it is not perhaps surprising that life writing has a growing significance in women's history (Polkey 2000); individual lives can act as a prism for the exploration of wider debates and discussions, and indeed serve as the focus for a number of case studies in this volume. Sallie McNamara's analysis of Lady Eleanor Smith's Society Column in the *Weekly Dispatch* in the late 1920s demonstrates how frivolous, even gossipy media texts can be used to explore the boundaries of cultural groups. Her writing indicates those who belonged, and what behaviour was frowned upon or viewed sympathetically by the cultural elite in the inter-war period. Alternatively, Glenda Strong demonstrates how the journalistic writing of Diana Rowntree sheds light on the tensions and challenges that came with undertaking the competing roles of architect, journalist, wife and mother in the early post-war period.

Lee Miller's war photography provides another personalised focus on the interrelationship of history and media in Janet Harrison's chapter. This chapter, however, provides examples of the tight textual analysis that is needed if historians are to genuinely engage with the media texts. If careful analysis of texts is needed, so too is an understanding of the debates that surrounded the consumption of media texts and attempts to regulate what should or should not be included in the media representations. Regulation takes many forms: government intervention, the restrictions of the economic imperative to make a profit and cultural and social taboo. Adrian Bingham's chapter demonstrates how Page 3 of *The Sun*, a media practice which in some countries would have been considered unacceptable and which feminists have frequently criticised, has come to be seen as a British tradition. Furthermore, Fan Carter's chapter in examining Peter Luff's attempt to introduce the *Periodicals (Protection of Children) Bill* in 1996 demonstrates how some areas of sexuality in print media have produced disapproval, concern and moral campaigning. She suggests the campaigns to regulate teenage magazines in the 1990s are an example of a media panic.

A theme across a number of chapters is the potential role the media takes as a public sphere (Habermas 1962), as a site of debate and discussion or perhaps even as a site for the working through of ideas, whereby the discourses articulated in media texts are ambiguous, suggesting the tensions, anxieties and preoccupations of an era. This is demonstrated both by Maggie Andrews's exploration of sexuality in wartime film and her discussion of the gendering of social problems films of the 1960s. Both suggest that media texts can be read not as evidence of behaviour, norms and practices at a particular historical moment, but rather indications of discursive struggles and contestation. In a sense they perhaps offer a way into the interior landscape of living in an era, of what Raymond Williams termed 'the structure of feeling' (1961) of a particular historical moment rather than its material conditions. Perhaps this is why drawing upon analysis of media texts may problematise and complicate the standard histories of any given period, offering instead strands of the complex and contradictory nature of change. Rachel Ritchie's exploration of the representations of youthful femininity in *Woman* magazine in the late 1950s and the 1960s convincingly challenges any simplistic notions of the long sixties as one of Cultural Revolution (Marwick 1998). Marriage, it is suggested, remains the defining feature in many women's lives. Maggie Andrews's discussion of the reportage of global humanitarian politics in the magazine *Marie Claire* in the 1990s also suggests the need to take on board the multiplicity of contradictory discourses of femininity and feminism which operate in media texts and indeed, it is argued, culture more generally. Furthermore, it points to the politics contained in popular media texts, a theme which is also explored in Paul Elliot's examination of the prostitute in 1980s British Cinema. Indeed as Elliot argues, 'historical analyses of media and filmic texts should always be mindful of the political and social dimensions of aesthetic forms'.

This book is organised chronologically into four parts: the era of enfranchisement 1900–1939, women in war and peace—the 1940s and 1950s, the Cultural Revolution of the long sixties, and the eighties and nineties of Thatcherism and its legacy. The themes, focus and emphasis of this volume interweave; no chapter takes one single line of enquiry in analysing its case study. Although the chapters are intended to be able to be read and utilised individually, it is as a whole that they attempt to provide a stimulus for those interested in interdisciplinary work across the boundaries of history and media studies. Inevitably there are, as we are more than well aware, too many silences within this volume in relation to the representation of women of colour, the diversity of female sexuality and the exploration of working-class media consumption. In part these are the silences of media representations themselves. For the majority of the twentieth century the media has been white, middle class, southern, straight and male. The spaces and places that women occupied were often done so conditionally. Being represented in the media or taking on a role in media production often required a degree of conformity to dominant discourses of femininity and the negation of other areas of women's lives, for example, their sexuality if they worked for the

BBC in the inter-war years. Little wonder then that there are conspicuous absences in the documents that have survived to produce a range of histories of women and the media. Inevitably, the low status of many media texts geared towards women, and particularly towards working-class women, has not aided their chances of survival for use by twenty-first century historians and skews the historical research that is undertaken. Furthermore, there is a serendipity of chance in the production of a volume like this; in the meetings and contacts, which brought these chapters together, in the timing which meant that particular research was ready for publication at this specific juncture in time. We acknowledge the problems in this, but hope that this collection will encourage further academic work on gender across the disciplinary boundaries of History, Film, Media and Cultural Studies and stimulate discussion about how these approaches can be further integrated with other areas of Women's History.

BIBLIOGRAPHY / SOURCES

Alexander, Sally. 1994. *Becoming a Woman and Other Essays in 19th and 20th Century Feminist History.* London: Virago.

Andrews, Maggie, and Mary Talbot, eds. 2000. *All the World and Her Husband: Women in the 20th Century Consumer Culture.* London: Continuum.

Andrews, Maggie, Charlie Bagot-Jewitt, and Nigel Hunt, eds. 2011. *Lest We Forget: Remembrance and Commemoration.* Stroud: The History Press.

Andrews, Maggie. 2012. *Domesticating the Airwaves.* London. Continuum.

Beauman, Nicola. 1983. *A Very Great Profession: The Woman's Novel 1914–1939.* London: Virago.

Beetham, Margaret. 1996. *A Magazine of Her Own? Domesticity and Desire in Women's Magazines, 1800–1914.* London: Routledge.

Bell, Melanie, and Melanie Williams. 2009. *British Women's Cinema.* British Popular Cinema. London: Routledge.

Bruley, Sue. 1999. *Women in Britain since 1900.* Social History in Perspective. Basingstoke, UK: Palgrave Macmillan.

Byerly, Carolyn M., and Karen Ross. 2005. *Women and Media: A Critical Introduction.* Oxford: Wiley-Blackwell.

Cook, Hera. 2005. *The Long Sexual Revolution: English Women, Sex, and Contraception 1800–1975.* Oxford University Press.

DiCenzo, Maria, and Lucy Delap. 2010. *Feminist Media History: Suffrage, Periodicals and the Public Sphere.* Basingstoke, UK: Palgrave Macmillan.

duGay, Paul, Stuart Hall, Linda Janes, Hugh Mackay, and Keith Negus. 1996. *Doing Cultural Studies: The Story of the Sony Walkman.* London: Sage.

Evans, Jessica, and David Hesmondhalgh. 2005. *Understanding Media: Inside Celebrity.* Maidenhead, UK: McGraw Hill.

Gledhill, Christine. 2003. *Reframing British Cinema, 1918–1928: Between Restraint and Passion.* London: BFI Publishing.

Habermas, Jurgen. (1962) English Translation 1989. *The Structural Transformation of the Public Sphere: An Inquiry into a Category of Bourgeois Society.* Cambridge, MA: The MIT Press.

Hall, Stuart. 1981. 'Notes Towards Deconstructing the Popular.' In *People's History and Socialist Theory*, edited by Ralph Samuel, 81–89. London: Routledge.

Harper, Sue. 2000. *Women in British Cinema: Mad, Bad and Dangerous to Know*. London: Continuum.

Hobson, Dorothy. 1982. *Crossroads: The Drama of a Soap Opera*. Michigan: Methuen.

Humble, Nicola. 2001. *The Feminine Middlebrow Novel 1920s to 1950s: Class, Domesticity and Bohemianism*. Oxford University Press.

Johnson, Richard. 1986. 'The Story So Far: And for the Transformations.' In *Introduction to Contemporary Cultural Studies*, edited by David Punter, 277–313. London: Longman.

Langhamer, Claire. 2000. *Women's Leisure in Britain*. Manchester University Press.

Light, Alison. 1991. *Forever England: Femininity, Literature and Conservatism between the Wars*. London: Routledge.

Marwick, Arthur. 1998. *The Sixties—Cultural Revolution in Britain, France, Italy and the United States, c.1958—c.1974*. Oxford University Press.

Morgan, Sue. 2006. *The Feminist History Reader*. Oxford: Routledge.

Morgan, Sue, Keith Jenkins, and Alan Muslow. 2007. *Manifesto for History*. Oxford: Routledge.

Mulvey, Laura. 1975. 'Visual Pleasure and Narrative Cinema.' *Screen* 16 (3): 6–18.

Nicholas, Sian. 1996. *The Echo of War: Home Front Propaganda and the Wartime BBC, 1939–45*. Manchester University Press.

Noakes, Lucy. 1997. *War and the British: Gender and National Identity 1939–91*. London: I. B. Tauris.

Oram, Alison. 2007. *Her Husband was a Woman! Women's Gender-Crossing in Modern British Popular Culture*. London: Routledge.

Polkey, Pauline. 2000. 'Reading History through Autobiography: Politically Active Women of Late Nineteenth-Century Britain and Their Personal Narratives.' *Women's History Review* 9 (3): 483–500.

Rappaport, Erica. 2001. *Shopping for Pleasure: Women in the Making of London's West End*. Princeton University Press.

Rowbotham, Shelia. 2012. *A Century of Women: The History of Women in Britain and the United States in the Twentieth Century*. London: Verso Books.

Showalter, Elaine. 1987. *The Female Malady: Women, Madness and English Culture, 1830–1980*. London: Virago.

Showalter, Elaine. 2009. *A Literature of Their Own: British Women Novelists from Brontë to Lessing*. London: Virago.

Summerfield, Penny. 2008. 'War, Film, Memory: Some Reflections on War Films and the Social Configuration of Memory in Britain in the 1940s and 1950s.' *Journal of Cultural Studies* 1 (1): 15–23.

Thane, Pat. 2010. *Women and Citizenship in Britain and Ireland in the 20th Century: What Difference Did the Vote Make?* London: Continuum.

Thornham, Sue. 2007. *Women, Feminism and Media*. Edinburgh University Press.

Waters, Melanie, ed. 2011. *Women on Screen: Feminism and Femininity in Visual Culture*. Basingstoke, UK: Palgrave Macmillan.

Williams, Raymond. (1961) 1966. *The Long Revolution*. Harmondsworth, UK: Pelican Books.

Williams, Kevin. 2009. *Get Me a Murder a Day! A History of Media and Communication in Britain*. London: Bloomsbury Academic.

Winship, Janice. 1987. *Inside Women's Magazines*. London: Rivers Oram Press/ Pandora List.

Zweiniger-Bargielowska, Ina. 2001. *Women in Twentieth-Century Britain: Social, Cultural and Political Change*. London: Longman.

Part I

Women and Media in the Era of Enfranchisement, 1900–1939

Suffrage agitation, whether involving peaceful protest, mass demonstrations or more militant activities such as non-payment of tax and window smashing, has perhaps dominated histories of women in the Edwardian era. Yet when writing the first history of the movement, Ray Strachey emphasised that even as early as 1928, *The Cause* (1988) was about more than the vote. Groups of women campaigned on a range of issues in the late nineteenth and early twentieth century including improved access to education and maternity grants. Arguably, the campaign for women's suffrage can be seen as the tip of an iceberg; beneath the surface the fluid and unstable discourses of femininity were being contested in a range of areas and media texts. Thus 'the Woman Question', as it became known, framed debates about what activities were suitable for women. Rosie Whorlow and Sallie McNamara's chapter on women motorcyclists traces some of this contestation around the suitability of motorcycling as a leisure activity for women as it was played out in the pre-World War One motorcycling press.

Popular mythology and some history has presented World War One as liberating for women (Marwick 1977; Braybon and Summerfield 2012) but recent historiography has suggested a more nuanced and complex picture of both the era and the increasing participation of women in paid wartime work. The Representation of the People Act in 1918 gave women over thirty with some property, and almost all men, the right to vote. In 1928, women were enfranchised on the same terms as men. Academic debate continues over what activities precipitated this change, Pugh arguing that by 1908 public opinion was convinced by the arguments for women's suffrage (2002) but that it was delayed by the machinations and self-interest of party politics, while Purvis places greater significance on militant suffrage activities both prior to and at the outbreak of war (1999). During World War One '[t]he number of women employed increased from around 4.9 million in 1914 to around 6.2 million in 1918' according to Gerry Holloway (2005), although they were not necessarily welcomed. A significant number of those who went to work in wartime munitions factories, a job which would exist only for the duration of war, came from domestic service or had been engaged in casual, temporary or piece work prior to the war.

Many married women, if they could afford it, were less than enthusiastic about paid work outside the home, seeing it as a double burden on top of their domestic duties, and were not necessarily reticent to leave work at the end of the war. The inter-war economic crisis hit traditional industries which were male dominated; ship building, mining and steel suffered and unemployment rose. A hesitant and uneven recovery occurred in the nineteen thirties with many of the job opportunities in new industries such as the growing car industries in the midlands or female employment in service and entertainment industries.

The inter-war period saw the development of the British Broadcasting Company (BBC) and its transformation, under the directorship of John Reith, into the public service / publically funded broadcaster, the British Broadcasting Corporation. The growth in newspaper consumption continued, as the period also saw what Curran and Seaton describe as the 'era of the press barons' (2003). The Harmsworth brothers controlled newspapers 'with an aggregate circulation of over six million—probably the largest press group in the western world' (Curran and Seaton 2003, 39). Both Kate Murphy's and Sallie McNamara's chapters demonstrate how women carved out working opportunities within these media industries. Murphy charts how a series of women who worked in the BBC Talks department, particularly those involved in the production of morning *Household Talks*, produced programming which enhanced and enriched other women's lives. Employment patterns were not the only things disrupted by wartime and the economic crisis that followed, and Sallie McNamara explores how one woman writer, Lady Eleanor Smith, through her newspaper gossip column, articulated the complex reworking of the boundaries of society in a time of uncertainty and change. Opportunities to pursue a literary career or work at the BBC, like the freedom facilitated by cars and motorcycling, were arguably available only to educated, often single, women of the wealthier classes. (Many jobs such as the civil service, nursing and teaching operated a marriage bar.)

By the 1930s, however, media consumption made leisure opportunities widely available to working-class women and enabled them to broaden their horizons. The radio which was 'the friend in the corner' (Moores 2000, 28) brought education, news, current affairs and, especially when listening to European commercial stations such as Radio Luxemburg, entertainment into the majority of homes. The weekly or even twice-weekly trip to the cinema was a staple entertainment for many women. For many, the glamour and spectacle of Hollywood productions and stars were the most popular, but British stars such as Gracie Fields, Jessie Matthews, Cicely Courtneidge and George Formby helped maintain the British industry with audience-pleasing light entertainment. Publications such as *Picturegoer* emphasised the more down-to-earth attributes of British stars, while

Fields's working-class background was positively embraced both in film and in the popular press as she was constructed as a 'national treasure', or the 'Lancashire Britannia' as Jeffrey Richards has argued (Richards 1984).

The rise in leisure activities such as radio and cinema attendance was one example of the contradictory nature of the inter-war years (Pugh 2009; Gardiner 2000). The worldwide economic depression by no means affected everyone or every region in the same way; for those with staple jobs the cost of living went down; consumer culture in the form of new chain stores (Winship 2000) and mass entertainment rose whilst Butlins opened their first holiday camp in 1936 at Skegness. Simultaneously, maternal mortality rates rose (Webster 1982) and for many women, as Elizabeth Roberts's oral history has documented (1995), the struggle to manage was unrelenting. In these circumstances at the outbreak of World War Two, both feminism and femininity were variable, unstable and intertwined. The Six Point Group campaigned for both equal pay for teachings and satisfactory legislation for widowed and unmarried mothers. Alternatively, women's organisations such as the National Federation of Women Institutes campaigned for greater recognition, support and acknowledgement of the skill of rural domestic housewives (Andrews 1997). The 'home fit for heroes', which had been fought for in the First World War, became culturally increasingly significant in the 1920s and 1930s with women expected to play a central role in it; what this role was, however, was both variable and contested.

BIBLIOGRAPHY / SOURCES

Andrews, Maggie. 1997. *The Acceptable Face of Feminism*. London: Lawrence and Wishart.

Braybon, Gail, and Penny Summerfield. 2012. *Out of the Cage: Women's Experiences in Two World Wars*. London: Routledge.

Curran, J., and Jean Seaton. 2003. *Power without Responsibility: The Press, Broadcasting, and New Media in Britain*. London: Routledge.

Gardiner, Juliet. 2010. *The Thirties: And Intimate History*. London: Harper Press.

Holloway, Gerry. 2005. *Women and Work in Britain since 1840*. Routledge. Kindle edition.

Marwick, Arthur. 1977. *Women and War 1914–1918*. London: Harper Collins.

Moores, Shaun. 2000. *Media and Everyday Life in Modern Society*. Edinburgh University Press.

Pugh, Martin. 2002. *The March of the Women: A Revisionist Analysis of the Campaign for Women's Suffrage, 1866–1914*. Oxford University Press.

Pugh, Martin. 2009. *We Danced All Night: A Social History of Britain between the Wars*. London: Vintage.

Purvis, June, and Sandra Holton. 1999. *Votes for Women*. Women and Gender History. London: Routledge.

Richards, Jeffrey. 1984. *The Age of the Dream Palace: Cinema and Society in Britain 1930–1939*. London: Routledge & Kegan Paul.

Roberts, Elizabeth. 1995. *Women and Families*. Oxford: Wiley-Blackwell.

Strachey, Ray. (1928) 1988. *The Cause: Short History of the Women's Movement in Great Britain*. London: Virago Reprints Library.

Webster, Charles. 1982. 'Healthy or Hungry Thirties?' *History Workshop Journal* 13 (Spring 1982): 110–129.

Winship, Janice. 2000. 'New Disciplines for Women and the Rise of the Chain Store in the 1930s.' In *All the World and Her Husband*, edited by Maggie Andrews and Mary Talbot, 44–60. London: Continuum.

1 Representations of Women's Motorcycle Riding 1903–1914
'Elated, Exhilarated and Emancipated'

Rosey Whorlow and Sallie McNamara

INTRODUCTION

This chapter brings together two aspects of what social researchers Charles Booth and B. Seebohm Rowntree (in Beck 2008, 456) referred to as a 'national urge for leisure' in the late Victorian and Edwardian period: motorcycling and magazines. It suggests that motorcycling magazines served as prisms for an exploration of the boundaries of acceptable femininity in the pre-World War I era. James Walvin (1978, 123) has argued that 'by the turn of the century . . . it was widely accepted that everyone had a right to the enjoyment of leisure'. Peter Beck goes on to comment that what was deemed 'acceptable, educational and "improving" forms of "leisure"' (Beck 2008, 457), for the industrial proletariat, were activities which included brass bands, choral societies, municipal parks, 'organized, codified modern sports and various activities provided by voluntary associations with church and chapel affiliations' (Beck 2008, 457). The degree to which women accessed and utilized the new leisure opportunities remains an area of historical debate (Beavan 2005; Beck 2008). Within the national urge for leisure cycling became an increasingly popular pastime, which Clare S. Simpson notes peaked for women around 1896–97 (2007, 49). *The Times* claimed in 1898 that 'the bicycle brought a new dimension to British social life in the 1890s . . . few corners of British society remained untouched by cycling' (Beck 2008, 457). Simultaneously, the sport of motorcycling grew and although perceived as a masculine sport, it was one in which women were increasingly visible.

The growing popularity of motorcycling was evidenced by the production of publications specifically aimed at Motor Cycle enthusiasts of this period: *The Motor Cycle* was published by Liffe and Sons in 1903, whilst *Motorcycling Magazine* was introduced by Rivals Temple Press in 1910. Simpson has argued that for middle class women the bicycle offered 'unique opportunities to move spontaneously and independently beyond accepted geographic and social boundaries' (2007, 49–50). She further draws attention to both the class base of bicycling and motorcycling and the special significance of the sport for women in furthering social change by challenging conventional practices, beliefs and values (Simpson 2007, 49). Both domestic and financial constraints worked against the participation of working-class women in cycling, an issue accentuated 'by the reluctance of upper- and middle-class women as well as working-class men to share their sport' (Beck 2008, 465). Simpson points out that women's participation in cycling was not always viewed in a positive light and similar claims can be made for motorcycling. Consequently, media texts became a space within which slippage occurred between debates over women's participation in motorcycling and wider contestation over gender roles and women's place in society.

The Edwardian period has left historians with a plethora of sources to draw upon to gain some understanding of the experiences of women who lived at this time. Magazines like *The Motor Cycle* and *Motorcycling Magazine* provide access to the everyday assumptions, preconceptions, concerns and experiences of Edwardian women generally as well as those who were Motor Cycle enthusiasts. Situated within the broader context of shifting discourses of gender in the period, these magazines demonstrate how women utilized what might be considered predominantly masculine media spaces for their own purposes. Crucially, motorcycling media enabled women to challenge the 'myth' of the Motor Cycle as being a 'man's' machine at a point in time when women were campaigning for increased participation in a range of areas once considered as masculine spheres. There has been much discussion of the suffrage campaigns in the period, and how these provoked wider debate about women's roles (Joannou and Purvis 2009). However, it is important to note that battles about what constituted acceptable femininity were not solely confined to women's suffrage, but were disseminated throughout popular culture. This chapter suggests that women contributors and readers appropriated spaces within the motorcycle media to share and discuss the challenges, experiences and emancipatory potential of motorcycle riding.

THE SIGNIFICANCE OF MOTORCYCLE
JOURNALISM IN TURBULENT TIMES

The Edwardian period was a complex transitional time when Britain was moving away from the values of the Victorian period (Van Vuuren 2011, xiii). Three areas facilitated this: Edwardian leisure, issues of gender and the New Woman, and developments in the press and magazines. The 'urge for leisure' must, as Beck argues, be viewed 'against a backdrop of urban, industrial and demographic change . . . reductions in working hours and increased spending power' (Beck 2008, 456). Access to specific sports and leisure, while dependent on class and economics, was also gendered. Although women, with the necessary leisure time and economic standing, were starting to participate more widely, Beck comments:

Sport reinforced rather than challenged gender stereotypes, and it remained difficult for women either to infiltrate key sports defining masculinity or to undermine existing perceptions of womanliness. Women were firmly excluded by most sports associations. (2008, 464)

Debates concerning the 'New Woman', the sexually independent woman seeking opportunities for self-development outside of marriage, were also important (Showalter 1992, 38–39) for she was seen as a deviant woman, a signifier of gender crisis, notably in a series of associated novels (Beetham 1996, 117). Linking leisure and attitudes to gender, Sally Ledger has drawn attention to concerns around the New Women on bicycles, garbed in bloomers, who were seen as 'a product of the campaign for rational dress at the *fin de siècle*' (1997, 26) and perceived to be 'creating fears of the "unwomanly woman"' (1997, 26). As Ledger notes, the recurrent theme of *fin de siècle* cultural politics was instability, and gender was arguably the most destabilizing category (1997, 22) due to the increasingly vociferous campaign for female suffrage. During the Victorian period women's rights had become an established issue with some significant progress being made by the women's movement, and the issue of women's suffrage was firmly on the political and social agenda. Lucy Delap has suggested many historians of the Edwardian era have equated suffrage activism and feminism, assuming 'that the main focus of Edwardian politics was the acquisition of the vote' (cited in Ardis 2009, 628). However, positioning Edwardian feminism within such a narrow focus misses the ways that in this 'tense and formative period' there was division and conflict between ideas of women's emancipation' (Ardis 2009, 628.). Much of this conflict was played out in the public sphere within the press and magazines. During the late Victorian and early Edwardian period the cultural meaning of 'printedness' changed with the expansion of both publishing and reading, and literacy levels had increased as a consequence of the widespread elementary education that had been introduced by Foster's 1870 Education Act. One of the driving imperatives of the New Journalism of the late nineteenth century had been the incorporation of women readers within the daily press, which aimed to deliver those female readers to advertisers of domestic and fashion products who provided much of the financially lucrative advertising in newspapers (Conboy 2011).

The *Motor Cycle*, priced at 1d. and often referred to as the 'Green un', included multiple photographs of riders on their Motor Cycles, alongside pages of adverts for new Motor Cycle designs and related products such as clothing or tools. It used to full advantage the more sophisticated 'printedness' offered by the developments in design and illustration; photographs and advertisements provide visual evidence of changes in design and attitudes towards consumer artefacts. Although advertisements were crucial for generating revenue, they also contributed to forming communal and imagined identities. Motor Cycle magazine editors were aware of the potential market offered by female riders, and in providing women with a space to explore the possibilities of motorcycling, encouraged the marketing opportunities and consumer choices that accompanied women's participation in the sport. The popular press and specialist publications created a public sphere where women could contest issues around gender and leisure (Hall 1981). Furthermore, as Lucy Delap's work demonstrates, 'periodicals and the communities of readers they created were perhaps a more important means of intellectual networking than formal political organizations' (Ardis on Delap 2009) and Sarah Pedersen has pointed out that readers' letters pages can create important spaces for the formation of newspaper communities to articulate their views, arguing that: 'A newspaper's "Letters to the Editor" column represents its readership in a unique way and can provide a useful "thermometer" with which to measure the extent of critical debate and discussion a particular issue generated in a locality' (2002, 657).

Conboy notes that although women had always contributed to early print culture in England, they had often been implicitly excluded from discussions within the early public sphere because of its male construction (2011, 67). The Motor Cycle magazines contained the voices of women; although predominantly catering to the male reader they often contained regular 'ladies' pages and advertisements targeting a female readership. This gave women a voice in the debates over gender and the parameters of acceptable femininity and feminism, not merely in the gendered spaces of female magazines, but by creating a public sphere in the more 'male' media of the Motor Cycle magazine (Habermas 1962). The discussion of appropriate gender roles and femininity located in a space outside of the central political domain thus offered an avenue of debate which was used to legitimate women's active participation in the developing leisure and sports opportunities of the era. Tracing the discussion of gender issues in the Motor Cycle periodical press suggests shifting attitudes to women's riding and broader tensions concerning female roles in the early twentieth century.

Although there is some limited research in relation to the history of Motor Cycle design and the rise of the Motor Cycle industry (Alford and Ferriss 2007), motorcycling for British women has only been looked at in relation to the inter-war period when there was a significant rise in Motor Cycle sales, and importantly, some concentrated attempts at marketing motorcycling to a female market (Koerner 1998, 2007). Steve Koerner addressing some of the discourses relating to concern about the suitability of women's motorcycling in the inter-war period draws, in his analysis, on the Motor Cycle press. However, many of the concerns the media expressed about inter-war women riders, such as Marjorie Cottle and Jessie Enniss, were a continuation of themes and issues over the physiological suitability of riding for women previously expressed in the Edwardian period. One theme was the challenge of attracting new women riders while maintaining their femininity (Alford and Ferriss 2007; Koerner 2007), which had

JULY 10th, 1905.   MOTOR CYCLE   615

THE LADY MOTOR CYCLISTS' PAGE

MOTOR CYCLISTS OF THE GENTLER SEX.

FROM the date of its birth, *The Motor Cycle* has always encouraged the development of an efficient motor bicycle for ladies, and though the actually perfect article has yet to be produced we feel confident that we shall not have long to wait before a really practical lady's mount will be placed on the market. Meanwhile, however, the sport has found favour with the gentler sex, and though their number among the great army of motor cyclists are not strong, each one possesses enthusiasm, and the possession of enthusiasm does much towards the furtherance of a cause. Mrs. Kennard has a handsome-looking 2 h.p. Phœnix, with two-speed gear. She, as all our readers know, is quite an old hand at motor cycling, and we doubt not that the time will come when ladies will see they owe her a real debt of gratitude.

Mrs. Frank Hulbert is another lady who is a really enthusiastic motor cyclist, and her views on the subject are extremely sensible. While in conversation with her the other day, she told us that she much preferred the motor to the pedal bicycle in traffic, "for the simple reason that one can get out of the way of other traffic so much more easily."

"I really can't understand," said she, "why more girls don't take up motor cycling. It may be due to nervousness, though they won't suffer from that complaint long. I fear it is because they cannot afford the initial outlay. The mud, dust, and oil on one's dress are also rather a nuisance; in fact, that is what troubles me most."

"But surely you can wear a sort of Holland overall?" we nervously ventured to suggest, fearing we were treading on dangerous ground now that the subject of dress had come into the conversation.

"Oh, that is an excellent idea. You mean something one can slip on over one's ordinary clothes, and take off immediately on dismounting."

Starting.

"Do you find any trouble in starting your motor bicycle?"

"Well, it is a little bit hard sometimes, especially uphill, but then my husband generally gives me a push, and off I go."

"Now, what is your idea of the lady's motor bicycle, as you know it?" we asked.

"My machine has carried me well for over two years. Sometimes I wish it would go a little faster. You see, it is only a low-powered machine, and my husband and his friend ride 3½ h.p. machines, so that I feel I am keeping them back. On some hills I have come across my little motor sometimes requires more muscular help than I care to give it, and then my husband catches hold of my shoulder and helps me up. Yes, I agree with you, a two-speed gear is what

we want. It would be such a help in starting, and I could also get up the hills all right."

"You really think then, that motor cycling for ladies will become popular?"

"I don't see why it shouldn't," replied Mrs. Hulbert. "Every girl I know who has taken it up likes it immensely, and I have never heard of any of my friends giving it up."

A Few Well-known Lady Riders.

"How many motor cycling ladies do you know of?" we asked.

"Well, let me see. Of course, you know of Mrs. Kennard; then there is Miss Hind (I believe she rides a Singer); Mrs. Wildman Baker, who is most

Mrs. Frank Hulbert (top left hand) and Mrs. Wildman Baker.

Figure 1.1 The Ladies Page in 1905 discussing the challenges and suitability of motorcycling for ladies (*The Motor Cycle* July 10, 1905). Image by kind permission of Mortons Archive.

already been circulating in the Motor Cycle press prior to World War I. Koerner's work is mainly focused on the industry, and the reasons for the failure of *concentrated* campaigns to significantly boost sales to women. He has acknowledged that 'from nearly the beginning, only a small proportion of women were active motorcyclists' (Koerner 2007). An analysis of motorcycling magazines between 1903 and 1914 provides a greater sense of this 'small proportion' of women riders and the processes involved in stabilizing the cultural meanings associated with motorcycling during its earliest development.

DISORDEREDLY WOMEN RIDERS

The number of women motorcyclists was much lower than bicyclists and car drivers, and was to remain so, but the meaning of all these sports to the participants and bystanders were interrelated. Despite bicycling becoming more affordable to the working class, women's participation in all forms of leisure and sporting activities was class specific and carried financial implications. Participation of middle- and upper-class women in the pleasures offered by automobiles and Motor Cycles had already won a degree of social acceptance at a time when, according to Virginia Scharff, there was 'unprecedented debate over women's right and capacity to step into public life. . . . Where the distinction between public and private spaces served as a boundary defining proper masculine and feminine roles' (1991, 23). In this cultural climate 'women's inroad in the automobile world reverberated with cultural significance' (Romalov 1995, 94). The Motor Cycle offered women the opportunity to move out of their private worlds and into the public sphere with more ease than the car and more speed than the bicycle. To some extent the Motor Cycle could be seen as a hybrid of the two technologies, offering the advantages of both. It was a bicycle with an engine, temperamental and often unreliable, fast but physically unstable; wide open and vulnerable to the physicality of the environment. Nevertheless, the Motor Cycle was more affordable than the auto car, enabling those women with the necessary financial background to go out alone, with fewer social restrictions.

However, the Motor Cycle, like the car, soon became associated with cultural fears about the anti-social nature of its users and its potentially damaging impact on society. Gary Johnstone has noted that 'the general impression of the Motor Cycle . . . was constructed in the wider media as a 'madcap invention', fit for horse frightening, and ridden by over-exuberant young men often referred to as the upper class hooligan or scorcher' (1994, 21). This negative image, linking the Motor Cycle with delinquency and disorderedly behaviour, consolidated the 'myth' of the Motor Cycle as a masculine artefact. Both male and female enthusiasts addressed this in the pages of *The Motor Cycle* and *Motorcycling* where negative and masculinized representations placed women in a position in which they needed to defend both their moral and physical suitability to be riders. The magazines offered women a public forum of debate in which to do this. As Bonnie Frederick and Susan McLeod argue (1993), any discussions of women's experiences that involved journeys, whether short or long, provide insights into women's relationship with both the public and private spheres and the ways they attempt to negotiate and renegotiate the boundaries of propriety and freedom. In an article in *The Motor Cycle* Muriel Hind described to her readers the feelings she experienced on her first solo ride on her brother's Motor Cycle when she wrote: 'I was elated, exhilarated and enchanted with my own performances, and full of the valour of the ignorant . . . I felt emancipated. I could go where I liked, and even at 18 a certain amount of liberty is a boon not to be despised' (December 26, 1906). Thus, the magazines gave women a voice to express their rising elation in the newfound freedoms the Motor Cycle offered them. These media spaces also enabled women to sidestep the political aspects of women's rights and moral rightness, while still utilizing the magazines to push at gender boundaries and more practical constraints placed on women's leisure.

The novelty aspect of a woman on a motorcycle did, however, attract negative responses and public outrage, which the women correspondents shared with their readers, often getting supportive responses from other women riders. For example, in 1903 Mary E. Kennard (c1850–1936), a politician's daughter, romance writer, and a prolific contributor to *The Motor Cycle*, described in her column 'Wake Up Ladies' an incident whereby she was riding in Coventry. 'A censorious prying old woman . . . accosted her thus' to inform her that the split skirt she had been riding her 2/3/4hp De Dion Tricycle in was indecent as it was 'open down the front ma'am'. She had then 'continued to follow in my wake eyeing me so intently that very soon I found myself pursued by a small crowd of ill-mannered factory girls' (May 27, 1903). In her 1910 fortnightly column 'The Lady Motorcyclist' Muriel Hind wrote 'that it is still rather uncommon to see a girl riding a motor-bicycle'. She added that even 'as far back as 1901' . . . 'I remember one day in Southampton a policeman had to 'move on' a crowd that had collected around my motor bicycle, which I had left outside a shop' (*Motor-cycling* October 25, 1910). Such accounts provide insights into the ways that the early Motor Cycle was a novel spectacle drawing crowds of curious onlookers, but a woman rider attracted not only attention but also sometimes ridicule and hostility.

In sharing their experiences the women journalists and commentators generally framed their narratives reassuringly within socially acceptable boundaries of femininity which their male counterparts were generally comfortable with. They were often subtle in their approach, reassuring all that their femininity was being respectfully maintained. An article by 'Atlanta' which encouraged women to take up riding and challenge the prejudices she felt were circulating around women riding demonstrates this. Concerning the need for a woman to maintain an appropriate appearance when riding, she wrote: 'This is an issue of importance to every woman, excepting perhaps a few of the extreme suffragettes and "ultra bluestockings"' (*The Motor Cycle* May 6, 1908). Importantly, in framing any type of challenge to conventionality in terms of femininity, women motorcyclists very carefully distanced themselves from the more potentially inflammatory politicization of women's rights and women's suffrage campaigns of the era. While the 'Woman Question' was clearly an unspoken subtext in debates about women's freedom, this was mainly only hinted at in discussions of women's motorcycling which were framed in liberal feminist discourses. Initially, equality of opportunity between the sexes referred to just riding and, later in the decade, it shifted to focus on participation in competitions. This minimized potential offence to readers. The 'Woman Question' and the emergence of the 'New Woman' imagery within media and literature were familiar and much-debated aspects of late Victorian and Edwardian culture (Ledger 1997). This conflict was not totally avoided within motorcycling magazines; there were occasions when women riders provoked hostile debate over the suitability of riding for the 'fairer sex'. The editorial response demonstrated the editors' role as cultural intermediaries, often refereeing in what were sometimes hostile debates; while their progressiveness was evident in their decision to publish all sides of the issue, there were some limitations. When debate had raged for a period of time, editorial support, designated columns and features for women were suspended for several months, suggesting an editorial desire not to alienate the predominantly masculine readership and detrimentally affecting magazine sales.

Intermittently in the period 1903–1914 female contributors encouraged their readers to seek out like-minded women to share their interest. On several occasions between 1905 and 1910 writers such as Muriel Hind and 'Diana' called for women to form their own ladies Motor Cycle clubs to further a sense of shared female experience and community. Several of the women writers, such as Mary Kennard, who wanted to share their encounters and contributed to the magazines, were already established writers of Edwardian literature. Other female contributors used their interest in Motor Cycles for leisure to become regular journalists in both *The Motor Cycle* and *Motorcycling* magazines. Muriel Hind was the most prolific of these writers to merge a riding career with her writing career; as her journalistic contributions grew, so did her semi-professional engagement with riding. Hind became a test rider for the Motor Cycle manufacturers who built Rex machines, was a successful competitor in the developing forms of Motor Cycle sports, but used her writing to become a voice in the issue of equality of women's rights. Having been given a regular page in *The Motor Cycle*, in 1905 she attempted to create a public forum to discuss suitable travel tips, necessary riding skills, practical mechanics, and advice on costume problems. She was also outspoken in attempting to provide moral support to other women riders in the face of sexism and public affronts to their femininity.

Miss Muriel Hind and her newly-acquired mount, a 5 h.p. Twin-cylinder Rex, on which sh
accomplished the best hill-climbing performance in the A.C.U. Quarterly Trials last month.

Figure 1.2   Muriel Hind, one of the most active and prolific advocates of motorcycling for Edwardian ladies, on her 5h.p Rex (*The Motor Cycle* February 12, 1908).
Image by kind permission of Mortons Archive.

An analysis of writing in *The Motor Cycle* and *Motorcycling* between
1903 and 1914 reveals contributors to the periodicals sought either to uphold
or challenge the entrenched masculinization of motorcycling. This poor
public image of the sport was an ongoing issue in *The Motor Cycle* (and
other print media) with the readers' letters pages full of both complaints
about misrepresentation, and pleas to the over-enthusiastic to show some
restraint. The editorial voice of the magazine worked hard to negotiate the
tensions reflected in the problems of poor public image coupled with harsh
treatment at the hands of the local village bobby. It often included warnings of police traps, with readers of both genders writing in with updates of

police locations and tales of unjust prosecution, as well as other unpleasant experiences of prejudice and heckling from the public. If male riders got a negative response, then female riders were more often castigated and heckled; although their writing suggests many women shrugged this off in fairly good humour. Those that did not soon gave up, as one noted:

> I passed an old looking Phaeton on the road, whose occupants were an old lady and gentleman . . . As I drove past them the old man turned away with a look of ineffable disgust. Evidently I was not a creature fit for a respectable old couple to look at. But one can laugh especially when one recollects the similar experiences one had some years ago when ladies first began to bicycle (*The Car* no.14, August 27, 1902).

This was not a unique response; the pages of the magazines were full of motorcyclists, both male and female, telling how they were often ridiculed by the public and in the wider press. Hind was one of those who directly challenged this, but she was not alone.

WAKING UP LADY MOTORCYCLISTS

Mary Kennard's column 'Wake Up Ladies', which was aimed specifically at women enthusiasts, demonstrates how discussions about women motorcyclists were framed by competing and overlapping debates about feminism and femininity. Mrs Kennard was already established as a prolific writer of fiction who had published over thirty novels and volumes of short stories between 1883 and 1903. Her novels, mostly stories based around sports and romance, were very popular and widely read, and many went through several editions (Ledger 1997). As her novel writing tailed off she continued to write focussing on the motoring press, publishing a number of articles in *The Car* magazine from 1901 as well as *The Motor Cycle* magazine from 1903. In the latter, she initially wrote encouraging women to take to two wheels, ending up with her own regular ladies page, 'Wake Up Ladies'. Although this was a regular feature for several months, unfortunately it disappeared abruptly after a number of the readers expressed essentialist concerns over the issue of Motor Cycles and their suitability for the 'fairer sex'. The designation of articles and regular pages for the lady rider, by the lady rider, resulted in calls for their regulation, both on the road and in sporting competitions, which became an on-going issue in the Motor Cycle press. Initially in 1903, *The Motor Cycle* stated that it had an editorial policy which had 'persistently advocated motorcycling for women', and it was always glad to hear of a machine likely to popularize the sport amongst the fair sex (September 23, 1903). However, there were limits to this, as when Mary Kennard presented an argument for women as 'equal but different'.

The most prevalent discourse within Mary Kennard's articles was her enthusiasm to encourage women to ride. Her rallying call, though, was limited to those women who, in her words, 'could develop the necessary faculties and sensibilities to cope', although she was keen to warn that motorcycling was by no means suitable for all women (June 3, 1903). Further, while she did appear to be negotiating essentialist discourses of the period, she was doing so within careful limits while also negotiating issues of women's rights. At a time when the suffrage movement was prevalent there were few direct insights into her political beliefs. She voiced her opinion that she believed in equality of the sexes and stated in 'Wake Up Ladies' that 'women nowadays are capable of so much more . . . they will conquer the Motor Cycle as they have already conquered the majority of sports and past times' (June 3,1903). She was also very clear in indicating the parameters of this statement. While it might be considered potentially radical, given the sensitive climate of gender politics, her comment was made more 'palatable' for her audience by the 'equal but different' feminism within which it was articulated:

And if they do so with feminine grace and tact, men will surely welcome them cordially and do their utmost to assist and 'instruct'. But ladies, be careful in one respect. They must not attempt to ape their male companions either as regards dress or performance. That would prove fatal to their best interests. Nobody wants them to ride from Lands-End to John-O-Groats in record time, and then pose as professionals who have gone one better than professionals. [Which is where the debates were later to go.] But the sensible woman has a natural intuition of the fitness of things. It is to her I appeal . . . she will eventually ride the Motor Cycle with nerve, courage, intelligence and perseverance. (June 3, 1903)

Although the editorial of the magazine stated that it supported and encouraged the 'fairer sex' to ride ladies' Motor Cycles, it would appear that many of the readers did not share their sentiments. During October and November of 1903, the Letters to the Editor pages repeatedly discussed the suitability of woman's riding. Seen within the context of wider social concerns over the shifting position of women, this debate was stimulated by a series of articles in the *Daily Mail* (1903) entitled 'The Deterioration of Women' in which Mr H. B. M. H. Mariott-Watson discussed the threat that activities such as athletics and cycling would have on the physique of the female body. The effects seem to mimic the physical caricatures of women suffragists and suffragettes in the popular press at the time. Marriott-Watson's article referred to the potential dangers of overtaxing the feminine physique, fearing that in conforming to standards that were not theirs but men's, women would become asexual, resulting in them 'shooting up tall, flat-chested, colourless and lacking in reasonable proportions. They would become dried and atrophied by rough wear and their unseemly habits' (The *Daily Mail* September 21, 1903). The article generated much debate from the national readership, lasting several weeks. Within such a climate a heated debate about the suitability of motorcycling for women emerged in the readers' letters pages of *The Motor Cycle* magazine with a particularly vitriolic exchange between S. M. J. R. and 'Woman-an Engine Driver'. A very angry S. M. J. R. wrote to the editor of *Motorcycling* as follows:

> I saw a lady motorist riding a Singer lady's machine for the first time somewhere in Cambridge, and without being ungallant, I don't want to see another. Her nervousness was pathetically obvious, and her facial expression was an index to the sustained nervous tension under which she was labouring. I am sure the natural constitution of the gentler sex is not such that they can abstract any pleasure or physical good from such a pastime as motoring, which requires strong nerves, and a cool and ready hand and head. . . . I am sure that if motorcycling is engaged in by ladies, they will be a source of considerable danger to both themselves and other users of the road, and I pity the poor men when the ladies of the household come home from a hard ride a bundle of nerves. (*The Motor Cycle* October 21, 1903)

This discussion draws upon essentialist discourses of femininity, prevalent in the early twentieth century, where women were classified as mentally and physically inferior to men. These discourses can also be identified in the supporters of women's riding. In one of Mrs Kennard's early articles her husband also wrote a short piece which praised her as 'an exceptional woman' due to her calmness of nerve (*The Car* no.14, August 27, 1902). S. M. J. R. too commented on the exceptionality of women who could control such a machine, but like Mr Kennard, felt these were the exception. Discourses articulated by writers such as S. M. J. R.'s served to infantilize women by rendering them as irrational, in need of protection and guidance, and physically both at risk, and worse still, a danger to others. Thereby the reference to women's 'fragility', 'nervousness' and 'irrationality' furthermore constructed them as a form of public enemy. There were also fears that the long-term effect of women participating in physically 'unsuitable' activities would be to threaten their role as mothers of the future of the British nation. The 'fair sex' was in danger of becoming 'less fair' due to the intense strain that motorcycling activities placed on the weaker constitution of the female body. This in turn, it was feared, would result in 'malformed and unattractive women' (Cahn 1994, 15). One American doctor went so far as to link cycling with a condition that he called 'bicycle face'. This condition was recognizable by the hardening of the facial muscles, a protruding jaw, wild staring eyes and a strained expression (Cahn 1994, 15). No doubt S. M. J. R. would have attributed this ailment to his nervous Singer-riding Cambridge lady had he known of it. Obviously aware of concerns about the physicality of motorcycling in relation to the perceived fragility of the female body, in her earlier articles Mrs Kennard was at pains to reassure her readers that no fatigue was experienced as a result of riding, and that rides of up to sixty miles could safely be undertaken with no undue stress. In one article she included a quote from her doctor whom she said enthusiastically greeted her riding as health-giving as long as limits were maintained. These debates were imbued with a language based on pseudo-medical and scientific knowledge which endorsed the essentialist difference of the female body (Cahn 1994, 159) and as such were potentially controlling and limiting discourses. S. M. J. R.'s fears could also be interpreted as embodying turn-of-the-century discourses of insecurity around traditional masculinity in the era of women's suffrage campaigns.

One woman rider, who signed herself 'Woman-an Engine Driver' provides evidence of a distinct counter-discourse to these critiques of women riders, although it was not previously found in this journal or found again for a while. It explicitly linked women's participation in motorcycling to the far more radical (and unpalatable) feminist intentions raised by the women's rights politics of the New Woman and suffragette movement. 'Woman-an Engine Driver' began by making a clear distinction between 'ladies', who, she suggested, presided at washtubs, and 'women', and pointed out that she preferred to label herself 'a woman'. Towards the end of her letter she made a radical political statement, even more surprising perhaps is that it was published. She referred directly to S. M. J. R. and wrote:

> despite my best efforts it seems probable that there is still some time between him and the day he seems to dread—the period when absolute equality in all things, subject to an individual capability, will be afforded to all human beings. (*The Motor Cycle* October 28, 1903)

S. M. J. R.'s response to this letter started with a paternalistic trivialization of her points by stating 'that in response to her gentle vapourings, they are pointless'. He continued:

> I should be very sorry to be forced to conclude that 'Woman-an Engine Driver' is a 'new woman' . . . She has completely misunderstood my letter and it seems to have drifted into that old chestnut, so-called 'woman's rights'. I referred to motor cycling for women purely from a physical and constitutional point of view . . . and whilst I take the audacious liberty of crossing pens with your fair correspondent, it is only my conviction that I am right which forces me to do so'. (*The Motor Cycle* November 11, 1903)

It would appear that S. M. J. R. had the last word for the time being, as the editorial written in November noted that this 'seems to occupy the minds of many of our correspondents, as we have received numerous letters on the subject, only a small number of which we have been able to publish' (November 11, 1903).

The series which started in 1905 catered primarily to the wives of male motorcyclists, with articles on how to dress, and the pleasures of riding in Motor Cycle sidecars; whilst by 1912 debates over women's suitability for riding a Motor Cycle on the road had shifted to focus on their suitability to participate in competitions such as speed trials, endurance and hill climbs. One such debate followed the accident of a Miss Hough during a hill climb at Sutton Club events at Harley Bank. From the sources cited it appears her accident not only resulted in her own injuries, which required hospitaliza-tion, but also injured some spectators as she lost control of her bike. The article commented on how she struck a slight dip at a road centre and '[s]he took the curve and spectators who had been warned proved to be her undo-ing' (*The Motor Cycle* May 23, 1912). Under the heading 'Should ladies be allowed to race', the editor, drawing once again on essentialist discourses of gender, wrote:

> One cannot but admire the pluck and courage of a lady who is willing, nay anxious, to try their prowess in a speed event. . . . The average lady is not possessed of the self-restraint, or presence of mind, which a man can command and we know we have many supporters in recommend-ing that ladies are discouraged from taking part in speed events! (*The Motor Cycle* May 23, 1912)

The writer went on to comment on having seen three ladies experience severe falls over the past year. Writing from her hospital bed, Hough, however, confirmed that her injuries were not serious and argued in her own defence:

> I should be very sorry indeed should our entries be refused in the future as I do not think that there is any more danger in racing for women than men. I certainly have fallen, but mine is not the first accident that has happened in the hill climb, often an expert man rider has come to grief. (June 27, 1912)

Hough's spirited defence of women's participation in the sport drew attention to the perhaps myopic approach of the motorcycle press in not only singling out accidents that involved women but seeing them as evidence that it was not suitable for women to participate in this particular leisure activity.

CONCLUSION

Specialist journals such as *The Motor Cycle* provided a lively public sphere within which journal editors played the role of intermediaries, shaping and refereeing the hostile debate about the suitability of riding for the 'fairer sex'. This examination of motorcycling magazines, however, sheds light on more than discussions about women's participation in this particular pastime, whether as riders, passengers or participants in competitions. Analysis of these magazines also demonstrates that historians can find evidence of contestation over the social construction of femininity and even discourses of feminism in some seemingly unlikely areas of print media. For historians of women, this emphasises that an understanding of the growth of early twentieth-century feminism should not be reduced to discussions of the more high-profile suffrage campaigns.

BIBLIOGRAPHY / SOURCES

Alford, Steven E., and Suzanne Ferriss. 2007. *Motorcycle*. London: Reaktion.

Ardis, Ann. 2009 [September issue]. Book Review of Lucy Delup. 'The Feminist Avant-Garde: Transatlantic Encounters of the Early Twentieth Century.' *Modernism/Modernity* 16 (3): 627–628.

Ardis, Ann. 2011. 'Making Middlebrow Culture, Making Middlebrow Literary Texts Matter: The Crisis, Easter 1912.' *Modernist Cultures* 6 (1): 18–40.

Beavan, B. 2005. *Leisure, Citizenship and Working-Class Men in Britain, 1850–1945*. Manchester University Press.

Beck, Peter J. 2008. 'Leisure and Sport in Britain, 1900–1939.' In *A Companion to Early Twentieth-Century Britain*, edited by Chris Wrigley, 453–469. Chichester, UK: Wiley.

Beetham, Margaret. 1996. *A Magazine of Her Own? Domesticity and Desire in the Woman's Magazine, 1800–1914*. London: Routledge.

Cahn, Susan K. 1994. *Coming on Strong: Gender and Sexuality in Twentieth-Century Women's Sports*. New York: The Free Press / Macmillan.

Conboy, Martin. 2011. *Journalism in Britain: A Historical Introduction*. London: Sage.

Dyhouse, Carol. 1989. *Feminism and the Family in England 1880–1939*. Oxford: Basil Blackwell.

Frederick, Bonnie, and Susan H. McLeod, eds. 1993. *Women and the Journey: The Female Travel Experience*. Pullman: Washington State University Press.

Habermas, Jurgen. 1962. English translation 1989. *The Structural Transformation of the Public Sphere: An Inquiry into a Category of Bourgeois Society*. Cambridge, MA: The MIT Press.

Hall, Stuart. 1981. 'Notes Towards Deconstructing the Popular.' In *People's History and Socialist Theory*, edited by Ralph Samuel, 81–89. London: Routledge.

Jaoannou, Maroula, and June Purvis. 2009. *The Women's Suffrage Movement: New Feminist Perspectives*. Manchester University Press.

Johnstone, Gary. 1994. *Classic Motor Cycles*. Osceola, FL: Motorbooks International.

Koerner, Steve. 1998. 'Four Wheels Good; Two Wheels Bad: The Motor Cycle versus the Light Motor Car 1919–39.' In *The Motor Car and Popular Culture in the 20th Century*, edited by David Thomas, Len Holden, and Tim Claydon, 151–176. Aldershot: Ashgate.

Koerner, Steve. 2007. 'Whatever Happened to the Girl on the Motorbike?' *International Journal of Motor Cycle Studies* (March). Accessed October 9, 2009. http://ijms.nova.edu/March2007/IJMS_Artcl.Koerner.html.

Ledger, Sally. 1997. *The New Woman Fiction and Feminism at the Fin De Siècle.* Manchester University Press.

Pedersen, Sarah. 2002. 'The Appearance of Women's Politics in the Correspondence Pages of Aberdeen Newspapers 1900–1914.' *Women's History Review* 11 (4): 657–674.

Romalov, Nancy. 1995 [Spring issue]. 'Mobile Heroines: Early Twentieth-Century Girls' Automobile Series.' *Journal of Popular Culture* 28 (4): 231–243.

Scharff, Virginia. 1991. *Taking the Wheel: Women and the Coming of the Motor Age.* New York: Free Press.

Showalter, Elaine. 1992. *Sexual Anarchy: Gender and Culture at the Fin de Siècle.* London: Bloomsbury.

Simpson, Clare S. 2007. 'Capitalising on Curiosity: Women's Professional Cycle Racing in the Late-Nineteenth Century.' In *Cycling and Society*, edited by Dave Horton, Paul Rosen, and Peter Cox. Aldershot, UK: Ashgate.

Van Vuuren, Melissa S. 2010. *Literary Research and the Victorian and Edwardian Ages, 1830–1910.* Lanham, MD: Scarecrow.

Walvin, J. 1978. *Leisure and Society, 1830–1950.* London: Longman.

PERIODICAL SOURCES

The Car, 1902
The Motor Cycle, 1903–1912
Motorcycling, 1910
The Daily Mail, 1903

2 From *Women's Hour* to *Other Women's Lives*
BBC Talks for Women and the Women Who Made Them, 1923–39

Kate Murphy

INTRODUCTION

At approximately 5 p.m. on May 2, 1923, an elegantly-dressed woman was gestured towards a microphone in the first purpose-built studio of the fledgling BBC. Princess Alice, the Duchess of Athlone, had been invited officially to open *Women's Hour* (not to be confused with today's *Woman's Hour*).[1] Her inaugural talk on 'The Adoption of Babies' would have been heard by an audience of several thousand listening in on their 'cat's whiskers', an early wireless technology (Moores 1988). The British Broadcasting Company, under the leadership of John Reith and now six months old, had recently moved to its new premises at Savoy Hill, next to London's Savoy Hotel. Here, and later from 1932 at Broadcasting House, hundreds of eminent women, and men, would take part in the BBC's impressive range of talks aimed at its ever-expanding female audience. And the audience did grow exponentially. There is no gender breakdown but listener figures grew from around 150,000 in January 1923 to nine million by January 1927, when the British Broadcasting Corporation was created by Royal Charter. At the outbreak of the Second World War, the figure was approaching thirty four million (Pegg 1983, 7).

The Duchess of Athlone was not alone in the Savoy Hill studio on May 2nd; her inaugural talk was coupled with that of the famous couturier Lady Duff Gordon who spoke on 'Fashions'. This mix of the worthy and light-hearted, of domesticity, social issues and escapism would provide the blueprint for women's programming in the inter-war years. *Women's Hour*'s producer (or Talks Assistant as the role was designated in the 1920s and 1930s) was Mrs Ella Fitzgerald, a former Fleet Street journalist. Fitzgerald, recruited to the BBC in April 1923, was the first of four female Talks Assistants responsible for women's programmes prior to the Second World War. She, and her successors Elise Sprott, Margery Wace and Janet Quigley, shaped the content and style of these broadcasts which were broadened and embedded into the morning schedules during the regime of Hilda Matheson, the first Director of Talks 1927–1932. As salaried BBC staff, all five women were ostensibly treated as equals to their male colleagues, in terms of promotion and pay. The Corporation was unusually enlightened in terms of the employment of women in the inter-war years (Murphy 2011). Even its marriage bar, introduced in 1932, was negotiable, if the woman concerned was viewed as valuable to the BBC.

Talks were to be a mainstay of radio in the inter-war years. With production techniques rudimentary, a scripted and rehearsed 'live' talk was the cheapest and most straightforward way to deliver the spoken word. Talks were central to the Reithian ethos of public service broadcasting, an 'instrument of democratic enlightenment' that could both inform and educate the British people (Scannell and Cardiff 1991, 13). The importance of the early BBC talk has been widely explored by Asa Briggs in his expansive history of the BBC and by Paddy Scannell and David Cardiff in their authoritative social history of British broadcasting (Briggs 1961, 1965; Scannell and Cardiff 1991). Only recently, however, have talks aimed at women in the 1920s and 1930s come under scrutiny. Michael Bailey has contended that the BBC's gendered broadcasts, with their focus on women's civic and domestic responsibilities, propelled the female audience towards a routine of ordered housewifery and childrearing (Bailey 2009). Maggie Andrews has examined how the public role of wireless, as it entered the private domain of the home, offered women listeners a range of 'expert' domestic viewpoints as they were in turn addressed as consumers, managers and homemakers (Andrews 2012). Issues of gendered broadcasting in the inter-war years have similarly been investigated in the U.S., Germany, Australia and Sweden (Hilmes 1997; Lacey 1996; Johnson 1988; Nordberg 1998).

This chapter takes an alternative perspective; rather than view women's talks through the lens of the listener or broadcaster, it considers these programmes from the viewpoint of the women who made them. This is an approach favoured by David Hendy who has argued for biography to be reappraised as a valued tool in media history, enriching our understanding of the BBC by exploring the backgrounds and motivations of employees (Hendy 2012). Fitzgerald, Sprott, Wace and Quigley were largely autonomous. Unlike the prestigious evening talks, daytime talks aimed at female listeners were not a high priority for the BBC, thus those producing these programmes did not face the same managerial scrutiny as others in the Talks Department. However, although they were empowered to address female listeners in what they believed were their best interests, the position was an onerous one. Whereas in newspapers and magazines, women could pick and choose what to read, wireless generally offered a single choice.[2] With an audience that encompassed women of all ages and social classes; married and unmarried; homemaker and employee; in town and countryside; providing a programme that would appeal to all was an almost impossible task. Rather, the breadth of women's talks reflected what each producer considered would best meet the needs of her audience; whether a talk on electricity, a farmhouse recipe or revelations of a mill girl's life. As Director of Talks, Hilda Matheson considerably expanded their range and complexity.

The BBC was born into an era of rapid change for women; their status had risen with the extension of the vote in 1918 (albeit only to those aged over 30), and, under the 1919 Sex Disqualification (Removal) Act, the opening up of the professions (Lewis 1984; Banks 1993; Beddoe 1989; Nicholson 2007). Young women, with their short hair and increasingly short skirts, were on the ascendant, flocking into the workplace, looking for fun and anticipating a very different future from that of their mothers (Alexander 1995). But barriers persisted in education and employment, most noticeably in the proliferation of marriage bars, and a married woman's place remained firmly in the home (Dyhouse 1995; Oram 1996; Giles 2004; Cowman and Jackson 2005). It was this captive daytime audience that talks aimed at women predominantly addressed. By examining the processes by which these talks came to air, new light can be shone onto the lives and expectations of both the women who listened, and of those who made them.

ELLA FITZGERALD

Little is known of Fitzgerald prior to her recruitment to the BBC apart from her place of birth, Dutch Guinea, and occasional references to Fleet Street (*Ariel* April 1936, October 1937). It is probable that her maturity, she was thirty five when she arrived at Savoy Hill, and her excellent contacts made her a good choice to oversee *Women's Hour*, with its requirements for two speakers on varied topics, six days a week. To address the diversity of her audience, Fitzgerald introduced regular broadcasts on, for example, cookery, poultry keeping, infant care, beauty and bridge and 'shamelessly' exploited former newspaper colleagues, several of whom broadcast without fees, just for the novel experience' (*Prospero* June 1969).

Edith Shackleton of the *Evening Standard* was one such contributor, making her first appearance on the programme in October 1923 when she gave a talk on journalism (*Radio Times* October 19, 1923). With the job market for women expanding, careers were a particular focus of Fitzgerald's, the earlier talks on how to become a house decorator or hairdresser giving way to less common female professions such as solicitor, x-ray operator, optician, welfare worker and analytical chemist. This proliferation of career opportunities for women was similarly reflected in an explosion of employment advice books, many written by outspoken feminists (Brittain 1928; Eyles 1930; Strachey 1935; Cole 1936). Marion Cran, whose gardening talks made her one of the BBC's most popular broadcasters of the interwar years, first appeared on *Women's Hour* in August 1923, confirming the growing acceptance of women as horticulturalists (Horwood 2010). Fitzgerald herself gave two talks each week including an early consumer item, 'In and Out of the Shops', for which she used her lunch-hour to gather material (*Prospero* June 1969). Reflecting on her time producing *Women's*

Hour, Fitzgerald was palpably proud that the MPs Nancy Astor, Margaret Wintringham and Ellen Wilkinson had graced the airwaves. The three were amongst the first women to take their seats in the House of Commons following the Parliament (Qualification of Women Act) 1918 which enabled women to stand as MPs.

In December 1923 a change was introduced to the way *Women's Hour* was run; a National Women's Advisory Committee (NWAC) was established to offer guidance to the programme, one of a number of advisory committees established by the early BBC to give it more credibility (WAC: R16/219: National Women's Advisory Committee (NWAC) 1924–1925). Seven eminent individuals were invited to sit on the NWAC, each signifying an area of women's lives the BBC deemed important to reflect. They were Lady Denman (Chairman of the National Federation of Women's Institutes), Margaret Bondfield (MP), Lilian Braithwaite (actress), Dr Elizabeth Sloan Chesser (physician), Mrs Violet Cambridge (Honorary Secretary of the Women's Amateur Athletic Association), Mrs Hardman Earle (Ministry of Food and Public Kitchens, First World War) and Evelyn Gates (Editor-in-Chief, *The Women's Yearbook*). Within weeks of its first meeting, and with Fitzgerald in attendance, two significant decisions were made; firstly to hold a plebiscite of listeners' views and secondly to abolish the *Women's Hour* name.

The plebiscite was Fitzgerald's suggestion. Two members of the NWAC appeared on *Women's Hour* on February 2, 1924 to establish at what time women could most easily listen and which subjects were preferred. Mrs Hardman Earle put forward the case for 'practical talks on topics relating to the welfare of the home'; Miss Evelyn Gates supported the argument 'that women looked to the wireless as a potential means of brightening their leisure hours' (*Radio Times* October 17, 1924, article written by Fitzgerald). These viewpoints encapsulated a thorny dilemma about programming for women: should it focus on domesticity or provide escapism, taking women out of the home? In her *Radio Times* article, Fitzgerald described how the plebiscite had galvanised the listener, with seventy five per cent of responses imploring the programme 'to abandon at once and for ever' all talks on domestic subjects.[3]

> Is it to be wondered at then that for 'the cure of constipation' we substituted a tour of Constantinople, that talks on the English country-side replaced those on the stocking of the kitchen cupboard! That instead of a series of talks on diets, we have debates on topical questions, that addresses on careers and hobbies have succeeded those on calories and how to dye the bathroom curtains?

As a result of the plebiscite, domestic subjects were reduced by a quarter to one third of the output, with new items introduced such as book reviews, travel talks and profiles of historical women (NWAC Minutes April 30, 1924).

Ironically, by the time Fitzgerald wrote her *Radio Times* article in October 1924, *Women's Hour* had ceased to exist. At the February meeting of the NWAC there was unanimous agreement to abolish the name (NWAC Minutes February 20, 1924). No reason was given as to why it caused such offence but a dislike of special treatment for women was part of the on-going feminist debate of the early 1920s. Divergent views were expressed by women's groups such as the National Union of Societies for Equal Citizenship (NUSEC) and the Six Point Group, centring on whether women should seek first to identify themselves as citizens rather than as women (Banks 1993; Law 1997). As a result of the NWAC decision, from March 24, 1924, *Women's Hour* was no longer listed in the schedules. Instead, from 4 p.m., 'two talks of general interest but with particular appeal to women' were interlarded with the afternoon concert (NWAC Minutes April 30, 1924). The NWAC met only one further time, on December 12, 1924. In September 1925 it was disbanded, by which time only one talk of interest to women was being broadcast. It appears that by getting rid of the title, the focus on women's issues was reduced, resulting in the demise of the NWAC and fewer programmes for women. In 1990, *Woman's Hour* campaigned to save its name for just this reason (Feldman 2000).

Fitzgerald's responsibilities may have diminished, but she continued to offer an array of female-related daytime talks such as 'Choosing a School', 'Psychology and the Shop Assistant' and 'A Woman in the Wild—Tiger Shooting' (*Radio Times* May 18, 1925, September 20, 1925, February 19, 1926). Two of her regular broadcasters became so popular their talks were published as books: *My Part of the Country* by 'A Bonnet Laird' and Mrs C Romanne-James' *O Toyo Writes Home*. In November 1926, Fitzgerald's three-and-a-half year association with talks for women came to an abrupt end when she was transferred to the new position of Assistant on *World Radio,* a foreign-programme supplement to *Radio Times*. Fitzgerald would go on to become Assistant Editor in 1928, retiring as Overseas Press Officer in 1947. Her move to *World Radio* came within weeks of Hilda Matheson's arrival at the BBC who, in January 1927, began her tenure as the BBC's first Director of Talks. One of Matheson's first tasks was to replace Fitzgerald and she appeared keen to appoint a new Talks Assistant who could cover a larger field of work (WAC: R13/419/1, Organisation of Talks Department October 1926). In the event, Elise Sprott, an established member of the Department, assumed the role, which was to create a tension between the two women and influence the direction of women's talks.

HILDA MATHESON AND ELISE SPROTT

Hilda Matheson was invited to the BBC by John Reith, coaxed away from her job as Political Secretary to Nancy Astor MP (Hunter 1994; Carney 1999). An Oxford graduate, Matheson was a brilliant intellectual who is credited with the transformation of BBC Talks (Scannell and Cardiff 1991; Avery 2006). Now aged thirty-eight, she moved on the fringes of the Bloomsbury set and introduced to the airwaves the likes of H. G. Wells, Harold Nicolson and Virginia Woolf. In late 1928, the novelist Vita Sackville-West was invited to broadcast and a two-year love affair with Matheson ensued.

Elise Sprott could not have been more different. She joined the full-time staff as a Talks Assistant in January 1925. Already an experienced broadcaster, she had regularly worked with Fitzgerald, giving her first talk, on European travel, in June 1924. Sprott originated from Cumberland and her fulsome pre-BBC career included motor engineering, volunteering as a nurse in the First World War and working for Herbert Hoover's Children's Relief Fund (*News Chronicle* July 29, 1939). Unlike Matheson, she had not been to university, which was to exacerbate problems between the two women. Prior to taking on responsibility for women's talks, Sprott had worked on the Department's broader output which included religious services, charitable appeals and the monthly Boy Scout and Boys' Brigade bulletins (WAC:R13/419/1, Organisation of Talks Department October 1926).

There is little direct evidence that Matheson and Sprott had an uncongenial relationship. However, in her letters to Sackville-West, Matheson shared her dream of finding a 'frightfully intelligent young woman of robust and excellent judgement' (Matheson to Sackville-West January 28, 1929). Sprott (nick-named 'Sprottie') did not fit the bill; a year older than Matheson, she was neither modern nor intellectual and appears to have been politically naïve. Matheson on the other hand, was sophisticated, urbane and undoubtedly progressive in her views. Sprott and Matheson took very different approaches to women's programming. While Sprott was a supporter of the domestic, Matheson was committed to widening the output, in particular enlightening women as citizens and, like many of her contemporaries, was an enthusiastic advocate of adult education.[4] The first indication of Matheson's desire to extend the scope of women's talks came in January 1927. Within days of becoming Director of Talks, the afternoons were revitalised with a schedule of programmes made in conjunction with the National Federation of Women's Institutes, including series on 'Citizenship in Practice', 'Health and Common Sense' and 'Village Life in Other Lands.'

A further experiment was initiated in January 1927; a weekly *Household Talk*. This was overseen by Sprott and was almost certainly her idea (WAC: R13/419/1: Talks Section Duties October 1927). The scope of *Household Talks* was modest but practical. The first few weeks included talks on decorating a small flat, making a lampshade and luncheon and pancake recipes; by the close of the year the series was encompassing modern methods of washing clothes and warm winter drinks. Sprott ensured the talks were given by appropriate experts including Mrs Cottington Taylor, the Director of the Good Housekeeping Institute and Mrs Clifton Reynolds, an expert in household appliances whose own home was 'equipped with every modern convenience and labour-saving device' (*Radio Times* September 2, 1927). *Household Talks* proved immensely popular and at the request of listeners, from August 24, 1928, merited a designated page in *Radio Times* with Sprott as point of liaison.

Sprott's enthusiasm for household talks was intense and it is doubtful that, without her input, Matheson would have given them the same priority. In her book *Broadcasting*, Matheson emphasised the huge value of such talks but also made clear her commitment to talks that were 'outside the common round of household drudgery' (Matheson 1933). In 1928, the vote was extended to all adult women; those over the age of twenty-one were now officially citizens. Matheson was eager to inform and educate these newly enfranchised young women about their civic responsibilities, introducing series such as *A Woman's Day* broadcast from November 1928. Here a female councillor, juror, magistrate and MP, amongst others, described their work and distinguished speakers included Margaret Bondfield MP, Dame Katherine Furse and Evelyn Emmett of the London County Council. In the run up to the 1929 election, the first at which all adult women could vote, the evening series *Questions for Women Voters* included discussions on equal pay, the marriage bar and whether boys and girls should have the same education.

In many ways, Sprott and Matheson complemented each other. While the BBC had an important role to play informing women about the wider world, it was a fact that the majority of daytime listeners were domestically orientated. Sprott and Matheson represented these two different needs. Sprott also conceived the idea of involving the listeners themselves in *Household Talks*, suggesting to Matheson that they contribute recipes and household hints, which would be professionally read out, and for which they would be paid a small fee (WAC: R51/239, Scheme for Special Series of Listeners' Contributions to Household Talks July 7, 1928). An appeal for Listeners' Contributions in *Radio Times* solicited more than 1,300 entries (*Radio Times* August 24, 1928, September 21, 1928). *A Listener's Household Talk* was first broadcast on September 24, 1928 and continued monthly thereafter, possibly the earliest example of listener input at the BBC. In October 1928, bolstered by the success of Listeners' Contributions, Sprott approached Matheson with a new venture; a daily rather than a weekly household talk (WAC: R51/239 October 2, 1928, Sprott to Matheson). The logical time for the new programme, she believed, would be 10:45 a.m., 'when housewives are about their work and . . . early enough not to interfere with the shopping'.

Discussions about the best time for women's talks had dogged the BBC since the earliest editions of *Women's Hour* and would continue throughout the 1920s and 1930s. The issue was never resolved because of the variance in women's listening habits linked not only to personal preference but also to age, social class, domicile and marital status. Nevertheless, on January

7, 1929 at 10:45 a.m., the experiment of *Morning Talks* began, soon to become a mainstay of the inter-war schedules. Although Sprott suggested this significant change to women's programming, Matheson had a strong input in the final content. Sprott had proposed somewhat mundane topics, for example talks on the principles of cooking, household art and domestic law (WAC: R51/239 October 3, 1928, Sprott to Matheson). While many of these ideas were realised, when *Morning Talks* came to air, far bolder series were also scheduled, initiated by Matheson. These included the feminist writer Ray Strachey's weekly *Woman's Commentary* on social affairs and *The Week in Parliament*, a vehicle through which women MPs spoke of the workings of Westminster. Nancy Astor made the first broadcast on November 6, 1929 and the series still exists on BBC Radio 4 today, as *The Week in Westminster*.

Sprott instigated a further series aimed at homemakers, *Housewives News* (WAC: R51/241: Housewives News October 10, 1930, Sprott to Matheson). The five-minute weekly consumer bulletin came to air in September 1931 and was both produced and presented by Sprott. However, by this time Sprott had been moved out of the Talks Department to other duties and Matheson herself was to resign shortly afterwards, ostensibly over disagreements with Reith about the direction of Talks (Carney 1991, 71–83). There is a lack of clarity about Sprott's departure but it was undoubtedly linked to the arrival of Oxford graduate Margery Wace. Matheson had finally found her 'robust young woman' who joined the Talks Department in September 1930 initially as an assistant to Sprott (WAC: R51/646: Women's Programmes undated document c.1931). In June 1931, the Control Board (Reith's inner circle of top managers) reported the ousting of Miss Sprott by Miss Wace, 'a more efficient junior' (WAC: R3/3/7: Control Board Minutes June 30, 1931). It was agreed that Sprott should be transferred to the newly created position of Women's Press Representative, with responsibility for publicity in connection with women's interests. Sprott would make a great success of her new job, travelling the length and breadth of the country to promote BBC women and women's programmes. She retired in 1945, as Head of Lecture Section.

MARGERY WACE

Twenty-five year old Margery Wace was Matheson's perfect appointee. Not only was she Oxbridge educated but, prior to her arrival at the BBC, had been secretary to the Oxford branch of the League of Nations and to the classicist and internationalist, Professor Gilbert Murray. Unlike cheerful 'Sprottie', who could be unsophisticated in her dealings with contributors, Wace was earnest and politically astute. For the first eighteen months she worked directly to Matheson, who retained her interest in women's talks. However, after Matheson left the BBC in early 1932, Charles Siepmann, the new Director of Talks, handed over full responsibility for *Morning Talks* to Wace. Now able to impart her own vision, she refocused on the domestic but in a manner she believed would both empower women and benefit wider society. Writing in *Radio Times* in 1935, Wace stressed her conviction that the mother in the home was crucial to social cohesion:

> The nation's health, both physical and mental, is in the housewife's hands. By her skill and knowledge she must often make a very small sum provide adequate food; by sharing her family's interests, and by keeping her mind alert, she must provide a happy atmosphere in the home. We want to help her (*Radio Times* November 1, 1935).

Child and maternal welfare were topics of serious political discussion throughout the inter-war years (Lewis 1990) and Wace's series *A Doctor to a Mother* can be viewed as part of this wider debate. It also demonstrates her verve, conviction and fresh approach to *Morning Talks*. Writing to Siepmann in early 1932 she suggested new arrangements for the BBC's child welfare talks which were 'potentially among the most important in the programme, capable, in time, of a real and lasting effect on the nation's health' (WAC: R51/75 January 26, 1932, Wace to Siepmann). Wace insisted that, because of this, not only should the most authoritative material be obtained but also the best speakers. She urged a change in the way they were chosen, maintaining that, rather than depending on doctors in administrative positions, GPs should be used because not only did they have personal experience with child patients, but also used less jargon. *A Doctor to a Mother* aired from October 1932 and was soon augmented by other Friday morning series on child and maternal health such as *Common Sense and the Child* and *The Mother's Health*. In planning these programmes, Wace showed meticulous care. For example, in January 1934, for a series on the health of the school child, she wrote to the Matron-in-Chief of the London County Council requesting a meeting to discuss the problems facing school nurses (WAC: R51/75 January 30, 1934, Wace to Matron-in-Chief, County Hall). Wace wanted her child welfare talks to tackle difficult issues such as stammering, shyness and obstinacy as well as more established subjects such as baby care (WAC: R51/239 April 7, 1932, Wace to Quigley). The Friday morning talks by doctors continued up until the Second World War. Hilda Jennings and Winifred Gill, in their 1939 report on listening habits in Bristol, made specific reference to these talks, which they believed had a positive effect on the working-class housewives who listened (Jennings and Gill 1939). Michael Bailey has argued that these talks empowered women, according them a new role as medical auxiliaries (Bailey 2009).

Another series initiated by Wace was *How I Keep House* in which housewives themselves spoke about their domestic routine (Andrews 2012, 46–50). In September 1934, *Radio Pictorial* ran an article headlined 'The Housewife's Friend' in which they wrote excitedly about Wace's journey around the country to meet potential contributors: 'So far, her search has taken her to Norfolk to see a farm worker's wife, to Scotland to visit a fisherman's and to Reigate to visit a policeman's home' (*Radio Pictorial* September 21, 1934). The series was also enthusiastically previewed in *Radio Times (Radio Times* August 17, 1936). Wace was not the first BBC producer to use 'real' people as contributors, but this was the first time the device was used on *Morning Talks*.

To find her contributors, Margery Wace had indeed been conscientious. She approached organisations as diverse as the Amalgamated Union of Building Trade Workers and the Ministry of Agriculture. Writing to the General Secretary of the National Union of Railwaymen, Wace indicated that, in order to fit the series, the railwayman's wife she was seeking should have young children, family earnings of not more than £2 a week and the reputation of being a good housewife (WAC: R51/240 October 30, 1934, Wace to Marchback). The notes sent to potential speakers indicate the specific and personal nature of the talks. The women were asked to describe exactly what they spent their housekeeping on as well as the daily routine of their lives. The essence of the series was that the women should be working-class housewives, so by definition not used to public speaking. Wace therefore oversaw their scripts and before each broadcast, the individual woman was extensively rehearsed. As Maggie Andrews has indicated, giving a voice to ordinary women, rather than experts, was a bold departure for the BBC and the series was well received (Andrews 2012, 49). A congratulatory letter from a Scottish miner's wife recounted that, despite running a home for nearly nineteen years, the talks had taught her many useful hints (WAC: R51/240 October 5, 1934, Letter from Mrs M Henry).

Wace's output was prodigious; in 1935 the six talks she produced each week were acknowledged to be the most in the Department. The other Talks Assistants, all male, were responsible for, on average, four talks series a year (WAC: R13/408/2, General Talks Department document February 28, 1935). Possibly because of her proven value to the BBC, in the summer of 1936 Wace was moved to the expanding Empire Talks Department, where she was promoted to Empire Talks Director in 1938. In 1944, now married to a BBC colleague, she would die tragically young, shortly after the birth of their first child (obituary, *The Times* January 13, 1944). One of her final acts as *Morning Talks* producer was to organise, with Elise Sprott, the BBC's Women's Conference. Held at Broadcasting House in April 1936, it was hosted by Sir Stephen Tallents, the newly appointed Controller of Public Relations, and was attended by almost four hundred women representing more than sixty different organisations including the Women's Freedom League, the Electrical Association for Women, the Central Committee on Women's Training and Employment, the Mother's Union, the Women's Co-operative Guild and the Over Thirty Association. The Conference had as its focus *Morning Talks*, in particular the content and the timing of programmes (WAC: R44/86/1: Women's Conference 1936). Thus, the issues that had exercised the NWAC were still of concern to the BBC twelve years on. Although the Women's Conference was viewed positively, the outcome was indecisive, indicating the impossibility of pleasing the diaspora of women, who had vastly differing tastes and daily routines.

JANET QUIGLEY

The replacement for Margery Wace was Janet Quigley. Quigley, an Oxford graduate like Matheson and Wace, had a varied working life before the BBC which included publishing, bookselling and a stint in the Publicity Department of the Empire Marketing Board (WAC: L1/784/1, Janet Quigley staff file). She was recruited to the BBC in 1930 as an Assistant in the Foreign Department where her main responsibility was American relays, that is, arranging simultaneous broadcasts from the USA.[5] Highly regarded by BBC managers, Quigley was thirty-four when she joined the Talks Department in August 1936.

Like Wace, Quigley's main duty was to supervise *Morning Talks*. In this she maintained the high standards and professionalism of her predecessor but with a lighter touch. While she retained the Friday morning series on child wellbeing, which she acknowledged were of real service to listeners, she introduced new programmes such as *Tea Time Talks* and *Five o' Clock* aimed at the family 'sitting round the tea table, waiting to be entertained' (*Radio Times* September 25, 1936). Quigley's distinct approach is apparent from an illuminating sequence of memos dating from November 1936, soon after her arrival in the department. These reveal Quigley's personal crusade to give air-time to 'The Beauty Racket', a subject she felt passionate about. As Carol Dyhouse has identified, the use of cosmetics was much debated in the inter-war years (Dyhouse 2010, 64–68). Because this was a controversial topic, Quigley needed the go-ahead from the Director of Talks, temporarily J. M. Rose-Troup (Siepmann had been sideways moved in October 1935). In her initial memo, she stated that if she had a mission in life it was 'to save people, and particularly badly-off-women from the tyranny of advertising', claiming that beauty advertisements were 'the most pernicious of all' (WAC: R51/397/1: Talks Policy November 9, 1936, Quigley to Rose-Troup). Quigley was particularly incensed that women of all ages were either being conned into spending large sums of money they could ill-afford on products with doubtful benefits or believed they were doomed because they were unable to purchase the new face powder or anti-wrinkle cream. Her series, in contrast, would show women how they could keep 'skin, hair and hands in good condition and also indulge in moderate cosmetics for ten shillings a year!'

Rose-Troup was impressed but because of the contentious nature of the series felt duty bound to approach the Controller of Programmes, Cecil Graves (November 17, 1936, Rose-Troup to Graves). Graves' response was curt. Having discussed the idea at Programme Committee, there was concern that the fury of the manufacturers would be raised if the BBC were seen to be suggesting that women could make themselves beautiful by soap and water alone. In addition, from the point of view of *Radio Times* advertisements, which included beauty products, it would be difficult (November 19, 1936, Graves to Rose-Troup). Quigley was not to be deterred. In July 1937, she re-presented her 'considerably modified' ideas to Sir Richard Maconachie, the new Director of Talks, assuring him that she was no longer 'burning with indignation at recent revelations of the ramp behind the beauty trade!' She hoped that an occasional series of talks on the care of the skin, hands and hair might be included in the autumn *Five o' Clock*, a new 'more feminine' edition (July 6, 1937, Quigley to Maconachie). Maconachie again proposed the series to Graves, citing as his excuse 'the quenching of Miss Quigley's spirit' (July 14, 1937, Maconachie to Graves). That Quigley's programme finally went ahead is confirmed in *Radio Times*. The listings for October 21, 1937 include a *Tea Time Talk*: 'Making the Most of your Looks.'

Quigley introduced a plethora of other new series including six talks on *Careers* in collaboration with Ray Strachey of the Women's Employment Federation and a long-running series entitled *Other Women's Lives*. Amongst the eclectic mix of speakers were Mrs Edward Harvey who ran a general store in a working class district of Liverpool, the film critic Winifred Holmes, Agnes Smith, a 'doffer' in a cotton factory and Olga Collett, the Supervisor of Female Staff at ICI.[6] One series that aroused particular interest was *Mistress and Maid*. The 'servant problem' remained a worry for the middle-classes throughout the inter-war years (Light 2007; Delap 2011) and the subject had been reflected twice before on the BBC ('The Domestic Service Problem' Autumn 1924; 'The Future of Domestic Service' Spring 1930). Quigley's series, broadcast in early 1938, was the BBC's most extensive exploration of the issue with sixteen different viewpoints aired in twelve programmes. Like previous series, there was no debate as to whether servitude was intrinsically wrong; rather, as an article in *The Listener* explained, the different speakers expressed views on why they thought the servant shortage had arisen and how best the situation might be dealt with, highlighting issues of status, flexibility and pay (*The Listener* February 23, 1938). Quigley was satisfied the subject had been given a thorough airing; her report indicated particular pleasure that, in many households, mistress and maid had listened and discussed the talks together (WAC: R51/397/2 April 29, 1938, Janet Quigley Quarterly Reports). The correspondence had also been impassioned, as Quigley explained, 'We have been hailed, on the one side, as the courageous spokesmen of a maligned and inarticulate class, and, on the other, accused—usually by contented servants—of stirring up unnecessary trouble'.

During her years in charge of *Morning Talks*, Quigley further developed programmes for women. While maintaining a number of long-running series such as the doctors' talks to mothers, she also placed greater emphasis on programmes for younger and more modern women. 'For the Young House-wife' was praised for its 'up-to-datedness'; her talks on beauty and simple cosmetics introduced a sparkle previously missing (*Radio Times* October 29, 1937). Quigley continued her expansive interest in women's talks into the Second World War, producing many key programmes, including *The Kitchen Front* (Nicholas 1996). Later she would become a trailblazing editor of *Woman's Hour* (Skoog 2010 and in Chapter 6, this volume), retiring in 1961 as Assistant Head, Talks.

CONCLUSION

The BBC broadcast an impressive range of women's talks during the 1920s and 1930s. The topics selected, the speakers used, the production values exhibited were invariably those of the individual woman producer concerned. With its enlightened attitude towards the employment of female staff, the BBC provided an environment where these women could thrive; they were trusted and respected and, provided they didn't stray into areas of controversy, they were largely left alone. Although seldom light-hearted, talks for women fitted the Reithian principles of the BBC: to inform, educate and entertain. They addressed their daytime audience essentially as homemakers and mothers, offering insights on issues of health, domesticity and citizenship, but also providing stimulation and escapism. As Hilda Matheson noted, radio offered women 'a preparatory course to help them to catch up, to feel less at a disadvantage, to keep abreast of wider interests' (Matheson 1933, 189–90). Ella Fitzgerald, Elise Sprott, Hilda Matheson (in her role as a producer of women's talks), Margery Wace and Janet Quigley all had a strong sense of their listeners and were dedicated to producing talks they believed would enhance women's lives. The diversity of the audience meant that there was certainly dissatisfaction with the talks that were offered, but for many, they were a lifeline to the outside world, as a letter to *Radio Times* confirms. Commenting on Ray Strachey's *A Woman's Commentary* in February 1929, a listener from Manchester wrote:

> Such talks come as a god-send to women bursting with mental energy, yet who must stay close to work-a-day household duties. To one, at least, the task of cleaning a kitchen went down a little better whilst listening to the intelligent observations of an intelligent woman.

NOTES

1. *Women's Hour* was one of a trilogy of programmes that included *Children's Hour* and *Men's Hour*. *Men's Hour* was short-lived; its final broadcast was October 9, 1923.

2. At some points in the schedule there would have been an alternative broadcast from a provincial or regional BBC station.
3. Fitzgerald's interpretation of the figures was inaccurate: 57% had voted against domestic topics, i.e., 187 out of 326 letters received (NWAC Minutes February 20, 1924).
4. For example, Matheson was Secretary of the Joint Committee of Inquiry into Broadcasting and Adult Education, chaired by Sir Henry Hadow, 1926–1928 (WAC: R14/145/Education: Adult Education).
5. Quigley was suggested to the BBC by her flatmate and former Oxford University friend Isa Benzie, who became the BBC's Foreign Director in 1933.
6. Olga Collett would become the BBC's first female Outside Commentator in 1937.

BIBLIOGRAPHY / SOURCES

Alexander, Sally. 1995. *Becoming a Woman and Other Essays in 19th and 20th Century Feminist History*. New York University Press.

Andrews, Maggie. 2012. *Domesticating the Airwaves: Broadcasting, Domesticity and Femininity*. London: Continuum.

Avery, Todd. 2006. *Radio Modernism: Literature, Ethics, and the BBC, 1922–1938*. Aldershot, UK: Ashgate.

Bailey, Michael. 2009. 'The Angel in the Ether: Early Radio and the Construction of the Household.' In *Narrating Media History*, edited by Michael Bailey. London: Routledge.

Banks, Olive. 1993. *The Politics of British Feminism, 1918–1970*. Aldershot, UK: Edward Elgar.

Beddoe, Deirdre. 1989. *Back to Home and Duty: Women between the Wars 1918–1939*. London: Pandora.

Briggs, Asa. 1961. *The Birth of Broadcasting: The History of Broadcasting in the United Kingdom*, vol. 5. Oxford University Press.

Briggs, Asa. 1965. *The Golden Age of Broadcasting: The History of Broadcasting in the United Kingdom*, vol. 2. Oxford University Press.

Brittain, Vera. 1928. *Women's Work in Modern England*. London: Noel Douglas.

Carney, Michael. 1999. *Stoker: The Life of Hilda Matheson*. Llangynog, UK: Michael Carney.

Cole, Margaret. 1936. *The Road to Success: Twenty Essays on the Choice of a Career for Women*. London: Methuen & Co.

Cowman, Krista, and Louise Jackson, eds. 2005. *Women and Work Culture in Britain c1850–1950*. Aldershot, UK: Ashgate.

Delap, Lucy. 2011. *Knowing Their Place: Domestic Service in Twentieth Century Britain*. Oxford University Press.

Dyhouse, Carol. 2010. *Glamour: Women, History, Feminism*. London: Zed Books.

Dyhouse, Carol. 1995. *No Distinction of Sex? Women in British Universities, 1870–1939*. London: UCL Press.

Eyles, Leonora. 1930. *Careers for Women*. London: Mathews and Marrot.

Feldman, Sally. 2000. 'Twin Peaks: The Staying Power of *Woman's Hour*.' In *Women and Radio: Airing Differences*, edited by Caroline Mitchell. London: Routledge.

Giles, Judy. 2004. *The Parlour and the Suburb: Domestic Identities, Class, Femininity and Modernity*. London: Berg.

Hendy, David. 2012. 'Biography and the Emotions as a Missing "Narrative" in Media History: A Case Study of Lance Sieveking and the Early BBC.' *Media History* 18 (3–4): 361–378.

Hilmes, Michele. 1997. *Radio Voices: American Broadcasting, 1922–1952*. Minneapolis: University of Minnesota Press.

Horwood, Catherine. 2010. *Gardening Women: Their Stories 1600 to the Present*. London: Virago.

Hunter, Fred. 1994. 'Hilda Matheson and the BBC, 1926–1940.' In *This Working-Day: Women's Lives and Cultures in Britain 1914–1945*, edited by Sybil Oldfield. London: Taylor and Francis.

Jennings, Hilda, and Winifred Gill. 1939. *Broadcasting in Everyday Life: A Survey of the Social Effects of the Coming of Broadcasting*. London: BBC.

Johnson, Lesley. 1988. *The Unseen Voice: A Cultural Study of Early Australian Radio*. London: Routledge.

Lacey, Kate. 1996. *Feminine Frequencies: Gender, German Radio, and the Public Sphere, 1923–1945*. University of Michigan Press.

Law, Cheryl. 1997. *Suffrage and Power: The Women's Movement 1918–1928*. London: I. B. Tauris.

Lewis, Jane. 1990. *The Politics of Motherhood: Child and Maternal Welfare in England 1900–1939*. London: Croom Helm.

Lewis, Jane. 1984. *Women in England 1870–1950: Sexual Divisions and Social Change*. Brighton, UK: Wheatsheaf Books.

Light, Alison. 2007. *Mrs Woolf and the Servants: The Hidden Heart of Domestic Service*. London: Fig Tree.

Matheson, Hilda. 1933. *Broadcasting*. London: Thornton Butterworth.

Moores, Shaun. 'The Box on the Dresser: Memories of Early Radio and Everyday Life.' *Media, Culture and Society* 10 (1): 23–40.

Murphy, Kate. 2011. 'On an Equal Footing with Men? Women and Work at the BBC, 1923–1939.' PhD diss., University of London.

Nicholas, Sian. 1996. *The Echo of War: Home Front Propaganda and the Wartime BBC, 1939–1945*. Manchester University Press.

Nicholson, Virginia. 2007. *Singled Out: How Two Million Women Survived without Men after the First World War*. London: Viking.

Nordberg, Karin. 1998. *Folkhemmets Röst: Radion som Folkbildare 1925–1950*. Stockholm/Stehag: Brutus Östlings Bokförlag Symposion.

Oram, Alison. 1996. *Women Teachers and Feminist Politics 1900–1939*. Manchester University Press.

Pegg, Mark. 1983. *Broadcasting and Society 1918–1939*. London: Croom Helm.

Scannell, Paddy, and David Cardiff. 1991. *A Social History of British Broadcasting 1922–1939*. Oxford: Blackwell.

Skoog, Kristin. 2010. 'The "Responsible" Woman: The BBC and Women's Radio 1945–1955.' PhD diss., University of London.

Strachey, Ray. 1935. *Careers and Openings for Women: A Survey of Women's Employment and a Guide for Those Seeking Work*. London: Faber and Faber.

3 Lady Eleanor Smith
The Society Column, 1927–1930

Sallie McNamara

INTRODUCTION: THE SIGNIFICANCE OF
LADY ELEANOR SMITH'S SOCIETY COLUMN

When Patrick Balfour in discussing the post-1918 generation remarked that 'a salient feature of the post-war epoch has been the increased appetite of the public for every form of gossip' (1933, 1), he was commenting both on society at large and a feature of the popular press. Society columns appeared in the *Daily Express*, *Weekly/Sunday Dispatch* and magazines such as *The Bystander* and *Tatler* in the inter-war era; however, there are different academic perspectives on the status of these columns. Histories of women and journalism see society news as something of a marginal area, a space often occupied by female journalists. Chambers, Steiner and Fleming comment that until the turn of the 20th century, and often beyond that, 'women occupied a "ghetto status"'. They 'were often confined to marginal areas of news—fashion, domestic issues and a form of 'society news,' that is essentially glorified gossip about the lives of the rich and famous' (2004, 15–16). However, this 'ghetto status' would appear to exist only when occupied by female journalists as Balfour's comments included reference to prominent society columnists (or paragraphists as they are also known). He provided a brief history referring to Lord Castlerosse (*Sunday Express*, started 1926) and Lord Donegall in the *Sunday News* while particular praise is given to the Dragoman (Tom Driberg) in the *Daily Express* for providing a critical commentary which covered society, sport, the Army, politics, the stage, literature and art (Balfour 1933, 101). In contrast, this chapter focusses on Lady Eleanor Smith's editorship of the society column in the *Weekly/Sunday Dispatch* from 1927–1930: its name was changed from the *Weekly* to the *Sunday Dispatch* at the end of 1928.

When considering women's relationship with different media forms, there are a number of significant issues to consider. While Balfour referred to Lady Eleanor Smith, commenting that he helped edit her page, he does not point out that she was the first woman to be *named* as the editor. Society columns used pseudonyms and it was thus not obvious who the authors were; *Tatler* and *Bystander*, for example, used 'Evelyn' and 'Blanchette',

In her flat in Grosvenor Square during the war

Figure 3.1 Lady Eleanor Smith in her flat in Grosvenor Square during the war. Courtesy Lady Juliet Townsend.

respectively, while the *Weekly Dispatch* used the name 'Lorgnette' prior to Smith's editorship. The 1920s and 30s can be seen, therefore, as an important moment in terms of women's roles within the largely male press. Secondly, while histories of women and journalism are critical of what they call the 'ghetto status', acknowledgement and analysis of all areas of women's involvement in the press is vital to assess the contribution of the gossip column to twentieth century media development. Thirdly, Smith's own background was important; women may not have been at the political centre in terms of actually wielding power, but they did have privileged access to its dissemination. In terms of central political figures, Smith was the daughter of the first Earl of Birkenhead, a Cabinet Minister in Lloyd George's government who became Lord Chancellor in 1919. Birkenhead was a close friend of Churchill, and the family were often invited to Blenheim Palace; her autobiography gives vivid descriptions of holidays and Christmases spent there (Smith 1939, 47–52). Lady Eleanor Smith was somebody whose family was at the centre of society, and while she may not have been politically powerful, she was close to those who were, something that was made apparent in her column.

Furthermore, Smith was also a former 'Bright Young Person', as immortalised by Evelyn Waugh in *Vile Bodies* (1930). Smith was described by Cecil Beaton as 'Lord Birkenhead's eccentric daughter' (1985, 36), 'terribly alert and sharp like a bird' (1985, 67). He stated that she talked at a rattling pace and used 'extraordinary obsolete and long words' (1985, 80). Her friends were from different backgrounds and included socialites and debutantes as well as artists, dancers and those from gypsy and circus backgrounds. She was passionately interested in gypsy life, having first encountered gypsies as a young girl when they camped near the family home. She travelled with gypsies both in Britain and in Spain, and learnt to speak Romany. She claimed (fictitiously) that her father's grandmother, Bathsheba, was a gypsy (Birkenhead 1953, 18–19). Smith was also fascinated by circus life and did publicity for the Great Carmo Circus; the painter, Dame Laura Knight, also travelled with this circus, using it as subject matter for her work. Smith's interest was such that she was the first President of the Circus Friends Association, formed in 1934.

Balfour intimates that Smith was a somewhat reluctant columnist, and that while she was adept, 'Lady Eleanor, who has since become a Romantic novelist of exceptional talent, never admired the view from her 'Window in Vanity Fair' and soon retired behind its curtains' (92). These comments were endorsed in her brother's memoir of her which pointed out: 'She detested Society, despised gossip writers, and refused to attend parties, so that an odder appointment could scarcely have been made' (Birkenhead 1953, 64). Smith endorsed this but noted that her involvement with the column had helped her own writing career in that she 'learned to write briefly and . . . learned to write fast. These are valuable lessons for any writer' (Smith 1939, 119). Apart from the society column Smith also wrote film reviews for the *Evening Standard*, and brief comments on films also appear in 'From My Window in Vanity Fair'. Her departure from the *Weekly Dispatch* in 1930 coincided with the publication of her first book, *The Red Wagon*, and until her death in 1945 she went on to publish eleven more novels and short stories, her autobiography, *Life's a Circus: Reminiscences of Lady Eleanor Smith* (1939), and, with John Hinde, a book on the circus, *British Circus Life*, published posthumously in 1948. Her books were extremely popular (McNamara 2008) such that five were adapted for screen and/or stage; her fame is perhaps also attested to by her appearance on *Desert Island Discs* with Roy Plomley in 1943. While editing the society column would, as she stated, prove to be a good training ground for a writer, it also allowed her to cover some of the issues and people she *was* interested in, for example, the arts and gypsies, while also offering a space to criticise those she disliked.

Smith could not however be described as feminist as her comments prior to the introduction of what became known as the 'Flapper Vote' in 1928 demonstrated. The Representation of the People Act in 1928 extended the voting franchise from women over 30 to all women over the age of 21; Smith, however, the previous year asserted:

> I do not in the least desire a vote, but it looks uncommonly as though I am about to have one. The whole idea seems to me absurd; the majority of twenty-one year old girls are not only profoundly ignorant of politics, but also entirely indifferent to them.
>
> I doubt whether one out of six could give a correct list of Cabinet Ministers.
>
> I heard a girl of twenty inquire the other day who was Prime Minister. I asked a pretty manicurist yesterday what she thought of the proposal. 'Oh, it doesn't interest me', she answered, 'and it won't make any difference to me, either. I shan't bother to vote'. (April 17, 1927)

Her next reference to the newly enfranchised was on January 20, 1929, when she asked her 'flapper friends' what they would do (if anything) with the Flapper Vote. She suggested ignorance amongst this group and stated: 'Most of them had never thought about it all. Others thought that there were only two parties they *could* vote for—Conservative and Labour' (emphasis in original). Finally, she suggested the decisions of all of them were influenced by any but political reasons, and went on to discuss the family explanations for women's voting patterns.

The layout of the column is important to note in that many of the paragraphs were interspersed with ones critical of a member of the social group, for example:

> Tuesday.—At a shoe-shop this morning I heard a shrill, angry female voice pouring forth a flow of violent abuse at an employee.

> I turned, and recognised a well-known woman, frequently extolled
> in "Court" columns for her poise, her grace, and her charming man-
> ners. (March 27, 1927)

This demonstrates the format where a story was often developed, but
broken up by something seemingly unrelated. The one above is an example of the criticism of some members of the elite social group, which was
not unusual, and it is likely that the people referred to were recognised
by others in that circle. It indicates an element of policing appropriate
behaviour within society itself: Smith herself was antagonistic towards
some aspects of society, and these criticisms were voiced in both her column and her later work. (Her novel *Tzigane* (1937), for example, developed this, presenting 'Society' people with condescending responses to a
talented gypsy dancer.)

For historians, the society column is of significance as it can reveal
important perspectives on the society of the time. Major debates may well
have been played out on the front pages, but other concerns, such as the
Flapper Vote, were discussed elsewhere and perhaps passed off as of no real
importance. The wide-ranging subject matter of Smith's column, as Balfour
noted, could include society as well as the arts, politics, sport and military
issues, and offered an informal, gossipy approach, suggestive of 'insider
knowledge' which illuminated concerns, anxieties and the reworking of
who was an 'outsider' to society. Discussing national identity and everyday
life, Tim Edensor comments: 'It is worth exploring . . . the boundary-making
processes which operate within national identities, ways of delineating who
does and who does not belong to the nation, for battles over exclusion and
inclusion are always ongoing' (2002, 25). Edensor is referring to the means
by which national identities are created, and as he argues, these are continually being remade, and identities either permitted or expelled are subject to
change. The society column is a potentially vital area for the exploration of
cultural boundaries, for the working through of concerns around national
and cultural identity as they often carried criticism or praise of individuals
and groups. It could work to mark symbolic boundaries and draw attention
to what disturbs cultural order, that is, what is 'matter out of place' (Douglas 1966, 35). Smith's society column thus provides an interesting source
to explore the perspective and boundaries of the aristocratic/elite groups
who figured most prominently in the content and suggest much about this
group's formation (and re-formation) in the inter-war period and how this
was being played out. Issues of group identity can be identified perhaps
predictably in relation to class, and to Americans, which will be discussed
below. Furthermore, study of Smith's perhaps more unexpected discourses
on the arts and gypsies/Romanies sheds light on the complex, contradictory and unstable nature of identity construction in the era and also draws
attention to women's and the media's role in relation to this.

THE SHIFTING TERRAIN OF THE RULING CLASS

Smith's own 'marginal centrality' enabled her, and her column, to become an important focus for the exploration of cultural boundaries, boundaries which were themselves in flux. The early decades of the twentieth century saw a great deal of change at all levels of society as traditional patterns of power and control were threatened. Aristocrats, or representatives of upper class and landed elites, those who might popularly be seen as powerful groups, were increasingly under pressure as class boundaries were, through political, economic and social forces, experiencing a period of transformation. Ross McKibbin argues that between 1918 and 1945 a large part of the upper class collapsed into the upper middle class and states that the post-1945 businessmen and financiers were 'socially a mixed lot' (McKibbin 1998, 42) while David Cannadine refers to the 'increasing impoverishment of many landowners' (1994, 66) and to the belief that the traditional class model no longer applied in this period as established hierarchies were undermined (Cannadine 1998, 128). The rise of Labour as the second party, along with the increasing marginalisation of the House of Lords meant that 'politics and government no longer functioned hierarchically: it was now impossible in practice for peers to be prime ministers' (1998, 127). He also refers to the massive sales of land, houses and works of art following World War I that 'portended the end of the traditional, ordered, stable rural world in Great Britain' (Cannadine 1998, 127). However, although there were challenges to traditional modes of authority, Cannadine also points out that:

> For all the resonance of the politically polarised vision of society, this remained a grossly exaggerated picture. Most people recognised that British society was still very 'finely graded', into 'discrete social layers', which comprised 'an impossibly complex series of steps' (1998, 136).

Joanna Bourke has drawn attention to concerns about borders and boundaries in the inter-war period, which operated at both local and national levels in relation to class, community and nation. She comments on the fear and/or dislike felt in local communities of 'strangers' from other parts of Britain. One example given is of a shopkeeper in a Kent village who during the hop-picking season sprayed Jeyes Fluid over everything 'as a form of "barricade against the horde of invaders": after all, "who could tell what horrible germs were lurking in the clothes of those scruffy looking cockneys? He was quite sure they never took a bath"' (1994, 167). There was a perceived hierarchy as similar comments were made by cockneys who jeered at the gypsy pickers (1994, 192). In looking at national borders, Bourke suggests that debates about immigrants in the first half of the twentieth century centred on the Irish and the Jews (1994, 192) and that 'foreigners' were seen to threaten local constructions of the 'body' and all the rules of respectability which followed these constructions (1994, 204). In 1928, Lieutenant-Colonel A. H. Lane wrote in *The Alien Menace*:

> Where the foreigner has taken up his abode, respectable neighbour-hoods become evil colonies where the most elementary laws of sanitation are disregarded. The alien drives away the clean-minded natives and fills the vacant space with double the number of human beings for which it was originally intended. (cited in Bourke 1994, 204).

Overall, there were tensions around issues of identity, with concerns over class and national boundaries. While the class system was still in existence, it is clear that the traditional land-owning elites were experiencing some challenge as they lost land—and power—alongside a growing middle class whose formation, as McKibbin notes, was changing with their impoverishment (1998). Ruling elites have always adapted to such challenges as new money, either from business or overseas, and specifically the U.S., or the Americans as they were referred to, were assimilated through marriage.

'FROM MY WINDOW IN VANITY FAIR': A MODERN VIEW

Lady Eleanor Smith's column ran from 1927–1930; it covered a range of people and topics, including contemporary celebrities, aristocratic and those from theatre and film, the arts, also including commentary on and criticism of the manners and behaviour of some of her contemporaries. While the column was edited by Smith, Patrick Balfour noted that he wrote for it, and in her autobiography Smith also referred to paying others, including the Duchess of Westminster and Lady Dufferin, to give her a story (Smith 1939, 120). However, columns in other papers, such as those by Castlerosse and Driberg, give them the credit as authors, regardless of other possible contributors, and my discussion will similarly credit Smith as the editor/author. It is important to note the name of the column changed when Smith took over, from 'Lorgnette' to 'From My Window in Vanity Fair'. This title, said to have been chosen by Smith (January 23, 1927) shows she was keen to create distance from the past as 'Lorgnette', a pair of eyeglasses or opera glasses with a short handle, had connotations of age, both from the elderly and the previous century. 'From *My* Window in Vanity Fair' [my emphasis] obviously was linked to William M. Thackeray's book *Vanity Fair: A Novel without a Hero* (1947–1948), which satirised early nineteenth-century society. The 'My Window' part of Smith's title shows a voyeuristic quality, but importantly, it placed her at the centre of society without being specific about her location. This distancing from the past was important; it showed a difference between ideas of 'age', as opposed to those of 'tradition'. The new twentieth century, and the death of Queen Victoria, heralded a desire to break with the past, a wish to move away from what were seen by many to be the old-fashioned and constricting values of the nineteenth century and Victorianism (Nicholson 2003, xiii–xix; White 1970, 94). While 'age' can be seen to have negative connotations, tradition was seen to be linked to values quintessentially 'English' or 'British', which it is suggested were a feature of the column.

In her debut column on January 30, 1927, the first person to be discussed was the Prince of Wales. The monarchy clearly represented continuity, the Prince also representing traditional values and notions of Englishness. His dancing partners were discussed, as Smith stated he was recently seen 'charlestoning', which was clearly modern, and she further commented on his preference for short partners. Interestingly, historian Juliet Gardiner has pointed out that 'the Prince of Wales was no more competent on the dance floor than he was in many other areas of life', and has referred to his 'two left feet' (2010, 627). Unsurprisingly, his dancing ability was not questioned or criticised in Smith's column, nor was his hedonistic lifestyle. This opening discussion was important in setting up Smith's relationship with the world under the microscope. Not only did she have access to the centre (i.e., the centre of society), the prince's favourite partners were said to be the daughters of her friends.

The Prince of Wales featured regularly in the column. On April 24, 1927, there was a reference to his summer residence in Summerfold, Ewhurst, Effingham near Guildford and comments on the prince's popularity:

> Let us hope that the curiosity of inquisitive visitors will be overcome before the Prince goes into residence in July at Summerfold. I was told by someone who stayed with him at Sandwich that on one occasion H. R. H. was actually prevented from dressing for dinner, as a crowd of tourists surged for the whole evening outside his bedroom, their faces pressed to the glass. (April 24, 1927)

She reinforced her access and proximity to the Prince by commenting on having stayed at Summerfold, noting that 'it is one of the most charming small houses I know' (April 24, 1927). That she commented on it being a 'small' house (though does not say in comparison to what) is suggestive; this is not displaying flamboyance or excess. The reference to the behaviour of 'inquisitive visitors', staring at the Prince of Wales, draws attention to one of the recurring themes in the column, and demonstrated the demarcation of group boundaries. On February 6, 1927, the Prince of Wales's visit to the theatre was apparently similarly marred by people in the stalls staring 'rudely and pointedly' at him. At the end of the show the audience made a dash for the main exit to see the Prince leave 'but he beat them by escaping through a special exit behind his box' (February 6, 1927). These snippets of gossipy information obviously continued to maintain the idea of the Prince's popularity, but also marked out the location of privilege and who was inside or outside of the group. They reinforced and reworked symbolic boundaries, as those who were part of the privileged circle would not have felt it necessary to stare.

Society columns have always commented on visitors from overseas, particularly those from the U.S. Patrick Balfour, for example, referred to 'certain ambitious American hostesses', and also to a Mrs Corrigan (1933, 102). In Balfour's discussion of the paragraphist Dragoman, who referenced Mrs Corrigan in his column, he suggested 'we are laughing with, The Dragoman' as he chronicled her activities in 1931/1932. Dragoman drew attention to her difference, that she was not 'one of us' (1933, 102). There was a sense of ambiguity as she was neither inside society nor outside, somebody who was unable to be categorised, and possibly writers adopted a more ironic tone in order to deal with her and other American visitors. Smith's column showed something of this ambiguity, as well as making more disparaging comments. On May 1, 1927 Smith referred to Mrs Corrigan 'taking her usual house again' and goes on to outline a 'cruel joke', a hoax, played on another American hostess some years before. (The suggestion is that this was *not* Mrs Corrigan.) Some guests had told the hostess that the Prince of Wales wanted to come to her party and dance, the woman informed her guests, and stood in the hall for half an hour awaiting his arrival. He did not, of course, attend the party. The humour was implicit, directed at the hostess and suggested her naiveté. Clearly she was not close to the Prince of Wales or she would have known of his whereabouts. However, Smith then explained that when the Prince heard of the hoax 'he expressed great indignation' and invited himself to dinner the following week (May 1, 1927). This cleverly recoups any anti-Americanism, which was transferred on to malicious, but anonymous, others.

Americans' lack of cultural knowledge was also suggested. One paragraph entitled 'Romulo and Remiet' reported that while in Rome, Lord Darling overheard two Americans standing by a statue of a wolf and explaining: 'That is the wolf that reared Romeo and Juliet' (February 26, 1928). Another paragraph included the following reference to Aintree and the Grand National in 1928: 'And the only way to find friends—dress loudly like the trainers and the American girls' (April 1, 1928). American wealth was further reported on in January 1928 when Smith included comments from Beverley Nichols who had been lecturing in the U.S. He recounted a dinner with William Randolph Hearst where '[it] was not until we were half-way through dinner that I noticed among the table-decorations in front of me, a full sized stag, horns and all, with a dozen unplucked partridges carelessly arranged around it' (January 29, 1928). The American houses were described as more palatial, perhaps over the top. Thus it was observed that John Hammond, 'the American Marconi', had built in Boston three mediaeval French houses 'brought across the Atlantic brick by brick and panel by panel' around a quadrangle, rather like that of an Oxford college. Nichols was apparently asked not only which room he wanted, but which *house* (January 29, 1928). Further it was observed that Bramshill Park in Hampshire was apparently copied by an American visitor, not in brick but in marble, while a French chateau (chateau de Ramboulliet) was built twice its size by a multi-millionaire for his son's 21 birthday present (January 8, 1928).

There were elements of contradiction in the column as other comments were welcoming towards Americans to Britain, and to members of the aristocracy who undertook the season in New York. Nevertheless, while there was no direct criticism, a view was created of America and Americans as lacking tradition, and, through their imitation of European style, insecure as to taste. Smith's column displayed what Martin Conboy argues is 'inferential racism' (2006, 94). He refers to the work of Benedict Anderson to discuss the 'style of representation' of national communities in print, and states:

> The language of this representation has a strongly normative inflection which aims to reinforce a sense of reader identity and in turn a strong sense of national community based not only on a sense of what is shared in common but also on what is shared as a common perception of external challenge or threat to that community. (2006, 94)

A strand of 'anti-Americanism' or fears of Americanisation have been a factor in British culture from Matthew Arnold onwards, and were also implicit in Smith's discussions of American visitors who participated in the social season. These perceptions related to notions of what constituted 'Englishness' or 'Britishness' at this particular time. Readers of the column were drawn into a privileged group and invited to view Americans as 'other'. There was thus a restatement of national identity.

CONSERVATISM MIXED WITH ASPECTS OF BOHEMIAN: THE ARTS, ROMANY/GYPSIES

As stated, the first column under Smith's editorship introduced the range of topics to be discussed and celebrities who would be referred to, and these became constants under her editorship. They were often comprised of her special friends and family including many references to socialites such as Theresa and Zita Jungman, the Guinness family, and Smith's own family—her parents, brother and sister. There was also a continuing juxtaposition of traditional and modern, through the references to members of the aristocracy and importantly via references to the world of the Arts. Her first column referred to Thomas Hardy and told a story of an American journalist going to Dorset to interview him where the journalist was teased by the elderly locals; these comments created links to both tradition via nineteenth-century rural Britain, and to the Arts (January 30, 1927). Smith's interest in the Arts was wide-ranging, moving from Hardy to include gypsy dance and ballet, both canonic literature and contemporary work. She commented on the work of her friends Cecil Beaton and Rex Whistler and referred to Vita Sackville-West and the Sitwells (November 27, 1927). She also referred to the abstract and *avant-garde* photographer Curtis Moffat and stated: 'He's American . . . though you would never in the world guess it' (January 30, 1927). He was mentioned again on February 20, 1927, described as 'probably the greatest living photographer and a remarkably interesting man as well'. In his favour, he married Iris Tree (daughter of Sir Herbert Beerbohm Tree) and set up a studio with Olivia Wyndham (sister of the millionaire, Richard 'Dick' Wyndham). Moffat's and Wyndham's exhibition of photography in June was described as 'brilliantly clever' (June 12, 1927). Also, although Moffat was an American, it was important that both he and Wyndham were part of Smith's set as from the comment above, that is, he's American but 'you would never in the world guess it'; there was clearly something in his manner that set him apart.

There was, however, inconsistency and uncertainty in Smith's discussion as not all contemporary experimental arts received the same praise and there were concerns when trying to understand some groups of contemporary artists, including writers such as James Joyce and Virginia Woolf, who received a somewhat ambiguous reception. It would seem that the upper classes were trying to navigate their way through these new ideas as many of the modernist literary elite were critiqued, if not ridiculed, in the column. They were perhaps also perceived to be beyond the boundary of her definition of upper class society. In a paragraph entitled 'Bloomsbury Again' she referred to the introduction in *Orlando* as an endorsement of 'cliquiness', which was used here as a disparaging term:

> After expressing her gratitude to eight dead and seven living authors, Mrs. Woolf says: 'I must content myself with naming'—a list of 43 people, among them her niece, her husband, her brother, her nephew and her mother-in-law, 'that most inspiriting of critics my brother-in-law, Mr Clive Bell': and a host of others, titled and untitled, whose reputation as authors I respect too much to damage by mentioning their names in a social column. (November 11, 1928)

Smith comments that Woolf's introduction to *Orlando* was a parody, but she went on to say, 'But it still remains an outstanding example of the clan spirit'. The criticism was implicit. Writer and painter Wyndham Lewis was criticised as a 'vitriolic highbrow'. She stated he was an American, far removed from 'real life', while Anita Loos, she suggested, was a 'grim realist' (March 13, 1927). Further criticism was reserved for Gertrude Stein, and she suggested '[no]-one outside the elite circles of which she is queen could possibly describe Miss Stein as intelligible or readable' (March 13, 1927). Two weeks later she commented on *transition*, the new modernist, surrealist and experimental literary journal. Under the heading 'Funny Miss Stein' she referred to the writing of Stein and James Joyce, citing extracts from the journal. Unlike the discussion of the work of Curtis Moffatt there was no attempt to situate either writer in the context of contemporary literary experimental or modernist writing. One extract from Stein's work is given, and is followed by the heading 'Yes: She Does!' under which Smith includes these comments and citations:

> A little later Miss Stein becomes poetic:
>> 'Suppose, to suppose, suppose a rose
>> is a rose is a rose.'
> Her essay finishes with this profound thought:
> 'Yes you do.
> Organisers.
>
> Yes you do.
> Organisation.
> Yes you do, and you, you do.
> To portraits and to prayers.
> "Yes you do." (March 27, 1927)

Smith's lack of intervention, other than referring to Stein's essay as it finishes with 'this profound thought', is as suggestive as direct criticism would have been. The poem does not follow the forms and modes of late Victorian poetry, and is thus perhaps unfamiliar to many readers of the column—and newspaper. However, Stein's own role within the *avant garde* is not indicated, nor her experiments with modernist stream of consciousness. Smith then moves on to discuss James Joyce, writing:

> Mr James Th' Joyce.—Mr. James has elected to express some of his thoughts in "Shelta," the tinkers' dialect. Here is a specimen of Mr. Joyce: "Sir Tristan, violer d'amores, fr over the short sea, had passencore rearrived from North Armorica on this side the scraggy istmus of Europe Minor to wielderfight his penisolate war." (March 27, 1927)

There were further extracts from Joyce's work in similar vein, interspersed with the statement: 'Lucidity.—In case you are bewildered, here is a more lucid passage'. Smith went on to comment that this reminded her of Lewis Carroll's 'Jabberwock' [*sic*] poem, 'Only the Jabberwock is funnier' (March 27, 1927). Here, and as with Gertrude Stein, there is no attempt to situate Joyce's work within modernist developments in literature; it is, rather, likened to Carroll's nonsense poem from *Alice in Wonderland* (1871). Smith then made a rather strange comment, that 'the author of "Ulysses" is a shy, silent, retiring man, sensitive, and easily shocked. Men who write shocking books are always like that'. However, the reference to Shelta, the tinkers' dialect, was a direct intervention by Smith; the authorial voice drew attention to her own knowledge. When commenting on Joyce the tone was more ambiguous as there was an element of trivialising his work (and perhaps deliberately misunderstanding it) while at the same time reincorporating him by commenting on his personal qualities.

I have referred to Smith's interest in gypsy/Romany life, and this was something shared by many artists and writers in the early part of the century. Virginia Nicholson, for example, refers to painter August John (and others), noting that John went to particular lengths to 'live for Freedom and the Open Road!' adopting clothing and a gypsy caravan for himself and his extended family (2002, 130). Smith's interest started when as a young child she encountered them camping near her family home at Charlton, in Oxfordshire, and she subsequently travelled with groups both in England and Spain. She learnt Romany and many of her books feature gypsy characters. Unlike many of her contemporaries, in her fiction there was no consistent attempt to romanticise either the gypsies (or indeed, any other group) or their way of life. The topic was first introduced to her column on February 27, 1927 utilising the device of an overheard conversation, a discussion as to whether or not there existed in England any 'genuine old-fashioned gypsies of the type beloved by George Borrow'. This led her to draw attention to her superior knowledge of Romanies by pointing out where groups could be found:

> I longed to take part in the conversation and to ask them whether they had ever visited the New Forest, at any time of the year, or Hampshire, during the season of hops and strawberries.
>
> As a matter of fact, any number of true 'black' Romanies are to be found not only in the South of England, but in many parts of Norfolk, Oxfordshire and Berkshire, to say nothing of Wales.
>
> One of our largest northern towns has a great encampment of nomads at its outskirts, which is known as 'The Redskin Village', and where magnificent gypsy types can be observed at any time of the year. (February 27, 1927)

At the same time the discussion noted their attractiveness to painters such as Augustus John and Alfred Munnings. Women were singled out for comment as they were 'uncommonly handsome' and 'nearly always more remarkable and dominant personalities than the men'. Thus her more intimate and informed knowledge was made clear as she went on to refer to her personal friendships: 'I know two young ladies of the Cooper (Vardomescro) tribe, whose good looks, intelligence and vivacity would create a sensation in any company' (February 27, 1927).

That Smith was overt in her championing of gypsies, and tried to counter other more dominant views, was made particularly obvious in a lengthy discussion in her column on May 29, 1927 when she referred to the Epsom

Derby where she hoped to meet many gypsies who camped there annually. Her autobiography confirms this was one of her happier moments on the column: 'I found myself among friends, and I brought back some sort of a story. This story found a certain amount of favour with the Editor' (1939, 119–120). They were said to be interesting and 'picturesque', and presumably not unlike people in her own social circle, in that some of the gypsies 'have not missed a Derby Day for twenty or thirty years' (May 29, 1927). She referred to Mrs Lemantine Stevens, and when describing her clothes said she was a 'gipsy [sic] straight from a Borrow book'. She went on to say that Mrs Stevens should be seen by every person:

> who imagines the pure bred gipsy to be dirty, thievish and ignorant. She has infinite claims to distinction, nineteen of which are her children, or *chavés*, as she calls them, all very much alive and healthy. The twentieth claim is that she is one of Mr. A. J. Munnings's favourite gipsy models. She figures prominently in two of his most famous pictures, 'Gipsies going to the Derby,' and 'The Downs at Epsom.' (May 29, 1927, emphasis in original)

The latter painting was reproduced above the column. This section continued with a brief discussion of Munnings, described by Lemantina Stevens as 'a deep one'. Intriguing links were made with the very wealthy as the caravan of a Mrs Whittles was described as 'a princely van', a huge structure, the interior of which is not unlike an extremely expensive yacht:

> It is upholstered in satin-wood; the curtains are of shot taffeta, bowls of roses are arranged on the tables, and the stove glitters as though it were made of silver. Cages of lovebirds dangle from the ceiling and the quilts on the beds are embroidered with silk wreaths of violets. (May 29, 1927)

The following also gives further insight into her style:

> Paying Business.
> 'How do you manage about water?' we asked our hostess.
> 'Oh,' she replied carelessly, 'we get it laid on wherever we stay.'
> Showmen are some of them extremely well-to-do.
> I know an ancient merry-go-round proprietor who is reputed to sleep every night on £4,000 in banknotes.
> The fair was the best part of the Derby—it was grand. (May 29, 1927)

In championing gypsies, she also drew attention to their ill-treatment. In the same column she discussed the plight of one woman camped in a Surrey village near London who had given birth to her twelfth child 'in a wretched tent through which the rain leaked'. Both mother and child were critically ill but requests for help, medicine and blankets were turned down by everyone, including the doctor, who 'refused to move out of his warm house to attend gipsies. The baby, of course, died'. Finally, she stated the clergyman refused to bury the child in the local churchyard 'for the child was not baptised'. The only editorial comment made was: 'A pleasant tale, is it not?' (May 29, 1927). While the concern would be shared, Smith's voice ran counter to views held in other sections of society, and her interest in gypsies, while shared by artists in the period, is more than an aesthetic appreciation of or liking for the 'other' or the 'exotic'. Her defence, particularly in the society column of a popular weekly newspaper, could be linked to Cecil Beaton's reference to her as 'eccentric' (1985/2003, 36), but I think shows someone who has no concerns when expressing views not shared by others within her social group; it emphasises her 'marginal centrality' and draws attention to the complexity of opinions within the upper class.

CONCLUSION

Smith's editorship ended in 1930, when the column was offered to Cecil Beaton at a salary of £1,000 per annum; he declined for fear of losing his independence (Balfour 1933, 45). The topics covered under her editorship were no less wide-ranging than those praised by Patrick Balfour in that as well as society she included sport, politics, the stage, literature and film, providing a critical commentary on the behaviour and mores of the elite social world of which she was part. Her column is therefore an important source for the historian. Firstly, it opens up further areas for exploration of women's journalism in the twentieth century, and secondly, it provides, in a more gossipy form, insight into other views on debates and issues outside of those discussed on the front pages of the press. Her later novels go on to show a discourse of conservatism mixed with some aspects of the bohemian (McNamara 2008), and elements of this are already apparent in her society column. She was critical of some of her group, usually about rudeness, and what she saw as the emptiness and vacuity of the lives of some society people. Her ambiguous yet anti-American comments no doubt found favour in some quarters, while her championing of gypsies probably had a more select audience.

BIBLIOGRAPHY / SOURCES

Balfour, Patrick. 1933. *Society Racket: A Critical Survey of Modern Social Life*. London: John Long.
Lord Birkenhead. 1953. *Lady Eleanor Smith: A Memoir*. London: Hutchinson.
Bourke, Joanna. 1994. *Working-Class Cultures in Britain 1890–1960: Gender, Class and Ethnicity*. London: Routledge.

Cannadine, David. 1994. *Aspects of Aristocracy*. London: Penguin.

Cannadine, David. 1998. *Class in Britain*. London: Penguin.

Chambers, Deborah, Linda Steiner, and Carole Fleming. 2004. *Women and Journalism*. London: Routledge.

Conboy, Martin. 2006. *Tabloid Britain: Constructing a Community through Language*. London: Routledge.

Douglas, Mary. (1966) 1984. *Purity and Danger: An Analysis of the Concepts of Pollution and Taboo*. London: Ark.

Edensor, Tim. 2002. *National Identity, Popular Culture and Everyday Life*. Oxford: Berg.

Gardiner, Juliet. 2010. *The Thirties: An Intimate History*. London: Harper Press.

Hall, Stuart. 1997. 'The Spectacle of the "Other."' In *Representation: Cultural Representations and Signifying Practices*, edited by Stuart Hall. London: Sage.

McKibbin, Ross. 1998. *Classes and Cultures: England 1918–1951*. Oxford University Press.

McNamara, Sallie. 2008. 'The Female Historical Novel 1918–1945: The Body, Boundaries and Social Space.' PhD diss., University of Portsmouth.

Nicholson, Virginia. 2002. *Among the Bohemians: Experiments in Living 1900–1939*. London: Penguin.

Smith, Lady Eleanor. 1939. *Life's A Circus: Reminiscences of Lady Eleanor Smith*. London: Longmans.

Vickers, Hugo. (1985) 2003. *Cecil Beaton: The Authorized Biography*. London: Phoenix Press.

White, Cynthia L. 1970. *Women's Magazines 1693–1968*. London: Michael Joseph.

Periodical Sources

Sunday/Weekly Dispatch, 1927–1930

Part II

Women in War and Peace
The 1940s and 1950s

The Second World War involved, with some regional variation, an unparalleled degree of disruption and interference in women's everyday lives. The evacuation of young children and many of their mothers, rationing, the blitz and the conscription of women in 1942 meant that the disruption of war was strongly felt on the Home Front. The privations of wartime laid new expectations on women, whether it was working in an aircraft factory, as an air-raid warden, undertaking night-time fire-watching or looking after evacuee children. Attempts to accommodate both these new expectations and maintain some continuity with pre-war femininities led to what Gledhill and Swanson have described as a 'refashioning' of femininity in the 'circulation of discourses, images, and narrative between official policymaking, social practices, cultural events, fashion, magazines, broadcasting, and films' (1996, 1).

Although euphemistically called a 'People's War', recent historiography has emphasised the Second World War was by no means experienced in the same way by different social classes or geographical regions (Calder 1992; Rose 2004). Nor did it evoke the unwavering support and sense of justification popular mythology has given it in the years since. Disorganisation, mismanagement, shortages and inequality of sacrifice threatened morale and could have undermined the war effort. The publically owned BBC, which soon became the only broadcaster, aired regular news, entertainment and public information which led it be called 'the voice of the nation'. Cinemas were initially closed as air raids, it was feared, could result in mass casualties. They were, however, quickly reopened when films were identified as able to boost morale and help keep up public spirits. A veritable industry of propaganda-style films were produced by the Crown Film Unit and the GPO with guidance on everything from eating to the desirability of factory work for women (e.g., *Jane Brown Changes Her Job* 1941).

Britain did not, however, really see itself as using propaganda (that was associated with fascism). Instead, the government had a Ministry of Information (MoI) which inserted tight control over the distribution of scarce resources for commercially produced magazines, newspapers and film, reserving them for those with MoI approval. Rare resources were allocated to the publication of women's magazines during the war, which was seen both as offering opportunities to educate housewives and boost morale (Vaughan-Rees and Waller 1990). Hence, British women, if wealthy enough, could afford to continue to read *Vogue* in wartime. Janet Harrison's analysis of the photography of Lee Miller which appeared in *Vogue* makes it clear that even within the pages of this glossy magazine the war was ever-present and Miller put a particularly domestic slant on the images that she took of war-torn Europe in the latter days of the conflict.

The 'accommodations' and slippage in discourses of femininity in wartime engendered anxiety in a number of areas; Maggie Andrews argues that these anxieties often crystallised around concerns over female sexual behaviour. The articulation of such concerns, in a range of media texts, has contributed to the perception that the Second World War was an era of sexual freedom. Statistical indicators are, however, at odds with media discourses and serve as a reminder that texts, such as the films examined, may articulate anxieties and fantasies rather than lived experiences.

The post-war peace did not necessarily live up to the dreams and expectations which had helped to sustain the population during wartime. Although the 'new Jerusalem' of the first majority Labour Government in 1945 was able to introduce a National Health Service in 1948 and a welfare state, Britain was financially crippled by war. The austerity and rationing of the post-war era was more extreme than it had been in the 1939–1945 period; in many ways women, and particularly housewives, bore the brunt of this (Kynaston 2008; Zweiniger-Bargielowska 2002). Kristin Skoog's chapter charts women's role in the production of *Woman's Hour*, which was introduced in 1946. Her study shows that women broadcasters and women's radio managed to tease out the contradictions of 'serving women's interests' to address the concerns of both working women and housewives. As Holloway points out, 'despite the assumption that women's involvement in the workforce would return to post-war levels, this was never the case. In fact, by the end of 1947 there were more women working than in 1939' (2005).

Within half an hour of the outbreak of war in 1939, the fledgling BBC television service had ceased broadcasting; when it resumed again in 1946 television programmes aimed at women soon became part of the planned output. Mary Irwin's chapter explores how some of these early 1940s television programmes portrayed the concerns and aspirations which were central to women's lives at the time, and therefore provide a useful historical source for an understanding of post-war British femininity. In the 1940s, however, television was generally reserved for the wealthy; it was not until the 'never had it so good' years of the consumerist 1950s that television became commonplace (Hartley 1999), particularly when 1,400,000 sets were sold in the weeks prior to the Coronation of Queen Elizabeth II in 1953, which was watched by an audience of approximately 22 million (Hill 1986).

The 1950s has been mythologised as an era of home and family, with the new young queen as an icon of this ideology; however, the post-war housing crisis meant that many found their dream home somewhat illusory (Langhamer 2005). Since the cult of domesticity (Giles 2004) has often been associated with the stay-at-home housewife, Glenda Strong's chapter which looks at Diana Rowntree, an architect, but also a wife, a mother and a journalist alongside Kristin Skoog's which examines the production and development of the BBC's perhaps most famous women's programme, *Woman's Hour*, are welcome reminders that the post-war era had a range of histories. Many women did not return to home and duty after the Second World War.

BIBLIOGRAPHY / SOURCES

Calder, Angus. 1992. *The People's War 1939–1945*. London: Pimlico.

Giles, Judy. 2004. *The Parlour and the Suburb: Domestic Identities, Class, Femininity and Modernity*. London: Berg.

Gledhill, Christine, and Gillian Swanson, eds. 1996. *Nationalising Femininity: Culture, Sexuality and British Cinema in the Second World War*. Manchester University Press.

Hartley, John. 1999. *The Uses of Television*. London: Routledge.

Hill, John. 1986. *Television and the Home 1926–1986*. London: BFI.

Holloway, Gerry. 2005. *Women and Work in Britain since 1840*. Oxford: Routledge. Kindle edition.

Kynaston, David. 2008. *Austerity Britain, 1945–1951*. London: Bloomsbury.

Langhamer, Claire. 2005. 'The Meaning of Home in Post-War Britain.' *Journal of Contemporary History* 40: 341–363.

Rose, Sonya. 2004. *Which People's War? National Identity and Citizenship in Wartime Britain 1939–1945*. Oxford University Press.

Waller, Jane, and Michael Vaughan-Rees. 1990. *Women in Wartime: The Role of Women's Magazines*. London: Macdonald and Sons.

Zweiniger-Bargielowska, Ina. 2002. *Austerity in Britain: Rationing, Controls and Consumption, 1939–1955*. Oxford University Press.

FILMOGRAPHY

Jane Brown Changes Her Job (1941)

4   A View from the Frontline
Lee Miller

Janet Harrison

INTRODUCTION

The three photographs used to illustrate this chapter were taken by Lee Miller in late 1944 to support her article 'Pattern of Liberation' published in the January 1945 editions of British and American *Vogue* but were not used in the final published article. They are clearly connected mirroring the content and style of the published article, and offer a unique insight into the impact of war on the ordinary everyday domestic world of women in the Second World War by making this world visible through an affective manipulation of a medley of different visual rhetorical devices from fashion photography to war photography synthesised with modernist and surrealist techniques: They contain underlying references to the art history she had encountered in her study and travels through the cultural and artistic capitals of Paris, Florence and Rome. That Miller was interested in the 'war's impact on civilians' (*Vogue* January 1945, 235) as noted by Carolyn Burke in her biography of Miller, was evident in this photojournalistic encounter. This particular article initially focussed upon the ordinary domestic lives of the women of Luxembourg, the geographic site for the piece, as they engaged with war, occupation and liberation at first hand and directed attention towards the disruption of the domestic everyday world of those who had been liberated and were caught between the departing enemy and the advancing army of liberation. This watershed world on the edge of Germany marked a slight hiatus in her photographic style. How was she to capture that edginess, the sense of foreboding of a world on a knife edge, a border space between two countries and two armies as well as cultural differences between the army of liberation and the indigenous one? Miller's photographs, had they been published, aimed to take the implied viewer, the magazine's original readership, into the heart of the situation and captured those fleeting conjunctions between people and things highlighting one of the central overarching themes of this article; that domestic disruption sat in parallel with the theme of liberation and the ongoing strategy of engaging the enemy across the frontier.

What was remarkable about Miller's images was the skill with which she manipulated the viewer by capturing the 'shrapnel' and dislocation of 'traumatic times' (Baer 2003, 7) through a synthesis of different photographic frameworks that resonated far beyond the initial first glance which disturbingly ruptured habitual ways of seeing. To encounter these images taken specifically for an up-market women's magazine, where they would have been, had they been published, sandwiched between articles and images on fashion, glamour and domestic harmony, was challenging at many different levels. They would have disrupted the viewer's system of knowledge and challenged their habitual subjectivities; and offered a splintered, fractured view of women's lives which was recognisable but which had been dislocated by war. War is a surreal experience and as Detlef Hoffman explains:

> Every photograph isolates, it cuts a moment and place out of the continuum of time and space. Through artistic translation it can enhance and direct the symbolising power of the subject. The part may stand for something more, perhaps for the whole and thus gains wider, larger meaning than the photographed object actually had. (cited in Hilditch 2010, 95)

The multilayered nature of Miller's photography had an explosive quality where different visual discourses and iconography were brought into play as she transformed little, often dismissed incidences of domesticity and ordinary women's experiences of war into images that have a resonance far beyond their seemingly inconsequential surface. As Baer suggests, photographs reveal a world that is 'splintered, fractured, blown apart' (2002, 4). Miller's photography for her article 'Pattern of Liberation' extrapolated an isolated moment, a fortuitous coming together of people and things, which the photographer cropped in such a way that she emphasised the fragility of women's lives, caught between opposing fields of interest.

Photography has had a chequered history as a source for historians, and war photography in particular has been fraught with problems as it is often perceived to be implicated within the propagandist regime of the culture in which it is produced. Miller was well aware of the potential impact of her images on her readership's views of the war and on the liberating forces. Knowing that they might be used to raise morale at home, she noted in a memo to Audrey Withers that accompanied her dispatch that she had no desire to 'commit [*Vogue*] to being rosy minded Polly-Annas' (Penrose 2005, 92). Her awareness of the pitfalls that faced war photographers and how her images could be manipulated and interpreted made her take a conscious decision to ensure that her eye-witnessing did not distort or overlook the realities of war and its impact on ordinary women's lives. Nevertheless, photography uniquely offers an immediate eye-witness record, testimony as Peter Burke suggests, to the actualities of events of the contemporary world around the photographer and the photograph; though there is the important caveat that such images need to be 'placed in "context", or better in a series of contexts in the plural' (2001, 187), including the cultural, political, and the material. They also need to be understood in relation to the artistic conventions of representation current at the time the photographs were created and the photographic conventions of the magazine in which they were intended to appear.

Consequently, this chapter is suggesting that Miller's images are viable sources of historical evidence through unpacking the various biographical, artistic and cultural contexts that would have impinged on her viewpoint, and which provide the framework for seeing those patterns of liberation as she suggests they impacted on ordinary women. This will entail a brief excursion into Miller's background in terms of her biography and her artistic development, which eventually led to her working for *British Vogue* and, because of her American background, *American Vogue*. The importance of her images appearing in such a prestigious woman's magazine should not be overlooked, as like other women's magazines before, during and after the war, *Vogue's* primary role was to encourage women's morale in wartime; something that was frequently tied up with maintaining a particularly glamorous version of femininity (Ballaster, Beetham, Fraser, and Hebron 1991; Gough-Yates 2002;). In the Second World War, as Rose has argued convincingly (2003), issues around the construction of proper femininity, the home front and the need to use female labour revealed the instability and contradictory nature of the discourses around femininity, opening up significant gaps which Miller exploited to illuminate the lives and domestic acts of resistance of those not normally seen in the glossy pages of *Vogue*. Three photographs used in the writing of her article 'Pattern of Liberation' alongside references to her text will be used to illustrate how she made visible the impact of war on what might otherwise have been hidden domestic lives.

BIOGRAPHY: THE COMING TOGETHER OF MILLER'S PHOTOGRAPHY AND *BRITISH VOGUE*

Born in Poughkeepsie, New York State in 1907, Miller initially briefly studied lighting, costume and theatre design in Paris, returning in 1925 to New York to continue her studies at the Art Students' League in New York. Her breakthrough into modeling for *American Vogue* happened by chance, when, according to the family mythology, she was saved by Condé Nast from being run over (Penrose 1985, 16). Miller's physical appearance fitted perfectly with the gamine femininity of the period and for the next three years she was photographed by, and learned from, some of the great American fashion photographers of the day, including Steichen, Nickolas Murray and Arnold Genthe. In 1929, she returned to Europe to study Italian renaissance art in Florence and Rome before settling in Paris, at the time the artistic center of Europe. Here she became a student of the American dada-surrealist artist and photographer, Man Ray, with whom she worked for the next few years as both model and pupil, before setting up her own studio first in Paris and then in New York in 1932, becoming a successful freelance photographer. In 1934, she married the Egyptian industrialist, Aziz Eloui Bey, and lived in Egypt for three years before returning to Paris in 1937 where she reconnected with her artistic friends, Picasso, Man Ray, Cocteau and Eluard, and rekindled her affair with the English painter, collector, critic and champion of Surrealism, Roland Penrose, who was to become her second husband. The outbreak of war in 1939 disbanded this tightly knit artistic circle in Paris and Lee Miller followed Roland Penrose to London, where she found work as a freelance photographer for *British Vogue*. She worked consistently for the magazine throughout the war, initially as a fashion photographer, before offering to do more serious articles on women in wartime (Penrose 1985).

Vogue during the 20s and 30s was, under Condé Nast, the premier glossy magazine of the period, devoted to Parisian Haute Couture. It employed significant *avant garde* and modernist photographers such as Alfred Steichen, Man Ray, Cecil Beaton and Horst to provide the rich and the wealthy with contemporary images of the current fashions from all the most important fashion houses and designers in Paris. Cutting-edge glamour and fashion were central issues, but *Vogue* also included articles on the famous and the fashionable across European, British and American society, from the current socialites, society hostesses, film stars, women with significant careers in the arts, and during wartime, women in the services. In its three formats, *French, American* and *British Vogue,* it held a mirror up to its wealthy female clientele and provided its readership with a range of intelligent articles on modern life and art, often written by well-known writers and luminaries, that reflected its readership's aspirations for opulence, glamour and intellectual currency.

During the war, British *Vogue* was under the editorial control of Audrey Withers, a graduate of Somerville College, Oxford and like many other women's magazines of the period, supported the war effort with rousing articles on how to use dress coupons effectively for maximum style. As Rose (2003) suggests, its emphasis was on glamour and how to maintain it rather than on privation. In choosing to encourage Miller's wartime photojournalist career by initially letting her do a piece on the WRNS, followed by another on the Evacuation Hospitals in Normandy, Withers ensured that Brogue, as British *Vogue* was affectionately referred to by its employees, fulfilled its patriotic duty as well as ensuring it maintained its remit to provide the cultured woman with articles that addressed contemporary events. Nevertheless, Withers was well aware of the incongruities in including Miller's wartime photojournalism complete with supporting articles written by Miller herself and described the effect of Miller's first contribution, 'Unarmed Warriors', based around the Evacuation Hospitals, as 'the most exciting journalistic experience of my war. We were the last people one could have conceived having this type of article, it seemed so incongruous in our pages of glossy fashion' (cited in Penrose 1985, 118). There is a certain disingenuousness in this comment that belies the astuteness of Withers's editorial decision to initially encourage Miller's aspirations to cover the war, and then to prominently position Miller's wartime photojournalism over the next eighteen months within the pages of British *Vogue,* sandwiched between articles on fashion, glamour and domestic issues, providing gravitas as Kate McLoughlin (2010) has remarked.

The ubiquity with which women were bombarded with images, articles and adverts from the outset of the war in all the key media from newspapers to magazines and radio situated them within the domestic sphere and emphasized this as their key role within wartime discourses on femininity. As Rose notes, 'Jenny Hartley astutely observed that the war made home visible' (cited Rose 2003, 136). The home front became a key theme in wartime propaganda with many articles focussed not just on women doing war work but on their responsibility for the 'second line of defense', which was identified as 'your house, my house and the house next door' (cited in Rose 2003, 136). The designation of women as defenders of the home front was linked to the need for creating a unified community based around the concept of the family, with all its traditionally domestic and gendered hierarchies that women's magazines of the period, including British *Vogue,* reinforced at the behest of government.

The fractured, often contradictory, nature of women's magazines with their household tips, articles on career women, agony aunt sections, fashion, glamour and advertisements for feminine goods offered the female reader contradictory versions of femininity. This was exacerbated in wartime with the mobilization of women into uniform as auxiliary workers doing the jobs that freed up and supported the men doing the heroic work of fighting at the front. The maintenance of femininity in wartime was, however, considered to be all important and women's magazines were crucial in raising morale, addressing issues raised by the ministry and maintaining the gender divide through its focus on glamorizing and feminizing the drab utility fashions and uniforms in the most economical ways possible. However, a particular emphasis was placed on women's traditional role as wives and mothers. The demand for labour within the wartime economy encouraged and, indeed, required many married women to work and to run their households alone; many needlessly feared this would change the traditional dynamics of the family unit.

The home front's designation as the 'second line of defence' reinforced its ancillary status despite the nightly bombing raids in the early years of the war when it became the front line (Rose 2003, 135–138). Lee Miller photographed many different aspects of this home front in *Grim Glory* (1941), which featured photographs of Britain during the Blitz by Miller and others that accompanied a text by Edward R. Murrow, a famous

American journalist of the period. The focus of *Grim Glory*, as the title suggests, was on the ordinary, 'routine scenes' (Murrow 1941, 3) and activities enacted by ordinary men and women in Britain during wartime. It was dedicated to Winston Churchill and the indomitable spirit of the common people' (Carter 1941, 1). Its aim was to reveal the impact of war on the ordinary people of England and how, despite the chaos and destruction, life carried on, to American audiences reinforcing attempts to encourage the U.S. to participate in the Second World War, something they strongly resisted until the Japanese attack on Pearl Harbor in December 1941. This focus on the home front and on women's defense of the home front was a theme of Miller's war photojournalism, most significantly in her article 'Patterns of Liberation' in 1945. Miller, as a participant in the creation of images as both a model during the 20s and later a fashion photographer for British and American *Vogue* during the war, would have been familiar with the contradictory discourses and the visual rhetoric of women's magazines, and through her fashion photography she was able to mobilize them with other visual discourses to punctuate the smooth, seamless, glamorous surface of *Vogue*.

ARTISTIC DEVELOPMENT:
CONTRADICTIONS AND FRACTURES

As Jean Gallagher (1998) has commented, Miller constantly questioned the notion of a stable unified subject position that was particularly pronounced in her career trajectory which took her from being a model in the photograph to the photographer and finally a war photojournalist. Miller's ability to slip and slide between subject positions is reinforced by Kate McLoughlin (2010) who suggests women occupy a triumvirate of seeing positions and experiences during war between 'those who are "seen" (those who are the news, or, at least, "help" to make it) . . . those who "see" (those who bring the news)' and a third 'undisclosed' category of '"the unseen" (those who remain, because they are unrecorded, camouflaged or behind the camera, invisible)' (2010, 336). Miller, according to McLoughlin, due to her various roles as model, photographer and correspondent, occupied all three positions which facilitated her ability to slip between these overlapping positions, thus revealing their inherent instability.

   This ability to slip in an out of focus and in and out of different subject positions was apparent in one of the first articles Miller wrote for *Lilliput* in October 1941 entitled 'I worked for Man Ray' (Heron and Williams 1996, 74). In this article the rather dominant 'I' of the title disappeared from the ensuing texts which focused the reader's attention on Man Ray, a well-known and very innovative fashion photographer for *Vogue*, a central figure of Breton's Surrealist Circle in Paris and exponent of photographic Surrealism whose work was frequently used to illustrate Breton's texts and discourses on Surrealism. Nevertheless, the initial 'I' of this article's title asserted Miller's relationship to Man Ray but the focus shifts to the pronoun 'he' and 'his' in relation to photographic and artistic working practices. This very pointed shift in the use of pronouns from the very assertive 'I' in the title to the very emphatic, repetitive use of 'he' and 'they' provides Miller with impeccable artistic credentials. She ironically included Picasso as a passing reference in the conclusion as she moved from the individual artistic 'he' to include 'everyone' who worked in collaborative artistic partnerships. This name dropping, referring to all the key artistic figures of Modernism and Surrealism, placed Miller at the centre of modernist innovative artistic practices in Paris. The magazine's cultured audience would have recognised these figures from exhibitions which had taken place in London during the 30s, culminating in the infamous *International Surrealist Exhibition* of 1936 at the New Burlington Galleries, London. The references to 'Picasso', 'Man Ray', 'Cubism, Dadaism and Surrealism' (Heron and Williams 1996, 74) in this article provided the artistic context for Miller's modernist visual rhetoric that she manipulated and synthesised with her knowledge of art history in her wartime images. Dada's nihilism and anti-establishment remit that ruptured the smooth, seamless surface of images through montage and Cubism's fracturing of the singular perspective to an abstracted multiple view of reality were as important to her surrealist focus on the chance encounters of mundane, everyday objects in odd juxtapositions. Her synthesis of the three enabled her to make visible the often hidden lives of the ordinary men and particularly women caught up in the chaos of war and to present them in ways that would engage her audience.

Added to this, it was photography's facility to capture the moment and the person, for as Jean Luc Nancy theorizes, photography 'grasps' (Nancy 2005, 106) the likeness of another subject that is estranged by the viewing position of the photographer and the 'luminous trace' (ibid. 106) that emerges as the final image. As Nancy posits, 'The sameness of this image is permeated with the alterity of its two concomitant subjects. . . . At this point at this moment, in this place the photograph in which time blinks and is distended as an immobile surface, the most exact and the most rigorous *nous autres* is produced' (2005, 104). Photography is, according to this argument, a validating process and this is an aspect of photography that Miller activated in her images when she recorded the impact of war and liberation on women, validating them as subjects through the process of photographic eye-witnessing.

This notion of eye-witnessing has a particularly visceral quality capturing the impact of experience as well as facts. Bracha Ettinger has suggested the concept of 'compassionate wit(h)nessing' (cited in Pollock 2007, 195) which provides a space in which both the viewer, the artists and the subject co-emerge through mutual understanding and recognition of a shared position and humanity, and in the case of Miller's work, through the shared cultural and pictorial references. This idea was intuitively understood by Miller as the responsibility of the war photojournalist and informed her use of a bricolage of visual rhetoric and verbal discourses in 'Pattern of Liberation', which drew attention to the impact of war on the everyday, domestic life of women. In so doing Miller validated women whose precarious lives had been damaged and disrupted by war, whose experiences were hidden from view, and turned them into thinking, speaking and acting subjects. An example of this can be seen in 'Maesy Bastion, interpreter to the US Civil Affair team, Luxembourg, 1945' (Figure 4.1).

Sitting on top of their haywain with crucial domestic, farm and child-care items, a mother, two children and grandmother were poised mid conversation with a well-dressed blonde woman and an American army officer. The sharp diagonal between the two sets of figures and the close cropping of the image behind and above the woman and children created a sense of impending disaster and suggested the precariousness of their lives as they were forced to flee by the liberating forces. This diagonal sweep to the figures below was pulled up by the advancing but blurred figure of the soldier on the right that forced the eye of the viewer to move up the right-hand-side of the image to the looming presence of the lorry in the centre between the foreground figure of the army officer, the haywain and the bicycle wheel. The juxtaposition of civilian transport with the mechanics of war was subtle but very telling and revealed the visual dexterity with which Miller conjured up the situation, weaving together the main narrative of war which was momentarily halted by the hidden narrative of the small family which was threatened and disrupted by the onward sweep of 'liberation'. The foregrounding of the different women here was equally important, as she presented the seen and the usually unseen women within the same frame. The well-dressed woman on the right, identified in the accompanying text as Maesy Bastion, was, through the social and political affiliations of her family and her brother's membership in the resistance, a visible woman who was able to speak and act with authority in her pivotal role as interpreter between the American army of liberation and the ordinary Luxemburger. The normally hidden or unseen women were the mother and grandmother in the small family unit atop the haywain. Miller behind the camera was the seer who made her position visible through her text.

The use of diagonals and the crisscross lines of broom or farm implement handles ironically revealed the vulnerability of these women whose only defence was very mundane, basic domestic and farm implements. However, they were rather pointedly spiky, cocked and aimed, one at the American officer, which suggested the inherent tension and an underlying suspicion of the liberating force. The image bristled with tension and the sense of a dark future was captured in the darkness created by the shadow of the haywain in the left hand bottom corner. This formed another set of diagonals which pointed back down the road behind the wagon to the sweep of the major narrative of liberation that threatened to engulf them but was momentarily

Title: Maesy Bastion, interpreter and explainer to the US Civil Affairs team
Location: Luxembourg
Date: 1945
Photographer: Lee Miller
Negative Number: 6106-234
Notes: VN
Credit Line: © Lee Miller Archives, England. All rights reserved.

Figure 4.1   Maesy Bastion, interpreter to the US Civil Affair team, Luxembourg, 1945, by Lee Miller. © Lee Miller Archives, England 2013. All rights reserved.

shifted off course. The angle of vision was modernist in its abstraction and shattering of a singular point of view, the myriad of criss-crossing diagonals ensured that the viewer's eye found it difficult to rest in one single place but was constantly drawn across the image. Equally, it was surrealist in its use of 'convulsive beauty', that bretonesque belief in the importance of random chance encounters of things and people in dynamic tension.

Beneath these modernist frameworks of seeing, however, was a visual echo to Pieter Brugel, the Elder, (1525/30–1569) a Flemish Renaissance artist, famous for his graphic images of war and genre paintings of Flemish life during a period of religious upheaval between Catholic and Lutheran factions. The focus of his attention is on the ordinary lives of the Flemish people used allegorically and ambiguously to critique current social, political and religious beliefs. Amongst his most famous work is his painting of Dulle Gret (1562), an ordinary peasant woman who led an army of other peasant housewives armed with cooking utensils to Hell to destroy the root causes of the common army practice of wanton rape, pillage and looting that devastated ordinary women's lives, their food supplies and subsistence domesticity. Thus she is a symbol of female resistance armed with ordinary domestic utensils who takes up arms against a conquering power. The subliminal reference here added another deeper dimension to Miller's image of other historical wars and invasions with their rather more gory impact on the ordinary people. It is this that sends a slight shiver down the spine of the viewer. This latter day Dulle Gret, poised at the entrance to the hell mouth, has little defence against the impending onslaught that was suggested in her precarious balancing act on top of the straw bedding, yet her vocalising cuts across the foreground and bars the onward sweep of the war narrative. It was a momentary but important stalling that was emblematic of the many hidden domestic narratives swept aside by the war but foregrounded by Miller.

Miller's photographs were 'unconventional in different ways' (Sim 2009, 48). Firstly, as Sim suggests, they did not provide traditional images of heroism and glory. For example, in the above image the male figure is mute, a passive onlooker, outside the petit narrative of the women, but inexorably linked to the narrative sweep of the war through the juxtapositioning of the lorry behind him, that is trapped between his head and the wagon. Secondly, according to Sim, they avoided the visual conventions of propaganda, with the exception of her images of Dachau and Buchenwald, as Miller focused on the seemingly insignificant incidents within the main sweep of history rather than the panoramic view. Finally, Miller rarely produced images of the more violent and horrific spectacles omnipresent in wartime. The 'horrorific spectacle of war' (2009, 48) was, nonetheless, always the subliminal undercurrent often inherent in her choice of historical pictorial referencing that creates the visceral shiver in the viewer. The essence of Sim's argument is that Miller's war photography sought 'to dialectically engage the viewer through . . . unusual viewing positions and, at times, manipulation of the gaze' (2009, 48). Miller achieved this by conflating the viewing position between the 'seeing subject and visual object' (2009, 57) that forced the viewer to engage at a personal and sometimes intimate and by extension ethical level with what was being depicted. Miller achieved this, Sim goes on to explain, by inserting herself as photographer into and often inside the experience as spectator and as recorder choosing a point of view that located the viewing experience of the viewer within the experiences of those being photographed.

THE AUTHORIAL VOICE OF MILLER'S
VIEW FROM THE FRONT LINE

The unconventional viewpoint of the Maesy Bastion photograph was apparent in the way in which Miller focused on a particular incident from a very close up position in the midst of the action, in this case in the midst of a discussion between the mother figure and the well-dressed woman. The action was caught in *medias res* (mid action) and was, as such, an action photograph, but it was the centrality of the women that was the focus of attention here for without their co-operation the war could not move on. The image, taken close up and personal, placed both Miller and by extension the viewer simultaneously as both outsiders and insiders, 'wit(h)nesses' to the discussion. The witnessing position was established in the American Army officer's equivocal position as the silent onlooker which offered the American audience a point of reference. His outsider role was captured in his stance and in the pointed aiming of the implement handles. The real business was being carried out by the women, whose marginal status was encapsulated in their positioning off centre but whose dialogue and sight lines cut across the field of vision and created a visual barrier.

The insider or witness position was situated in the figure of Maesy Bastion. The foregrounding of her on an equal plane with the Army officer provided her with the authority needed to enact her role, which was prioritised by the clarity of focus and definition of her stance, with her black coat anchoring the image and drawing the eye into the frame. She was at first glance the focal point of the image which suggested the importance of such women was pivotal rather than peripheral, although her off-centre positioning suggested she was still ancillary. In line with current perceptions of femininity in wartime, Maesy Bastion represented a single young woman volunteering her services in the defence of the home front whilst maintaining a version of idealised feminine glamour through her clothes and Veronica Lake hair style which sat rather oddly in the midst of a potential warzone. In Maesy Bastion, Miller provided the implied magazine's reader with a figure with whom they could identify; her youth, glamour, wealth, status and class were equivalent to their own. Her job was to mediate between class, culture and gender with an implicit suggestion that there was social and political responsibility inherent in this role.

The women on the haywain represent the family, that bastion of British war- and peacetime culture wherein women have had a primary role as mothers and carers of all. The iconographic reference to the figure of the Madonna situated this young mother within a readily identifiable cultural framework of femininity that linked this image to the wartime remit of the good feminine citizen but with a crucial difference inherent in her ability to speak and thus assert her subjectivity. The cross of the haywain's framework echoes the religious iconography inherent in the Madonna and child motif and was superimposed between the viewer and the group seated on the haywain, suggesting subliminally to the viewer the sacrifices they were making for the greater good of others and thus, in a muted way, their heroism was made a visible and meaningful symbolic act. The iconic framework Miller used tapped into the viewer's cultural heritage that provided this anonymous family with a visibility normally denied them by their drab clothing. It likewise accentuated their precariousness; however, the mother figure was not a mute subject but caught in the act of speaking back and importantly down to Maesy Bastion in a paradoxical cultural and social shift that subtly implies a critique of the magazine's readership, whose social position would have ignored and denied such women any sense of subjectivity or importance and thus rendered them both mute and invisible.

In the published article that these photographs mirror, 'Pattern of Liberation', Miller described the exodus of people and things fairly graphically: 'Bundles were stacked patiently in doorways, being passed out of windows, falling off ridiculous carts. Kids sat patiently, like bundles on top of bundles. Women were scrubbing floors again and closing shutters' (Penrose 2005, 117). As with her photographs she took the magazine's readers straight into the situation and created a sense of purpose and hurry by piling up phrases with active verbs and rounding off the image with reference to domestic chores to be completed before the family moved on. This sense of domestic order sat at odds with the ensuing mayhem but marked the defiance of these women in the face of chaos. Its triviality, even futility, was one of the many seemingly hidden actions of defiance that women used to wage war against the enemy, and which en masse would have been an uncomfortable irritant to the enemy. Throughout this piece Miller repeatedly gave visibility to the seemingly trivial actions of the ordinary woman and children, providing instances of small, often hidden acts of defiance. The daughter of the family with whom she was billeted, for example, wore the forbidden *'ecossais'* plaid skirts (Penrose 2005, 115) underneath her coat throughout the German occupation. These hidden acts of resistance were woven into the larger narrative of the war as they intersected across and with one another, and punctuated the main narrative of war.

The sense of being caught between two opposing armies was also established in 'Boy refugee, Luxembourg, 1944' (Figure 4.2). The photograph of the young boy portrays him seated on bundles and suitcases in front of signposts which pointed left to Luxemburg and right to Echternach, the border

Figure 4.2   Boy refugee, Luxembourg, 1944, by Lee Miller. © Lee Miller Archives, England, 2013. All rights reserved.

town that became the site of the first American offensive into Germany. Here the pattern of liberation took on a darker aspect as in this portrait of a young boy seated awkwardly on a pile of suitcases and bundles that have been carefully labelled for ease of transportation and identification.

In this photograph, the child has become emblematic of this country, caught between two opposing forces, seated on the cusp between signposts pointing in opposite directions. As Calvocoressi (2002) highlights, Miller used the genre of portraiture to enable her to represent the traumas of war in a visual vocabulary that the magazine readers would be able to comprehend. The potential for sentimentalising the child was avoided by the slightly awkward way in which he was seated as if dumped, a deflated putto whose inertia suggested the deeper psychological damage inflicted on the innocent. His slightly bemused, petulant expression was accentuated by the lopsided alignment of his woolly hat. He could be mistaken for a truculent schoolboy with his satchel waiting to go unwillingly to school but for the lacklustre questioning eyes that stared unrelentingly out at the viewer. It was a disturbing gaze in its unrelenting emptiness, a blank stare that interrogated, haunted and followed the viewer, questioning their complicity and position in relation to the war. This was not some childish adventure or schoolboy prank but reality that has left him immobile, petrified, an object amongst other objects.

That Miller found the effect of war on children particularly disturbing was reflected in this image which aimed to bring her readership face to face with the psychological damage of war, at an affective, visceral, child's view of events. The child was a visual metonym for those other young lives affected by the war and the use of portraiture provided a clear framework in which hidden psychic damage was articulated. In her role as witness, Miller manipulated the gaze to confront the disruption of ordinary young lives at a very personal and recognisably ordinary, child's level of vision. She placed the viewer on the same visual plane as the child by using an angle of vision that would have required her to get down to the boy's level of seeing. Thus she was both 'witness' to his situation and 'with' him, a space she vacated for the viewer to imagine the horrors he may have seen and heard. While Miller clearly eschewed the sentimentality of propagandist imagery, the photograph was charged with emotion that was visceral in its proximity and focus.

The disruption of liberation was felt by young and old alike—a point that Miller addressed in images of the elderly whose stories were otherwise rarely reported. In the haywain image (Figure 4.1) the grandmother figure was a visible member of the family group but was situated outside the immediate conversation, an indication of her position outside the main narratives. The grandmother was thus portrayed as part of the domestic furniture, her head framed by the rooftop behind her; however, Miller foregrounded narratives of the elderly in another photograph: 'Lt. Paul A. Villard cheers an old Dame, Luxembourg, 1944' (Figure 4.3). Once again

Title: Lt. Villard cheers an old dame.
Location: Luxembourg
Date: 1944
Photographer: Lee Miller
Negative Number: 6106-23
Notes: FP
Credit Line: © Lee Miller Archives, England. All rights reserved.

Lee Miller Archives
Photographs by Lee Miller 1907-1977

This photograph/document is the copyright of the Lee Miller Archives
© Lee Miller Archives, Farley Farm House, Muddles Green, Chiddingly,
East Sussex, BN8 6HW, England.
Tel: ++44 (0) 1825 - 872 691 Fax: ++44 (0) 1825 - 872 733
E-mail: archives@leemiller.co.uk

Figure 4.3   Lt. Villard cheers an old dame, Luxembourg, 1944, by Lee Miller. © Lee Miller Archives, England 2013. All rights reserved.

Miller offered a view of liberation that cut across the narrative flow of traffic on a town street and captured the momentary intersection of different lives within one frame. It set the foreground event in parallel with the middleground and background and revealed a wide range of visualities that she exploited and co-opted to create her photograph.

There was something very postmodern about Miller's ability to focus on petit narratives that offered different viewpoints on liberation, which, here, were collapsed into one frame. The ostensible point of focus was the figure of the elderly woman in the GI jeep. Dressed in an outmoded style of dress, she was being treated to a ride in a jeep, the often glamorised workhorse of the U.S. army. The jeep's shattered windscreen suggested it had previously been involved in conflict but it was now being used to ferry to safety an elderly woman, who was clearly not fazed by the experience, if a little uncomfortable at the attention, caught in the action of her hands clutching and twisting a clean neatly folded hankerchief. There was a certain ironic humour in this odd juxtaposition of jeep and the well dressed, elderly woman that transported this incident into the realms of the romantic war movies. Yet the underlying classical allusion to the ferryman of Hades who in Greek Mythology transported the souls of the recently dead provided a chilling subtext to this image of an elderly woman who was waiting her turn to cross the flood of refugees chaperoned by GIs. For those who spotted this allusion, this odd juxtaposition revealed quite tellingly the hiatus created by the war, but as with the small family on the haywain, Miller punctuated the grand sweep of history by bringing it to a momentary full stop. The elderly woman's storyline was paralleled by the ox cart driven in the opposite direction loaded with neatly stacked household goods and the firmly shuttered up house in the background. These fragments of different parallel narratives mirror the style of reportage that catalogued a myriad of domestic actions and incidents that have to be logistically handled by the GIs. Equally, they revealed Miller's ability to co-opt a wide range of both classical and contemporary popular visual culture to make her point.

The sartorial splendour of the elderly woman would have reminded her implied readership of the old fashioned dress codes of their own grandmothers who would have such clothes to signal the importance of an occasion. In this image with its accompanying written dialogue the black coat became a marker of rigid resistance like the black coat of Maesy Bastion. This elderly woman's black coat anchored the image in an easily identifiable fashion framework familiar to *Vogue* readers, but their visual reading would have been jolted by the situation and the model. As Miller had made clear in her article, women had used clothing as a feminine weapon of defiance; choosing to dress in her best hat and coat may well have been a subconscious act of resistance that here interrupted the course of the war momentarily but would have been another form of irritant to the occupying enemy.

Clothing during the war was contentious for both the Germans and allied forces as the drab utility clothing and rationing in Britain highlighted. To dress ostentatiously in Britain was to be provocative and jeopardise the war effort. For the German occupying forces clothing was used to identify otherness and used to destroy individuality and personal identity or as a way of segregating peoples as in the striped clothing of concentration camp prisoners. Thus by choosing to dress smartly or wear the *eccosais* would have been to assert individuality and cultural defiance against the dehumanising Nazi war machine that threatened individuality and cultural difference.

As an elderly woman, her position within this gendered economy was peripheral and as a result she would have been excluded, even threatened; but her immobility in terms of her domestic, physical and sartorial codes cuts across the easy narrative flow of traffic and thus figures a certain kind of resistance. As part of a generation of women who would have dressed in their best for almost all external visiting, she was asserting a moral code and ritualised order in the face of chaos in much the same way as women who left their houses clean and tidy addressed the task of scrubbing floors before leaving, eliminating foreign bodies from their houses. As with all gestures, there was a certain futility and ephemerality in such actions, which meant that they were often overlooked and missed; but in these images and accompanying text Miller renders them indelibly visible.

CONCLUSION

In 'Maesy Bastion, interpreter to the US Civil Affair team', Miller deliberately aimed/intended to mobilise the *Vogue* reader's gaze to focus on unseen incidents in the ordinary lives of those rarely the focus of wartime photography. Interestingly, in two of these photographs of civilian evacuees, the GI played only an ancillary role. She shifted the normal perspective for photographing refugees from the panoramic view of mass migration and the mainstream movement of arms to a more personalised individual perspective that aimed to bring home the impact of evacuation on everyday domestic life. With the exception of 'Boy refugee', these were not, however, images of abject, stricken subjects fleeing from the enemy, but identifiable, individualised, active subjects whose actions and narratives paralleled those of the GIs whose story took over the last part of Miller's 'Pattern of Liberation' article. Through photography Miller validated the experiences and subjectivities of women and children. To have attempted to insert these unsung, and usually, unseen heroines of war into the glossy pages of *Vogue* would have been quite a coup and would have forced her privileged readership to reconsider their relationship to these other, unseen women. Nevertheless, in focussing very particularly on the impact of war and on the minutiae of the everyday domestic world of these women, Miller, as in her article, aimed to address her audience at an intimate but universal level. She quite literally intended to bring home visually to *Vogue* readers the impact of war, and provided women with a space in which to engage with and rethink their relationship to society. By focussing on the domestic Miller revealed its fragility and instability, charting both how women and children's lives were subject to catastrophic change from without, but also their spirit of resistance.

BIBLIOGRAPHY / SOURCES

Ballaster, Ros, Margaret Beetham, Elizabeth Fraser, and Sandra Hebron. 1991. *Women's Worlds: Ideology, Femininity and Women's Magazines*. London: Palgrave Macmillan.

Baer, Ulrich. 2002. *Spectral Evidence: The Photography of Trauma*. Cambridge, MA: The MIT Press.

Burke, Carolyn. 2006. *Lee Miller: A Life*. New York: Borzoi Books / Random House.

Burke, Peter. 2001. *Eyewitnessing: The Uses of Images as Historical Evidence*. Ithaca, NY: Cornell University Press.

Calvocoressi, Richard. 2002. *Lee Miller: Portraits from a Life*. London: Thames & Hudson.

Carruthers, Sarah L. 2000. *The Media at War*. London: Macmillan Press.

Carter, Ernestine. 1941. *Grim Glory: Pictures of Britain under Fire*. London: Lund Humphries/Scribner.

Gallagher, Jean. 1998. *World Wars through the Female Gaze*. Carbondale & Edwardsville, IL: Southern Illinois University Press.

Gough-Yates, Anna. 2002. *Understanding Women's Magazines: Publishing, Markets & Readership in Late Twentieth Century Britain*. London: Routledge.

Haworth-Booth, Mark. 2007. *The Art of Lee Miller*. London: V&A Press.

Heron, Liz, and Val Williams. 1996. *Illuminations: Woman Writing on Photography from the 1850s to the Present*. Durham, NC: Duke University Press.

Hilditch, Lynda. 2007. 'Aesthetics of War: The Artistic Representation of War in Lee Miller's WWII Photographs.' In *The Turn to Aesthetics International Conference Papers*, edited by Jonathan Harris, 51–57. Liverpool Hope University.

Hilditch, Lynda. 2010. '"Surreal Documentation": Lee Miller's Artistic Representation of Dachau and Buchenwald.' In *Inside the Death Drive: Excess and Apocalypse in the World of the Chapman Brothers*, edited by Jonathan Harris, 77–98. Liverpool University Press.

McLoughlin, Kate. 2011. 'Glamour Goes to War: Lee Miller's Writings for *British Vogue*, 1939–45.' *Journal of War and Culture Studies* 3 (2): 336–349.

Murrow, Edward R. 1941. Introduction to Carter, Ernestine. 1941 *Grim Glory: Pictures of Britain under Fire*. London: Lund Humphries/Scribner

Nancy, Jean-Luc. 2005. *The Ground of the Image*. Translated by J. Fort. Bronx, NY: Fordham University Press.

O'Sullivan, S. 2006. *Art Encounters/Deleuze and Guattari: Thought beyond Representation*. London and New York: Palgrave Macmillan.

Penrose, Anthony. 2005. *Lee Miller's War*. London: Thames & Hudson.

Penrose, Anthony. 1985. *The Lives of Lee Miller*. London: Thames & Hudson.

Pollock, Griselda. 2007. *Visual Encounters in the Virtual Feminist Museum: Time, Space and the Archive*. London: Routledge.

Rose, Sonya O. 2003. *Which People's War?* Oxford University Press.

Salvio, Paula S. 2009. 'Uncanny Exposures: A Study of the Wartime Journalism of Lee Miller.' *Curriculum Inquiry* 34 (4): 521–536.

Sim, Lorraine, 2009. 'A Different War Landscape: Lee Miller's War Photography and the Ethics of Seeing.' *Modernist Cultures*. 4 (2009) 48–66.

Sliwinski, Sharon. 2010. 'Visual Testimony: Lee Miller's Dachau.' *Journal of Visual Culture* 9 (3): 389–408.

Summerfield, Penny. 1998. *Reconstructing Women's Wartime Lives: Discourse and Subjectivity in Oral Histories of the Second World War.* Manchester University Press.

Zox-Weaver, Annalisa. 2003. 'When the War Was in *Vogue*: Lee Miller's War Reports.' *Women's Studies* 32 (2): 131–164.

PERIODICAL SOURCES

Vogue 1939–1945

5 Prostitution, Adultery and Illegitimacy
Tortuous Couplings and Unstable Sexual Repression in Wartime Film

Maggie Andrews

INTRODUCTION

The Second World War has almost mythical status in 20th century Britain. Although recent scholarship has begun to challenge the perceptions that war was a time of freedom and liberation for women (Summerfield 1998; Holloway 2005; Hall 2000), nevertheless the idea that wartime was an era of sexual licence continues to pervade twenty-first century popular culture. This representation of the past owes much to the numerous media depictions of women in romantic if tortuous wartime relationships found in fictional films which are the focus of this chapter. Recent scholarship has suggested that although 'the Second World War disrupted existing sexual lives and in some cases provided new sexual opportunities (Hall 2000, 133), the degree to which such opportunities were utilised and by whom is open to question. Furthermore, statistical indicators, such as the increase in illegitimacy or divorce rates, which suggest that sexual promiscuity increased in wartime, need to be examined critically. Hall has noted that it is hard to ascertain whether the rise in reported cases of venereal diseases, for example, were a consequence of the new opportunities for sexual activity or new opportunities for health inspection and treatment. Analysis of texts such as *Waterloo Bridge* (1940), *Brief Encounter* (1945) and *The Holly and the Ivy* (1952) suggests film sheds light perhaps not on sexual behaviour—something which is particularly difficult to research—but on the stretching, reworking and rejecting of discourses surrounding sexuality which both construct the place of sexuality within culture and give meaning to sexual practices. This chapter builds upon recent feminist scholarship on cinema, autobiography and fiction in the 40s and 50s which have unpicked the idealisation of marriage in this era (Geraghty 2000; Langhamer 2006; Harper 2000; Fink 2011; Thane and Evans 2012). Films provide the historian with ample evidence of the complex and contradictory discourses surrounding sexuality by offering glimpses of the lexicon of images, narratives and interpretations which enable individuals to make sense of their everyday experience.

Selecting texts across a twelve-year time span draws attention to the temporary, contingent nature of the social constructions of sexuality. For as the Second World War developed, so too did the anxieties of social commentators, politicians, the chattering classes and general public over women's sexual behaviour, anxieties which had to be navigated at both an individual and collective level as the war ended and the people's peace was constructed.

Waterloo Bridge, a film set in First World War London, was made in the US and released in the first year of World War Two. It is the story of an ill-fated love affair between a Duke's nephew, Roy Cronin, and Myra, a ballet dancer. *Brief Encounter* was a critically acclaimed film released as war ended which followed the tortuous relationship of Laura Jesson, a respectable married mother and wife, who falls in love with a doctor Alec Harvey. *The Holly and the Ivy* is set in an emotionally and sexually repressed postwar Norfolk vicarage within which an extended family gathers for Christmas. In each film women face complex moral dilemmas which encourage audiences to engage in ethical debates about female sexual behaviour in wartime. The idea of errant female sexuality and sexual longing raised in all three films is cocooned in narratives of romance. War and its consequences are portrayed as having disrupted, destroyed and subverted the progress of relationships which are tortuous. Romance is ultimately thwarted, a victim of the circumstances of war. In this they mirror many historians who suggest that marriage, home, and family—which had been dreamed about by so many during the war—was rendered unattainable by the mental scars of warfare and Britain's appalling post-war housing crisis in the 1940s and 1950s (see Thane 2003; Andrews 2012; Allport 2009).

What is perhaps most significant in these films is that errant sexual behaviour is not reserved for working-class girls or even the aristocratic women who, as Sue Harper has pointed out, were frequently an 'enabling device for images of wayward females' in wartime (Harper 1996, 208). The focus of each text is on the respectable middle-classes. It is the daughters of teachers and vicars who become prostitutes, unmarried mothers and women who are emotionally if not physically unfaithful to their husbands. Thus, within *Waterloo Bridge, Brief Encounter* and *The Holly and The Ivy,* repressed, forbidden areas of female sexuality threaten to erupt uncontrollably into polite middle-class society. The cultural significance of representations must be understood in relation to the historical importance of sexuality to constructions of class in the nineteenth and early twentieth century when, as I have argued elsewhere (Andrews 2003), women's sexuality, sexual desire or rather its negation was one of the defining characteristics of middle-class culture. It enabled the nineteenth century bourgeoisie to differentiate themselves from the amoral working classes and the immoral aristocracy. Consequently, wayward sexuality amongst middle-class women suggested uncertainty and potentially fluidity around boundaries of class and nation, particularly given the centrality of the middle class to 'the people' of the notion of the 'People's War' (Noakes 1997; Rose 2003).

Cultural assumptions linking wartime with women's sexual promiscuity predated wartime or indeed any evidence of changes in women's behaviour. As war was declared, many of the tensions and moral panics of the First World War resurfaced; the prostitute and the 'enthusiastic amateur' caused particular concern. Anxieties which initially focussed upon young girls did not however dissipate as war progressed; rather they were joined by increasing concern over what married women were getting up to when their husbands were occupied fighting the enemy. Attempts through cultural governance to regulate sexuality only served to exaggerate its significance, for as Danaher, Shirato and Webb point out, 'discursive and regulatory attention paid to sex and sexuality means that we are continually being called to focus on it, to think about what is approved and what is not. This makes sex very important' (2000, 144). How this played out in people's lives during the Second World War is of course somewhat harder to fathom. When the war ended nervousness around women's sexual behaviour was managed, at both the national and individual level, by narratively constructing war as a different space, the extraordinary. In the second half of the twentieth century, women's perceived sexual permissiveness in wartime began to be understood in terms of 'we weren't really immoral there was a war on' (Costello 1985, 23). Wartime thus began to be viewed as a licenced discursive space. As reassuring and unthreatening as this narrative may be for a culture which perceives sexuality and sexual morality as important constituents of identity construction, it is a generalisation and over-simplification which needs careful critical interrogation.

NARRATIVES OF WOMEN AND SEXUALITY IN THE SECOND WORLD WAR

Early historians of the Second World War suggested sexual behaviour was one of many areas of social change precipitated by the upheaval of total war (Costello 1985; Marwick 1968). Moral restraint was apparently eroded by the fear of imminent danger or the freedom from family and community ties offered by the mobilisation of women for war work and in the armed forces. Furthermore, greater involvement in the workplace apparently gave women new economic and social independence and also contributed to a shift in women's sexual behaviour. According to Costello's *Love, Sex and War 1939–45*: 'everywhere, men and women turned to one another for affirmation of life amidst death and destruction' (1985, 26). Chastity and sexual repression were apparently the victims of a new hedonistic culture which set Britain on the path towards the permissive society of the 1960s. However, evidence is hard to establish and scholarly work, particularly by feminist historians, has suggested a range of more complex histories of the period; Penny Summerfield and Nicole Crockett argue that 'the construction of the Second World War as a time of heightened eroticism when sexual inhibitions were thrown to the winds is something of voyeuristic invention' (1992, 440). Their interpretation owes much to the Foucauldian approach to sexuality in recent scholarship, which sees sexuality not so much as a physical force to be restrained 'by the cultural matrix' (Weeks 1989, 24) but instead as 'something which society produces in complex ways . . . the result of diverse social practices'. Thus '[s]exuality is not given, it is a product of negotiation, struggle and human agency' (Weeks 1989, 25). Arguably since the latter part of the nineteenth century the media has increasingly played a role in this negotiation and struggle, providing narrative representations through which individuals can explore their ideas of approval, disapproval, acceptability, normality and taboo.

Evidence of concern and even disapproval of women's sexual behaviour and morality is easy to locate in wartime media and is indicative of commonly expressed anxieties; the *Norfolk News and Weekly Press* reported that the Bishop of Norwich had warned that 'nothing is more alarming than the decay of personal standards of sexual morality . . . nothing threatens more the future of our race. When men and women grow loose in morality, they endanger their own eternal salvation and they endanger too the England of tomorrow' (Rose 2003, 78–79). Women who joined the armed forces were the objects of aspersion and particular critical social comment. Maureen Wells recounts how she listened in shock as Cathy, the daughter of one her mother's old school friends, and an officer in the Women's Auxiliary Air Force (WAAF) explained that 'she is a strong believer in free love for young girls and practices it, adding: "My dear I assure you that 75 per cent of the WAAFs will never see virginity again and what's wrong?"' (Hartley 1994, 208). The representativeness of such memories is hard to ascertain for as Summerfield and Crockett (1992) affirm, the existence of such discourses does not mean they were accepted or internalised, rather they may have met with resistance, appropriation, negotiation and rejection. There are many indications, as Claire Langhamer has pointed out (2003, 2006) that the fantasies of the majority of young girls were about romance rather than free love. Celia, the heroine of the wartime film *Millions Like Us* (1942) was portrayed looking at recruitment posters for the armed forces in the employment exchange. Her daydreams about life in the Women's Royal Navy (WRN), the WAAF or the Auxiliary Territorial Service (ATS) suggest such work could be a prelude to romance. Joining any of the armed forces was seen as providing opportunities to meet an array of handsome men in uniform.

Women in uniform were in a particularly perilous position, simultaneously portrayed as masculinised, having lost their femininity by putting on a uniform and as women whose role involved not only serving their country but also sexually servicing the men in the forces. Publicity posters and radio broadcasts portrayed the WRN, WAAF and ATS as glamorous, with their uniform worn over figure-emphasising corsets. While this may have encouraged women considering volunteering in advance of the introduction of their conscription from the end of 1941, popular descriptions of the ATS as 'officer's ground sheets' and the WAAF as 'officer's cockpits' did little to reassure their parents. The government organised an investigation by the Women's Services (Welfare and Amenities) Commission into immorality in the armed forces in 1942 which contradicted popular perceptions.

In 1945, despite a paucity of evidence, the senior ranks of the RAF remained 'very concerned about the rising rates of unmarried pregnancy in the WAAF which they believed had reached an inexcusable level' (Thane and Evans 2012, 67). For some women, however, pregnancy offered a welcome alternative to the domestic drudgery and marching which made up life in the services; pregnancy could be utilised to dodge conscription or in 1945 speed up their discharge. Mary Lee Settle's account of her first days in the WAAF provides evidence of such strategies being employed:

> 'I'm going to work my ticket' Tina said . . . I heard that because I didn't know what it meant. Tina had already picked up more of the language . . . The officer in charge illuminated: 'In the event of pregnancy, fire, catastrophe, act of God you are released from active service at the termination of three months. I looked around at Tina who was smiling. I knew what 'working one's ticket' meant (Settle 1984, 40–41).

If promiscuity and pregnancy provided one way for some women to navigate the challenges of wartime, others saw romance and marriage as more acceptable alternatives. However, both films and women's magazines suggest wartime relationships were problematic (Waller and Vaughan-Rees 1987). Women who were spatially separated from their loved one for long periods of time found themselves facing moral dilemmas about sexual behaviour as they were tempted to fall in love, or lust. Media texts suggest women agonised over what they should do and what they should tell their husband. Some historians may question the usefulness of using films and magazines as a historical source, but they were all commercial products; they published what their sales and audience research suggested women wanted to read. Consequently, they may provide historians with a sense of the concerns and dilemmas at a particular historical juncture. In magazines, editorial pages and the answers to readers' letters, alongside along wartime propaganda posters can be perceived to be attempting to exert a culturally determined regulatory framework which advocated self-restraint. This can also perhaps be identified in *Waterloo Bridge*. The trauma and uncertainty caused by the mobilisation of both the armed forces and civilians was one of the most immediate effects of the initial months of the Second World War, when evacuation, conscription of men, war work and billeting disrupted many people's lives. This initial 'phoney war' when there was little bombing or armed conflict nevertheless disturbed normal patterns of courtship;

hurried marriages took place as the young men were called up, moved from one part of the country to another, undertook training or awaited embarkation to a combat zone. The uncertainty, separation and accelerated speed of romance and courtship in wartime were also structuring elements of the early scenes in *Waterloo Bridge*.

Wartime's capacity to create new opportunities for courtship and interaction with the opposite sex is touched upon when Myra and Roy meet on Waterloo Bridge during a World War One Zeppelin raid. An air raid siren and plethora of men in uniforms signified the special circumstances of war. The consequent rush to a shelter forewarns of Roy's impetuous and childlike plans for a speedy courtship and marriage which disregard any potential pitfalls and trample upon Myra's career as a ballet dancer. Myra risks her job to see her fiancé off to fight on the Western Front and finds herself ill and destitute after he is reported missing. Initially looked after by a friend, she turns to a life of prostitution in order to survive. Roy's unexpected return poses an ethical dilemma; she is torn between disclosure and deceit and chooses instead suicide. Women too, the film suggests, are victims of war. *Millions Like Us* (1942) was produced just after conscription for women was introduced and features no sexually promiscuous women, and no moral dilemmas. Instead Celia, a respectable working-class girl, finds romance, marriage and widowhood. As the film ends she has replaced her relationship with her husband with camaraderie with other women and a proper shared commitment to war work.

Waterloo Bridge addressed one of the moral dilemmas around sexuality faced by young women in wartime, which was also the focus of many column inches in women's magazines. What was an appropriate level of sexual engagement and commitment to give to boyfriends who were going to risk their lives in war? Should young women have sex with them and risk an unplanned pregnancy and possibly an illegitimate child or resist men's advances and let them go potentially to their death with the relationship unconsummated (Waller and Vaughan-Rees's 1987)? Hasty marriages were one solution and provided financial security and respectability to women on the home front although the return of a comparative stranger on leave or at the end of the war was not without its problems (Allport 2010).

The representation of Myra in *Waterloo Bridge* as a victim and a fallen woman who follows her altruistic and caring friend into prostitution is at odds with propaganda posters aimed at combatting VD which portrayed prostitutes as exploiters and polluters of the armed forces. 'Hello Boyfriend, Coming My Way?' asked a poster warning of the dangers of VD explaining: 'The easy girlfriend spreads syphilis and gonorrhoea, which unless properly treated may result in blindness, insanity, paralysis and premature death' (Costello 1985, 31). The discursive construction of virile young men in the armed forces as under threat from prostitution was established in the nineteenth century and indeed led to the inspection and regulation of women deemed to be prostitutes in garrison towns between 1864–1885

(Walkowitz 1982). Furthermore, Lucy Bland has drawn attention to First World War anxieties over the transmission of venereal diseases, which led the government to consider using the criminal law to regulate the transmission of venereal disease (1985, 203). The 'amateur' prostitute in particular was held responsible for the transmission of the disease (Bland 1985, 206). Juliet Gardiner has suggested that in wartime prostitution was an area in which women worked long hours to take advantage of unprecedented demand and rising prices. 'Martha Watts who had come to London via a marriage of convenience with an elderly man, soon after the outbreak of war, had very soon notched up 400 court appearances through successful participation in a seller's market' (2004, 606). Significantly and perhaps surprisingly, given U.S. involvement in the production of *Waterloo Bridge*, Myra's actions were not condemned in the film. Her prospective mother-in-law is sympathetic when she hears Myra's story. Roy remains unmarried after her suicide, faithful to her memory; he keeps the lucky charm she gave him and revisits Waterloo Bridge when he is called to fight for his country again at the outbreak of the Second World War.

AS THE WAR ENDS: COMING TO
TERMS WITH BRIEF ENCOUNTERS

Brief Encounter never mentions the war, but it is a structuring absence within the text. The film's account of a married housewife's tortuous unconsummated romance echoes concerns expressed about adulterous relationships during the war which were heightened in the post-war era as men were slowly demobbed and returned home. Laura and Alec face an ethical dilemma about whether to prioritise their feelings for one another over loyalty, duty and, importantly, respectability, which is ultimately resolved when Alec and his family emigrate to Africa. Laura is left to return to home, husband and children with only a yearning for sexual adventure (Smart 1996) or at least something more than hum-drum post-war idealised domesticity is likely to provide.

Anxiety as to what women had been up to when men were absent in wartime was exaggerated by the number of foreign troops stationed on British soil. Nazi propaganda suggested American troops were 'lend-leasing' British women (Costello 1985, 32) and 'transgressive sexual behaviour during the war years was particularly associated with non-British' others (Costello 1985, 32). The Americans had a reputation as 'overpaid, oversexed and over here' (Hall 2000, 145). The female body in many ways was perceived to be in danger in wartime; its boundaries vulnerable to be breached by enemy action, bombs, bullets, shrapnel, shots and colonisation from invading and occupying forces—even if the GIs and Canadian troops were part of the allied army. The wife, mother and sweetheart were the emblem of the homes that ideologically war was being fought to protect, gender and nation were intrinsically intertwined (see Rose 2003). Perhaps at the back of soldiers' minds was a concern that women had not been worthy of the sacrifices of war. Divisions between idealised wives or mothers and morally dubious and corrupting women appeared a little fluid. Thus when Laura in *Brief Encounter* decides not to go home on time but to meet Alec in his friend's flat, she begins a slippery slope to immorality. She removes her headscarf, a tentative step towards greater intimacy, but they are interrupted and she furtively scuffles away via the service or servants' entrance, an indication that as morality slips so does class status. The sordidness of the encounter is further emphasised when unable to face going home she sits on a street bench and a policeman suspects she may be a prostitute.

Women faced moral dilemmas around the degree to which they disclosed any wartime misdemeanours. Laura is emphatic she must never admit to what she has done to save her husband pain, a view endorsed in many magazines, particularly when men were away. Sometimes the consequences of a wife's infidelity were clear for all to see. Thane and Evans point out that 'a substantial new group amongst mothers of illegitimate children were the married women who became pregnant when their husbands were away at war' (2012, 57). Allan Allport suggests that '[i]n the eighteen months that followed the end of the war in Europe, scarcely a Sunday went by without at least one story in the *News of the World* about a returning serviceman killing or assaulting an errant wife or lover—or in a few cases being preemptively killed by them before he could act himself' (2010, 84). Undeniably, the news coverage was disproportionate, nevertheless 'Britain in 1945 was a country tormented by sexual suspicion' (2010, 85). 'The number of divorce petitions in England and Wales rocketed from about 9,970 in 1938 to 24,857 in 1945 and to a post-war peak of 47,042 in 1947 . . . two-thirds of these immediate post-war divorces were initiated by husbands who came home to find their wives had been unfaithful' (Waller 2010, 356). This was at least the reason given, and it was in a couple's financial interests for the husband to take on the role of the injured party if he was in the armed forces. Those in the forces could obtain cheap, quickie divorces, however for some couples this may have been a mutual decision given the speed of some marriages at the outset of war and the years and experiences which had intervened.

One of the overwhelming emotions in *Brief Encounter* is of thwarted love, the idea of an emotionally intense and fulfilling relationship which has no future within a society in which it is forbidden. Andy Medhurst's seminal work on the text emphasises potential queer readings, arguing the forbidden, the repressed and the tortuous unconsummated heterosexual relationship between Laura and Alec can be seen to be standing in for homosexuality (1991) at a historical juncture when homosexual sex was a criminal act, carrying a prison sentence. This is not, however, the only reading of the text, and homosexuality was not the only forbidden sexual relationship. Adultery was also seen as problematic, when the object of a woman's affections

was a foreign serviceman or a prisoner of war. Social disapproval particularly increased when women's husbands had been injured or were prisoners of war. Longing separation was the experience of many couples whose
relationships were not forbidden. Government control of people's working
and domestic lives interfered with personal relationships, splitting couples
up, placing uncertainty and geographical distance between partners. *Brief
Encounter* articulates separation and absence, setting a number of sequences
in a railway station, the scene of so many wartime partings. Alec Harvey, the
embodiment of Laura's yearning, leaves for Africa with his wife and family
at the end of the film; coping with men going overseas to do their duty was
an all too recognisable emotional experience for many women in the audience. War separated women from their husbands, men they had had affairs
and intense relationships with. Mavis Bunyan's husband was sent abroad in
August 1944, and she wrote to him: 'Today it is eight months since I saw
your dearly beloved face and in that time my love and longing for you has
increased to such a desperate need. It has become so overpowering that I have
no will or wish to do anything' (Hartley 1994, 214).

Brief Encounter may have gained both critical and middle-class approval
because of its narrative privileging of denial, duty and suffering in silence.
Laura's return to her home, to duty, could be interpreted as promoting
repression and restraint. More sympathetically, Smart describes Laura as
'a woman who has the courage to face boredom and drudgery and knows
the limitations of her situation' (1996, 102). Arguably for the audience,
Laura's decision is unconvincing; there is little conviction in the idea that
she will be happily married. Rather what this film suggests is the instability
of the sexually repressed polite middle-class home and family on which the
post-war reconstruction was to be built. The 'nice' middle-class domestic
unit of the Home Counties was portrayed as central to post-war peace
in documentary films like *Diary for Timothy* (1946). Yet *Brief Encounter* suggests that perhaps these homes harbour secrets and uncontrollable
passions which could erupt unexpectedly. Discourses of women's sexual
promiscuity which caused anxiety in wartime were equally problematic to
the construction of the people's peace. If, as *Brief Encounter* suggests, the
discursive finger of suspicion pointed at even middle-class housewives, it is
not perhaps surprising that for many it was hard to rebuild marriages in
the post-war world.

THE HOLLY AND THE IVY: ILLEGITIMACY

The Holly and the Ivy was set in a quintessential English small town in
the years after the war, as snow fell, carol singers visited, log fires burnt
and one family's secrets seethed in a Norfolk vicarage Christmas. Passions do indeed erupt from beneath the repressed, respectability of this
middle-class home. Elder daughter Jenny longs to give up her role as her

widowed father's housekeeper to marry and go abroad. When the two younger members of the family spend Christmas Eve getting drunk in a local hostelry, alcohol loosens Michael's tongue and he tells his father that no one in the family can speak the truth, something he elaborates on the following morning with the revelation that his sister had an illegitimate child. There was an increase in illegitimacy during wartime and it became an area of concern, but it does not necessarily imply that there was greater sexual promiscuity. Thane and Evans point out that in 1938–1939 the Registrar General estimated that 30% of children were conceived out of wedlock, being born within eight-and-a-half months of their parents' marriage (2012, 54), a percentage which increased for mothers under twenty years old. This figure fell significantly during the war, while the number of illegitimate births rose (2012, 55), suggesting that wartime disturbed the normal patterns of courtship whereby marriage generally took place when a pregnancy was discovered. Indeed, Thane and Evans point out that the total number of pre-married conceptions and unmarried deliveries fell during wartime (2012, 55). For women who conceived an illegitimate child in the 1930s and 1940s, there were a limited range of options: illegal abortion, adoption or to have the child and risk social condemnation, struggling with economic hardship and if they continued to work, the problems and expense of childcare. Arguably for middle-class women illegitimacy carried a greater stigma although some changed their names, or moved away to avoid this condemnation. An increasing number of women, like Margaret in *The Holly and the Ivy*, chose to keep their babies and return to work in the 1940s and 1950s (Thane and Evans 2012, 57). As one of this new type of unmarried mother, Margaret employed a nanny jointly with a friend and lived an independent life. Her illegitimate child, however, had remained hidden from her family, although he became a reason for living after her lover had been killed in combat. For other women adoption or illegal abortion enabled mothers to hide their pregnancy, and magazines in the immediate post-war period carried articles and adverts encouraging women to adopt babies. When Margaret returns to participate in the family Christmas her child has died of meningitis and her life has become meaningless. Given in Margaret's new role as a vicar's housekeeper, she would not have been confined to the vicarage but also would have been involved in the parish church and the town, it is convenient that her illegitimate child has been removed. Single and childless once again, Margaret is placed in the same position as a woman who has had an abortion, which to some extent can be swept under the carpet. Both she and others refer to her child as 'all over and done with now'. Although her child has died, the spectre of abortion remains in the background for many of the audience, repressed like so much else in this vicarage.

Margaret's behaviour would have elicited social condemnation during wartime, as her child's father was an American GI. Tinkler has drawn attention to concerns expressed about the 'alleged wave of immorality in

Blackpool', in the *West Lancashire Evening Gazette*, which focussed upon young women's relationships with men in the armed forces. On July 28, 1941, Alderman Grime described many women's enthusiasm for a man in uniform as 'a crisis of promiscuity and, more specifically of female behaviour' (Tinkler 2006, 201). Alderman Grime was by no means an isolated voice yet there are indications that as war progresses so did a softening of attitudes towards illegitimacy and an acknowledgement that it was not necessarily associated with promiscuity. In *Nella Last's Diaries* (Malcolmson 2012), kept for Mass Observation, she discusses a friend whose daughter had an illegitimate child, and whose fiancé was moved away by the Armed Forces before they had chance to marry. Nella does not condemn this girl and is full of empathy for the mother. Likewise, there is no condemnation of Margaret's behaviour at any point within *The Holly and the Ivy*; the death of her son, Simon, and her struggle coping with pregnancy and grief alone elicit strong sympathy from both her sister and father. Margaret's rejection of her London social life and career and her return to home, duty and family stresses the narrative construction of wartime as a period of aberrant sexual behaviour which too is 'over and done with', a different time with different social norms. Yet Margaret's shift from independent woman to her father's housekeeper narratively jars. It seems incongruous; not least because her Aunt Biddy, miserable and bitter at having wasted her life looking after her parents, serves as a warning to Margaret and the audience that her planned course of action inadvisable. Once again it is through the range of characters, the discomfort of the decisions made that the film encourages its audience to engage in ethical debate. Arguably, there is an acknowledgement also that even in a vicarage sexual repression is unstable, families are far from ideal and relationships are tortuous.

CONCLUSION

Arguably these texts were examples of the Pandora's box on sexuality that a discursive fixation on sexuality unleashed; ethical debates about the position of women and sexuality had started and rumbled on, in post-war Britain, for many years to come. The stretching, shifting and challenging to discourses of sexuality which appeared to be taking place in wartime film erupted into many other spaces and places in the post-war era. Carol Smart points out that in 1951 the Royal Commission on Marriage and Divorce was set up in 'response to pressure both within and outside Parliament' (1998, 3). The infamous *Report of the Departmental Committee on Homosexual Offences and Prostitution* under Lord Wolfenden's chairmanship was published in 1957, and lengthy campaigns for changes to the law on abortion led to the 1967 Abortion Act. Perhaps then these films provide an important source for historians trying to identify the traces of discontent beneath idealisation of romance, home and marriage in many wartime media. Furthermore, they begin to suggest the difficulties, sacrifices and problematic relationships that women encountered in wartime which fuelled post-war changes.

BIBLIOGRAPHY / SOURCES

Aldgate, Alan. 2007. *Britain Can Take It: British Cinema in the Second World War*. London: I. B. Tauris.

Allport, Alan. 2010. *Demobbed: Coming Home after the Second World War*. Yale University Press.

Andrews, Maggie. 2003. 'Calendar Ladies: Popular Culture, Sexuality and the Middle Class, Middle Aged Domestic Woman.' *Sexualities* 6 (3–4): 385–403. .

Andrews, Maggie. 2012. *Domesticating the Airwaves*. London: Continuum.

Bland, Lucy. 1985. '"Cleansing the Portals of Life": The Venereal Disease Campaign in the Early Twentieth Century.' In *Crisis in the British State 1880–1930*, edited by Mary Langan and Bill Schwarz, 192–208. London: Hutchinson and Co.

Calder, Angus, and Dorothy Sheridan. 1984. *Speak for Yourselves: A Mass Observation Anthology 1937–49*. London: Jonathan Cape.

Cook, Hera. 2004. *The Long Sexual Revolution: English Women, Sex and Contraception 1900–1975*. Oxford University Press.

Costello, John. 1985. *Love, Sex and War: Changing Values, 1939–45*. London: Collins.

Danaher, Geoff, Tony Shirato, and Jen Webb. 2000. *Understanding Foucault*. London: Sage.

Evans, Tanya. 2011. 'The Other Woman and Her Child: Extra-marital Affairs and Illegitimacy in Twentieth-Century Britain.' *Women's History Review* 20 (1): 47–65.

Fink, Janet. 2011. 'For Better or for Worse? The Dilemmas of Unmarried Motherhood in Mid-Twentieth-Century Popular British Film and Fiction.' *Women's History Review* 20 (1): 145–160.

Gardiner, Juliet. 2004. *Wartime Britain 1939–45*. London: Hodder Headline.

Gledhill, Christine, and Gillian Swanson, eds. 1996. *Nationalising Femininity: Culture, Sexuality and British Cinema in the Second World War*. Manchester University Press.

Hall, Lesley. 2000. *Sex, Gender and Change in Britain since 1800*. London: Macmillan.

Harper, Sue. 2000. *Women in British Cinema: Mad, Bad and Dangerous to Know*. London: Continuum.

Hartley, Jenny. 1994. *Heart Undefeated: Women's Writing in the Second World War*. London: Virago.

Hately-Broad, Barbara. 2002. '"Nobody Would Tell You Anything": The War and Foreign Offices and British Prisoner of War Families during World War II.' *Journal of Family History* 27 (4): 459.

Higonnet, Margaret R., Jane Jenson, Sonya Michel, and Margaret Collins Weitz. 1987. *Behind the Lines: Gender and the Two World Wars*. Yale University Press.

Holloway, Gerry. 2005. *Women and Work in Britain since 1840*. London: Routledge.

Klein, Hodger. 1997. *Beyond the Home Front: Women's Autobiographical Writings of the Two World Wars*. Basingstoke, UK: Macmillan.

Malcolmson, Robert. *The Diaries of Nella Last: Writing in War and Peace*. London: Profile Books.

Marwick, Arthur. 1968. *Britain in the Century of Total War: Peace and Social Change 1900–1967*. London: Bodley Head Ltd.

Medhurst, Andy. 1991. 'That Special Thrill: *Brief Encounter,* Homosexuality and Authorship.' *Screen* 32 (2): 197–208.

Noakes, Lucy. 1998. *War and British Gender and National Identity 1939–9*. London: I. B. Tauris.

Langhamer, Claire. 2006. 'Adultery in Post-War England.' *History Workshop Journal* 62 (1): 86–115.

Langhamer, Claire. 2006. 'Love and Courtship in Mid-Twentieth-Century England.' *Historical Journal* 50 (1): 173–196.

Langhamer, Claire. 2003. '"A Public House is for All Classes, Men and Women Alike"': Women, Leisure and Drink in Second World War England.' *Women's History Review* 12 (3): 423–443.

Rose, Sonya O. 2003. *Which People's War? National Identity and Citizenship in Wartime Britain 1939–1945*. Oxford University Press.

Settle, Mary Lee. (1966) 1984. *All the Brave Promises*. London: Thorsons.

Summerfield, Penny. 1998. *Reconstructing Women's Wartime Lives: Discourse and Subjectivity in Oral Histories of the Second World War*. Manchester University Press.

Summerfield, Penny. 1988. 'Women, War and Social Change in Britain in World War II.' In *Total War and Social Change*, edited by Arthur Marwick, 97–103. London: Macmillan.

Summerfield, Penny, and Corinna Peniston-Bird. 2000. 'Women in the Firing Line: The Home Guard and the Defence of Gender Boundaries in Britain in the Second World War.' *Women's History Review* 9 (2): 231–255.

Summerfield, Penny, and Nicole Crockett. 1992. '"You Weren't Taught That with the Welding": Lessons in Sexuality in the Second World War.' *Women's History Review* 1 (3): 436–454.

Thane, Pat. 2003. 'Family Life and "Normality" in Post War British Culture.' In *Life after Death: Approaches to a Cultural and Social History of Europe during the 1940s and 1950s*, edited by Richard Bessel and Dirk Schumann. Cambridge University Press.

Thane, Pat, and Tanya Evans. 2012. *Sinners? Scroungers? Saints? Unmarried Motherhood in Twentieth-Century England*. Oxford University Press.

Tinkler, Penny. 2006. 'Sexuality and Citzenship: The State and Girls' Leisure Provision in England, 1939–45.' *Women's History Review* 4 (2): 193–218.

Walkowitz, Judith. 1982. *Prostitution and Victorian Society: Women, Class and the State*. Cambridge University Library.

Waller, Jane, and Michael Vaughan-Rees. 1987. *Women in Wartime: The Role of Women's Magazines 1939–1945*. London: Macdonald Optima.

Waller, Maureen. (2009) 2010. *The English Marriage: Tales of Love, Money and Adultery*. London: John Murray.

Weeks, Jeffery. 1989. *Sex, Politics and Society: The Regulation of Sexuality since 1800*. London: Longman.

Weeks, Jeffery. 1997. *Sexuality*. Oxford: Routledge.

FILMOGRAPHY

Waterloo Bridge (**1940**)
Brief Encounter (**1945**)
Diary for Timothy (*1946*)
The Holly and the Ivy (**1952**)

6 Striving for Editorial Autonomy and Internal Recognition
BBC's *Woman's Hour*

Kristin Skoog

INTRODUCTION

On November 29, 1951, Janet Quigley wrote a two-page document to the Editorial Board of Talks Division about the staffing issue in *Woman's Hour*. Quigley was nearly a year and a half into her appointment as Editor and *Woman's Hour* was running in its fifth year. From the document it is clear that the programme's journey had not been smooth and was still, in 1951, an area of negotiation within the BBC:

> As I understand it *Woman's Hour* was started some five years ago in rather a hurried and haphazard way: 'Let us have a daily programme for women and put in a woman to run it'. Now Marjorie Wace in her time fought a great battle for so-called women's interests and succeeded in getting the Corporation to take very seriously their programmes for women.

Quigley goes on to outline the problems encountered by successive editors, stating:

> It is time that *Woman's Hour* moved from a hand-to-mouth struggle for existence to recognition as an established programme with a high listening figure whose claims to staff and money should be looked at on the basis of its worth to the Corporation (BBC Written Archives Centre hereafter WAC R13/408/6: Quigley to Editorial Board November 29, 1951).

Quigley's words provide an entry point for this inquiry. On the one hand they highlight the growth and development (since the inter-war period) of programmes made especially *for* women and often *by* women, and what a significant role these played. On the other hand she also demonstrates how this expansion was contested, showing that the development of radio programmes for women was a continual struggle for resources and recognition. It tells us something about the perceived status of women's radio within an institution such as the BBC and also the determination of the women involved in this type of programming.

Women have had a long relationship with the radio. Kate Lacey (2005) has argued that women's radio in the inter-war period bridged the private and the public, integrating women into the public sphere. In the British context the BBC developed specific programmes and talks aimed at the female audience early on—many with a domestic flavour and focus (Bailey 2009; Andrews 2012; Chapter 2 in this volume). These talks and programmes continued into the 1940s. Sian Nicholas's (1996) study of the wartime BBC examines programmes such as *The Kitchen Front*, *Mostly for Women* and *Woman's Page*, and argues that these programmes changed from being mainly domestic in focus to more outward looking, covering topics such as equal pay and careers for women. This chapter will further explore women's radio by examining in more detail the production and development of the BBC's perhaps most famous women's programme, *Woman's Hour*, which built on a long tradition of programmes for women broadcast by the BBC. It was introduced in October 1946 at 2 p.m. on the BBC Light Programme (the BBC's response to the demand for more popular entertainment and output) and attracted listeners in the millions, the majority of whom were working class. *Woman's Hour* was produced and presented mainly by women, just as programmes for women in the inter-war period and during the war had been. Although the first presenter was a man, Alan Ivimey, he was replaced by Joan Griffiths in December 1946 and Olive Shapley in February 1949. In 1951, the 'trio', Marjorie Anderson, Margaret Hubble and Jean Metcalfe, took over. *Woman's Hour* was aimed at housewives and had a strong focus on the domestic setting including childcare, cooking and health, although as will be discussed this focus is much more complicated. Maggie Andrews (2012) has highlighted the programme's construction of the housewife as a consumerist citizen, which also reflected representations of women found in many women's magazines at the time. Moreover, Anne Karpf (1987) and Sally Feldman (2000, 2007) have drawn attention to *Woman's Hour*'s reputation for being pioneering and controversial (covering issues such as equal pay, the menopause) and how it provided companionship and advice to its listeners. Very little however has been said about the early development and the actual production of *Woman's Hour*.

There has been a tendency within media studies to focus on the text or reception, and not so much the areas of production, and in particular production of women's own media or feminist media (Byerly and Ross 2006). Liesbet van Zoonen has argued that studies of production are important since 'communicators' decisions are shaped by institutional factors such as policy, organizational structure, work routines and power relations within the organization' (1994, 47). Histories within national contexts suggest that women's radio and women broadcasters were often marginalised within broadcasting institutions (Hilmes 1997; Badenoch 2008). Michele Hilmes (1997, 131), for example, has argued that in histories of broadcasting, production has almost always been male dominated, or as she says, 'so we are led to believe'. As Hilmes shows, women in American broadcasting were involved from the beginning in the development of key genres such as the serial drama and the magazine format. Women broadcasters and women's radio thus contributed immensely to the development of radio (and television) as tools of communication, information and entertainment. Furthermore, Hilmes has argued for the importance of daytime radio, that it was here in 'the hidden, subversive, and publicly disparaged space,' women found a place and the careers of key women broadcasters were built (1997, 154). As this chapter will argue, there are parallels here to be made with the British context.

This chapter is about recognising the role that women's radio played in mid-century Britain and the role women broadcasters have played in the development of British broadcasting. An examination of the production process of *Woman's Hour* will demonstrate that institutional and organisational structure had a considerable impact on the outcome of the programme. *Woman's Hour* initially fought for editorial autonomy and control, and against prejudice and disrespect from other members of staff, at a time when traditional gender roles overall were being challenged and contested. Furthermore, this chapter will suggest that initially working out what a programme for women should be about proved rather difficult. Preconceptions about the female audience and women's radio surfaced within the BBC and so setting out a clear editorial policy for *Woman's Hour* required a redefinition of so called 'women's interests'. This case study is therefore a contribution to the ongoing revisionist work within women's history which challenges the image of post-war Britain as a particularly stifling place for women. Recent histories have complicated this narrative of the 1950s considerably and shown women were given an increasing role as mothers, workers, voters (citizens) and consumers (Thane 1994; Zweiniger-Bargielowska 2000; Thane 2003; Holloway 2005). The need for women's labour continued after the war and between 1947 and 1949 the government campaigned to encourage older women, as well as married women, into paid employment. Women were acknowledged as playing an important part in the nation's economy, and taking up paid work—whether for single or married, working- or middle-class women—became more accepted (Holloway 2005). Concerns about both domesticity and work affected the post-war woman and gave her a central role in the rebuilding of Britain. In her analysis of femininity and film in the 1950s, Melanie Bell makes the valid observation that 'the contours of normative femininity were clearly under pressure, being transformed and rendered increasingly ambiguous by the greater economic, social and sexual freedoms that many women experienced' (2010, 10).

By studying the production and editorial process of *Woman's Hour* it is possible to see how the changing role of women in this period was reflected (and challenged) within the programme. The 'duality' of women's experience was felt in radio and impacted on the schedule when the

Woman's Hour repeat, aimed at working women, was introduced. The programme makers had a close connection and awareness of the audience and responded to their changing needs. *Woman's Hour* promoted the democratic and intimate radio style now taken for granted. For example, the BBC Home Service in the 1960s moved towards programming that was more personal in style using 'real people rather than experts' and incorporating listeners' letters into programmes, providing greater interaction between guests, producers and experts, helping Britons to realise that it 'was both possible—and desirable—to talk' (Hendy 2007, 232), aspects which were already incorporated in *Woman's Hour* in the post-war period, as will be discussed below.

SETTING UP A PROGRAMME FOR WOMEN

Woman's Hour was one of several programmes aimed at the female audience introduced on the Light Programme after the war. Programmes such as *Housewives' Choice* (1946), a music request programme broadcast in the mornings, and the domestic serials *Mrs Dale's Diary* (1948) and *The Archers* (1951), all became hugely popular and indicate the female audience was important for the BBC. *Woman's Hour* was deliberately placed as a separate unit outside programme departments (the Home, Light Programme and the Third) but with a close relationship to the Light Programme and the Talks Department (later Talks Division), which supplied both the producers and the material. The intention of this was 'to preserve the programme's character as a magazine eminently suited to experiment and expansion' (WAC R13/408/5: Report from Evelyn Gibbs February 17, 1948). The BBC did not have separate departments for its women's programmes but it clearly produced 'units' whose main focus was to create these programmes.

The immediate success of *Woman's Hour* meant that the small production team was under pressure from the start. Within its first weeks a demand for a more efficient and a better-staffed production was already put forward. The programme did not have an editor but an 'Organiser'. This post was held by Nest Bradney, who had already, at the start of the programme, complained about the need for more secretarial help and better facilities (WAC R51/640/1: Bradney to Collins, October 16, 1946). Beside Bradney, the production team was made up of Pat Osborne, who selected records, while Peggy Barker (and other producers through her) supplied material for talks. Scripting and production were done by Leslie Perowne (WAC R51/640/1: Memo October 16, 1946). Norman Collins, the Controller of the Light Programme (often referred to as the creator of *Woman's Hour*) realised the urgent need for more resources and staff and in a memorandum to the Director General, William Hayley, at the end of October 1946, echoed Bradney's concerns, and in particular raised the issue of the need for a full-time editor. Collins further suggested that the editor must be able to 'cater for all tastes and [. . .] be as aware of the interest aroused by the Mountbatten wedding in Romsey Abbey as by Basil Henriques's remarks on Juvenile Delinquency' (WAC R13/408/5: Collins to Director General October 30, 1946).

Collins' remark says something about the expectation as to what topics a woman's programme should cover. Rosalind Coward (1986) has written that 'to try to understand the history of *Woman's Hour* is to try to unpick the contradictions which reside in that most ambiguous of terms, "serving women's interests."' As Murphy (Chapter 2 in this volume) identifies, this notion of defining women's interests was already a challenge in the interwar period, when the BBC's women's programmes first developed. The 1930s is of course in many ways a different context from post-war Britain, providing different possibilities and challenges for women. Broadcasters catering to diverse audiences, with different needs and expectations, were confronted in both periods by changes in women's lives. In their choice of topics and approaches they aimed to improve women's lives whether as homemakers or employees. As the war drew to a close there was much internal debate in the BBC, however, about how to continue the wartime output. In November 1945, one member of staff who had experience working in commercial radio, and had seen the 'terrific response' to women's programmes, suggested that the BBC ought to do something similar. This would be an hourly programme including items on household hints, fashion, childcare and a radio doctor (WAC R34/949: Inns to Chalmers November 23, 1945). This approach was further echoed in March 1946 when a Talks Producer suggested that fashion, dress-making and gardening should be part of the proposed daily women's programme (WAC R51/299/1: N.G. Luker to Chalmers March 13, 1946).

Woman's Hour had at its start an explicitly domestic feel and addressed the audience mainly as homemakers and mothers, consistent with pre-war women's programmes and talks. The first programme in October 1946 was promoted in *Radio Times* with a photograph which featured a swirling ribbon and the text: 'Today's Recipe', 'Your Winter Clothes', 'Children in the Home', 'Your Health Problems', 'Putting Your Best Face Forward', 'Answering Your Questions', and 'Mother's Midday Meal' (*Radio Times* October 4, 1946). But not long after its start the focus turned to subjects such as current affairs, women's employment, and other areas of national and public interest. Early on Collins told producers there was too much focus on cookery and more serious talks and discussions were needed on topics affecting domestic life (WAC R51/642: Collins to Assistant Controller Talks October 14, 1946) and requests were also made to include regular talks on current affairs and Parliament (WAC R51/640/1: Assistant Director of Talks to Director Talks October 19, 1946). In 1948 it was reported that the programme had moved 'towards more serious subjects' and that this was due to listener demand (WAC R34/422/1: Chalmers to B.

E. Nicolls March 19, 1948). There were reports on new government legislation and equal pay, as well as coverage of women's groups and of the Conservative and Labour parties' women's conferences. This move towards a
broader definition of what a 'woman's interest' might constitute appears to
have been steered as much by listeners' requests as by producers' or senior
management initiatives. Hence *Woman's Hour* should be seen as a continuation of the more outward-looking programmes for women introduced (by
women such as Janet Quigley) during the war.

Women were expected to (and did) participate in public discourse, something which further complicates images of the post-war woman and post-
war domesticity and reveals that the housewife was no longer expected to
be isolated within the four walls of the home. Prejudice however remained;
one BBC announcer left a message in a log book commenting on a current
affairs series in *Woman's Hour*:

> The first one—today—has been all about the Comet. I should have
> thought this quite unsuitable for *Woman's Hour.* Surely the yardstick
> for this sort of thing is to say "Is this more suitable elsewhere?" If
> you have to say "yes", then put it there. In this case, your most inter-
> ested audience is obviously children. Whey [sic] not have made up a
> feature of all the worry, work and general preparation leading up to the
> Dress Show the Queen went to at Claridge's? There are plenty of things
> reported in the papers which are of exclusive interest to women and
> I'm dead certain the Comet isn't one of them! Women, on the whole,
> distrust anything mechanical (WAC R15/244: Engelman to Editor,
> *Woman's Hour* November 17, 1952, emphasis in original).

Whether this comment was meant as a joke or a serious point remains
uncertain but the implementation of a programme especially for women
suggests institutional and gendered prejudice, not least in the way the programme team was treated in terms of resources and lack of editorial autonomy and control.

In this period the Talks Department was growing steadily in size and
going through internal restructuring, which consequently impacted on
Woman's Hour, especially in the pursuit and appointment of an editor for
the programme. Although a request was made and approved in the autumn
of 1946, an editor was not appointed until July 1947 (WAC R51/640/1:
Memo, William Haley November 25, 1946). *Woman's Hour*'s first editor
was Eileen Molony, a Talks Producer who was also given a clerk and secretary, which improved the workload and staffing situation. Molony however
did not stay long and neither did her replacement, Evelyn Gibbs, who was
appointed in 1948 (and left in 1950). Both women made strong points about
the difficulties in running the programme. Two recurring themes appear:
a lack of resources (including staff) and not being able to exert editorial
control. Molony produced a very detailed and in many ways interesting

report of her time as editor and she made clear that there was confusion over editorial lines of command:

> When I took over the programme, the Controller of Talks, Mr. Collins and subsequently AD(T) [Assistant Director of Talks] impressed upon me the necessity of my taking responsibility for the general professional level of the Programme as well as its adjustment to the audience. Here in practice there seems to be some confusion. Furthermore responsibility appertains also to the Head of Talks Department who is responsible for the quality of all Talks output. The practical results of this system is [sic] often bewildering to the Talks Producer who may receive two or three sets of widely differing and often contradictory criticisms. Thus, the Chief Producer (who does not study the special audience) may criticise a production qua talk without reference to the special points which the Editor has been trying to make (WAC R13/408/5: 'Report on *Woman's Hour*' February 5, 1948).

She continued to explain in the report that, for example, a talk which had been approved by the editor of *Woman's Hour* and the Light Programme management might then be considered too simple in its tone and content by the Head of Talks Department. She argued that this 'double supervision' was unnecessary since as the editor of the programme she:

> [I]s well placed to offer criticism of presentation and production because of her special knowledge of the audience. She also knows in detail what the Controller of the Light Programme wants and in practice she must brief the Producers. Moreover, so long as the Editor has no say in the choice of Producer she <u>can only</u> exercise her control by discussion and criticism. It would seem only logical that the Producers should work to her and the Head of Talks Department exercise his responsibility by sampling rather than by editing before transmission (WAC R13/408/5: 'Report on *Woman's Hour*' February 5, 1948, emphasis in original).

This was a tentative effort to assert a degree of autonomy, in so far as BBC editorial structure would allow. It is also about establishing power relations, staking out her role as editor, and being recognised as a professional in her own right. Due to its placement as an outside 'unit' the programme fell between 'supply' and 'output', in other words, supply departments such as Talks might have set a certain standard or editorial preference, whereas the output (the Light Programme or the Home Service for instance) relied on other policies. It appears as if this process affected the output; press material from the late 1940s reveals that the programme was criticised for talking down to listeners and this seems to have been a result of various editorial interference, and as the *Evening Standard* suggested, producers not being familiar with the audience they were aiming for (Radio dept.

February 15, 1947). This problem persisted and was not entirely resolved until Gibbs took over as editor in 1948 and was given full editorial control of the programme:

> [I]t is surely essential that the practical difficulties of this arrangement should be overcome so that *Woman's Hour* may become not indeed a microcosm of broadcasting as a whole, but a programme where material of interest and value to a specific audience may be given its most suitable and effective presentation (WAC R13/408/5: 'Report on *Woman's Hour*', by Evelyn Gibbs, no date).

Relying on supply departments such as Talks posed other problems and the material reveals that internally *Woman's Hour* was seen not to be a prestigious programme to work on, as observed by Gibbs in 1950:

> I think there is a lot to be said for this way of running *Woman's Hour* as opposed to a small production unit, but the Editor's job would be made much easier if the responsibilities of all the departments concerned could be more clearly defined and agreed. As it is, they are most of them inclined to regard *Woman's Hour* as something outside and additional to their own work. The result is that nearly always *Woman's Hour* work is given to the most junior or least experienced producers and in moments of stress our needs are entirely ignored (WAC R51/640/7: Gibbs to ACT, '*Woman's Hour* Report' June 5, 1950).

One example of this was the regular current affairs item. In 1949, it was brought to the attention of the Controller of Talks that *Woman's Hour* had been allocated five different Talks Producers in the past eighteen months to produce current affairs talks (WAC R51/128/1: Assistant Controller of Talks to Controller of Talks September 9, 1949). This lack of internal recognition and prejudice from fellow staff did put a strain on the women behind the programme. One of the regular producers, Isa Benzie, who pioneered medical and health talks, expressed clear frustration in 1951 to the Chief Assistant in Talks:

> I wonder if you could help over the attitude which producers not working for *Woman's Hour* take in their ignorance for that programme? The weight of this programme is resting on the shoulders of people who can tolerate a very severe amount of work year after year; and who can tolerate also, and also year after year, the ever-repeated exhibition of fellow producers' contempt (WAC R51/640/10: Benzie to Chief Producer December 4, 1951).

Within the BBC, *Woman's Hour* was clearly being sidelined. The internal structure complicated the editorial process and it is striking that allowing the programme greater autonomy and control was so problematic. The unit behind *Woman's Hour* possessed strong audience awareness and was further encouraged with the appointment of Janet Quigley as editor in June 1950 which gave the programme a stronger sense of identity and crucially a sense of control and ownership that had been absent before.

KNOWING YOUR LISTENERS

Quigley's career and involvement in women's programmes at the BBC spanned the 1930s to the late 1950s. She was without a doubt a key figure in the development of women's radio at the BBC; she expanded and broadened talks and programmes for women, showing an inspiring dedication and determination (Nicholas 1996; Chapter 2 in this volume). Quigley left the Corporation in 1945 when she married, but returned in 1950. The records make it clear that the Controller of Talks, Mary Somerville, was very keen to see her as editor for *Woman's Hour* and Somerville certainly supported her appointment (WAC L1/784/1: Janet Quigley). The pair had both worked for the Corporation in the 1930s when Somerville had become BBC's Director of School Broadcasting in 1931 and Quigley had been an Assistant in the Foreign Department since 1930. Together their knowledge of broadcasting and its possibilities helped *Woman's Hour* gain new strength and vigour in the 1950s.

Quigley firmly believed that a producer or editor must know the programme and the audience to whom they were broadcasting. She often emphasised working 'hands-on' and did a lot of work herself in the studio (Quigley 1958, 53). Quigley's appointment took the staff on the programme to: editor, deputy editor, compère, two secretaries and one clerk (WAC R51/640/7: Gibbs to ACT, '*Woman's Hour* Report' June 5, 1950). In a report a month into her new position she gave a good insight into the situation, observing that the programme was not produced as an entity and there was not enough communication between producers, speakers and editor (WAC R13/408/6: Report from Editor to Controller Talks, '*Woman's Hour*: reorganisation' July 3, 1950). Quigley suggested a scheme whereby producers would work more closely with the programme and producers would take turns, being responsible for the whole production of *Woman's Hour* for a week at a time. In this experiment she wanted to include the more experienced producers such as Elisabeth Rowley, Isa Benzie, Peggy Barker and Marguerite Scott. It was also Quigley, Benzie and Rowley who would later create the *Today* programme in 1957, and thus it is tempting to suggest that *Woman's Hour* was an important stepping-stone in this process. Quigley was also keen to develop reporting, interview techniques and mobile features (WAC R13/408/6: Report from Editor to Controller Talks, '*Woman's Hour*: reorganisation' July 3, 1950). Material examined suggests that the internal relations within the *Woman's Hour* unit were working well once clear leadership and direction were achieved. Quigley's previous experience of producing women's programmes proved invaluable for the programme's continued success and development.

A key feature of the longevity and the continued success of *Woman's Hour* lies in its ability to connect with and respond to the listeners. This was a staple aspect of the programme from the start in 1946. A few weeks after its first broadcast it was reported that the programme received more than a thousand letters per week (WAC R51/640/1: Collins to Director General October 30, 1946). Eileen Molony stated in 1948 that it was crucial for the editor and the producers to have access to the letters since these gave an enormous insight into audience attitudes (WAC R13/408/5: 'Report on *Woman's Hour*' February 5, 1948) which in turn sometimes resulted in listener participation. For instance, in December 1948 it was suggested that *Woman's Hour* should run a regular discussion 'in which listeners are invited to take part' (WAC R51/640/5: Editor Woman's Hour to Bentinck December 8, 1948). In 1949 it was noted that one of the producers recorded a 15-minute discussion once every four weeks with the editor and listeners to the programme (WAC R51/640/6A: Marguerite Scott, 'Listeners Discussions for *Woman's Hour*' February 1, 1949) and in 1951 Quigley introduced an experimental theatre series in which 'ordinary' people (instead of professional critics) reviewed a theatre production on the programme (WAC R51/640/11: Scott- Moncrieff to Boswell March 31, 1952). Quigley saw the programme as a co-production between the listeners and the producers:

> *Woman's Hour* has come to be regarded by many of its listeners as a kind of club. Far from being confined to passive listening, membership of this club takes an active form: listeners write about the programme and about themselves, they criticise, encourage, suggest and occasionally broadcast. This co-operation in building the programme insures that it is really their own and forges a chain that links listeners to us and to each other (1953, 5).

Listener's letters were taken seriously and it is therefore possible to argue that the female audience took part in shaping BBC radio programming in the post-war period. This indicates how interactive and ahead of its time the programme really was. Interestingly, other studies show that women's radio has tended to forge very strong bonds and connections between its producers and audience (Hilmes 1997; Badenoch 2008). For example, Karin Nordberg (1998) has examined the Swedish Radio's women's programmes (1930–1950) and argues that in Sweden women radio producers had a different relationship to the audience compared to their male counterparts, employing a much more subjective and less authoritative style. One key broadcaster was Ingrid Samuelsson, who in the 1940s, in similar style to Quigley, introduced listeners to the microphone, clearly understanding the potential for discussion and dialogue over the air (Nordberg 1998).

Nordberg suggests it created a conversation in the ether, opening up a space for women to discuss, debate and voice their questions and outlooks. Clearly, parallels can be made with *Woman's Hour*.

THE WORKING WOMAN

A problem faced by *Woman's Hour* was how to reach and cater to the working woman. During the war, women had been mobilised into work and in the post-war period the introduction of part-time work and the abolition of the marriage bar facilitated significant changes. The programme was keen to respond to the development of the increasing employment of women and did so mainly in two ways. The first strategy was to address the working woman with a steady flow of editorial items in the regular programme covering women and work. For example, in 1948, features producer Eileen Hots put together a programme on 'Women in Industry: Qualified Women Engineers' which introduced a range of women engineers and a detailed description of how someone could become an engineer (WAC: Programme as Broadcast Transcript, *Woman's Hour,* 'Women in Industry': Qualified Women Engineers' by Eileen Hots December 16, 1948). The second strategy, which was deployed after lengthy negotiation, was to introduce a weekly repeat.

The demand for a repeat of the programme had begun in April 1948. At this point the programme received a flow of letters from women in industry asking for a programme they were able to listen to (WAC R51/640/4: Acting Controller Light Programme to ACT April 14, 1948). Later the same year, the National Federation of Business and Professional Women's Clubs complained about the timing of the programme. Mary Somerville (at that point Assistant Controller of Talks) referred the query to the management of the Light Programme and the Home Service but with no luck, prompting her to reflect 'it is a pity to overlook the claims of the outside working woman in these days' (WAC R51/642/1: 'Resolution from National Federation of Business Women' December 1, 1948; Somerville to CLP and CHS December 17, 1948). Women's groups such as the National Federation of Business and Professional Women's Clubs continued to lobby the programme. Mary Hill, one of the programme's producers, suggested in March 1951 to Janet Quigley that the reputation of *Woman's Hour* would improve among some women's groups if they could broadcast a programme in the evening or at the weekend (WAC R51/640/9: Hill to Editor March 28, 1951). Quigley brought the request to the management once again and emphasised that the pressure came from both individual women and women's organisations. She reiterated the argument put forward by these women and made the point that there was not really a difference 'between women with home interests and women with careers' (WAC R51/ 640/10: Quigley to Controller of Light Programme July 2, 1951).

Quigley's plea had an impact, and in August 1951 the first repeat was broadcast on Sunday afternoons under the title 'The Digest'. The repeat was well received amongst listeners and women's organisations such as the National Federation of Business and Professional Women's Clubs (WAC R51/640/11: Editor, *Woman's Hour* to CT and CLP January 25, 1952). There is, however, a paradox here. As stated earlier, Quigley had made the point that there were no differences between women with home interests and women with careers, but she would later argue that because 'The Digest' was placed on a Sunday afternoon, it did not fully cater to the working woman (it was described as 'family listening'):

> The fact that it was placed on Sunday afternoon defeated the ends of the original project as it at once became apparent that, far from selecting material from the previous week's programme that would be of most interest and service to business and professional women who can't listen to the daily programme, we were forced by considerations of the actual audience which included fathers, husbands and children to choose instead the items of least specialised interest [. . .] I still think we have an obligation to the growing body of women who work either whole or part-time outside their homes (WAC R51/640/13: Editor, *Woman's Hour* to CT November 24, 1952).

The result of this was that after much discussion a 'new' version was introduced in 1953 broadcast on a Sunday morning. This time it was called 'Home for the Day' and became quite a success. In 1954 the Controller of the Light Programme, Kenneth Adam, who was very supportive of Janet Quigley, was full of praise: 'I think "Home for the Day" is <u>so</u> good these days it ought to be on Sunday afternoons in the autumn' (WAC R51/ 640/17: Controller, Light Programme to Mr. Pelletier April 22, 1954, emphasis in original). Its success was also confirmed in a listener research report the same year: '[O]n the whole, the evidence suggested that "Home for the Day" was thought to offer some very interesting and often unusual talks and discussions, and was generally much appreciated' (WAC R9/9/18: LR/54/1043 August 24, 1954). The programme was important in acknowledging the working woman, but at the same time the 'separation' and creation of something for a 'special audience' also sent mixed signals, undermining the initial project of appealing to all women.

Quigley's persistence not only resulted in the introduction of a repeat, she also fought against a decision to cut the programme's airtime in the summer of 1951, and by expressing her frustration won *Woman's Hour* more staff and more money. In September 1951 the budget for the programme increased from £325 to £355 per week (WAC R51/640/8: A.R Bell to Editor September 1, 1950). In December 1951 another extra £10 was allocated to cover for extra editorial assistance (WAC R51/640/10: Controller Light Programme to Postgate December 12, 1951). Slowly the

BBC began to acknowledge the success of the programme. Quigley left *Woman's Hour* in 1956 when she was promoted to Chief Assistant in Talks (the post was later renamed Assistant Head of Talks Department (Sound)) and she retired in 1962 (WAC L1/784/1 Janet Quigley). *Woman's Hour* continued to thrive after her departure and has now been running on the BBC for over sixty years, a testament to its importance in the schedule and to its listeners.

CONCLUSION

This chapter demonstrates the importance of studying the site of production (when possible) to fully understand how programmes are shaped by institutions, organizational structure, policy and also individuals. *Woman's Hour* was a relatively small unit within the BBC that was not so well regarded by some as other parts of the Corporation. This exposed the programme to patronising attitudes and a continuous lack of resources and support. Although the programme attracted millions of listeners and played a key part in the schedule, it was treated as something 'outside' and 'additional'; not a key priority for producers or the management in the 1950s. This study of *Woman's Hour* indicates the challenges women broadcasters and women's radio faced in an institutional setting in the post-war era when they were marginalised and often had to withstand gendered stereotyping. The women behind *Woman's Hour* fought to further the programme's development and continued existence but they *also* fought for their own professionalism to be taken seriously and recognised. Women broadcasters in the late 1940s and 1950s may not have been organised or fought loud campaigns, but they clearly showed an awareness of being professionals in their own right. The women working on *Woman's Hour* established and pioneered broadcasting techniques and styles developing and refining the magazine genre. It was an interactive programme with a dialogue between the producers and the audience; listeners' demands and suggestions had an impact on the editorial process and the final output. Daytime radio, therefore, provided an important public space for women, and the programme sought to learn more about its audience and to represent not only the housewife but also the working woman. By doing so it acknowledged and perhaps further challenged the representation of women in post-war Britain.

NOTES

I would like to acknowledge and thank the staff at the BBC Written Archives Centre, Peppard Road, Caversham Park, Reading, RT4 8TZ, UK, abbreviated above as WAC.

BIBLIOGRAPHY / SOURCES

Andrews, Maggie. 2012. *Domesticating the Airwaves. Broadcasting, Domesticity and Femininity.* London: Continuum.

Badenoch, Alexander. 2008. *Voices in Ruins: West German Radio across the 1945 Divide.* Basingstoke, UK and New York: Palgrave Macmillan.

Bailey, M., 2009. 'The Angel in the Ether: Early Radio and the Constitution of the Household.' *In Narrating Media History*, edited by Michael Bailey. London; New York: Routledge.

Bell, Melanie. 2010. *Femininity in the Frame: Women and 1950s British Popular Cinema.* London: I. B. Tauris.

Byerly, Carolyn M., and Karen Ross. 2006. *Women and Media: A Critical Introduction.* Oxford: Blackwell Publishing.

Coward, Rosalind. 1986. *The Listener,* October 23.

Feldman, Sally. 2007. 'Desperate Housewives: 60 Years of BBC Radio's *Woman's Hour.*' *Feminist Media Studies* 7 (3): 338–341.

Feldman, Sally. 2000. 'Twin Peaks: The Staying Power of BBC Radio 4's *Woman's Hour.*' In *Women and Radio: Airing Differences,* edited by Caroline Mitchell. London: Routledge.

Hendy, David. 2007. *Life on Air: A History of Radio Four.* Oxford University Press.

Hilmes, Michele. 1997. *Radio Voices: American Broadcasting, 1922–1950.* London; Minneapolis: University of Minnesota Press.

Holloway, Gerry. 2005. *Women and Work in Britain since 1840.* London: Routledge.

Karpf, Anne. 1987. 'Radio Times: Private Women and Public Men.' In *Out of Focus: Writings on Women and the Media,* edited by Kath Davies, Julienne Dickey, and Teresa Stratford. London: The Women's Press.

Lacey, Kate. 2005. 'Continuities and Change in Women's Radio.' In *More than a Music Box: Radio Cultures and Communities in a Multi Media World,* edited by Andrew Crisell. Oxford: Berghahn.

Nicholas, Sian. 1996. *The Echo of War: Home Front Propaganda and the Wartime BBC, 1939–45.* Manchester University Press.

Nordberg, Karin. 1998. *Folkhemmets Röst: Radion som Folkbildare 1925–1950.* Stockholm/Stehag: Brutus Östlings Bokförlag Symposion.

Quigley, Janet. December 1958. *Brown Book.* Oxford: Lady Margaret Hall Archives.

Quigley, Janet. 1953. Foreword to *The Book of Woman's Hour: the Words behind the Voices* by Joanna Scott-Moncrieff. London: Ariel Productions Limited.

Thane, Pat. 2003. 'What Difference did the Vote Make? Women in Public and Private Life in Britain since 1918.' *Historical Research* 76 (192): 268–285.

Thane, Pat. 1994. 'Women since 1945.' In *20th Century Britain: Economic, Cultural and Social Change,* edited by Paul Johnson. London: Longman.

Zoonen, Liesbet van. 1994. *Feminist Media Studies.* London: Sage Publications Ltd.

Zweiniger-Bargielowska, Ina. 2000. *Austerity in Britain: Rationing, Controls, and Consumption, 1939–1955.* Oxford University Press.

7 *Women's Viewpoint*
Representing and Constructing Femininity in Early 1950s Television for Women

Mary Irwin

INTRODUCTION

In June 1946, the BBC television service, having closed down on the commencement of war in 1939, began broadcasting once more. One feature of this relaunched service was the provision of afternoon magazine programmes made specifically for women. The focus was on topics considered to be of particular value and interest to a female audience: domestic advice about the management of home and family life, items on hobbies and how to spend leisure time as well as panel discussions which took a female perspective on contemporary social issues. These now little known or remembered early television programmes are valuable archived sources for augmenting historical understanding of women's lives and experiences in the early years after the war. This chapter explores key examples of early television made for women that addressed the variety and complexity of women's lives; simultaneously, the programmes worked towards constructing for the female audience something of a sense of what it was to be a woman at this historical moment. The reality of working women's lives set against persisting hegemonic discourses about the desirability of domesticity created complex definitions of women's roles in the period of post-war reconstruction. Television acknowledged both women's role at home and their stake in the world beyond domesticity, at the same time building bridges and making connections between both worlds. The selected programmes encompassed different public and private discourses of femininity and challenged any rose-tinted nostalgic notions surrounding 'cosy' domestic femininity of the 1950s, perhaps best exemplified by the commercial popularity of the picturesque re-imagining of the 'vintage' post-war home and associated kitchenware stocked by UK high-street retailer Cath Kidston selling vintage fabrics, wallpapers and brightly-painted junk furniture. In *Understanding Postwar British Society* Penny Summerfield comments on the changes in women's lives in the immediate post-war period, noting that 'women's role in marriage and the family appeared to be quite different, coinciding in a dramatic expansion of paid work for married women' (Summerfield 1994, 58). Furthermore, Maggie Andrews' scrutiny of the idealisation of the so-called 'new Elizabethan' age has argued that '[t]he era has been typified in popular mythology as one of long and happy marriages, domestic contentment and harmony. A more careful examination of the first 15–20 years that followed the war suggests a more contradictory and complex picture' (Andrews 2012, 114–5) and points out that, '[t]he role of the housewife was often idealised but an increasing number of women were in the workforce' (Andrews 2012, 117).

RESEARCHING EARLY TELEVISION

Working with early television sources where no recorded examples of the programmes exist necessitates developing a sense of the programme as viewed experience from available archived sources. Jason Jacobs's pioneering reconstructive work on early television drama at the BBC is very important in this context where he reassembles previously 'invisible' texts (2000), allowing for their deployment as moving image historical archives. It is Jacobs's framework which will be utilised to analyse programmes in this chapter. He explored archived institutional production material and documentation held at the BBC Written Archives Centre in Caversham to re-examine and contest assumptions about both the aesthetics and production techniques to be found in early television drama, suggesting: 'Given the absence of primary material the study of this period needs to reformulate traditional notions of textual analysis. These are texts that do not exist in the original audiovisual form but exist instead as shadows, dispersed and refracted amongst buried files' (Jacobs 2000, 14). He calls his work 'the reconstitution or reconstruction using this written material, of 'ghost texts' (Jacobs 2000, 14); it enables critical attention to be placed upon television previously given scant consideration, or dismissed simply because no easily accessible recording was available. Following Jacobs, I draw on available extant archival evidence found in the BBC Written Archives such as: studio floor plans, set lists, scripts, production files and programme listings to reconstruct and explore the series under consideration, and to consider the competing discourses of femininity that the programmes set up. My work reinstates programmes which have disappeared from television history because there is no visual record. As this chapter demonstrates, it is, in fact, in returning to such primary sources that it is possible to form fuller and more nuanced understandings of the television made for women and of its resonance with their lives and experiences.

A broad range of early women's television series existed offering a variety of contrasting perspectives on women's lives at the period. Taken together, they had much to say about the breadth of concerns and interests which played a part in women's lives. As will be demonstrated, the range of subjects they tackled acted to extend what might be imagined as the primary interests of women. Social historian David Kynaston's scholarship on post-war Britain usefully nuances the complexity and conflicting nature of the roles women took on and which are identifiable in early women's television. Kynaston chronicles the centrality of the role of homemaker and mother to popular public discourses of the 1950s, citing a *Woman's Own* magazine article which said of the kitchen, 'A woman's place? Yes it is! For it is the heart and centre of the meaning of home' (Kynaston 2010, 568). It continued, 'The place where, day after day, you make with your hands the gift of love'. Further, 'Yet however exalted, a housewife did not exist on the same plane as a mother' (Kynaston 2010, 570). He suggests the 'idealised mother' figure took the centre stage (Kynaston 2010, 568) although, 'contrary to subsequent mythology, the 1950s were not entirely bereft of ambitious, independent-minded women' (Kynaston 2010, 572). The investigation of women's television texts substantiates and develops such material further; the resulting synthesis of written and moving image texts offered in this chapter begins the process of analysing their combined address to questions of women's post-war identity. A general overview of the diet of women's programmes broadcast between 1947 to 1953 will be followed by a detailed analysis of two contrasting formats which best illustrate the breadth and range of women's lived experiences, responsibilities and concerns in this historic moment.

Programmes produced by the BBC for women in this first post-war period were *Designed for Women* (1947), *For the Housewife* (1948), *Leisure and Pleasure* (1951), *About the Home* (1951) and *Women's Viewpoint* (1951). These series were broadcast in an early-afternoon slot (most usually on or around three o'clock) and customarily ran for thirty to forty minutes. *Designed for Women* was the first television programme created specifically for women. It was a magazine strand containing a mix of instructive talks, book reviews and suggestions for leisure activities, recipes and practical cookery demonstrations. Early women's radio formats in the U.K., Europe and the U.S. have been discussed by Kristin Skoog (2009), Kate Lacey (2004) and Michelle Hilmes (1997). The television magazine format owed much to the earlier development and use of magazine format programmes for women on radio as Andrews has suggested, pointing out that '[a]fternoon television programming needs to be understood in relation to radio programming. BBC personnel such as Olive Shapley moved between [radio magazine] *Woman's Hour* and television' (Andrews 2012, 137). Shapley and other colleagues, such as radio and television producer Mary Adams, brought their previous broadcasting expertise with them. While acknowledging early women's television's great debt to the innovations of radio, it is equally important to acknowledge that television took this radio inheritance and reconstituted it for a very different medium, tackling the challenge of the visual presentation of an aural format. This required the development of a quite different set of professional production and broadcast skills.

This magazine formula was extended by *Designed For Women*'s replacement *Leisure and Pleasure*, which extended the range of items covered and broadened the variety of guests invited to take part. *For the Housewife* focused specifically on domestic and household management and was replaced in 1951 by *About The Home* which again, as in the case of *Leisure and Pleasure*, was an extension of the original format, refined and developed to suit the changing social and cultural demands of Britain in the middle and later 1950s, specifically in this case to encompass growing consumer choice and availability of goods which followed the material shortages of the early 1950s. The final format of *Women's Viewpoint* was concerned with providing a female or perhaps more accurately an implicitly proto-feminist perspective on then current social and public issues.

The chapter will focus on the *For the Housewife* and *Women's Viewpoint* programme strands, as they offered interesting and useful insights into very different aspects of women's lives in a Britain which was struggling with rationing, hardships and shortages. Yet at the same time Britain was also growing more hopeful about the new possibilities brought about by the end of war. While *For the Housewife* mobilised a range of very practical concerns around how to manage a household when money and resources were in short supply, *Women's Viewpoint* presented women in the public sphere, debating issues of particular interest to contemporary women.

For the Housewife

What is clear when the 'ghost traces' of *For the Housewife* are examined is that it there was nothing of the 'fluffily' feminine or lightweight about the concerns and the perspective of the *For The Housewife* strand of women's television. In fact the programme's focus, contents and advice were single-mindedly practical; very much a product of the times in which the programme was produced and broadcast. Britain in 1948 was a worn-down country struggling to get back on its feet in the aftermath of war. 'It had been an extraordinarily hard six years since the end of the war—in some ways even harder than the years of war itself' (Kynaston 2008, Afterword, 597). As Susan Cooper writes, 'War ends tidily in the history books with the signing of a document. But there was no single finishing line for the shortages of food, clothes and fuel and all the aspects of austerity which gave a cold grey tint to postwar life' (Cooper 1964, 56). Ina Zweiniger-Bargielowska enumerates the practicalities of day-to-day austerity life:

> In World War Two the civilian population coped with extensive rationing of food and clothing as well as severe shortages of most other foodstuffs as economic resources were diverted towards the war effort. The end of the war did not mark any relaxation, and indeed food rationing was more extensive and rationing levels were lower and more volatile during the late 1940s than in wartime. For many foodstuffs and domestic consumer pre-war consumption goods, levels were not surpassed until the mid-1950s. (Zweiniger-Bargielowska 2001, 54)

For the Housewife chimed in with such sentiments, and in reading the programme's address it is possible to discern a call to the women who generally undertook much of the practical burden of daily life, at a time when getting hold of basic household necessities was an ongoing challenge. The programme offered its female viewers a call to action, demonstrating to them how best to cope with the tasks of managing and maintaining their house and feeding their family in the context of the social and domestic conditions which were the everyday reality of Britain in this period. *For the Housewife*'s ethos was to make the best of what you had and stretch it a little further, when the option of going out to a local shop for an extra pint of milk or a loaf of bread was simply not available. *For the Housewife* aired for around thirty minutes and comprised two items. One was on cookery, offering either a recipe to prepare, or a demonstration of a cooking or baking technique, while the other segment offered advice, guidance and frequently an expert demonstration of how best to accomplish a practical household task. In a note on the series for a possible advertisement for contributors circulated to women's magazines, programme producer S. E. Reynolds wrote that experts 'must be outstandingly good on their particular subject, talk lucidly and demonstrate in a practical manner under studio conditions' (WAC T32/166, TV Talks 1948–1949; S. E. Reynolds' draft advert for women's magazines September 2, 1948).

The series' core team of presenters included Philip Harben, formerly compère of a radio cookery format and frequent presenter on food and cookery, who subsequently went on to become the first 'celebrity chef' on British television. He was accompanied by Joan Robins, an established cookery writer; and W.P. Matthew, billed as television's first DIY expert. Like Harben, Matthew had also begun his career as a radio 'expert', moving to television in the 1940s.

The programme production files make it possible to reconstruct some sense of the visual style of *For the Housewife*. Preserved drawings of studio floor plans show how the space was organised and the set dressed to set the tone for the programme. Careful examination of these set plans allows for an interpretation of the address to the female audience, and provides an opportunity to reflect on who this female audience might have been. The set was designed to resemble, more or less, a tasteful middle- or upper-middle-class drawing or living room, which was the customary setting for afternoon women's television programmes of the period, situating the programme in a broadly domestic, feminine setting.[1] The layout plans indicate the simulation of a well-proportioned room furnished with comfortable chairs, occasional tables and tasteful décor and ornamentation. Specifications to dress the room in a set list of properties for a 1949 edition included full-length, buff sateen curtains with scalloped pelmets, a Georgian fireplace, potted plants and a recessed bookshelf (WAC T32/166, TV Talks, props list November 22, 1949). Such a room seems to have been designed to replicate the kind of rooms in which it was implicitly understood that the audience themselves might be watching; the programme was providing a 'home from home' situated within a television space. A sense of the corporation's own values also seems implicit in such a set: 'This is the kind of room we are accustomed to', it suggests. 'We are inviting you into our drawing room'. The programme's female presenters were themselves also extremely well turned out, as can be seen in contemporary photographs which showed neatly dressed hostesses wearing smart suits with carefully styled hair, prepared to meet and greet the guests they have invited into their 'homes'. Andrews suggests the set was 'a pseudo-domestic space presenting domesticity as a performance' (2012, 137), while, 'at one level, the audience was positioned as a friend dropping in on a domestic conversation, just as in the fireside chat of early radio discourse' (2012, 138). As *For the Housewife* was structured around domestic chores, a replica working kitchen area formed part of the set, furnished with a stove, a cooking table, a set of nesting tables, practical cupboards and this time, utilitarian grey curtains as a backdrop. This was the site of the practical demonstration and instruction which were a key aspect of the series (WAC T32/166, TV Talks, props list November 22, 1949). The kitchen set also suggested the amply sized kitchen of a fairly comfortable, middle-class home. I will discuss later the significance of the middle-class address of the programme and the way in which it adds to our understanding of female middle-class life in this period.

For the Housewife's weekly broadcast contents allowed for a sense of how a woman running a house in such circumstances might practically proceed. Programme files provide a rich source of information for the kind of items which might be found in the weekly broadcast and give a sense of the priorities and tasks which concerned the viewer. What was to be found was predominantly guidance on how to undertake a wide range of demanding household activities. The programme also pointed to areas where there were shortages, what measures could be taken, and what in the eyes of the programmes' producers and experts were ongoing difficulties that viewers would need help with. What is most apparent was the wide range of jobs which women at home were assumed to be tackling and be in need of support with, alongside a range of suggested solutions to household challenges. Starting with household tasks, and specifically those inside the house, there were items on fairly small-scale yet labour-intensive domestic undertakings, such as polishing furniture, caring for linoleum, mending fuses, the preparation of furniture for spring cleaning, cleaning silver and a talk on the latest domestic hardware. There were even more demanding tasks covered, such as how to replace the springs in the seat of a cushion, pad the seat of a chair, sand a chest of drawers, clean carpets, prevent burst pipes and in an item on women and engineering advice, maintain a toolbox and use tools. Such vigorous manual labour was in contrast to pervasive discourses of 1950s femininity: the idea of the mother at the heart of the family kitchen baking cakes, referred to earlier in Kynaston, or in the reimagining of some kind of idealised post-war feminity also evoked by the Cath Kidston fashion brand.

Matthew Hilton points to the historical conditions which dictated the manual labour and make-do-and-mend central to the contents of *For the Housewife*. He stresses the scale of shortages and official control of goods and supplies which people were forced to negotiate and explains the particularly challenging early post-war socioeconomic context in which women as consumers would be working to feed their families and manage their homes (2003). Citing lack of consumer agency, he describes governmental control of consumption where 'wartime controls saw unprecedented state intervention in supply, distribution and consumption, stretching the sphere of governmental activity well beyond the usual boundaries of bread and milk' (Hilton 2003, 137). This situation continued with equal and sometimes even more stringent measures into the late 1940s and early 1950s.

For the Housewife gave advice on tackling tasks which related directly to such shortages and the pressing need to find ways round the absence of daily necessities. There were items on how to make soap substitutes and also how to cure home-grown tobacco. Outside the house the practical work continued with advice on growing bulbs and herbs and even an item on keeping bees for honey. Many activities seemed to be centred on finding ways of growing and cultivating your own food where food was difficult to come by. Cookery items combined the preparation of modest, manageable savouries and puddings made from whatever was available in perhaps a garden or an allotment (for example cherry cobbler, summer fruit pudding and duck flan) with the production and preservation of foodstuffs such as curing bacon, jugging hare and making marmalade. Also in the production files are complete scripts for longer items, featuring experts who were invited on to the programme to take part in extended interviews about their own specialisms. Two preserved scripts dating from 1950 illustrate what the experts said about selecting wallpaper and paint for the home (WAC T32/166, TV Talks January 1, 1950, January 28, 1950). They fill in valuable detail about managing such tasks in the conditions of Britain at this time. In one interview the viewer learns about the first issue of wallpaper to the public since 1940 and an industry moving toward normality now that war was over. This interview provided detailed information about pre- and post-war wallpaper prices and, according to the script, included visual examples of available wallpaper samples. Asked about then present-day styles and choices, the expert, Mr Lee, said, 'In showrooms most customers are to be found in front of brighter paper', going on to say, 'People are more house conscious. [It was] impossible for housewives to buy furniture and curtains and carpets, they would like to if they had bottomless purses and unlimited choice, so they brighten up their home with wallpaper'. Such an excerpt illuminates the difficulties facing women in furnishing a home while at the same time highlighting how significant the purchase of some rolls of eye-catching wallpaper would be in boosting morale in the home.

Similarly, in the second extract, the opening remarks of interviewer Joan Gilbert indicated something of the appearance of early post-war urban Britain. She says, 'The importance of paint is brought home to us all by the shabby appearance of London and other towns at end of [the] war when no painting was possible'. The purchase and application of paint in order to counter the aftermath of wartime urban damage and deterioration underpinned the item. There was specific information on the effect of different weather conditions on the condition of paint, and then advice for housewives on undertaking their own home painting chores. The final section had Gilbert taking part in a structured practical session with an invited painter, Mr McIver, in which he instructed her on how to prepare and paint some wooden furniture. Both these interviews, like the items on cooking, cleaning and domestic upkeep, made it clear that the address of *For the Housewife* articulated the experience of coping with a climate of austerity in which women were struggling just to live ordinary lives and the physical effort that the upkeep of a home required.

The series and its address also provide further useful insights into the particularities of how life was changing for different classes of women at the time. *For the Housewife* emphasised hard, practical work in the home, and yet this address is at odds with the factual information about television ownership in the period. 'In the late 1940s television programmes could only be received within an expanding but limited radius of fifty miles from Alexandra Palace' (Kynaston 2008, 212). Further, 'Sets were still expensive to get, and by 1948 owned by a mere 4.3 % of the adult population'. He continues, 'A poll returned by viewers to the BBC in this year revealed that they were predominantly suburban and middle class [. . .] Although television gradually began to be owned by people from less prosperous backgrounds, by 1950 there was still only one home in 20 with a set' (Kynaston 2008, 214). Asa Briggs points out that 'at the end of 1947, 48% of TV sets in use were owned by 12% of the population and 9 out of a 1000 better-off 'Class 1' families had one, as against less than 1 in a 1000 in Class 3' (Briggs 1978, 230).

Women watching *For the Housewife* could therefore be supposed to be reasonably affluent, metropolitan and middle-class. These were not necessarily women who had to take on the primary responsibility for the demanding household tasks on which the series concentrated. One implication is that women who would have had domestic help before the war now had to take a bigger role in managing their households themselves, and the programme reflected this new reality. As Lucy Delap points out: 'being employed or engaged as a servant had been a widely shared experience for large numbers of women at the start of the century', continuing, 'this was not so for the generations working after World War Two' (Delap 2011, 1). Perhaps the BBC was reinforcing the message that everyone was in effect in the business of reconstruction together, and was a series like *For the Housewife* reinforcing the spirit of 'making the best of things' that was part of the patriotic, early post-war ethos? Also worthy of consideration is that times were tough for everyone, war had affected everyone, scarcity and shortage were likely to have impacted on the affluent middle class as well as less prosperous working-class families.

Women's Viewpoint

Women's Viewpoint, in contrast to *For the Housewife*, considered very different aspects of post-war women's lives; it was a live and unrehearsed twenty-minute panel discussion format, broadcast, like *For the Housewife*, in the early afternoon 'women's slot'. The format comprised a panel of women who discussed and debated pre-selected topics of particular interest to women in this period and was described by producer David Bryson in the following terms: 'On Tuesday a new discussion forum will be launched: an unrehearsed discussion by women, for women, of subjects of special interest to women. A regular for-women-only discussion forum is something new in British broadcasting' (WAC T32/ 363 TV Talks).

Women's Viewpoint's subject matter demonstrated early women's television's engagement with a diverse range of topical issues and, in its use of an 'expert' all-female panel, the deployment of a new and innovative women's television programme format. This was broadcast television for women which put the spotlight on the 'public' woman, active in the public sphere in her role as citizen. The panellists were tasked with engaging with issues of public significance and of particular significance to women, and most importantly their primary consideration was to look at such issues from a female perspective. Also worthy of note is that in *Women's Viewpoint*, a format had been created which both acknowledged and foregrounded the idea that women might have a distinctive take on then-contemporary social issues and that there were issues of specific interest of women. While the series initially invited well-known women, prominent in society, to be part of the panel, the production files record that plans were being made to invite women to participate who were perhaps more representative of the women who watched the programme: engaged, 'ordinary' women who were actively involved with the life and running of their local community, for example. David Bryson, the programme's producer, wrote of it: 'Later, viewers' representatives and others well known in their local community may join the group' (WAC T32/ 363 TV Talks). The implication is that these 'ordinary' women would be presenting the perspective of a woman with a stake in the public sphere, be it of paid or charitable work, and would represent the views of other women in such a position—likely to be balancing work and family.

So what was *Women's Viewpoint* like? Again, although no recordings of the programme exist, it is possible using the programme production files to establish a sense of the layout of the studio in which the series was filmed, the form and content of the programme, and biographical detail about the women who participated in the programmes. Specified on the studio plan drawings, as in the studio set of *For the Housewife*, are, as before, comfortable sofas, armchairs, occasional tables decorated with vases of flowers, bookcases, as well as a writing desk, and also an upright armchair positioned by a standard lamp; a good place to sit and read, perhaps. The details of the writing desk, the bookshelves and a well-lit place to read suggest that this room may even be a study or a small private library, certainly a place which is even more conducive than the family living room of *For the Housewife* to the thoughtful discussion and debate which should arise from the programme. The women who took part in the discussion were to be seated around a table positioned in the centre of the set. The programme notes make it clear that while this is a discussion programme, the setting will be what the producer deemed as one more suitable to women. 'Sofas and easy chairs' have been brought in to replace 'the uncompromising table battle-stations and name cards' of the 'In the News' format [another live television discussion format]. Further, 'there will be battles and controversy on occasion but not the intensity and all-in wrestling—a sport in this country still reserved to the male sex. The hope is that there will be room for reminiscence and anecdote as well as agreement" (WAC T32/ 363 TV Talks). The notion of repackaging a programme format, in this case, the discussion panel, to make it 'a better fit' for its female participants, suggests that this latter television format was seen implicitly as a male form.

The discussion, made to look as if it was taking place in a domestic setting rather than a studio, can be seen as a way of feminising the format; viewers were being welcomed not into a studio, but rather a more convivial environment where the panellists would look and feel comfortable as they participated in discussion. Whilst this discussion would be challenging and lively, the inference is also that it would not have the aggressive, combative edge that men would bring. In fact, the notion of the feminised discussion is highlighted by the assumption that women in discussion together, as a gender, would bring a gentler, more decorous approach to proceedings, where agreement is assumed and proceedings made more palatable by the introduction of some telling detail or anecdote from participants' personal lives and experiences. In stressing the demure behaviour which is being assumed of women's panellists, seated in their 'feminised' environment, it seems that battles, controversy and sharply conflicting opinions—the stuff indeed that makes for compelling discussion programmes—were *not* to be expected from ladies. Unfortunately, it is impossible now to see the panellists 'in action' as no recordings remain. However, the kind of high-powered public women participating in *Woman's Viewpoint*, a number of whom were Members of Parliament and notable public figures, seem unlikely to have been any less intense or impassioned than male counterpoints when debating the finer points of an argument, or in any need of a more comfortable physical and less threatening environment in which to carry out debate. It is perhaps worth considering whether this feminised setup was a strategy of containment to make opinionated, powerful women more palatable for the afternoon television slot.

The first edition of *Women's Viewpoint* entitled 'Is There a Woman's Viewpoint?' included Dame Vera Laughton Mathews, a leading figure in the woman's naval service; Lady Violet Bonham Carter, active in liberal politics and former governor of the BBC; Margery Fry, a penal reformer and also another former governor of the BBC; and finally Jill Craigie, writer, filmmaker and feminist. The second programme tackled the position of women in parliament and politics; most of the panel for this were involved in political life, although with varying political allegiances. The discussion was chaired by Labour MP Jennie Lee and the panel comprised Dame Vera Laughton Mathews, Lady Megan Lloyd George, Liberal MP, and Pat Hornsby Smith, Conservative MP. The subsequent programmes looked at the subjects of girls' education, considering in particular if girls were taught the wrong things in schools, and whether their education was just a pale imitation of boys' education? Participants included Lillian Charlesworth, head of Sutton High School for Girls and recently president of the Headmistresses' Association, and E. Arnott Robertson, writer and broadcaster. In the 1950s the issue of girls' education was under debate and developments were afoot: 'Changes in the education system meant that the school-leaving age was raised, more girls were being educated to secondary level and more were progressing to colleges and fulfilling jobs' (Holloway 2005, 195). The next topic was women's magazines, and the panel in this instance featured Mary Grieve, editor of *Woman*, and Audrey Withers, editor of *Vogue*. The final topic was how far has the state increased or decreased the importance of the family, featuring again Jennie Lee and President of the Women's Liberal Foundation Doreen Stephens, who was soon to be editor of BBC Women's Programmes (see Irwin 2011 on Doreen Stephens' career at the BBC). Also to be found in the documentation on the programme were future plans as to what topics the programme would like to feature. Such discussions would have a special bearing on the home and family life, or on the social and economic position and standing of women. This would include rationing, divorce, married women at work, adoption, equal pay, psychology and bringing up children, nursery schools, the National Health Service and the effect of television on home life. The idea was that initially, there would be the public figures mentioned, and it was hoped that later on in the series, viewers' representatives and less well-known women would be invited in (WAC T32/ 363 TV Talks).

The diversity of topics planned is striking. There were debates about the quality of girls' education, women's contemporary relationship with politics, the influence of women's magazines in daily life, and an exploration of whether the state had increased or decreased the importance of the family. These were topics which might not have been predicted as part of the discourses surrounding women's lives in the seemingly conservative early 1950s. What is evident is that here were women as citizens engaging with the political and social and cultural conditions of their daily lives. The concerns around girls' education were central in a period where understandings of women's career and prospects were bound up with the centrality of marriage and what kind of education was appropriate for girls.

The ideas for future programmes are very interesting and again are not what might have been predicted, for example: the experiences of the working woman, the issues of equal pay and divorce and topical concerns about bringing up children, including the relevance of psychology and the possible influence of watching television. That the programme had intentions of tackling such issues, topics of relevance to any contemporary discussion about women's experiences in the period, speaks to women's television's understanding of the complexities of women's lives. *Women's Viewpoint* also presented women in the role of acknowledged and well-respected public figures. These were women who were active in a variety of roles, encompassing politics, the arts, social reform and the armed services. Women were represented here as an acknowledged part of British public life. The remaining traces of *Women's Viewpoint* make clear that women were not only considered in their domestic roles, but were also understood and shown to have had concerns and interests beyond home and family. Of course, the women selected for the panel were from the upper and upper middle classes and the address of the programme was, as with *For the Housewife*, an implied middle-class one. Yet it is noteworthy that *Women's Viewpoint* had ambitions to include a wider circle of women in its future broadcasts. Additionally, all or many of the issues under consideration would have an impact on the lives and experiences of British women in the period, regardless of class. *Women's Viewpoint* did not continue beyond the four episodes described in this article. The experiment stopped, and there is nothing in the programme documentation to explain this. One can only speculate as to why this happened: for example, did the format simply not work well in practice or, perhaps, did practical budgetary concerns, always a pressing issue in the production of women's television, prompt this termination? What must be acknowledged, however, is that in *Women's Viewpoint* there was a programme format that sought to provide intelligent and socially engaged viewing for its female audience and a format, moreover, that moved away from the established domestic television magazine formats that had been a staple of early television up to that point.

CONCLUSION

The analysis of *For the Housewife* and *Women's Viewpoint* offered in this chapter demonstrates the significance of early women's television as an important historical source for scholarly work on histories of women's lives in early post-war Britain. The lack of critical interest in seemingly inconsequential records of obscure women's television series means that valuable data about women's lives and experiences has until now been largely hidden. These series which have been uncovered by exploration of their production files and discussed here grant access to something of the concerns and aspirations which were seen to be at the centre of women's lives in these times, adding to an understanding of the historical figure of the British post-war woman. The reconstruction of these programmes evidences the subjects and debates presented on a weekly basis to a contemporary female viewer and how such programmes conceptualised and spoke to her. Such findings work alongside social histories of women's' lives, augmenting sources such as oral histories and magazines to help develop the picture of everyday femininities. They also provide practical evidence in the form of broadcast series and featured debates of the issues around women, work and education which were of particular significance in this period. The inclusion and integration of archive television sources are of significance in the development of rich, full, feminist histories of women's lives.

NOTES

I would like to acknowledge and thank the staff at the BBC Written Archives Centre, Peppard Road, Caversham Park, Reading, RT4 8TZ, UK, abbreviated above as WAC.

1. Examination of the associated production files related to all the early women's television formats of the period discussed here—*Designed for Women, Leisure and Pleasure, About the Home*—revealed that all had studio set plans which indicate that the programmes were broadcast from similar drawing room sets.

BIBLIOGRAPHY / SOURCES

Andrews, Maggie. 2012. *Domesticating the Airwaves: Broadcasting, Domesticity and Femininity*. London: Continuum.

Briggs, Asa. 1978. *The History of Broadcasting in the United Kingdom, Volume IV: Sound and Vision*. Oxford University Press.

Delap, Lucy. 2011. *Knowing Their Place: Domestic Service in Twentieth Century Britain*. Oxford University Press.

Hilmes, Michele. 1997. *Radio Voices: American Broadcasting, 1922–52*. University of Minnesota Press.

Hilton, Matthew. 2003. *Consumerism in 20th-Century Britain*. Cambridge University Press.

Holloway, Gerry. 2005. *Women and Work in Britain Since 1840*. London: Routledge.

Irwin, Mary M. 2011. 'What Women Want on Television: Doreen Stephens and BBC Television Programmes for Women, 1953–64.' *Westminster Papers in Communication and Culture* 8 (3): 99–122.

Jacobs, Jason. 2000. *The Intimate Screen: Early British Television Drama*. Oxford University Press.

Kynaston, David. 2008. *Austerity Britain, 1945–1951 (Tales of a New Jerusalem)*. London: Bloomsbury Publishing.

Kynaston, David. 2010. *Family Britain, 1951–57*. London: Bloomsbury Publishing.

Lacey, Kate. 2004. 'Continuities and Change in Women's Radio.' In *More than a Music Box: Radio Cultures and Communities in a Multi-Media World*, edited by Andrew Crisell, 144–166. Oxford: Berghahn Books.

Skoog, Kristin. 2009. 'Focus on the Housewife: The BBC and the Postwar Woman.' *Networking Knowledge: Journal of the MECCSA Post Graduate Network* 2 (1).

Summerfield, Penny. 1994. 'Women in Britain since 1945: Companionate Marriage and the Double Burden.' In *Understanding Post-War British Society*, edited by Peter Catterall and James Obelkevich, 58–73. London: Routledge.

Zweiniger-Bargielowska, Ina. 2001. *Women in 20th-Century Britain*. London: Longman.

8   'But What about Mum?'
Journalist Diana Rowntree

Glenda Strong

INTRODUCTION

Reporting from an Aegean cruise, the venue for the 1966 Konstantinos Doxiadis urban planning symposium, where thirty or more professionals discussed models for city structures in which children could grow up feeling at home with global transport networks, and fathers might lunch with their children, Diana Rowntree wrote: 'the women members of the symposium made such a squawk at the thought of midday cooking that the full revolutionary significance of [the] suggestion was missed' (1966, 6). The 'squawk' is significant and is typical of Rowntree's prose. On the surface she was reporting on town planning issues, but the subtext is wry indignation. The suggestion that parenting might become a shared vocation rather than the role of the person behind the cook-top was not a topic for discussion and 'squawk', a pejorative term generally used to describe women's exclamations, was perhaps used ironically in this 1966 *Guardian* newspaper article which is entitled 'Talking about Planning for the Family', and the pun was intended. Rowntree went on to ask: 'But what about Mum? Is she to be tethered to the pedestrian world in spite of her global capabilities? This never got discussed, although some elegant brows were knitted' (1966, 6). The article written in the mid-60s encapsulates some of the significance and fascination of Diana Rowntree (1915–2008), a journalist, architect, wife, mother, interior designer, feminist and academic; a woman who was, to use David Kynaston's term, an 'activator', an opinion former, a catalyst (2010, 280). She criticised the critics and drew a substantial following by working vigorously in the public domain using journalism as her vehicle. Rowntree's career as a journalist had begun in 1956 when she wrote for a year for *The Architectural Review*, for an audience with a very specific knowledge and gender base. She then moved, in 1957, to *The Manchester Guardian* newspaper, where she became their first architectural correspondent and over the course of fourteen years developed her own journalistic voice, a voice that is positioned against the larger picture of women finding their voice and their place within the workforce as professionals during the era of second wave feminism. Diana Rowntree was an 'activator'. She was prepared to be critical of city planners, the built environment and the Council for Industrial Design. She was critical of fashion and passing trends and believed fervently that architectural design modernism was the way forward. She wrote on professionalism, the role of the architect and the nature of architectural practice and paralleled these concerns with the larger debates concerning 'women's two roles', a discourse that remains relevant today.

This study of Rowntree's journalism aims to provide insights into the tensions, traumas and ideological battlegrounds that one woman architect engaged in during the post-war period. A study of Rowntree serves therefore both to provide evidence of how media history can illuminate wider studies in design history and acknowledges the significance of life writing in recent women's history (see Bornat and Diamond 2007; Polkey 2000). Research into Rowntree's journalism must, of necessity, travel from journalism through to other life history sources; including her 1964 advice manual, *Interior Design,* which specifically targets the amateur housewife, a readership most likely drawn from her burgeoning following at *The Manchester Guardian.* Similarly important is her much later 1994 architectural reader, *Buildings Face the Future,* specifically Chapter 11, 'The Gap', in which a mature Rowntree reflects back on life at the news desk, architectural discourse, and its associated feminine values. This chapter will initially discuss Rowntree's role as a pioneer, covering her work as an architectural correspondent and a woman with an overt agenda: a passion for the modern-built environment, and a covert agenda: her commitment to women's business. The second section looks at her role as an architect and mother, using Lees-Maffei's premise that to be a woman in design is difficult and coping strategies are needed. One such coping strategy is 'super-performance (2008, 68). Specifically, Rowntree's journalistic presence is an essential component of her professional architectural life, and in the larger picture, for the workplace life of other female designers. Finally, it will be suggested that for women to position themselves professionally in the workforce they must imagine a place where this is possible, and thus a feminist vision of the future is needed, a utopia. Rowntree's utopia, evidenced in her journalism, is focused squarely on design modernism; she writes evangelically on the subject, and believes it can deliver the equality and freedom so desired in the second wave of feminism. But the products of modernism are a tricky affair.

THE PIONEER

In 1957, Rowntree was *The Manchester Guardian* newspaper's inaugural architectural correspondent and, at a time when the men in the newsroom had no interest in architecture, she built up a substantial readership base. In 1940, Diana was newly married and one of only thirty-eight women who were registered with the Royal Institute of British Architects (RIBA) as professional architects; the word 'architect' was a legally protected term. Her journalistic and architectural accomplishments were more interconnected than they may at first appear and provide an important case study within women's and media history. Perhaps she had been encouraged by her suffragette mother when she decided to enter this predominantly male profession. Gillian Harrison had become the first female fellow of the Institute in the United Kingdom in 1931, only nine years earlier. The first female Associate member was Ethel Mary Charles. Elected in 1898, she had practised with her sister Bessie Ada Charles, who became the second female member of the Institute in 1900.

In the post-war era it was difficult to be a woman and work in design: feelings of inferiority, isolation at home, and debates about which buildings were suitable for women to design presented impediments. Coping strategies were needed (Lees-Maffei 2008) and joining the all-female cooperative, Jane Drew Architects, was one such strategy. However the 'feminist glow of this enterprise diminished when Drew unwisely told Diana to go out in the lunch hour to buy her infants vests' (MacCarthy 2008, 32). This early initiative into a male-dominated field but within the safety of the female cooperative was not enough for Rowntree, who wanted more. As Langhamer notes, the 1950s were not as cosy as we might imagine. The prevailing norms of the time embodied 'near universal, stable long lasting marriage' and a 'smug conventionality', however 'tense domesticity and anxious conformity' bubble below the surface (Langhamer 2005). Rowntree was in her mid-thirties and about to begin her journalism career. It seems no accident that her printed voice emerges (her first articles in 1956) during these tense societal times. Furthermore, Rowntree's body of work exists in the larger context of the professionalization of women in design— their impediments and coping strategies, when 'interior decoration' became 'interior design' in the post-war period, are already well documented. Both architects and interior designers dismissed the decorators as inferior, amateur, feminine and linked to the past (Lees-Maffei citing Sparke 2008, 8). Rowntree was practising at the high point of these tensions. In the post-war period most interior designers were trained architects, and in the spirit of modernity and Gesamtkunstwerk (the total work of art) the interior was the architect's domain (Lees-Maffei citing Sparke 2008, 8). In the spirit of the times, Rowntree aligned with the 'normative maleness' of architecture (where 'normative maleness' refers to the conventional male stereotype), a 'normal' coping strategy which compensated for the cultural devaluation of the feminine. In the spirit of Gesamtkunstwerk her journalism covered the full range of design topics available to the architect/interior designer: everything from city planning and the state of the built environment to motels and university buildings, but also TV sets, plywood chairs, textiles, Swedish hollowware and glass tableware. The more feminine 'interior decorator' was not permitted this scope and remained within the confines of the interior: TV sets to tableware.

Rowntree knew her very specific audience: in 1956, readers of *The Architectural Review* were a mostly male, modernist, architectural elite. Her article 'Oxford College Barges' was a plea for the reconsideration of boathouse design. The first line invited the reader in by using a conversational style; Rowntree told a story and stated a problem, her writing began gently and informatively. Problems were outlined in seminar-like style and, uniquely, she proposed design solutions by using her own annotated sketches, bringing her architectural drawing skills directly into journalism. Her solution called for a type of boathouse 'that presents man directly to water' (1956, 38). 'Man' here was perceived to be universal, so that this statement could have been seen as inclusive. Rowntree goes on to confidently draw comparisons with other iconic waterside buildings and was critical when she wrote: 'consider Venice or English watermills—do often rise sheer out of the water . . . but if these boathouses could not rise out of the water, they could have flattered it with colour and tone. This they have not done' (1956, 38). Having led the reader gently, she was ready to land her punch: 'Unfortunately the disease the existing Oxford boathouses suffer from is one that threatens to consume the whole of England. What has happened on the Isis shows exactly how subtopia creeps in' (1956, 42). The mention of 'subtopia' was a leap because the early part of the article is detailed and specific to the local issue at Oxford but then Rowntree panned out towards the general state of architecture in England, the debate of the day being led by journalist Ian Nairn who coined the term 'subtopia', which represented 'a visceral, largely intelligentsia-led dislike, even hatred of suburbia' (Kynaston 2010, 419). David Kynaston has drawn attention to the young and passionate Ian Nairn who had written his first piece for *The Architectural Review* in March 1955, and three months later wrote the review's special edition, *Outrage*, arguing that city and country are losing their distinctiveness and that soon 'the end of Southampton will look like the beginning of Carlisle, the parts in between will look like the end of Carlisle or the beginning of Southampton' (2010, 420). In closing her article, Rowntree again became conscious of her elite audience. The significance of Oxford was a given and the words she chose were mannered and polite:

> It is on their [the public's] behalf that I urge Christ Church to use the same magnanimity in its dealings with tenants and architects, to give the scheme the consideration and revision that it deserves and to apply it in the broadest and most amenable way when suggestions arise (1956, 42).

It is important to note that the tone used by Rowntree in this 1956 *The Architectural Review* article was very different from that of her future writing and had had seven A4 pages, complete with illustrations, within which to unpack her argument. She was confident of her subject matter, she had something to say and knew it. She was not going to get this much space at

The Manchester Guardian newspaper but at the latter she found a very different kind of space where her feminist values and her more personal agenda resurfaced. From 1957, at *The Manchester Guardian* newspaper, and later when it became *The Guardian* newspaper, Rowntree wrote on a wide range of architectural subjects. In a similar vein to her work at *The Architectural Review*, she criticised new buildings and books on building, reported on international architectural conferences and design shows and promoted the role of architect while all the time eulogizing design modernism. The noteworthy departure from *The Architectural Review* was that it added her personal agenda to her remit. Her newspaper columns now became a forum where she worked to create a space for the professionalization of female artists and designers and comments on their struggle to be taken seriously in what Lees-Maffei describes as a move from taste to skill. This shift was facilitated by the use of journalism and advice manual authorship, in order to establish the writer as an expert in their field and therefore promote their practice (2008, 1).

On average, Rowntree contributed articles to *The Manchester Guardian* between two and four times a month. Articles in a section of the newspaper entitled 'Mainly for Women' appeared far less frequently, as little as twice a year with less than ten in total in her fourteen years on the payroll. She was an infrequent voice on these pages where women were so clearly the intended audience. Closer examination raises the question as to why these specific articles were located in this section. The answer is that the common ground the articles shared was their reference to rooms that women inhabited: specifically kitchens and bathrooms; rooms where a traditional feminine role was firmly in place. Rowntree's 1959 article 'Therapy in the Waiting Room' was located in 'Mainly for Women' because men did not take their children to the doctor's surgery. The article was bounded by advertisements for gold and silver brocade court shoes and Chanel-styled fashion photo shoots so that these pages were clearly signposted as 'not for men'. Her in-depth article was about the design of a doctor's waiting room for the Council for Industrial Design (COID) at the Design Centre. In one highly skilful move Rowntree positioned her own architectural/interior design work *and* her profession in the public domain both at the Design Centre and in the newspaper. Rowntree stated: 'in the humbler sphere of the waiting and consulting rooms, interior designers have something valuable to offer the doctor', and inferred perhaps that this may have come as a surprise to doctors (1959, 6). Her article outlined the practical, aesthetic and psychological concerns to be taken into account in the design and in true Rowntree prose she wryly noted that the main problem of bringing a waiting room to life was that '[y]ou have somehow to silence the accusations of that row of empty chairs (1959, 6). The small number of Rowntree articles that appeared in 'Mainly for Women' may indicate that (with the exception of her advice manual, *Interior Design*, which is squarely pointed at a female readership) Rowntree did not wish to position herself in a domestic ghetto. In *A View from the Interior* Lynne Walker describes this ghetto as a place that 'limited women's opportunities and reinforced sexual stereotypes; however, it also directed women architects to the most socially useful area of architecture—housing' (1989, 100).

The strength or weakness of the notion of the domestic ghetto is not the topic of this chapter but it is important to note that Rowntree was consciously positioning both herself and the framework of architectural discourse. Her later 1994 architectural reader *Buildings Face the Future* served as a potent reflection on her journalism of the period. Here she speculated that, while the field was male dominated, the practice of architecture might possess feminine qualities that result in its marginalisation in the media and that when it does find space the general nature of architectural criticism was 'boorish' (1994, 74). When comparing critiques on fiction to those on architecture she noted:

> Rudeness in literary criticism tends to be oblique, subtle or restrained. Buildings and their architects can expect full, frontal attack. I do not know whether to regard this lack of space for architecture as the reason for the boorishness or its outcome. In either case I presume that the connection is significant (1994, 74).

THE ARCHITECT AND THE MOTHER

Rowntree's writing style had frequent double meanings and her message and meaning was never far from the reader. The headline for an urban planning symposium, 'talking about planning for the family', was an interplay between town planning and contraception, for women re-entering the workplace; 'The Kitchen and the T-Square' hinted that a woman's place was in the office (1966, 6). It is important to note that in her later writing Rowntree referred to the architect (the male paradigm) using feminine pronouns wherever possible and thus drew attention to her championing of women; her word play consistently brought in feminine values and found parallels between architects and mothers at every opportunity:

> Architects, like mothers, are prepared to work very long hours if their children + [sic] designs need them to. . . . The fee agreement . . . does not specify hours—and the same can be said of marriage vows, or whatever may serve as an agreement between mothers of young children and the fathers (1994, 74).

In her architectural discourse, Rowntree was not rejecting domesticity, but rather saying 'I am this *and* that', 'architect *and* mother'. In this way, she was not just referring to architects and mothers but to all women. Thus Rowntree was part of Butler and Scott's 'feminist plural'—'the "we" of feminism founded on an identity common to all women' (1992, 132). This was not a feminism based on differences between women, as the later 1960s New Left would describe as having many divisions: 'radical, liberal, socialist, cultural, lesbian, and Third World feminisms' (Bammer 1992, 57). However, in a more critical vein, it is worth noting that Rowntree's feminism existed mainly in white academic upper middle class circles. The latter is said not to dismiss Rowntree's contribution but rather to reinforce it. In their 1956 sociology text, *Women's Two Roles*, Myrdal and Klein noted that the very few women who were fortunate enough to become professionals were in the intense and admiring gaze of the rest of their societal class. These pioneers were critical; they must succeed at work, marriage *and* motherhood so that 'all women may take comfort' and if they fail damage was done to all as well (1956, 151). The stakes are high: the new working professional woman cannot get it wrong. Unreasonably, she was accountable for success across all arenas.

In a 1966 *Guardian* newspaper article, 'The Kitchen and the T-Square', Rowntree is at pains to point out that Anne Acland took only five hours to find work as an architect after the seventeen-year gap needed to raise children. Rowntree was signposting to her readers: 'you can do it too, it's not hard'. Rowntree quoted Acland's creative frustration in: 'A bitter little broadcast, "My T-square in the Kitchen"', where domesticity was less than ideal; the report described the success of the architectural practice Acland, Barron and Smith, and observed: 'it will only be by the merest chance that you will discover she still has a formidable domestic career'. Later Rowntree noted that in Acland's '"spare" time—I suppose she must mean railway journeys—she is writing a cookery book, "Cooking Ahead," for people like herself who have to do it all at weekends' (1966, 8). Inverted commas around 'spare', and reference to trains and forward planning denoted that there was not really any spare time; Acland's was not a life of ease but rather one planned with militant care and attained through hard labour. Myrdal and Klein, writing in the previous decade, had described the unrealistic expectation of balancing housewifery and paid work as something which should be done with ease. With reference to the nineteenth century notion of the 'lady of leisure' (1956, 145), they spoke of a virtuous housewife who prepared daily home-baked bread with apparent ease and without revealing the sixteen-hour working day needed to achieve this. Thus the feminine ideal of the 'lady of leisure' was presented as in direct conflict with the hard work of running a home and at best confused the next generation of women. In 1950s and 60s Britain there were many reasons for women to go 'out' to work and engage in the battleground of balancing work and home. But as Myrdal and Klein note, married women without their own income had a financial position 'similar to that of a minor' (1956, 146). In the same vein, Kynaston points to extensive evidence that the main power struggle between women and men in 1950s Britain was over money and birth control (2010, 590) and this was exemplified in Rowntree's journalism with upfront headings such as 'Talking about Planning for the Family' and 'The Kitchen and the T-Square'. Furthermore, Kynaston cites Kate Fisher's research which notes, contrary to popular belief, that:

> Not only was 'men's knowledge of birth control more extensive than women's but that men were frequently given ultimate power to determine whether or not birth control would be used, what method was chosen, and the regularity with which it would be employed' (2010, 590).

Arguably, given the power struggle that Kynaston outlines, when Rowntree was reporting on architectural design discourse, women's plight would never have been far from the mind of her readers. In her 1961 article 'Crying Over the Kitchen Sink' Rowntree objected to expensively constructed and thoughtlessly planned contemporary kitchen designs and wrote that: 'The popular idea of 'the modern kitchen' in our country always strikes me with such sadness that I long to lean over the edge of the expensive sink and have a good cry' (1961, 6). To illustrate her case she cited two well-designed kitchens, one traditional American and the other modern British where both modernity and tradition had more to offer than the current marketplace had. This was a state of affairs that could move her to tears at the very location, the kitchen sink, which was both a woman's place and a refuge where her tears, as she stood with her back to the family, would have gone unnoticed. In Rowntree's view the modern kitchen should have pitched women out of domestic drudgery and into Le Corbusier's 'machine for living'. Under these high modernist tenets a kitchen should be conceived, designed and built in a rational manner so that counter heights, planning, and visual proportion function together seamlessly. Irrational design only frustrated the promise of a new age and a better life. In her advice manual, *Interior Design*, Rowntree describes the kitchen as a complicated place that must be designed in an organised manner so that things are simplified for the cook, the children and visitors. She writes: 'The best designers will always modify [their designs] to fit the particular space and people in question' revealing an attention to detail in terms of perfect fit and function (1964, 145). In 'Crying over the Kitchen Sink' Rowntree's concern was that women were not where they needed to be and that a stronger vision of the future was needed.

UTOPIA: A FEMINIST VISION OF THE FUTURE

For Rowntree utopia took on a physical, aspirational and symbolic form, that could become a built form through design practice and ideology which represented a 'machine for living' (Honour and Flemming 2009). In journalistic prose she urged her readers towards an architecture that would set them free, and a feminist vision of the future that argued for equality. Here architectural, journalistic and feminist discourses intertwine. Newly married herself, Rowntree encountered this physical utopia most directly at the Lawn Road flats in Hampstead where she and her husband Kenneth lived for 10 months in 1940. In a later 1963 *Guardian* newspaper article entitled 'The Ideal Client' Rowntree described Lawn Road as a building with 'an air of sweet reason' and drew attention to the fact that the architect's brief had been written by a psychotherapist in order to produce 'minimal dwellings for professional people' and a building so 'enthusiastically concrete that it looked almost soft from the moulds' (1963, 8). This now iconic building, designed by architect Wells Coates, was the first reinforced concrete block of flats in London. A pool of creatives, now also famous, lived there: Walter Gropius, Moholy-Nagy, Marcel Breuer and Jacques and Jacqueline Croag fled Europe and found refuge at Lawn Road. Rowntree describes housing these émigrés as a further architectural imperative or service to the profession that this now great building possessed.

According to Fiona MacCarthy, Rowntree said of the flats that '[i]t was a marvellous thing to live in a functional, light-drenched architecture' (2008, 32). It was not, however, a functional architecture that was designed for an aspiring mother, so for Rowntree this utopia could not last. In a 1996 radio interview she remembered her 1940s self and reminisced: 'we can't possibly have a baby here—it wouldn't do' (1996, tape 3), intimating that the management would have disapproved. It would seem that the Lawn Road flats were a professional domain and by inference a male domain. It is not the physical space that was at issue here, but the social space. This begs the question: Would Rowntree be the first woman to push a pram into this machine for living? And what would that mean?

That modernism promised time and a sense of self but did not promote or deliver feminine values has been well documented (Partington 1989). The backbreaking work of maintaining the minimalist home, the complete absence of servants and the new chores such as chauffeuring children to school meant there were always more chores to be done (Sparke 1995, 168). Rowntree's writing on her utopian 'machine for living' was aspirational, not practical. It had an evangelical ring: 'I do not think anyone has really experienced modern architecture until they have walked barefoot on pale grey marble or black quarry tiles that are heated to the temperature of a sunny beach' (1964, 69). In 1964, most women were lucky to walk on linoleum. While there was the desire for the modern home, there was also the financial impossibility of having one as home ownership rates continued on their downward trend. As a young mother with her dream on the back burner, Rowntree found herself living in what she later, in a 1996 radio interview, calls a 'non-village' (1996, tape 5). The Essex village of Lindsell, at the time, was a few houses strung out over two miles. Rowntree's house was primitive, the water had to be pumped, and they were poor, having lost her London income where she had been 'earning four pounds a week and living well' (1996, tape 4). In the same interview she lamented that they could have stayed at Lawn Road, there really was no reason to leave. She had possibly misjudged the seemingly inappropriateness of Lawn Road as a home for a young family and the personal price she would pay by leaving her physical utopia. Rowntree's time at Lawn Road had been idyllic but short and design modernism remained her fervent ideal; living in Lindsell, the importance of her journalism moved to the forefront of her life once again. For her utopia to manifest itself society had to change, and Rowntree's most effective campaigning vehicle became journalism, which enabled her to become an activator and catalyst for change. In 'Talking about Planning for the Family' she wrote: 'Suppose that both parents were tethered while their children were small? Then I suspect family planning would not only be a euphemism for contraception. Families would be planned indeed' (1966, 6). In a momentary low, Rowntree conceded some defeat, when in this same article she concluded that the idea of parenting as a visible vocation for both sexes would not find favour with the current generation of executives—although she had hopes for the next generation when she asked: 'what about the boys and girls in their identical bobbed hair and jeans?' (1966, 6). Indeed, what will they have to say about their future? Angelika Bammer has argued that the feminist movement may be underpinned by the 'idea of the future *as possibility* rather than as preset goal' (1992, 48), a process-orientated thinking without a specific end point in mind. It was the open-ended unpredictability and changeability of the outcome that makes this version of feminism emancipatory; thus the New Left, in the 1960s, was against the 'straight-jacketing of utopia' (Bammer 1992, 49). Unlike her more radical counterparts, Rowntree's vision of the future appears fixed and pragmatic; but in her own way, in the spirit of liberal feminism, she spoke out.

CONCLUSION

From modest beginnings Rowntree built a substantial readership base through journalism and her authorship of advice manuals, and repeatedly argued for a socially responsible built environment. In her own words, she believed that it was her role to 'draw attention to those aspects of architecture that were not being discussed' (1994, 98). By extension, her role included women's issues wherever and whenever she could slip them in. As consummate professional and mother of two, she knew home and work were a messy business. In a 1966 book review entitled 'Lighten our Darkness' she illustrated the full complexity of family life with her characteristic wry wit:

> As for kitchens—there is no doubt that the trickiest piece of the machine for living in is that dangerous vortex of family life where man, woman, children, unwashed crockery, half peeled onions, masterpieces

of model-making, sharp knives, grubby paintings, and dirty laundry are all drawn into a swirl (1966, 10).

The quiet insertion of the imperfect modernist 'machine for living' would not be lost on her readers; Rowntree knew there was no catch-all solution. Her utopia was a fixed ideal set against the pragmatic concerns of daily life. Conversely, the 1960s New Left found a much more radical and open-ended utopia, 'redefining it in such a way that it was freed of its repressive function as a signpost to a set future on an equally set path from which deviations were not allowed' (Bammer 1992, 49). It can be argued that Rowntree, although less radically orientated, was a feminist within her own rubric: she was a solitary figure in the newsroom where the patriarchal perspective was endemic. She was Trojan horse-like, working inside the system for change where she understood the male system but was not happy with it. She was a purposeful reflective practitioner who constantly imprinted the female voice at every opportunity. And in so doing became part of the larger project of recovering women's and media history.

BIBLIOGRAPHY / SOURCES

Bammer, Angelika. 1992. *Partial Vision: Feminism and Utopianism in the 1970s.* 2nd ed. London: Routledge.

Bornat, Joanna, and Hanna Diamond. 2007. 'Women's History and Oral History: Developments and Debates.' *Women's History Review* 16 (1): 19–39.

Butler, Judith, and Joan W. Scott. 1992. *Feminists Theorize the Political.* London: Routledge.

Honour, Hugh, and John Flemming. 2009. *A World History of Art.* London: Laurence King.

Kynaston, David. 2010. *Family Britain 1951–57.* London: Bloomsbury.

Langhamer, Claire. 2005. 'The Meanings of Home in Postwar Britain.' *Journal of Contemporary History* 40 (2): 341–362.

Lees-Maffei, Grace. 2008. 'Introduction: Professionalization as a Focus in Interior Design History.' *Journal of Design History* 21 (1): 1–17.

Myrdal, Alva, and Viola Klein. 1956. *Women's Two Roles: Home and Work.* 2nd ed. London: Redwood Press Limited.

Partington, Angela. 1989. *The Designer Housewife in the 1950s.* In *A View from the Interior: Feminism, Women and Design,* edited by Judy Attfield and Pat Kirkham. London: The Women's Press.

Polkey, Pauline. 2000. 'Reading History through Autobiography: Politically Active Women of Late Nineteenth-Century Britain and Their Personal Narratives.' *Women's History Review* 9 (3): 483–500.

Rowntree, Diana. 1994. *Buildings Face the Future.* 1st ed. Corbridge, UK: Architype.

Rowntree, Diana. 1964. *Interior Design.* 1st ed. Middlesex: Penguin Books Ltd.

Rowntree, Diana. 1956. 'Oxford College Barges.' *The Architectural Review* 120 (714): 36–42.

Rowntree, Diana. 1988. *Tracing Papers.* 1st ed. London: Gronow Press.

Sparke, Penny. 1995. *As Long as It's Pink: The Sexual Politics of Taste.* London: Pandora.

Sparke, Penny. 2008. *The Modern Interior.* London: Reaktion.
Walker, Lynne. 1989. 'Women and Architecture.' In *A View from the Interior: Feminism, Women and Design,* edited by Judy Attfield, and Pat Kirkham. London: The Women's Press.

NEWSPAPER ARTICLES

MacCarthy, Fiona. 2008. 'Obituary Diana Rowntree.' *The Guardian,* August 27.
Rowntree, Diana. 1959. 'Therapy in the Waiting Room.' *The Guardian,* November 4.
Rowntree, Diana. 1961. 'Crying over the Kitchen Sink.' *The Guardian,* January 11.
Rowntree, Diana. 1963. 'The Ideal Client.' *The Guardian,* September 26.
Rowntree, Diana. 1966. 'Lighten Our Darkness.' *The Guardian,* January 28.
Rowntree, Diana. 1966. 'The Kitchen and the T-square.' *The Guardian,* June 27.
Rowntree, Diana. 1966. 'Art for Living.' *The Guardian,* July 8.
Rowntree, Diana. 1966. 'Talking About Planning for the Family.' *The Guardian,* August 23.

RADIO INTERVIEW

Contributors: Rowntree, Kenneth, Rowntree, Diana, Bumpus, Judith, Rowntree, Adam. 1996. 'NLSC: Artists Lives: Professor Kenneth Rowntree interviewed by Judith Bumpus.' Corbridge: August 25.

Part III

The Long 1960s
Cultural Revolution?

The long 1960s, that is, the period from the middle of the 1950s to the mid-1970s, has been seen by historians such as Arthur Marwick as an era of Cultural Revolution. Both popular mythology and his research, which relies heavily on media sources, oral interviews and memories, suggest this was an era in which the rising prominence of young people and their sub-cultures, individualism, media and fashion spectacles were indicative of changing values. He argues that there was a spirit of new permissiveness, openness and shifting private morals (1999) leading to a reduction in deference towards authority and the breaking down of hierarchies of class, race and gender.

There is much historical debate about when, where and to what degree the changes actually took place in the long 60s and what the impact was on women. Legal and social changes included the introduction of the birth control pill (1961), the decriminalisation of suicide (1961) and of homosexuality (1967), the abolition of the death penalty (1965) and the introduction of legal abortion (1967). Such legislation was quickly followed by divorce reform which came into force in 1970, introducing divorce by mutual consent or after five years without the consent of an ex-partner. Many of these changes have been seen as giving women more control over their sexuality, relationships and private lives and facilitating the growth of second wave feminism (Cook 2005) evidenced by the first Women's Liberation Conference at Ruskin College Oxford in 1970. An alternative interpretation of events is put forward by Bocock, who identifies the long 60s as a historical moment when moral governance moved from being the responsibility of the legal system to one of self-discipline (1998). This is an interesting perspective and might explain the conservative strains which can be identified in many areas of the media alongside a greater diversity and liberalisation of media imagery.

There was certainly a greater media visibility of sexuality and youth, however, the relationship between these media discourses and women's lives is hard to fathom. Arguably, age, class, locality and marital status all constrained women's access to the supposed new freedoms on offer.

Furthermore, close analysis of media texts suggests the tenacity of traditional discourses of femininity even when faced with second wave feminism. Rachel Ritchie's chapter on *Woman* magazine argues that although social and cultural changes can be identified, young women continued to be offered a traditional trajectory for their life. In this it was expected to move towards becoming a fiancée, then bride and wife. Given that such magazines were commercial products, which women chose to purchase, these scripts of femininity must have retained a significant appeal.

Furthermore, whatever the idealism of some of the youth movements, Britain remained divided in the long 60s, fractured in many directions. Class divisions remained acute despite a greater diversity of the media representations of class; for example, the soap opera *Coronation Street* (1960) and the docudrama *Cathy Come Home* (1966) were set in solidly working-class homes and experiences (Laing 1986; Andrews 2012). The discontent and dissatisfaction of many working-class women, it is suggested in Maggie Andrews's chapter, was articulated through racist discourses in social problem films. The alienation and marginalisation may have been more pronounced when individuals were confronted with the visibility of consumerist youth culture brought into the homes via television. In the 1960s television was arguably central to mass domestic culture and, as Ellis points out, 'something the whole family shared or argued over' (2000, 46).

Women's participation in the workplace continued to rise despite the slow progress towards equal pay and twenty-four hour (or even eight-hour) nurseries which the Women's Movement demanded. The Equal Pay Act, although passed in 1970, did not come into force until 1975 when it was accompanied by the Sex Discrimination Act. Gillian Murray's chapter utilises the regional television news programme *ATV Today* to demonstrate the contested position of the female bus workers in the Midlands during the 1960s and 1970s. Like Andrews's chapter it suggests that tensions and conflict lay beneath the surface in many areas of women's lives. Furthermore, they also suggest that dreams of liberation were for many women very modest—about having an indoor bathroom, holding a steady and relatively well-paid job on the buses and getting by with a little less insecurity and anxiety than their parents and grandparents had had.

To many it is the supposed sexual revolution which epitomises the 60s (Marwick 1999; Cook 2005); for historians, analysing sexuality using media to study Women's History presents particular challenges. It could be suggested the sexual revolution identified by some as occurring in the 60s overplays the significance of media images on everyday lives and underplays the complexity of sexual lives in the 1950s, when such activities were more firmly kept behind closed doors (Thane 2013). Arguably, shifts in sexual practices were adopted much more slowly and in a much more piecemeal way and cannot really be identified until much later in the 1970s. Getting a divorce could still result in people losing their job in the early 1970s when many family planning clinics, as they were called, insisted on calling everyone 'Mrs' whatever their age. Furthermore, Adrian Bingham's chapter which provides careful historical contextualisation to the introduction of the Page 3 girl to *The Sun* newspaper in 1970 is a useful reminder that women do not necessarily benefit from the liberation and permissiveness of a supposed cultural revolution; and arguably, discourses of femininity that emerged in the 1960s brought already established representational practices of the pin-up into mainstream media and onto the breakfast table.

BIBLIOGRAPHY / SOURCES

Coronation Street (1960–)
Cathy Come Home (1966)
Andrews, Maggie. 2012. *Broadcasting the Airwaves: Broadcasting, Domesticity and Femininity*. London: Continuum.
Bocock, Robert. 1998. 'Choice and Regulation: Sexual Moralities.' In *Media and Cultural Regulation*, edited by Kenneth Thompson, 69–116. London: Sage.
Cook, Hera. 2005. *The Long Sexual Revolution: English Women, Sex, and Contraception 1800–1975*. Oxford University Press.
Ellis, John. 2000. *Seeing Things*. London: I. B. Tauris.
Giles, Judy. 2004. *The Parlour and the Suburb: Domestic Identities, Class, Femininity and Modernity*. London: Berg.
Laing, Stuart. 1986. *Representations of Working Class Life*. Basingstoke, UK: Palgrave.
Marwick, Arthur. 1999. *The Sixties: Social and Cultural Transformation in Britain, France, Italy and the USA*. Oxford Paperbacks.
Thane, Pat, and Tanya Evans. 2013. *Sinners? Scroungers? Saints? Unmarried Motherhood in Twentieth-Century England*. Oxford University Press.

9 Young Women and *Woman*
Depictions of Youthful Femininity, 1954–1969

Rachel Ritchie

During the 1950s and 60s, a raft of new women's magazines appeared on the market. Some, such as *She* (1955) and *Nova* (1965), were embryonic of the trend for targeting 'attitude' rather than demographics (White 1970, 287; Gough-Yates 2003, 2). Others, such as *Honey* (1961) and *Jackie* (1964), appealed to the youth market and were indicative of the post-war emphasis on youth and part of this shift, encouraging a growing perception of each generation as distinct rather than seeing adolescents as simply a younger version of their parents. This chapter explores how such discourses of age and generation featured on the pages of the well-established and best-selling women's magazine of the period, *Woman*, which billed itself as the 'world's greatest weekly for women'. It examines the publication's depictions of young women during the period from the end of rationing in 1954 to the close of the 1960s, analysing the dominant themes and tensions evident in representations of youthful femininity.

The study reveals that while social and cultural changes were apparent, these representations continued to present young women within a conventionally feminine lifecycle in which they moved seamlessly from one stage to the next: first girl-about-town to fiancée, then bride and wife. The study also demonstrates how such depictions catered to older women who read *Woman* and shows that developments in the mid to late 1960s partially disrupted this tightly defined vision. Although marriage and consumption remained central features, by the end of the period contributors increasingly recognized that not all young women's lives neatly fitted into this framework and challenges to hegemonic femininity began to feature more noticeably within the magazine.

Age and generation feature prominently in popular perceptions of the post-war period as well as scholarship on these decades. Age-focused concepts are central to many dominant narratives about Britain in these years: the notion of the 'birth of the teenager' in the 1950s, for instance, and a supposed 'cultural revolution' driven by a new generation in the 1960s. As Bill Osgerby observes in his influential account of post-war youth, the teenager became 'an ideological axis around which cohered debates about these more fundamental shifts in social and cultural relations' (Osgerby 1998, 28). More recently, the editors of a *Contemporary British History* special issue on post-war youth culture and popular music made a similar statement, arguing that youth serves 'as a metaphorical device to embody both the aspirations and anxieties of a particular historical time' (Garland et al. 2012, 266).

In this chapter, 'youth' and 'young' refer to those aged between 15 and 25. Even within these parameters, marriage was a dominant feature in women's lives. Average age at first marriage for women was 24.4, 23.1 and 22.6 years in 1951, 1961 and 1971, with marriage rates reaching the highs of 76.3, 83.0 and 97.9 per 1,000 respectively (Lewis 2001, 71). Despite these statistics, the figure of the young bride or young wife has received little attention in literature on youth in the 1950s and 60s. This reflects the relatively limited attention given to young women at all in such accounts. Osgerby laments this oversight, arguing that their experiences encapsulated change even more than the lives of their male counterparts did. An academic preoccupation with subcultures and counter-culture exacerbates such neglect as young women often occupied a marginal position with these spheres. However, work by feminists has accentuated the cultural spaces occupied by girls and young women. The private realm of the home was important, as was popular music and magazines (Osgerby 1998, 50–63). This study builds on such findings, not only by looking at a particular magazine but also by highlighting the centrality of the domestic world, with marriage at its core, within *Woman*'s depictions of youthful femininity.

Recent research by Selina Todd and Hilary Young on the 1950s and early 60s has found that many young women sought independence through marriage, however contradictory this strategy may seem (Todd and Young 2012, 462). Their findings also challenge common assumptions about a generational clash during these years, revealing instead 'widespread evidence of intergenerational cooperation between parents and children' (451–452). This study finds similar evidence in *Woman*, with an emphasis on continuity and connections across generations rather than divisions between them—although tensions increase notably as the 1960s go on.

This attention to links between generations is a new feature in terms of post-war women's history as well as writings about youth. Scholarship on the years after 1945 has often articulated a strong sense of hostility between older women and their coming-of-age daughters, perhaps most famously in Carolyn Steedman's *Landscape for a Good Woman*, which charts her relationship with her mother from an autobiographical perspective (Steedman 1991). Wendy Webster observes that such accounts portray the 1950s 'as a period in waiting for something else . . . The waiting is the daughters' perspective and what is awaited is their moment' (Webster 1998, xxi). However, while the focus here is on representations of youth, this chapter does not simply reiterate 'the daughters' perspective' found in many existing studies of post-war womanhood. Rather, by exploring how *Woman*'s writers, advertisers and readers depicted young women, it considers a variety of perspectives on both age and women's lives.

Woman is an ideal source for such an age-gender analysis. The 1950s and 60s were tumultuous years within the women's periodical industry; the new titles mentioned at the start of the chapter, for instance, posed a cumulative threat to *Woman*'s pre-eminent position in the market (for a full account of industrial developments, see Ballaster et al. 1991, 110–112; White 1970, 155–242). However, it was a 'Golden Age' in terms of circulation figures, with sales of *Woman* reaching over 2.5 million copies per issue during these decades (Keeble 2007, 96; White 1970, appendix iv). The size of its readership reflects the publication's mass appeal: it catered to women in their teens onwards, hence its pages contained a broad range of standpoints on age.

Despite (or perhaps because of) this enormous popularity, magazines such as *Woman* remain relatively neglected by historians of women and gender. Moreover, as Margaret Beetham observes, historians 'have rarely treated them as texts in themselves' (Beetham 1996, 6). This case study illustrates what a rich and enlightening source such media texts can be, drawing women's history and media history together by combining detailed textual analysis with a firm grounding in the wider socio-cultural context. The chapter also joins a growing body of scholarship specifically focused on young women and magazines, from studies by Alisa Webb and Penny Tinkler on the late nineteenth century and first half of the twentieth century to work by Fan Carter and Anna Gough-Yates on late twentieth and twenty-first century titles (Webb 2006; Tinkler 1995; Carter 2005; Gough-Yates 2012).

Literature on the women's periodical press has reached varied conclusions, portraying magazines as manipulative (propagating patriarchal and repressive ideals of femininity), helpful (offering guidance) and pleasurable (a site of leisure and escapism). Investigations have also employed a wide range of analytical approaches, from exploring reader practices to investigating the industry's economic and commercial facets (Hermes 1995; Gough-Yates 2003. For an evaluation of different theories, see Ballaster et al. 1991). The focus here is on representations within a sample of sixteen issues, one chosen randomly from each year of the study (1954 to 1969). Within this kind of analysis, the concept of 'preferred meaning' is crucial, although this is not to deny the possibility of other interpretations; while a journalist or advertiser may aim to communicate one particular meaning, readers can create others, even ones that were completely unintended (Kirkham 1996, 166).

There is frequently friction between publications: as Janice Winship noted in the 1980s, 'Each engages and embraces readers in a world of "we women" but assumes and constructs different definitions of who "we" are' (Winship 1987, 13, 28, 52, 55). Furthermore, the composite nature of magazines means that multiplicity is inherent even within them (Blix 1992, 58). Inside a single issue, there are different types of content (editorial, fiction, advice columns, features, correspondence and advertising) and three distinct elements (producers, advertisers and readers) (Tinkler 1995, 186). There are often disparities within these factions, let alone between them: two readers, for example, may express opposing views. Much of the emphasis in recent research has been on such intrinsic tensions; contributors to the *Design and the Modern Magazine* edited collection, for instance, accentuate the polysemic and fragmented nature of the publications studied (Aynsley and Forde 2007). Fragmentation and the presence of multiple voices affected the content of *Woman* too, as the rest of the chapter demonstrates.

FANTASY AND DREAMS: THE GIRL-ABOUT-TOWN

Depictions of young women appeared most regularly in the short stories that featured in every issue of *Woman*. These fictional examples figured prominently in the magazine, occupying an important position near the front. The commissioning editor and authors clearly regarded young single women as a popular character type as they were the central protagonist in twenty (69%) of the twenty-nine short stories in the sample used. Analysis of these stories shows why. The protagonist usually has an exciting job (student, florist, model) or works in an industry that has prestige (fashion, advertising, public relations). Such occupations symbolized the newfound confidence that came with economic prosperity during the 1950s. They were highly aspirational and represented an enviable lifestyle but, as employment structures changed and office work became girls' largest employer, they were potentially within reach of more young women than ever before (Todd and Young 2012, 455–456; Tinkler 2001, 44; Osgerby 1998 50–51). Such ambitions were not confined to young women themselves; Todd and Young argue that working-class parents encouraged their sons and daughters to '"have a go" and aim high' (Todd and Young 2012, 460).

These jobs signified glamour too. Although the stories do not present glamour as a desirable character trait, other understandings of the concept resonate strongly, particularly the link between glamour and what Carol Dyhouse describes as 'a dream of transformation, a desire for something out of the ordinary, a form of aspiration, a fiction of female becoming' (Dyhouse 2010, 3). These examples are literally 'a fiction', allowing readers the opportunity to daydream about other lives, whether feasibly attainable or not. The location of these stories further enhances this aura of glamour, with many set in London (for example, see 'Day of Always' and 'A Girl with a Halo', *Woman* May 15, 1965, 6–8, 12, 53 and July 2, 1966, 6–7, 10–12, respectively). This setting reflects the migratory pull of the capital for young men and women seeking adventure and independence and the city's association with fashionable youth cultures, particularly in the mid to late 1960s when 'Swinging London' was at its height. It was the obvious choice for authors looking to create a young female character living outside the confines of the familial home.

Such depictions of young women living independently were also indicative of a broader trend for contemplating 'a period away from home, of flat sharing or city living, before settling down' (Dyhouse 2010, 150). The origins of this post-war 'girl-about-town' lay in inter-war magazines, when fiction writers began to depict young women living in bedsits and working in places such as department stores. As Judy Giles argues, such characters tell us about contemporary understandings of gender: their work, leisure and living spaces 'would have resonated with symbolic meaning for their female readerships, suggesting a "modern" femininity' (Giles 2004, 128). Giles also observes that despite inviting reader identification, such stories 'were consumed, in the main, by married housewives living in the suburbs rather than by single women working in large cities' (Giles 2004, 128). Likewise, the readers interviewed by Janice Radway in her seminal study of women and romantic fiction were mainly wives and mothers. Furthermore, what these readers enjoyed most was 'the opportunity to project themselves into the story, to become the heroine' (Radway 1991, 56–57, 67). Radway's findings have implications for this study, indicating that as well as being aspirational, *Woman*'s short stories offered a form of escapism, with older readers taking vicarious pleasure in following the fictional antics of the girl-about-town. The distance between protagonist and reader thus reinforced the fantasy element inherent in such stories; dreaming about other lives is part of the purpose.

Romance has a dual function in this respect. On the one hand, it fuels the sense of escapism. On the other, the character's pursuit of or participation in a heterosexual relationship allows the reader to identify with her; it is the one point of contact between their contrasting lives. Mostly the plots concentrate on a single girl-about-town and the relationship that inevitably emerges with, for instance, a fellow commuter, neighbour or stranger they meet in the park (*Woman* September 17, 1955, 28, 37, 39; September 29, 1956, 29, 31; April 10, 1954, 9, 10, 12, 14, 16). Sometimes the unmarried protagonist is already 'courting' or engaged. The drama usually revolves around an argument or misunderstanding that either delays romance developing or challenges an existing partnership. The stories in a May 1965 issue illustrate both scenarios. In 'Laura Transformed', the male lead thinks that Laura will snub him because she is beautiful but also aloof, whilst in 'His Sort of Girl', Lisa's well-intentioned efforts to be more adventurous like her boyfriend's ex cause problems in the relationship (*Woman* May 15, 1965, 6–8, 69, 71, 73, 24, 74, 76).

At times, authors go as far as having the female protagonist question her feelings for her fiancé and her wish to marry him. Ultimately, though, events serve to assuage her concerns (*Woman* June 7, 1958, 16–18, 49, 51; September 27, 1969, 25, 27, 67, 69, 72). By the end of all twenty of these stories, the reader has no doubt that wedding bells are soon to follow. Even the rare woman character that resists romance ends up with a fairytale conclusion: although 'Mary-Ann thought falling in love an absurd extravagance', she eventually agrees to marry Mr Prendergast, one of the bosses at the advertising agency where she works (*Woman* April 10, 1954, 28–29, 35, 37, 38, 41). Indeed, as the reader indulges in escapist dreaming while following the escapades of the girl-about-town, the girl-about-town character is dreaming of marriage and her own transformation into a housewife and mother. Marriage is the assumed and only outcome in these stories, supporting Radway's claim that romances attempt to convince readers that 'heterosexuality is both inevitable and natural and that it is necessarily satisfying as well' (Radway 1991, 14). Its dominance certainly implies that marriage, or at least aspirations to marry, is *the* central feature in women's lives from girlhood, even if some individuals take a detour into single city living along the way.

DREAMING OF MARRIAGE:
THE YOUNG WOMAN AS BRIDE AND WIFE

Within *Woman*'s short stories, the prevalence of romance culminating in marriage creates a sense of seamless continuation across generations of women. This is apparent in other areas of the magazine too, which likewise portray heterosexual relationships leading to marriage as a commonality of female experience, uniting women of different ages wherever they were in the lifecycle. *Woman* provided a space in which readers of varying ages could dream about romance and weddings: young ones about their future engagement and marriage, older ones about their memories of that time. The inclusion of readers' reminiscences demonstrates this. In 1956, Mrs SC of Cardiff wrote to the letters page about how she had always admired her husband's immaculate appearance when they were dating; she later discovered that he had bought a new shirt every time he saw her (*Woman* September 29, 1956, 3–4). A similar mix of nostalgia and humour is evident in 'Wasn't It Romantic?', a 1962 feature containing readers' anecdotes about courtship and engagement (*Woman* February 24, 1962, 28).

While these examples introduce a nostalgic element to dreaming about marriage, references to brides and weddings highlight the notion of fantasy again. A 1954 article entitled 'A Marriage Has Been Arranged' told a mother's story of 'when a young girl's dreams come true' (*Woman* April 10, 1954, 27). Language suggestive of the supernatural and enchantment also formed part of this discourse: one 1957 advertisement claimed that 'Dreams come true in the magic of a James Walker Ring' and another from 1963 promoted wedding gowns 'which you can make up in Witchcraft Lace' (*Woman* March 23, 1957, 32; January 26, 1963, 57).

Although the institution of marriage incorporated women of all ages, the figure of the bride was always a young woman. This is perhaps unsurprising considering the low average age at marriage during this period, as detailed earlier. Alongside the fictional girl-about-town, the bride is central to representations of youthful femininity in *Woman*, representing the next step in young women's assumed lifecycle. Advertisements particularly depicted young women at this stage, as either fiancées or brides. In some cases, such as advertisements for diamond rings, the imagery suited the product (*Woman* September 29, 1956, 44; March 23, 1957, 32; December 12, 1964, 25). In other instances, advertisers chose these motifs in order to encourage consumption of their goods, presenting engagement and marriage as an important time in terms of training and preparing for domestic roles. As a 1956 advertisement for Belling cookers stated, 'Now you're engaged . . . *Now* is the time to think about the things you must have to start a home of your own' (*Woman* September 29, 1956, 28; emphasis in original). Similarly, a 1969 advertisement showed an older woman whispering to a young bride with the headline 'And a couple of things you ought to know about carpets' (*Woman* September 27, 1969, 5).

As well as reiterating the dominance of heterosexuality, these advertisements, like many others, reflected and reinforced the centrality of consumption in understandings of women's identity in this period, whatever their age. In the words of the magazine's editor, Mary Grieve, 'it dawned on the businessmen of the country that the Little Woman was now Big Business' and, as the highest circulation women's periodical, *Woman* was the ideal vehicle for advertising directly to them (White 1970, 97, 179). Young women occupied an important position in this market, with advertisers and manufacturers perceiving them as a distinct category—not children, but not like the older generation (Osgerby 1998, 50, 52). As early as 1954, *Woman* carried an advertisement for a range of Clarks shoes designed specifically for teenagers (*Woman* April 10, 1954, 34). Another footwear brand did the same the following year, claiming 'For your young income . . . Designed in America for the young and sophisticated' (*Woman* September 17, 1955, 55).

However, despite this age-based segmentation, gender identification ultimately triumphed. While age affected spending patterns and the kinds of items purchased, the role of consumer was a consistent feature in depictions of women across the generations. Every stage in their lives, not just youth, provided a marketing and sales opportunity. Moreover, the notion that all women were key consumers created a sense of unity and continuity. The advertisements featuring fiancées and brides exemplify this, revealing an underlying assumption that young women would progress effortlessly from one stage to the next, both as consumers and in terms of the typical mid-century female lifecycle.

The knitting pages in *Woman* further illustrate this accentuation of 'feminine' identity over age-based classifications. While the target audience for a pattern might vary according to age, the presumption that women readers of all ages participated in the act of knitting underlined a sense of unity and continuity across the generations. At the same time, knitting-related content reinforced the omnipresence of heterosexual relationships in the magazine. Patterns and advertisements encouraged women across the age spectrum to knit items for 'the man in your life' (*Woman* December 12, 1964, 34). This was in part about expressing love and affection; as one wool manufacturer extolled, 'He's your one and only. So cherish him. Care for him. Knit something for him. Something a bit different—could be this golf jacket' (*Woman* January 26, 1963, 42). It also had a practical motivation, forming part of the magazine's guidance to readers on clothing their families. *Woman* often featured patterns for children as well as adults, including special supplements such as their 1962 'Fifteen easy smart family knitteds [sic]' pullout (*Woman* February 24, 1962, 37–45). Viewed in this light, encouraging young women readers to knit for their 'one and only' was another way of positioning them within the seemingly seamless cycle in which they would progress through the stages to bride, wife and in the end mother—the assumed ambitions of them all.

The knitting patterns hint at the practical and perhaps rather mundane aspects of such a future. At the same time, they contain signs of socio-cultural changes affecting the lives of young women in the post-war period. The 1966 pattern for matching sweaters, for instance, was part of a trend for 'his and hers' clothing (*Woman* July 2, 1966, 20–21). Matching clothing signified the mid-twentieth-century ideal of companionate marriage, as suggested in pattern names such as 'Tailored companions' (*Woman* February 24, 1962, 37–45; Langhamer 2000, 139; Summerfield 1994, 59–60; Summerfield and Finch 1991, 17). Although this new relationship model was not exclusively a youth phenomenon, it was particularly apparent within the magazine's depictions of young couples. The issue featuring the matching sweaters pattern also contained 'A Well-Timed Dinner Party', in which *Woman* writers advised a newly wed couple about home entertaining. The piece conveys an impression of more egalitarian relationships with statements such as 'Gordon is willing to help', albeit by serving drinks, rather than cooking (*Woman* July 2, 1966, 14–16). Other guidance given by the magazine's writers, however, exposed a far less positive picture of married life for young women, as the following section demonstrates.

TENSIONS AND CHALLENGES:
YOUNG WOMEN READERS AND LIVED EXPERIENCE

Even though post-war youth cultures frequently challenged accepted behaviour and norms (Osgerby 1998, 41–47), references within *Woman* to groups such as the Mods did not necessarily undermine the magazine's typical depictions of youthful femininity. Two allusions to scooters, a potent symbol of youth and Mod culture, in the November 11, 1961 issue illustrate this. In one case, the young woman in the advertisement declared 'I was the scooter fan they always left standing' until she used Colgate toothpaste to eliminate her bad breath. In the other, a feature on Christmas presents, the reader sees what 'Teenager Penny' has purchased, including the gift for her 'scooter fan' boyfriend (*Woman* November 11, 1961, 29, 70). In both instances, the heavy emphasis on consumption and heterosexual relations reinforces dominant understandings of young women's, indeed all women's, lives, thus avoiding any suggestion of the potentially disruptive influence of youth culture.

However, disruption and tensions increased as the period wore on, in references to specific youth cultures as well as within representations of young women more generally. In 1968, a girl wrote to one of the magazine's 'agony aunts' complaining that her parents did not understand her student boyfriend's 'scruffy' appearance (*Woman* October 5, 1968, 14). This letter is indicative of the escalation in generational conflict in the mid to late 1960s, a shift that has been widely observed. Whereas attitudes towards youth in the 1950s and early 60s had been mixed, this began to change as hostility and discord became the prevailing discourses in British society (Gough-Yates 2012, 376; Todd and Young 2012, 456; Osgerby 1998, 97–100). As Garland et al. observe, 'Once "crisis" beset the "consensus" . . . youth and youth culture provided more negative motifs' (Garland et al. 2012, 267–269).

This 1968 letter is one of many examples of young women readers writing to *Woman* about their experiences. Such correspondence, along with the magazine's 'real life' features, often presents a different image of young women than the depictions of femininity explored in the first two sections. In particular, accounts of lived experience challenge the fantasies that its own pages perpetuated. For instance, the letters about relationships that filled *Woman*'s advice columns undercut the romantic and nostalgic dreaming discussed previously. A 1954 query from a nineteen-year-old married woman exemplifies this. She asks agony aunt Evelyn Home whether she should seek a divorce because she does not love her husband—her situation contrasting starkly against the idealized vision of courtship and marriage conveyed by short stories, advertisements and even older readers' reminiscences. Home's advice reinforces the widespread assumption that being a wife and mother is a woman's natural destiny and explicitly instructs the reader to embrace these roles: 'Become an expert cook and housekeeper, an ideal companion to your husband, a perfect sweetheart. And if you also become a mother—so much the better . . . before you know where you are, you will be happily in love again' (*Woman* April 10, 1954, 55). Her confident reassurance belies the fact that many women did not find satisfaction through domesticity. Moreover, the response cannot disguise the clear tension between this reader's experience and the raft of depictions in other parts of the magazine showing young women progressing effortlessly from courtship to marriage.

Like this reader, many young women did not move seamlessly from one stage of the lifecycle to another as contributors to *Woman* indicated they should. Throughout the sample, there were references to those whose did not step neatly from one stage to the next and whose lives did not fit within the boundaries of conventional femininity. Home's page, for example, regularly included correspondence about pregnancy 'out of wedlock', an occurrence that overtly disrupted the prescribed sequence of courtship followed by marriage and then motherhood (*Woman* March 23, 1957, 65, 67; September 12, 1959, 65; November 11, 1961, 77). This issue did not solely affect young women but was often conflated with teenage motherhood, as in a 1963 article that reported on a London County Council school for pregnant 13 to 16 year olds and included the statistic that one in eight London births was illegitimate (*Woman* January 26, 1963, 59).

The tone of this article implies that the capital was a site of sexual transgression, and in a society where sexual double standards still prevailed (Summerfield 1994, 68), such contraventions seemed to pose a particular threat to women. A 1969 'special investigation' went even further in portraying London as a place of danger. Labelled on the cover as 'A disturbing report on girls who leave home', the piece opened by outlining the capital's attractions, talking about 'the world of red London buses, bright lights, opportunities and freedom, gaiety and friends. A place where everything is Go, and Life is waiting to be lived' (*Woman* September 27, 1969, 8). While such statements echo the glamorous portrayals of London in the magazine's fiction, the rest of the article vehemently undermined this vision by emphasizing the dark underside of city living experienced by young women who had come to the capital as runaways. One interviewee had an abortion, while a quotation from another provides the bleak caption accompanying the report's main image: 'I felt I couldn't live with myself any longer. I reached Southwark Bridge and that was that . . . I jumped' (*Woman* September 27, 1969, 9).

Such divergent images of the capital, although common in the post-war decades (Mort 2010), created another area of tension in *Woman* and its depictions of young women. The report's frankness refutes the widespread belief that post-war women's magazines simply eschewed controversial issues, particularly as abortion had only been legalized in 1967 and suicide decriminalized in 1961 (Harrison 2009, 248–249, 290). The piece is also indicative of shifting social mores in the 1960s, suggesting an increased willingness to acknowledge transgression and deviation from the acceptable feminine norm. However, the report does not signal a sexual revolution transforming British society. Within the magazine itself, reactions to changes in sexual behaviour indicate a rather more fragmented and limited picture. In 1967, for example, Marje Proops, another of *Woman*'s agony aunts, praised the honesty of an unmarried seventeen-year-old mother-to-be featured in her column but criticized her attitude to sex as irresponsible: promiscuity is not freedom, she argued, but self-destruction (*Woman* December 2, 1967, 20).

This was not simply about an older woman condemning a younger one. There is no straightforward generation divide in terms of attitudes or experiences, as illustrated by Home's page in the same issue. The tone and outlook in two letters from a sixteen- and eighteen-year-old were completely different from both each other and the pregnant teenager addressed by Proops. The younger one expresses the continued sexual naiveté of some young women, asking the agony aunt 'to write a bit about how you have babies, etc.' as she has 'a steady boy friend' but does not know 'what's right or wrong about sex'. In contrast, the eighteen-year-old wished to marry the older divorcee that she was dating but feared her parents' reaction to this news and, as Home reminded, she could not marry him for another year without their consent (*Woman* September 27, 1969, 76). Even in 1969, the freedom available to young women often remained limited and in many cases, that freedom still took the form of marriage.

CONCLUSION

This chapter has considered a range of different voices, including writers, advertisers and readers, who shaped depictions of youthful femininity within *Woman*. In doing so, it has highlighted the importance of age as a category of analysis when studying women's lives and encouraged greater consideration of its influence. The study's focus on multiple perspectives, rather than concentrating just on the standpoint of young women themselves, has exposed a large degree of continuity in the representations of young women across the two decades. Throughout the 1950s and 60s, various contributors to *Woman* provided images of youthful femininity that centred on the figures of the girl-about-town, the bride and the young wife. The experiences of young women themselves, mostly expressed on the problem pages, often challenged such depictions, particularly in the second half of the 1960s. However, even such conflicts did not fundamentally destabilize marriage as the defining feature in women's lives, whatever their age.

Although there were changes, especially from the mid 1960s onwards, evidence from *Woman* reveals more piecemeal and limited socio-cultural change than is frequently assumed. As well as informing work on gender history, reiterating the shift away from 'the daughters' perspective' (and its emphasis on breaking with the past) that has dominated women's history in this period, such findings also contribute to the growing body of scholarship revising perceptions of social change in the 1960s (Varon, Foley, and McMillan 2008, 4–5; Thomas 2002). Indeed, many of the new opportunities that emerged for young women during the 1960s are notable only by their absence. There was, for instance, little indication of young women choosing to pursue a career; references to paid employment were mainly limited to fictional examples where the protagonist's job added an aura of glamorous escapism to the story and/or allowed her to meet eligible men. Similarly, there were few signs of the openings provided by the expansion of higher education or the burgeoning feminist movement. There were also few allusions to symbols of the supposed cultural revolution; no mention of the contraceptive pill, for example. These absences are not solely a consequence of sampling. It seems that, with some exceptions, contributors avoided topics that threatened to disrupt the circumscribed notions of youthful femininity (and womanhood generally) that prevailed within *Woman*. This avoidance may explain the two major silences within the magazine, race and homosexuality, although both warrant further investigation.

Certain tensions, though, could not be evaded. As with all women's magazines, *Woman*'s composite nature resulted in ambiguities and disparities, both within different elements of the publication and between them. Underlying many of the tensions discussed in this chapter was a conflict between lived experiences and fantasy. The pages of *Woman* provided both a mirror to readers' lives, from knitting for loved ones to arguing with them, and a looking-glass through which they could escape to a fantasy world. This fantasy took various forms, including glamour, romance and nostalgia. The concept of dreams and dreaming is crucial too, and older women were central to this. Indeed, catering to older readers shaped depictions of young women in the magazine. *Woman*'s enormous popularity indicates that this was a successful commercial strategy at the time, but it was not without repercussions for the future. The dominant vision of young women seen throughout this study, defined by consumption and heterosexual relationships leading to marriage, corresponded with the feminine lifecycle familiar to these older women. Although there was some accommodation of changing social mores as the 1960s wore on, there were still closely defined parameters. Young women whose lives did not fit neatly within these boundaries received only occasional reference, usually as an object of warning or pity. As a result, young readers looking for a magazine depicting a less prescribed way of life would have to look elsewhere, to one of the new titles emerging on the market.

BIBLIOGRAPHY / SOURCES

August, Andrew. 2009. 'Gender and 1960s Youth Culture: The Rolling Stones and the New Woman.' *Contemporary British History* 23 (1): 79–100.

Aynsley, Jeremy, and Kate Forde, editors. 2007. *Design and the Modern Magazine*. Manchester University Press.

Ballaster, Ros, Margaret Beetham, Elizabeth Fraser, and Sandra Hebron. 1991. *Women's Worlds: Ideology, Femininity and the Woman's Magazine*. Basingstoke, UK: Palgrave Macmillan.

Beetham, Margaret. 1996. *A Magazine of Her Own? Domesticity and Desire in the Woman's Magazine, 1800–1914*. London: Routledge.

Blix, Jacqueline. 1992. 'A Place to Resist: Reevaluating Women's Magazines.' *Journal of Communication Inquiry* 16 (1): 56–71.

Carter, Fan. 2005. 'It's a Girl Thing: Teenage Magazines, Lifestyle and Consumer Culture.' In *Ordinary Lifestyles: Popular Media, Consumption and Taste*, edited by David Bell and Joanne Hollows, 173–186. Maidenhead, UK: Open University Press.

Dyhouse, Carol. 2010. *Glamour: History, Women, Feminism*. London: Zed Books.

Finch, Janet, and Penny Summerfield. 1991. 'Social Reconstruction and the Emergence of Companionate Marriage, 1945–1959.' In *Marriage, Domestic Life and Social Change: Writings for Jacqueline Burgoyne*, edited by David Clark, 7–32. London: Routledge.

Garland, Jon, Keith Gildart, Anna Gough-Yates, Paul Hodkinson, Bill Osgerby, Lucy Robinson, John Street, Pete Webb, and Matthew Worley. 2012. 'Youth Culture, Popular Music and the End of "Consensus" in Post-War Britain.' *Contemporary British History* 26 (3): 265–271.

Giles, Judy. 2004. *The Parlour and the Suburb: Domestic Identities, Class, Femininity and Modernity*. Oxford: Berg.

Gough-Yates, Anna. 2012. '"A Shock to the System": Feminist Interventions in Youth Subculture—The Adventures of Shocking Pink.' *Contemporary British History* 26 (3): 375–403.

Gough-Yates, Anna. 2003. *Understanding Women's Magazines: Publishing, Markets and Readerships*. London: Routledge.

Harrison, Brian. 2009. *Seeking a Role: The United Kingdom 1951–1970*. Oxford University Press.

Hermes, Joke. 1995. *Reading Women's Magazines: An Analysis of Everyday Media Use*. Cambridge: Polity Press.

Keeble, Trevor. 2007. 'Domesticating Modernity: *Woman* Magazine and the Modern Home.' In *Design and the Modern Magazine*, edited by Jeremy Aynsley and Kate Forde, 95–113. Manchester University Press.

Kirkham, Pat. 1996. 'Fashioning the Feminine: Dress, Appearance and Femininity in Wartime Britain.' In *Nationalising Femininity: Culture, Sexuality and British Cinema in the Second World War*, edited by Christine Gledhill and Gillian Swanson, 152–174. Manchester University Press.

Langhamer, Claire. 2000. *Women's Leisure in England 1920–60*. Manchester University Press.

Lewis, Jane. 2001. 'Marriage.' In *Women in Twentieth-Century Britain*, edited by Ina Zweiniger-Bargielowska, 69–85. Harlow, UK: Pearson.

Osgerby, Bill. 1998. *Youth in Britain since 1945*. Oxford: Blackwell.

Marwick, Arthur. 1998. *The Sixties: Cultural Revolution in Britain, France, Italy and the United States, c1958–c1974*. Oxford University Press.

Mort, Frank. 2010. *Capital Affairs: London and the Making of the Permissive Society*. London: Yale University Press.

Radway, Janice. 1991. *Reading the Romance: Women, Patriarchy, and Popular Literature*. London: University of North Carolina Press.

Steedman, Carolyn. 1991. *Landscape for a Good Woman: A Story of Two Lives*. London: Rutgers University Press.

Summerfield, Penny. 1994. 'Women in Britain since 1945: Companionate Marriage and the Double Burden.' In *Understanding Post-War British Society*, edited by James Obelkevich and Peter Catterall, 58–72. London: Routledge.

Thomas, Nick. 2002. 'Challenging Myths of the 1960s: The Case of Student Protest in Britain.' *Twentieth Century British History* 13 (3): 277–297.

Tinkler, Penny. 1995. *Constructing Girlhood: Popular Magazines for Girls Growing Up in England, 1920–1950*. London: Taylor and Francis.

Tinkler, Penny. 2001. 'Growing Up: Girlhood.' In *Women in Twentieth-Century Britain*, edited by Ina Zweiniger-Bargielowska, 35–50. Harlow: Pearson.

Todd, Selina, and Hilary Young. 2012. 'Baby-boomers to "Beanstalkers": Making the Modern Teenager in Post-war Britain.' *Cultural and Social History* 9 (3): 451–467.

Varon, Jeremy, Michael S. Foley, and John McMillan. 2008. 'Time Is an Ocean: The Past and Future of the Sixties.' *The Sixties* 1 (1): 4–5.

Webb, Alisa. 2006. 'Constructing the Gendered Body: Girls, Health, Beauty, Advice, and the *Girls' Best Friend*, 1898–1899.' *Women's History Review* 15 (2): 253–275.

Webster, Wendy. 1998. *Imagining Home: Gender, 'Race' and National Identity, 1945–1964*. London: Routledge.

White, Cynthia. 1970. *Women's Magazines 1693–1968*. London: Michael Joseph.

Winship, Janice. 1987. *Inside Women's Magazines*. London: Rivers Oram Press.

PERIODICALS

Woman April 10, 1954–September 27, 1969.

10 The Gendering of Racism in Social Problem Films

Maggie Andrews

INTRODUCTION

The 60s is a period perceived by historians such as Arthur Marwick as one of Cultural Revolution (1999) when dominant values, attitudes and ideologies were, if not overthrown, at least challenged, stretched, undermined or dislodged; when respect for authority and hierarchies was apparently questioned and disrespect revelled in. Even those who question the degree to which the 60s was really an era of change acknowledge that critiques and challenges to hierarchies and dominant values bubbled to the surface and can be identified in a range of media texts. One key, identifiable area of questioning and shifting discursive frameworks in the era was race and race relations. The gendering of the racism in the sixties has been the focus of recent academic attention; for example, Wendy Webster's seminal book, *Imagining Home: Gender, Race and National Identity 1945–1964* (1998), explored the racially specific nature of post-war domestic ideals, while Lola Young's *Fear of the Dark Race, Gender and Sexuality in Cinema* (1995) drew upon a Media and Cultural Studies framework to analyse the conjunction of race, gender and sexuality in British film. In this work a strong reliance on discourse analysis to undertake close readings of texts was informed by an understanding of the historical context and imperialism. Bringing together the academic traditions of Women's History and Media Studies to look at the complexities of race, gender and class in the long 60s presents particular challenges and opportunities as this chapter will demonstrate through a focus on two films: *Sapphire* (1959) and *Flame on the Streets* (1962). Arguably, these films point to the contradictory and fluid nature of gendered discourses of racism in the era.

Analysis of these texts also serves to demonstrate why Women's History and Media and Film Studies are not the easiest companions. Trying to mesh together complex, contradictory and multiple women's histories of an era with the range of readings that polysemic popular media texts encourage necessitates complex approaches to both texts and historical eras, and suggests the need to tease out both contradictions and multiple layers of meaning in any popular text. The films this chapter focusses upon were deliberately discursive, structured to draw attention to different views and debates about race. At times, however, the texts attempted to nudge their audiences towards a liberal agenda, which saw racism as a sickness or a consequence of a lack of education. In *Sapphire*, for example, two policemen articulate differing positions in what was the contemporary debate over the 'race problem' as it was known. Similarly, *Flame in the Streets* articulated a range of differing views to encourage debate, reserving more extreme expressions of racism which led to street violence for those alienated from society. Indeed, I want to suggest when the debated terrain of historical analysis meets the contested field of textual analysis the consequence may of necessity be an untidy or messy history, as the historian attempts to juggle multiple interweaving and inter-related threads to structure material into the demands of academic history writing. An analysis of these films needs to combine Women's and Media History to navigate the inconsistencies and contradictions of interweaving, overlapping and interrelated threads of discourses around female sexuality, miscegenation, youth and domesticity. What follows, therefore, are a series of threads, all of which I would argue are important and relevant in understanding these films; they are not however finite, and readers will be able to identify other relevant threads worthy of consideration.

THE TEXTS IN THEIR CONTEXTS

Sapphire is structurally a whodunit; its opening shots showed the discovery of the body of a young student (Sapphire) on Hampstead Heath; the ensuing police investigation revealed her pregnancy and that she was 'passing' as white despite being mixed race. As the narrative unfolds, the senior policeman showed what was considered at the time to be a striking determination to carry his investigation to its conclusion. This conscientious investigation in the face of a potential black suspect who could have been charged with the crime was an indication of the film's liberal agenda. It transpired that Sapphire was murdered by her boyfriend's sister—Mildred Farr. The racism which motivated this killing was grounded in Mildred's own unfulfilled domestic life. Mildred and her twin daughters live with her parents, as she has been deserted by her husband. Her guilt was unequivocally established when she erupted into an uncontrollable diatribe of hate when Sapphire's brother entered her home, and touched her children's toys.

Flame in the Streets is a melodramatic narrative focussed on both the working and domestic life of Trade Unionist Jacko Palmer. He was initially portrayed as opposing racism in the workplace, as well as violence on the streets. He struggled, however, when faced with his daughter Kathie's relationship and plans to marry her black boyfriend and his unfulfilled wife, Nell's, overtly racist attitude to Peter. The narrative suggests Jacko's oratory was able to persuade the furniture-makers with whom he worked to accept

Afro-Caribbean Gomez's promotion but was more open-ended regarding Jacko's wife Nell. Domestic racism, it seemed, was more ingrained and harder to challenge. The closing image in the film portrayed Jacko and Nell standing on one side of a clearly divided kitchen while Kathie and Peter were on the other. This ending suggested both the potential for and the social discomfort in relation to mixed race relationships in 1960s Britain.

These films brought together a number of political, economic and cultural tensions which fed into historically located articulations of discourses of race and gender. The British Empire, which had been subject to much-justified criticism in the inter-war period, had, as Sonya Rose argues (2004), become increasingly fragile and incongruous during World War Two. The legacy of colonialism was, however, complex and multi-layered; Britain had relied upon citizens from a wide range of Commonwealth countries during the Second World War. Men and women from the Caribbean, India and Ireland, for example, had joined Canadians and Australians as both members of the fighting forces or on the Home Front to replace industrial workers who were fighting. As Kathleen Paul has pointed out, the passing of the 1948 British Nationality Act, which granted British Citizenship to all members of the Commonwealth, 'created a fundamental contradiction' (1997, xii) by enabling many people to enter Britain but not necessarily to really 'belong' or to be included in cultural constructions of the nation, something that quickly became apparent to the nearly five hundred, mainly ex-servicemen who arrived in the same year on the Empire Windrush. The reception that they and their families got from what they knew as the 'mother country' was in many cases much less than welcoming. As Roxy Harris astutely asserts, 'the colour problem was debated in parliament on television, in newspapers, magazines and on the radio. It was the big story of the 1950s' (2009, 484). The Notting Hill Riots (1958) and the racist murder of Kelso Cochrane walking home from hospital in 1959 did nothing to quell the growing anxieties about racial tensions.

Prime Minister Macmillan's 'Winds of Change Speech' in 1960 heralded the onset of the slow but steady dismantling of colonial relations and power structures which had been established in the nineteenth and early twentieth century; it was one of a clustering of elements which signalled discourses of race were shifting in post-war Britain. To some degree these were reactions to post-war economic migration from the Commonwealth in response to the labour shortages in both the National Health Service and London transport in the post-war era. The 1962 Commonwealth Immigration Act put upper limits on Commonwealth immigration and yet in 1964, Peter Griffiths won the Smethwick by-election against the national trend by utilising the racist elections slogan: 'If you want a nigger for your neighbour vote Labour'. Consequently, the Campaign Against Racial Discrimination was formed in 1964. The following year Malcolm X visited Britain, Martin Luther King was awarded an honorary doctorate from Newcastle University and the first race relations legislation was passed. Thus discourses of race and racism were varied, contradictory and contested: jazz music was popular, so was Enoch Powell's 'Rivers of Blood' speech in 1968, which with its dystopian prophesies of racial violence to come fanned the flames of racial tension.

Race in the 1950s and 1960s had become defined as a social problem and both *Sapphire* and *Flame in the Streets* can be identified as social problem films. If Lord Tyrrell, President of the British Board of Film Censors (BBFC) had felt able to loudly, but not necessarily accurately, proclaim in 1937 that: 'We may take pride in the fact that there is not a single film showing in London which deals with any of the burning issues of the day' (Hill 1986), the same could not be said of many of the films which were produced in the late 1950s and 60s, categorised as social realism or British New Wave, which intentionally engaged with contemporary social and political questions. Most significantly, all of these clusters of films privileged the representation of working-class life and explored subjects which would once have been considered taboo. John Hill argues that social problems were articulated in sexual terms (1986) with films containing a range of both moral panics and folk devils (Cohen 1973). Aberrant or perhaps threatening groups, whether working-class youth, young girls or black Britons, were codified by their supposedly identifiable sexual practices and were used to embody the social problems, although representations of such groups were not necessarily consistent and frequently contradictory. The films did not necessarily capture a mass market or immediate critical acclaim, judging by the BFI's Monthly Film Bulletin, but they are potentially rich source material for interrogation by historians, offering potential insights into what Raymond Williams described as the 'structure of feeling' of an era (1961). This is the contradictory and complex ways of seeing or envisioning which structured people's common sense and which give a sense of the complex and contradictory emotions that individuals living in the era would have had to navigate their way through. There are, however, challenges in analysing films which were produced in response to the Notting Hill Race Riots of 1958, and which brought racial tensions and anxieties over inter-racial sexual relationships into the public sphere, representing what Jim Pines has as described as one of those 'sporadic "moments" in which . . . race . . . featured prominently' (1981, 3). Given the imperialist construction of Britain as the 'mother country', there is a complex significance in the most virulent physically embodied versions of racism in both texts being articulated by mothers in apparent defence of the racial purity of their children's families and lives. They are indicative of an unravelling of discourses of race and Empire, particularly when linked to Enoch Powell's 1968 Rivers of Blood speech within which, as Wendy Webster points out, 'the story of the nation that he tells is about powerlessness and vulnerability in an English Street and it has at its centre the figure of a white woman' (1998, 185).

DISCOURSES OF RACE AND MISCEGENATION

Strategies to manage the anxieties created by female sexuality in nineteenth century and early twentieth century Britain frequently rested upon negation or displacement. As Jill Fields argues:

> Throughout the nineteenth century, depictions of black women in medical and scientific texts, and cultural representations emphasized their sexuality as animalistic, lustful, and deviant. Descriptions of black women's sexual difference that focused on their supposedly more primitive breasts, genitals and buttocks were a critical component in proving that Africans were a distinct, and distinctly lower race than Europeans (2006, 613) .

The discourse of black woman as eroticised beauty is evident in *Sapphire* who was codified as sexually promiscuous by her underwear—particularly her red underwear—and positioned as the binary opposite of Mildred Farr, whose quintessential white English femininity was affirmed by her job in a dairy. Narratively, black female sexuality can be seen as disruptive, responsible for beginning the chain of events which led to tragedy. Mildred's repressed white sexuality, however, did erupt in the violent stabbing of Sapphire; she was unable, it seems, to contain herself when Sapphire asked her if she could remember what it was like to be really wanted by a man. The repeated stabbing—or perhaps more accurately penetration—of Sapphire by Mildred's knife makes the killing a deeply sexual act. As Young points out: 'it is a socially aspirant sexually frustrated white woman . . . who becomes embittered and bigoted' (1995, 108). That white women were sexually frustrated is not, however, conveyed as entirely their fault; Jacko's wife Nell criticised the inadequacy of her husband's sexual skills; Mildred Farr was abandoned by her husband. Nevertheless, sexuality, which seethed, repressed beneath the surface of both these film texts, operated as a marker, an indication of aberrance and difference. For as Hall suggests, it is 'in the ritual exchange of stereotypes around the body between 'race', gender and sexuality, in which racism is deployed in its most violent and destructive fantasies' (2006, 20).

In exploring the inter-relationship between gender and race, these films provide important if uncomfortable source material for twentieth century women's historians to work with, for they articulated not merely a particular individual's sexual anxieties but also society's unsaid, unseen and repressed (Jackson 1981). The discomfort comes in viewing, with twenty-first century sensibilities, material which by the standards of their day can be seen as radical in attempting to confront and critique racism, yet perpetuated essentialist discourses of racial difference. Despite 'passing' for white Sapphire, for example, was signified as black by her love of music and dance, expressed in the blatant essentialism of the Tulip Club owner who remarks that all 'lily skins' can be identified by their response to the jungle rhythms of black music. The reference to music and dancing suggested racially different attitudes to the body and sexuality. The structuring absence framing much of the racist dialogue was a perception that the black body and black sexuality was more animalistic. As Young points out, *Flame in the Streets* makes a number of references to the animalistic or the transgressive sexuality of the black men within the film; Gomez's pregnant wife Judy remarked that she feels like she was carrying an elephant (1995, 107). The physicality of Jacko's wife Nell's racist sentiments were expressed through her repugnance at the idea of potential sexual activity between her daughter and her black boyfriend. She screamed at her daughter thus:

> I am ashamed of you when I think of you and that black man sharing the same bed.
> It makes my stomach turn.
> I feel sick.
> You're no worse than the whores in the high street.

Her abhorrence was also expressed over the prospect of mixed race children; she decried the prospect of Kathie having black babies. Discourses of black sexual promiscuity invariably leak into anxieties over miscegenation which Young (1995), echoing Laura Stoler's work on nineteenth century colonialism, points out, are an essential element of policing inter-racial sexuality. Seeking to ensure racial purity has a long history in the maintenance of white supremacy (1989, 634–60 in Rose 2004, 254). Fears of miscegenation were indeed a key strand in interweaving histories of gender and race in Britain in the twentieth century (see Bland 2005 and Rose 2004). They were, for example, strongly articulated by the birth control campaigner Marie Stopes in the 1930s who suggested mixed-race children should be sterilised (Rich 1990, 68). Caballero has asserted with reference to the decades between 1930s and 1950s that those who engaged in mixed-race relationships in Britain 'did so against social discourses and a set of attitudes which, particularly at an official institutional level, positioned them as unnatural, unsettling and unwanted' (2012, 49).

Perhaps unsurprisingly, then, children of mixed-race parentage haunted these films as the threatening 'other', though they never had an active role and were rarely seen. Sapphire, whose father was a white doctor and mother a black dancer, was shown as nothing more than a corpse—investigated, spoken about, but not seen. Comments about her suggest both communities perceived her as deceitful in 'passing' as white. Her premature death, her body found by a young family on a walk on Hampstead Heath, was an affirmation that miscegenation was a deadly threat to society. Interestingly, interracial relationships also serve as signifiers of the more liberated attitude to sexuality of the younger college generation who suggest a growing if slightly muted sexual freedom. In *Sapphire* David appears to have been genuinely unbothered by Sapphire's race and their college friends appear shocked by the racism of landladies and many others they interact with.

YOUTH: ROMEO AND JULIET

Anxiety over miscegenation and racial tensions were predicated upon strong, though historically inaccurate, representations within the films which suggested that the black and white communities were culturally and physically separate. There was more generally a noticeable paucity of representations of diversity and hybridity or any sense of the newly emerging post-colonial culture in popular film and media in the 1960s or for that matter in other areas of arts and literature. Caballero has noted that particularly in some geographical areas such as Newport: 'despite the warnings of violence, ostracism, hostility and isolation, women and men in Britain still actively and habitually crossed racial boundaries and formed relationships and families' (2012, 37). Indeed, Stephen Bourne's oral history interviews of wartime Britain suggested that in some areas, interracial relationships were accepted unproblematically (2010). At one level it could be argued that these films did little to shift the notion of a racially divided Britain, but rather reinforced the problematic discursive construction that there was a 'colour problem' in Britain in this era and this was a consequence of black people's presence in the UK. This is not, however, the whole story, for the younger generation are portrayed as engaged in interracial relationships, albeit ones which frequently end in tragedy. Interestingly, Smelik points out that in another social problem film, *A Taste of Honey,* which focuses on the plight of the pregnant young girl, its moments of happiness are situated in the interracial romance' (2003, 58). Indeed, within both *Flame in the Streets,* and I would argue, to some degree in *Sapphire,* interracial relationships are portrayed as part of the youthful sexual revolution.

Kathie in *Flame in the Streets* was a young woman who gave voice to different, perhaps idealised, discourses of femininity within which interracial relationships were signifiers of women's sexual self-determination. As a teacher who worked in an inner-city multi-racial school she became emotionally involved with a supply teacher, Peter, who had emigrated from Jamaica. Kathie is represented as aware this relationship was socially frowned upon and displayed a little anxiety about society's reactions to them. However, she remained not merely idealistic, but emotionally committed to change, seeing the right to a relationship with whomever she pleased, across racial boundaries, as her 'cultural revolution'. She criticised her mother's account of the material difficulties that she would face in interracial marriage. Indeed, she saw her mother's views and attitudes as out of date, old-fashioned and not relevant to her generation. To Kathie, in the words of Bob Dylan, 'The times they are a-changing' (Rosenstone 1969). The attitudes of the young were of particular significance because the long 60s is the cultural moment when youth was shifting to become more culturally central, more idealised and desirable. An example of these changing times can be identified in the portrayal of black and white children playing together in street games in *Flame in the Streets*. Indeed these children, untainted by the prejudices of their elders, built a bonfire together on Guy Fawkes Day; both racial groups are portrayed as involved in preparation for a traditional celebration of democracy and Britishness. With these children, there is the suggestion of hope for the future, albeit one that is dashed by racist violence.

The children's innocence and lack of prejudice chimes with the use of the Romeo and Juliet motif to both explore and critique racism within the films. The tragic 'unlikely couple' who are divided by family, class, racial, religious or age differences is a staple of western drama and arguably, cinema frequently constructs interethnic relationships as a tragedy which usually ends badly. Although as Smelik points out, 'The Romeo and Juliet motif places the locally embedded interethnic love relation within a familiar framework for the western spectator: the great tragedies of the Renaissance. This allows the filmmaker to represent the interethnic love relation as a classical drama of human pain, suffering and death' (Smelik 2003, 73). At one level, the use of this motif therefore can be seen as a strategy to engage the audience. However, it also framed the way in which the audience engaged with the text. It predisposes them to see all the interracial relationships as liable to end in doom or death. Indeed *Sapphire* opens with the discovery of Sapphire's corpse, and news of her death was something with which her boyfriend and fiancé, David, was literally weighed down. His shoulders were almost permanently hunched in mourning; his last line in the film was to affirm to Sapphire's brother that he really had loved her and to draw the audience's attention to the tragedy of the narrative of their relationship. Near the end of *Flame in the Streets*, secondary characters, the Afro-Caribbean Gomez and his white wife who were expecting their first child, were driven off in an ambulance after he has been injured in street violence. Despite his promotion at work early in the film, and the imminent arrival of their first child, their relationship was also steeped in tragedy.

The Romeo and Juliet motif also serves to draw attention to the youth, inexperience and perhaps naiveté of the interracial couples at the heart of each narrative. In *Flame in the Streets* Kathie and Peter are first seen at the swimming pool where he is shown teaching her to dive during half-term. They are then portrayed playing imaginary games, fantasising about what they would do if they were in Jamaica. These childlike activities, which emphasise their youth, can be seen as a strategy to avoid any representation of the black male as a potential rapist, an all too frequent motif in film and popular culture. It does, however, open the way for the black male characters to be seen as emasculated (Young 1995). A historical precedent of white men regarding rape as a right may also lie behind the unprepossessing character of David in *Sapphire* who, oppressed by his family, appeared incapable of taking control of his own life: his greatest misdemeanour was to attend the cinema during college term time, against his father's wishes. This scenario emphasised his youthful position and has added poignancy when it is remembered that in 1959, when this film was released, David if still under the age of 21 would not have been able to vote or indeed to marry without parental approval and permission.

Youth was not, however, unequivocally liberal in its attitudes within these texts. In *Flame in the Streets*, it was gangs of self-proclaimed white-trash, Teddy boys, who took up a menacing presence towards anyone non-white on the streets of Notting Hill. It was their actions which eventually led to violence on the streets. Working-class youth were therefore rather more problematically conveyed through the trope of youth as 'trouble' (Osgerby 1997). The four main protagonists, the youthful couples in inter-racial relationships, were significantly all educated, underlining the film's liberal agenda that education would combat racism. David and Kathie were both from working-class homes; they were the beneficiaries of the 1944 Education Act and the consequent expansion of secondary and higher education. They had responded to their parents' aspirational ideals and gone to college. Their rejection of their parents' values and prejudices, however, gave a voice to different and idealised discourses suggesting at least a questioning of hegemonic attitudes hinting at a cultural revolution beginning to take place in the long 60s. The audience too were being gently nudged towards a sense that through education racial tensions could be eliminated. The desire for change was not, however, restricted to youth; but what change meant, what needed changing, how change could be idealised, was envisaged very differently by different generations. The mothers and families of these college kids dreamed of a more mundane or materialistic future in which houses all had indoor bathrooms and children would not face the economic insecurity and hardship they had lived through when brought up in the depression years of the 1930s. Kynaston has argued the idea of family was at the core of post-war ideals in the 1950s: 'food, jobs and homes: such was the holy trinity'. This was to be

> the formula for the Tory votes and a widespread almost wholly welcome sense of security after the tumultuous upheavals and painful privations of the 1940s . . . for most people the future, not just in the kitchen, was indisputably modern—yet modern, they hoped, within a familiar reassuring setting' (2010, 697).

The white, working-class, aspirational parents who had struggled to get their children into higher education saw their dreams threatened by inter-racial relationships.

DOMESTIC RACISM

The family that was at the heart of British post-war culture, of the ideal of nation, of post-war planning and the new welfare state was, ideologically speaking at least, a very white one. As has already been pointed out, in both these films when the whiteness of these homes was questioned, virulent racism erupted. No wonder that the very many Commonwealth citizens who in 1948 had had their right to come to Britain affirmed could not really feel that they belonged in British culture. Anne McClintock has pointed out that

> nations are often symbolically depicted through the iconography of familial and domestic location, as domestic lineage and pedigree such as the 'Family of Nations', 'motherland' and 'fatherland', the British and Commonwealth, the 'Royal Family' and the US 'First Family'. In these ways, the family trope has been used to naturalize national hierarchy as a fusion of domestic interests' (McClintock 1995, 357).

Whatever the symbolic depiction of domesticity in the fifties and indeed the sixties, for many there was a gap between the ideal and lived experience. In *Flame in the Streets*, Nell's opposition to her daughter marrying Jamaican-born Peter rested not merely on his race, but on her desperate desire that her daughter should not have a life like hers. Nell was one of the many women for whom after the Second World War marriage became almost universal (Thane 1994) even if it was less than ideal. The domestic space, a place called home, was during the Second World War both disrupted and elevated as an icon to be fought for and protected. Nevertheless, a happy family life and domestic bliss proved a somewhat unattainable ideal in the post-war era for many women. The austerity years and housing crisis that followed the outbreak of peace meant that the home that was desired by many was realised by only a very few. For many women domesticity came with no inside sanitation, involved living with relations or living in a subdivided house, sharing taps and toilets with many other families.

Domestic comfort was Nell's aspiration for change in the 1960s; the modernity she longed for, not unreasonably, was an inside bathroom. She was one of those women who was tenuously clinging on to the individualist and consumerist, but unfulfilled fantasies of mid–twentieth century family life. In the 1950s and 60s Britain was in the midst of the housing crisis, even though between 1947 and 1966, the proportion of owner-occupier households had increased from 27 to 46.7% and state housing increased from 12 to 25.7% (MacFarlane 1981, 62). The increasing number of couples who sought to set up separate households at a young age, alongside a significant number of older people staying put in familiar surroundings, added pressure to the limited housing stocks. The population had grown from 38 million in 1921 to 46 million in the 1960s; the number of private households doubled from 8.7 million to 14.9 million. Wartime had taken its toll on the housing of Great Britain; nevertheless, a significant amount of housing stock was old and Ministry of Housing and local authorities classed approximately 1.8 million houses as unfit for human habitation in 1967 (MacFarlane 1981, 63).

Racism in these films was most strongly articulated by those with unsatisfactory domestic lives; significantly, both films focus upon respectable
working-class families who have their own front doors. They, however,
saw their own and their children's respectability and material well-being
as threatened by mixed-race relationships. An acute shortage of housing
was interwoven with racial prejudice to create particular problems for
interracial couples seeking housing in the 50s and 60s, something that
was explained to Kathie in *Flame in the Streets* initially by her mother,
but more precisely by Gomez's heavily pregnant wife. Judy lived in one
room in a divided house, having been unable to find better accommodation which will accept her and her black husband. Although the Rach-
man scandal did not hit the headlines until 1963, many were aware of
the practices of the activities of unscrupulous landlords like him. Rach-
man had, in the wake of the Conservative government's abolition of rent
controls in 1957, bought properties in Notting Hill, forced tenants out
and rented them to African Afro-Caribbean families who could find no
other accommodation. Immigrants consequently found themselves living
in some of the most squalid and overcrowded slum conditions in Europe.
The respectability and the capacity to rent those homes which defined
families as respectable was perceived to be threatened by interracial relationships and miscegenation. Rachman-style slums were not the life that
Nell wanted for her daughter, nor the one Mildred Farr aspired to for her
family. The physically or verbally violent gendered racism which erupted
onto the screen within these films was grounded in the very real material
struggles of working-class mothers.

Young critiques both these films suggesting a 'major flaw of the liberal
discourse of social realism of this period is the attempt to explain away
racism by locating it in individuals who are already pathologised "others"'
(1995, 10); but these individuals were the product of economic, social and
cultural forces which were out of their control. Nell's domesticity appeared
to be unappreciated, she did not feel needed and if not physically deserted
like Mildred Farr, Sapphire's murderer, she was emotionally deserted by
her husband. These women had bought the Cinderella myth, the dream of
domestic fulfilment, but prior to the second wave feminism of the late 60s
and early 70s, they were unable to find a language to articulate their anger
and discontent. Looked at from this perspective, racism became the public
discourse which they could draw upon to articulate their own personal
anger, grief and dissatisfaction which literally erupted into physical and
verbal violence. Arguably, too little attention has been given to how the
discourses of race and racism are played out in the home, where they are
rejected, adopted, stretched and renegotiated in private spaces as much as
public ones. Women's History's focus has frequently been on the personal,
the domestic and private; Veronica Strong-Boag points out that 'What
occurs out of sight, hidden away in bedroom, bathroom and kitchen, needs
to be recovered not only for itself, but because it influences, directly and

indirectly, activities carried out in public realms' (1978 , 4). Indeed, I would argue that the very unsatisfactory domestic lives of many of the women who articulated this gendered racism needs to be considered, not in terms of their individual pathology but as crucial ingredients in the articulation of racism in the 1950s and 60s.

CONCLUSION

Together these films suggest the need for an analysis combining Women's and Media History to navigate the interconnected threads of: domesticity, motherhood, sexuality, miscegenation, class, burgeoning youth cultures and female sexuality, which were interwoven to contribute to the structure of feeling shaping the lives of those who lived through the long 60s. This chapter has only been able to touch the surface of these threads. The untidy, or what is sometimes termed messy, history that has emerged from using the two films as a prism on the era is arguably a reflection of the untidy, contradictory, fluid nature of gendered racism in the long 60s.

BIBLIOGRAPHY / SOURCES

Bland, Lucy. 2005. 'White Women and Men of Colour: Miscegenation Fears in Britain after the Great War.' *Gender & History* 17 (1): 29–61.

Bourne, Stephen. 2010. *Mother Country: Britain's Black Community on the Home Front, 1939–45.* Stroud, UK: the History Press.

Caballero, Chamion. 2012. 'From "Draughtboard Alley" to "Brown" Britain: The "Ordinariness" of Mixedness in British Society.' In *International Perspectives on Racial and Ethnic Mixedness and Mixing*, edited by Rosalind Edwards, Suki Ali, Chamion Caballero, and Miri Song. London: Routledge.

Cohen, Stan. 1973. *Folk Devils and Moral Panics.* St Albans: Paladin.

Fields, Jill. 2006. 'From Black Venus to Blonde Venus: The Meaning of Black Lingerie.' *Women's History Review* 15 (4): 611– 623.

Hall, Stuart. 2006. 'Black Diaspora in Britain: Three Moments in Post-War History.' *History Workshop Journal* 61 (Spring 2006): 1–24.

Harris, Roxy. 2009. 'Black British, Brown British and British Cultural Studies.' *Cultural Studies* 23 (4): 483–512.

Hill, John. 1986. *Sex, Class and Realism: British Cinema 1956–1963.* London: BFI Publishing.

Jackson, Rosemary. 1981. *Fantasy: Literature of Subversion.* London: Routledge.

Kynaston, David. 2010. *Family Britain, 1951–57.* London: Bloomsbury.

MacFarlane, Leslie. 1981. *Issues in British Politics.* Harlow, UK: Longman.

Marwick, Arthur. 1999. *The Sixties: Social and Cultural Transformation in Britain, France, Italy and the USA.* Oxford Paperbacks.

McClintock, Anne. 1995. *Imperial Leather: Race, Gender and Sexuality in the Colonial Contest.* London: Routledge.

Osgerby, William. 1997. *Youth in Britain since 1945.* Oxford: Wiley-Blackwell.

Paul, Kathleen. 1997. *Whitewashing Britain: Race and Citizenship in the Postwar Era.* Cornell University Press.

Pines, Jim. 1981. 'Blacks in Film: The British Angle.' *Multi-Racial Education* 9 (2, Spring).

Rich, Paul. 1990. *Race and Empire in British Politics*. Cambridge University Press.

Rose, Sonya. 2004. *Which People's War?* Oxford University Press.

Rosenstone, Robert. 1969. '"The Times They Are A-Changin": The Music of Protest.'. *The ANNALS of the American Academy of Political and Social Science* 382 (1): 131–144.

Smelik, Anneke. 2003. 'For Venus Smiles Not in a House of Tears: Interethnic Relation in European Cinema.' *European Journal of Cultural Studies* 6 (1): 55–74.

Stoler, Ann Laura. 1989. 'Tensions of Empire: Colonial Control and Visions of Rule.' *American Ethnologist* 16 (4): 609–621.

Strong-Boag, Veronica. 1978. 'Raising Clio's Consciousness: Women's History and Archives in Canada.' *Archivaria: Journal of the Association of Canadian Archivists* 6 (Summer).

Thane, Pat. 1994. 'Women since 1945.' In *20th Century British Economic, Social and Cultural Change*, edited by Paul Johnson, 392–410. London: Longman.

Webster, Wendy. 1998. *Imagining Home: Gender, Race and National Identity, 1945–64*. London: Routledge.

Williams, Raymond. (1961) 1966. *The Long Revolution*. Harmondsworth, UK: Pelican Books.

Young, Lola. 1995. *Fear of the Dark: 'Race', Gender and Sexuality in the Cinema*. London: Routledge.

FILMOGRAPHY

Sapphire (1959)
Flame on the Streets (1962)

11 "Should Women Be Bus Drivers?"
Defending a Permanent Position for Women on the Buses in ATV's Regional Television News, 1963–1979

Gillian Murray

INTRODUCTION: WOMEN BUS WORKERS

Remembered as an iconic war-worker, the struggles of the female bus worker to secure a permanent position in a male-dominated industry in the second half of the twentieth century made her an ideal character for visual journalism and for ATV's regional news to illustrate a range of social questions raised by (married) women's employment. The contested position of the female bus worker was evident in local print and broadcast media in the Midlands during the 1960s and 1970s. The regional television news programme *ATV Today* broadcast six items on female bus workers between 1963 and 1979. Three visual themes were apparent in these news stories, namely: the connections made between women's physical mobility and social mobility, how the media maintained elements of novelty in framing the female bus worker, and how the synthesis of feminine and masculine tropes in the images studied changed over time. This chapter will analyze the changes in the gendered discourses used to support women working on the buses in contemporary regional news broadcasts and demonstrate that the frequency with which the television news featured women bus workers was symptomatic not only of the contested position of women in Midland bus companies, but also their effectiveness as visual subjects in framing discussions of 'women's changing place' in popular television journalism. Straddling the 'progressive era' of the 1960s and 70s allows exploration of the social and cultural influences within this process.

The increasing numbers of women entering paid employment outside the home has been widely recognized in women's history as a central social trend of the twentieth century (Smith Wilson 2005; Cowman and Jackson 2005; Todd 2005; Holloway 2005; Rowbotham 1999). Practitioners of women's film, television and media history have been interested in examining whether this social trend was apparent in cultural representations of female workers and what this demonstrates about the relationship between women, the media and social change (Bell and Williams 2010; Thumim 2002; Gledhill and Swanson 1996). As has been highlighted by Deborah Valenze in reference to female mill workers in the nineteenth century, an integral part of the social history of women's paid employment has been the visibility of women as workers, made apparent in media commentary (Valenze 1995, 97–103). In a twentieth-century context, Penny Tinkler's work on women smokers demonstrated the importance of 'the visual dimensions of social and cultural life' (Tinkler 2006, 5). In post-war Britain, the contradiction inherent in the idealisation of women as wives and mothers and the pressures on women to take up at least part-time employment provided the context for broader media debate on 'women's place' in society.

Data from census returns recorded the percentage of women working as tram and bus drivers, nationally, at 0.2% in 1951 and 1961, rising to 0.5% in the 1971 returns whilst comparable figures for women working as bus and tram conductors were significantly higher. Women made up 27% of all those working as conductors in 1951, 40.7% in 1961 and 40.6% in 1971. In contrast to the national trend, the percentage of women working as conductors in the Midlands fell from 69% in 1951 to 48.9% in 1961 and again to 30.5% in 1971.[1] Against a trend of rising numbers of women in the labour market, these figures show how gender and region remained significant in shaping the employment of women despite the legislative interventions of the Equal Pay Act (1970) and the Sex Discrimination Act (1975). Historically, certain areas of the Midlands had maintained high levels of female employment (Castle 1986; Grey Osterud 1986). These figures, however, suggest that this did not necessarily make it easier for women to break into male-dominated industries.

RESEARCHING THE ATV ARCHIVE

This chapter makes use of an archive of regional television news produced for the Midlands by Associated Television (ATV) between 1956 and 1981. In television history there has been relatively little research into the companies on the ITV network when compared with histories of the BBC, and less still into regional television. Natasha Vall has suggested that studying regional broadcasting is an effective means of questioning 'the region as a cultural space' and the limits of an area's 'cultural coherence' (Vall 2011, 7). Moreover, as Su Holmes has demonstrated, there has been little consideration of the role of 'ordinary' people in television history (Holmes 2006, 284–303). Considering the appearances of 'ordinary' women in the regional news is particularly productive, since as Patricia Holland has suggested, regional news dealt in completely different 'topics and imagery' compared to its national counterparts and consequently proposes it may have been more effective in engaging women (Holland 1987, 142). In paying attention to the constructions of 'ordinariness' of female bus workers and the extent to which the regional news maintained a distinctive regional address, this study will begin to address this gap.

The archived items are not complete programmes, but the film inserts which were scheduled into the evening news programme. Since the news programmes were broadcast live, the link segments and voiceovers are irretrievable. Historical research using the archival material originated by the companies contracted to the ITV network has a distinct set of challenges compared to similar research using the BBC archive; audio-visual evidence is relatively plentiful, but there remains a lack of 'written traces' for ITV programmes (Holmes 2007, 69–70). Working with these audio-visual fragments requires the researcher to start with the images and work outwards to reconstruct their historical context. Although centred on print media, recent discussions on ephemera resonate with the challenges of working with the material in the ATV archive. James Mussell's article, 'The Passing of Print', reminds scholars that ephemera are meant to be forgotten, and thus argues that when it accidentally survives it provokes a:

> distinct affectual shock that accompanies the rediscovery of something we had forgotten: this is not just nostalgia, an opportunity to recollect and reframe a moment from the past, but also a peculiar reminder of the constructedness of memory. . . . Of the different forms of printed ephemera, newspapers are a key resource for restoring the clutter of the everyday (Mussell 2012, 80–85).

Mussell's approach can be usefully applied to ATV's film inserts produced for the regional television news. The collection holds records of what have become known as defining moments of the late twentieth century, such as the Ugandan Asian crisis and the Miners' Strike. However, arguably the strength of the collection lies in the mundane, forgotten visions of the twentieth century. Restoring the 'clutter' to discussions of women's media history holds immense potential to challenge the accepted historiography of contemporary life in the region. This approach resonates with the project of recovering women 'hidden from history' as outlined by Sheila Rowbotham in the 1970s (1974), but also in more recent discussions by Joanne Meyerowitz, who has argued that practitioners should move beyond reductive readings of mass culture, such as those described in Betty Friedan's *The Feminine Mystique* (1963), to provide a nuanced picture of women's relationship with the media (Meyerowitz 1993, 1455–1482). Lastly, it is important to recognize that the ephemeral nature of the production of television news places limitations on what can be reconstructed from the television news archive. Having become detached from their production documents, a collection of the staff newspaper *ATV Newsheet* and contemporary local print media have been used to begin to reconstruct the context of the audio-visual material.

THE ICONOGRAPHY OF THE FEMALE BUS WORKER

The history of the making of the female bus worker's iconic image is an important aspect of the history of women's employment on the buses

Figure 11.1 Reg Harcourt interviews bus drivers and conductors at Walsall, May 23, 1963. *Midlands News*. Courtesy of Media Archive for Central England/ITV.

and is key to the three visual themes which will be commented on in this chapter. Firstly, the connections made between women's physical mobility and social mobility in the visualization of the female worker has been discussed in numerous historical contexts (Tinkler and Krasnick, 2008; Otto and Rocco, 2011). In her discussion of the invention of the New Woman in print culture during the *fin de siècle*, Michelle Elizabeth Tusan argued that as 'the invention of the identity of the New Woman took place in the women's press . . . Simultaneously, a counter image of the New Woman as a dystopic vision of a society gone wrong was promoted by the mainstream press' (Tusan 1998, 169). Tusan's point marks an important comparison with discussions of the female bus worker. By discussing the advantages and disadvantages of the female bus worker, she became a pivot for discussions of women's 'progress' at large. Situating the female bus worker within this tradition thus adds a valuable dynamic to the discussion, as it reveals how regional news providers used themes present in local industrial disputes to open up broader discussions of social change.

The second visual theme is an exploration of how the media maintained elements of novelty in their framing the female bus driver. Women were first employed as bus drivers and conductors during the First World War.

Figure 11.2   Anne Diamond interviews Stevie Fade on her decision to give up nursing and become a bus driver, Oxford, November 14, 1979. ATV Today. Courtesy of Media Archive for Central England/ITV.

Historians have described how the sight of women doing 'men's work' in masculine uniforms and visible positions of authority on the city streets was 'striking and shocking' for contemporaries (Jerram 2011, 120–121; Braybon and Summerfield 1987, 33–34). The professional portraits of these women in their uniforms included in Gail Braybon and Penny Summerfield's *Out of the Cage* indicates that the women working in these positions wanted to record their time in uniform (Braybon and Summerfield 1987, 33, 92). These images have a personal, memorialising quality, but the inspiration behind them, capturing the anomaly of the woman in uniform, remained powerful and was later harnessed in the production of propaganda posters for public consumption in the Second World War. One example, painted by E. H. Kennington for the London Transport Board in 1944, depicts a female conductor in a thoughtful pose. Titled 'Seeing it Through', it was one of six posters which focussed on the 'heroism of ordinary men and women' in a 'slightly monumental style' (Darracott and Loftus 1971, 41). Comparing these images reveals how a genuinely startling image to the public and workers alike could be recontextualized, maintaining its extraordinary quality across time, even if the female bus worker was not a 'new' sight to the public.

The third visual theme analyzes how the synthesis of masculine and feminine tropes in the visualization of the female bus driver changed over time. In their discussion of the cultural representation of the female war worker Christine Gledhill and Gillian Swanson have emphasised how at times images of women's war work were framed to provide 'the means by which it was possible to imagine the working woman without disrupting the image of woman as homemaker' (Gledhill and Swanson 1996, 1). Likewise, Penny Summerfield has explained that the heroism of women's war work was visually 'indicated by the "unfeminine" settings in which she was required to work and the signs that she was performing successfully there' (Summerfield 1991, 78). She has traced similar ideas in women's memories of war work, in descriptions of their 'creative synthesis of "masculine" and "feminine" styles' in their uniforms, hair and make-up (Summerfield 1991, 91). The success of the image of the female war worker lay in its ability to capture this synthesis of the masculine and the feminine.

THE 1960S: RECONTEXTUALIZING THE ICONIC WAR WORKER

The 1960s have been discussed as a period where television production was 'masculinized'. Holland defines the 'masculine turn' within the context of gendered understandings of the visual: 'The visual has continued to be linked with frivolity, triviality and a lack of seriousness, as well as an excess of emotion and even with femininity, which in the 1950s, itself had a distinctly frivolous air' (Holland 2006, 3). The feminine and the frivolous had been an important aspect of establishing television and television audiences in the 1950s, but increasingly came under criticism in the 1960s: 'Once television was fully established, as it was by the mid-sixties—the 1962 Pilkington Report and the advent of the third channel, BBC2, in 1964 being evidence of this—it seems that it must also, by virtue of its public centrality, be masculinized' (Thumim 2004, 79). Janet Thumim has discussed how this had consequences for 'feminine' programme content as well as implications for women working behind the screen and in vision on screen (Thumim 2004, 79–81). This was also apparent in ATV's regional television news programming. Pat Cox, who had read the *Midlands News* bulletin since it was first broadcast in 1956, left in 1965. Following a scheduling overhaul in October 1964, the regional news bulletin (6.07–6.15 p.m.) was followed by the regional news magazine *ATV Today* broadcast between 6.15 p.m. and 6.35 p.m., which preceded *Crossroads* from 6.35–7.00 p.m. This meant sacrificing the weekly news magazine programmes *Midland Montage* and monthly current affairs programme *Look Around*, which had had a strong female presence, with Pat Cox and Jenny Martin as reporters, and Julia James working as director. After 1964 a group of five male reporters, Lionel Hampden, Reg Harcourt, Barri Haynes, David Lloyd and John Swallow, dominated ATV's Midland news. The aim to cultivate an investigative journalist style is apparent in the staff newspaper, which described them as: 'the programme's presenters by night and the investigators by day' (*ATV Newsheet* August 1966, 6:8, 6).

Despite this turn, television news continued to be deeply structured by its position as a hook into the evening television schedule and the need to appeal to a local family audience. Using 'ordinary' Midlanders on screen provided a means for the regional news teams to anchor themselves as the region's news provider. The construction of the 'ordinary' Midlander at this time was based on the white, affluent working class who the regional news teams had ready access to at Midlands' factory gates. Since it was more difficult for news teams to approach the doorsteps of local terraced housing, the female worker was often constructed as an equivocal figure transcending her domestic and social roles; this is especially evident in the appearances of female factory workers. In contrast, as will be argued, female bus workers were presented as ciphers of social change. The regional television news may have sought male reporters and presenters to embody authority within the news programme, but the women of the Midlands appeared widely in their news reports, cutting across the news hierarchy. These diverse appearances of 'ordinary' women provide an index of ATV's imagined female audience and a means to explore how a domestic address continued to structure the regional television news.

The first regional television news story to feature female bus workers was an item broadcast in May 1963 over a decision by the Walsall Corporation Transport Undertaking not to recruit women platform staff (*Midlands News* May 23, 1963): ATV broadcast a two and a half minute report on the story, including an interview with Chairman of the Walsall Corporation Transport Undertaking Councillor L. B. Parkes, two female conductors and a male bus driver. The workers all stated their opposition to the new management policy, although no evidence has been found to date that this issue was formally taken up by their union. Visually the item makes a clear distinction between the management and workers' perspectives. The chairman is framed against the windows of high street shops, while the workers are neatly grouped in two rows, in uniform, at the station. The exact age of the women in this item is unknown, but they were conceivably older married women, the demographic central to the increase in women's employment during this period. They provide a poignant reminder that working-class social mobility within this period was based on the rise of the 'working wife' as well as the male affluent worker.

Turning to the reported testimony of the news item Councillor Parkes argued that men were being prioritised in light of local unemployment and the perceived longevity of the male career. Councillor Parkes made a similar statement in the *Birmingham Evening Mail and Despatch* (May 22, 1963, 9). The attack on female bus conductors must be understood in the context of an underfunded industry and a loss of status for male employees. For men, working as a conductor was an important step towards working their way up to the position of bus driver. John Rule has described the status of the post-war 'busman' as in decline compared to his inter-war predecessors; heavily reliant on overtime, which at times made up half of their take-home pay. This also contributed to discrimination against black and Asian employees at a number of bus companies (Rule 2001, 227–228). Thus, in accounting for the change in policy towards women the Undertaking drew upon dystopian visions of male unemployment and emasculation.

Unlike the print media reports, the television recordings by interviewing the workers themselves provided an insight into how women's position in industry could be publically supported. One of the female conductors responded to the relatively high rates of unemployment in the area by explaining: 'There are plenty other jobs if the men care to look for them' (*Midlands News* May 23, 1963). This was the bluntest statement of women's entitlement to work and a rejection of the notion of prioritising male breadwinners. It undermined the 'common sense' logic of the industry in the era, that is, that women should only seek to work in feminized positions as bus workers. It is important to note that the male bus drivers interviewed by Reg Harcourt publically supported their female colleagues. A second female conductor and a male driver presented their support for female conductors with reference to women's war work, stating: 'If they were glad of them [women] in the war, why can't they be glad of them now?' (*Midlands News* May 23, 1963). This declaration of support drew upon the public visibility of the female bus worker in wartime and exemplifies how this visibility was acknowledged as *proof* that women could do the job.

This testimony from the bus workers can be usefully compared to a vox pop item filmed in 1965 *(ATV Today* July 7, 1965). This item was an example of how the news teams revisited questions raised by local industrial disputes, but as 'soft' news items disconnected from a particular event, and thus framed them as broader social issues. The piece was set on-board a moving bus and opened with an interview with a male conductor followed by a segment with various vox pops of bus passengers. This meant the piece made a visually neat progression from the conductor along the bus to the passengers. The participants in the item were all asked the question: 'Should women be bus drivers?' The range of views expressed by the public and selected for broadcast by the news team were remarkably similar to the 1963 item, suggesting continuity in ATV's editorial line. Those who were sceptical about the employment of women as bus drivers cited women's lack of physical strength and ability to cope under pressure, which suggests that for some, female bus workers still required 'extraordinary' heroic qualities beyond the capabilities of 'ordinary' women. Reference to women's war work appeared in two out of the six vox pop responses and two out of three responses which supported female bus drivers. Like the 1963 item, the reference to war work was used to undermine all other criticisms of female bus drivers, with comments such as: 'They did it while the war was on, what's the difference now?' The memory of the work of the iconic wartime bus worker appeared as a frame of reference for the public, which the news team could safely broadcast as the progressive edge of public opinion. Together these news items suggest that the 1960s was a transitory moment for the female bus worker, a point where her 'extraordinariness' was remarked upon by some but normalized by others as men and women defended her right to work.

The framing of support for the female bus workers within a discussion of women's experience of war work raises questions over how this 'memory' was informed and constructed. Summerfield has questioned whether a focus on women in only four out of the fifty most popular war films produced in the 1950s and 1960s demonstrates 'public amnesia' over women's participation in the war effort. Although, in her conclusion she noted that films were by no means the only 'vectors of memory' in the field of cultural production (Summerfield 2009, 935–957). The evidence cited above suggests that ephemeral forms of media production were also important 'vectors' of cultural memory. The regional news provided a space for the re-presentation of the female bus worker, revealing how the memory of women's war work was bound up with subsequent commentary on how the experience of war changed society.

The idea that the First and Second World Wars were significant agents of social change, although now contested, was exemplified by Arthur Marwick's work in the 1960s and 1970s. As well as his written publications, a film he made for the Open University with Richard Dunn and Lisa Pontecorvo in 1970, 'Emancipation of Women 1890–1930', revealed his perspective on this aspect of social history (Dunn and Marwick 1970 British Pathé News). The film featured footage of women working as conductors during the First World War and a Punch cartoon which identified their work with women's suffrage campaigns. The film also quoted Elsie Inglis who transported teams of nurses to the front line: 'the ordinary male disbelief in our capacity cannot be argued away, it can only be worked away.' Although the film does not cover women's war work during the Second World War, the message of the piece was clear; that women *proved* they could do men's jobs was significant in struggles for women's emancipation. The testimony present in the regional news drew upon a popular cultural memory rather than a distinct regional experience. This commentary was blended in with regional workplace disputes framed around the female bus worker. Arguably, the questions which engaged with women's social position were more visible in the Midlands television news than in the national output of ITN, where there were no comparable stories during the 1960s.

THE 1970S: INTERRUPTING THE
ICONOGRAPHY OF THE FEMALE BUS WORKER

The 1970s has at times been referred to as a 'golden era' of current affairs television, although in her analysis Holland adds the caveat that the 'masculine, rationalist atmosphere' that prevailed in *This Week* meant there were difficulties in retaining female staff and covering 'issues of importance to women' (Holland, 2006, 60, 79–81). On the national news programmes, Anna Ford and Angela Rippon were lauded (inaccurately) as the first female newsreaders and subject to intense scrutiny in the press (Holland, 1987, 134–135). Developments in Midland news programming show that by the late 1960s women were reappearing in the production team. Sue Jay was the first woman to maintain a permanent position on the news team after the 1964 schedule overhaul. She joined the *Midlands News* team in 1968 and moved into the *ATV Today* team when the programmes merged. Ann Diamond joined *ATV Today* in 1979. Wendy Nelson started to present the news with Bob Warman in 1980 and became the first woman at the Midlands news desk since Pat Cox's departure in 1965.

Two short news items from the 1970s provide evidence that the contested position of the female bus worker in the labour force continued. These items would have appeared in the middle of the news programme accompanied by live voiceover and are therefore mute in archived form. Broadcast in July and October 1973 respectively the first covered the refusal of bus crews at Wolverhampton to work with female drivers, the second celebrated an award given to 'Britain's Best Woman Bus Driver', Christine Ahmed (*ATV Today* July 12, 1973). This contradiction indicates that the opportunities to celebrate women bus drivers did not address structural factors that allowed women to be excluded from the workforce. Two longer pieces featuring female bus workers broadcast in 1974 and 1979 invite further analysis. An item broadcast in 1974 was catalogued in ATV's news library under the label 'Sex Discrimination—Oldbury Bus Crews' (*ATV Today* May 5, 1974). Visually the workers were grouped far less formally than in the 1963 material; the one woman present on screen, a bus conductor, remained a visual novelty. Her long hair and dark glasses contrasted with the men who filled the screen behind her, some shook their heads visually confirming their opposition to female bus drivers. The male breadwinner argument remained as a justification for restricting women's right to work. The female testimony broadcast in this case revealed points of change. In response to a question about prioritising male breadwinners the female conductor replied: 'what about those of us who are single? I'm single.' This statement, first broadcast by ATV, suggested that women sought financial and social independence through paid employment.

Discussions of women's war work and 'natural' feminine aptitudes had been displaced in the workers' comments that the news teams used. The female conductor's response along with the title of the item 'sex discrimination' suggests that the perspectives raised by the Women's Liberation Movement had made an impact on the language permissible for broadcast on the regional television news. As Laurel Foster has discussed in her essay on women's magazines in the 1970s, the circulation of printed material by feminist groups may have been small, but their resonance could be seen in print media with far larger circulations such as *Cosmopolitan* and *Woman's*

Own (Foster, 2010, 93–106). However, although the news teams made use of the language of sex discrimination, other factors, such as their relationship with trade unions, also informed the presentation of this news story. Media research has revealed that news teams tended to explain industrial disputes as a problem within individual workforces (Philo, Beharrell, and Hewitt, 1977, 7). In this report, rather than providing the broader social context of the dispute, a few male trade unionists were presented as sexist. ATV made use of the language of women's liberation, but presented this news story as a 'battle of the sexes'. It would, therefore, be inaccurate to suggest that in using terms such as 'sex discrimination' ATV maintained a feminist editorial line.

On November 14, 1979 the local print media publicised a recruitment campaign by local hospitals experiencing shortages of nursing staff. The headline in the *Birmingham Evening Mail* read: 'WE SAY Your Hospital Needs You' and the article then went on to explain: 'The Kitchener style message was aimed at trained nurses—former State Registered or State Enrolled nurses who had left the NHS to raise families' (*Birmingham Evening Mail*, Wednesday November 14ᵗʰ , 1979, 4).

While the *Mail* attempted to appeal to women's 'feminine compassion' to persuade then to return to nursing, the news team at *ATV Today* took a very different angle on the story. The television news item followed an Oxford nurse who had left the profession and started work as a bus driver. The female bus driver was filmed extensively at the wheel of her bus, with close-up shots which framed her head and arms in profile; her pose meant she focused on the road ahead rather than looking into the camera. Thus the themes of physical mobility and social mobility were still referenced, but in this instance she was not being compared with male bus drivers. The discussion between Ann Diamond and the female bus driver focused on the difficulties of living on a nurses pay and how her income had doubled in her new job as a bus driver. The insert did not discuss the marital status of the bus driver, but implicitly implied that women had chosen work according to their economic position rather than as a means to express their 'feminine compassion'. This example reveals how local issues affecting women in the workplace were not only given space in the television news, but in synthesizing the popular and the vernacular the regional television news was able to accommodate a broader perspective on these issues and the local print media.

As well as the women's liberation movement the intervention of *On the Buses*, a successful 1970s sitcom, must be considered as it was the most popular contemporary representation of a British bus company. The programme ran for seven series over four years between 1969 and 1973 on the ITV network, produced by London Weekend Television, and subsequently led to three spin-off films. The glamorous 'clippies' in *On the Buses* were generally set up as out-of-reach love interests for the central characters, bus drivers Stan and Arthur, to maximum comic effect. The comparative point between *On the Buses* and *ATV Today* and their connection to social change is not the plotlines or characters of the sitcom but its interruption of the visual representation of the female bus worker. *On the Buses* revealed a disruption in the iconographic trajectory of the female bus worker. The *On the Buses* 'clippies' were highly made-up and stylised with mini-skirt uniforms and provided a definite departure from the synthesis of masculine and feminine traits required to create the stoic image of the wartime bus worker. Thus, *On the Buses* referenced the so-called sexual revolution rather than women's liberation. However, disturbing definitions of gender-based 'natural attributes' in the 1970s arguably displaced the need to accommodate the masculine in representations of the female bus worker. In turn this meant visually women did not have to be framed as 'exceptional' in performing their work for the television cameras. In very different ways *On the Buses* and the *ATV Today* items broadcast in the 1970s reflect shifting trends in the representation of female bus workers. In the sitcom, the presence of women in the bus company was presented as a disruptive influence on the male workers for comic effect. Likewise in *ATV Today*, rather than making reference to any 'feminine' inadequacies, it was the sexist attitudes of male trade unionists that were (perhaps unjustly) framed as the source of breakdown in working relationships in Midland bus companies. While their respective masculinities paralysed male workers, female bus drivers were framed getting on with their jobs.

VISUALISING SOCIAL CHANGE: OPENING UP THE TELEVISION ARCHIVE

This chapter has analyzed how support for women bus workers was articulated through the regional television news programme *ATV Today*. The inclusion of television news inserts allowed visual themes which were vital to the construction of the iconic image of the female bus worker to be carried through historical analysis of the 1960s and 1970s, when women struggled to become a permanent part of the industry. By paying attention to the differences between regional and national trends in television production it is possible to show how the 'ordinary' women of the Midlands remained constantly visible on screen, even in periods when conditions were not favourable for women's employment in the industry. As a visual form of journalism that sought to distinguish itself from national news programmes and to engage a family audience, local issues affecting women were not only given space in the television news, but could be presented very differently when compared to the local print media. Since the female bus worker was also visualized as a cipher for social change, questions of women's changing place in society was perhaps more visible in the regional television news compared to national news programmes. The visualization of women's physical mobility as bus workers continued to provide a useful means to present discussions of women's social mobility throughout the 1960s and 1970s. The arguments presented against the female bus driver remained consistent and most notably prioritized the male breadwinner; however, arguments used to support female bus workers changed significantly. This suggests that alongside feminist activism and other forms of media and communication the regional news did important work in normalizing the position of working-class women in the bus company.

In the 1960s news stories the legacy of women's war work was used to legitimize women's place in the bus company, against dystopian visions of the consequences of increasing numbers of working women. It also suggests that the regional television news was an important vector of cultural memory, synthesizing the popular image of the iconic and heroic war workers with contemporary local issues. In the 1970s regional news coverage, the contested position of the female bus worker meant she could still be framed as a novelty, but the undermining of discourses which revolved around men and women's 'natural' attributes meant there was less emphasis on the need to synthesize masculine and feminine qualities. Most importantly, this chapter has suggested that visual media has significant explanatory purchase when analysing the complexities of women's history in the twentieth century. In beginning to unpack the diversity of 'ordinary' women's experience in broadcast media, the interconnections between women's and media history emerge in clearer focus, providing valuable insight into the changing visual and discursive frameworks used to defend women on the buses.

NOTES

1. Census 1951, England and Wales, Occupation Tables, Table 1: Occupations of population aged 15 and over by industrial status, 13–15 and Table 20: selected occupations with status aggregates, 156–157; Census 1961, England and Wales, 10% sample, Occupation Tables, Table 1: Occupation by status, 4–5 and Table 26: Occupation and status, 165 & 172; Census 1971, Great Britain, Economic Activity part II, 10% sample, Table 4: Occupation by Status and Sex, 53–54.

BIBLIOGRAPHY / SOURCES

Bell, Melanie, and Melanie Williams, eds. 2010. *British Women's Cinema*. London: Routledge.

Braybon, Gail, and Penny Summerfield. 1987. *Out of the Cage: Women's Experience in Two World Wars*. London: Pandora Press.

Castle, John. 1986. 'Factory Work for Women: Courtaulds and GEC between the Wars.' In *Life and Labour in a Twentieth Century City: The Experience of Coventry*, edited by Bill Lancaster and Tony Mason, 144–147. . Warwick, UK: Cryfield Press.

Cowman, Krista, and Louise A. Jackson, eds. . 2005. *Women and Work Culture: Britain c. 1850–1950*. Aldershot, UK: Ashgate.

Darracott, Joseph, and Belinda Loftus. 1971. *Second World War Posters*. Imperial War Museum.

Foster, Laurel. 2010. 'Printing Liberation: The Women's Movement and Magazines in the 1970s.' In *British Culture and Society in the 1970s: The Lost Decade*, edited by Laurel Foster and Sue Harper. . Cambridge Scholars Publishing.

Friedan, Betty. (1963) 2010. *The Feminine Mystique*. Harmondsworth, UK: Penguin Modern Classics.

Gledhill, Christine, and Gillian Swanson, eds. 1996. *Nationalising Femininity: Culture, Sexuality and British Cinema in the Second World War*. Manchester University Press.

Grey Osterud, Nancy. 1986. 'Gender and the Organisation of Work in the Leicester Hosiery Industry.' In *Unequal Opportunities: Women's Employment in England 1800–1918*, edited by Angela V. John, 45–68. Oxford: Basil Blackwell Inc.

Holland, Patricia. 2006. *The Angry Buzz: This Week and Current Affairs Television*. London: I. B. Tauris.

Holland, Patricia. 1987. 'When a Woman Reads the News.' In *Boxed In: Women and Television*, edited by Helen Baehr and Gillian Dyer, 130–150. London: Pandora.

Holloway, Gerry. 2005. *Women and Work in Britain since 1840*. London: Routledge.

Holmes, Su. 2007. '"A Friendly Style of Presentation Which the BBC Had Always Found Elusive?" The 1950s Cinema Programme and the Construction of British Television History.' In *Re-Viewing Television History: Critical Issues in Television History*, edited by Helen Wheatley, 67–81. London: I. B. Tauris.

Holmes, Su. 2006. 'The "Give-Away" Shows –Who Is Really Paying? "Ordinary" People and the Development of the British Quiz Show.' *Journal of British Cinema and Television* 3 (2): 284–20.

Jerram, Leif. 2011. *Streetlife: The Untold History of Europe's Twentieth Century*. Oxford University Press.

Meyerowitz, Joanne. 1993. 'Beyond the Feminine Mystique: A Reassessment of Postwar Mass Culture, 1946–1958.' *The Journal of American History* 79 (4): 1455–1482.

Mussell, James. 2012. 'The Passing of Print.' *Media History* 18 (1): 77–92.

Otto, Elizabeth, and Vanessa Rocco, eds. 2011. *The New Woman International: Representations in Photography and Film from the 1870s through the 1960s*. University of Michigan Press.

Philo, Greg, Peter Beharrell, and John Hewitt. 1977. 'One-Dimensional News –Television and the Control of Explanation.' In *Trade Unions and the Media*, edited by Peter Beharell and Greg Philo, 1–22. London: Macmillan.

Rowbotham, Sheila. 1999. *A Century of Women: The History of Women in Britain and the United States*. London: Penguin.

Rowbotham, Sheila. 1974. *Hidden from History: 300 Years of Women's Oppression and the Fight against It*. New York: Pantheon Books.

Rule, John. 2001. 'Time, Affluence and Private Leisure: The British Working Class in the 1950s and 1960s. *Labour History Review* 66 (2): 223–242.

Smith Wilson, Dolly. 2005. 'A New Look at the Affluent Worker.' *Twentieth Century British History* 17 (2): 206–229.

Summerfield, Penny. 2009. 'Public Memory or Public Amnesia? British Women of the Second World War in Popular Films of the 1950s and 1960s.' *Journal of British Studies* 48 (4): 935–957.

Summerfield, Penny. 1991. *Reconstructing Women's Wartime Lives: Discourse and Subjectivity in Oral Histories of the Second World War*. Manchester University Press.

Thumim, Janet. 2004. *Inventing Television Culture: Men, Women, and the Box.* Oxford University Press.

Thumim, Janet, ed. 2002. *Small Screen, Big Ideas: Television in the 1950s.* London: I. B. Tauris.

Tinkler, Penny. 2006. *Smoke Signals: Women, Smoking and Visual Culture.* Oxford: Berg.

Tinkler, Penny, and Cheryl Krasnick Warsh. 2008. 'Feminine Modernity in Interwar Britain and North America: Corsets, Cars and Cigarettes.' *Journal of Women's History* 20 (3): 113–43.

Todd, Selina. 2005. *Young Women, Work and Family in England, 1918–1950.* Oxford University Press.

Tusan, Michelle Elizabeth. 1998. 'Inventing the New Woman: Print Culture and Identity Politics during the Fin-de-Siècle: 1997 VanArsdel Prize.' *Victorian Periodicals Review* 31 (2): 169–182.

Valenze, Deborah. 1995. *The First Industrial Woman.* Oxford University Press.

Vall, Natasha. 2011. *Cultural Region: North East England 1945–2000.* Manchester University Press.

VISUAL SOURCES

'Britain's Best Woman Bus Driver.' October. *ATV Today.*

Dunn, Richard, Arthur Marwick, and Lisa Pontecorvo. 1970. 'Emancipation of Women 1890–1930', available to view via British Pathé: reel one http://www.britishpathe.com/video/emancipation-of-women-1; reel two http://www.britishpathe.com/video/emancipation-of-women.

'Female Bus Conductors.' May 23, 1963. *Midlands News,* http://www.macearchive.org/Archive/Title/midlands-news-23051963-female-bus-conductors/MediaEntry/1398.html.

'No More "Clippies" for Walsall Buses.' May 22, 1963. *Birmingham Evening Mail and Despatch*, 9.

'Sex Discrimination—Oldbury Bus Crews.' May 5, 1974. *ATV Today,* http://www.macearchive.org/Archive/Title/atv-today-06051974-sex-discrimination-oldbury-bus-crews/MediaEntry/21182.html.

'Vox Pops: Female Bus Drivers.' July 7, 1965. *ATV Today,* http://www.macearchive.org/Archive/Title/atv-today-12071965-vox-pops-female-bus-drivers/MediaEntry/1400.html9 1973: http://www.macearchive.org/Archive/Title/atv-today-09101973-britains-best-woman-bus-driver/MediaEntry/20038.html.

'WE SAY Your Hospital Needs You.' November 14, 1979. *Birmingham Evening Mail*, 4.

'Wolverhampton Corporation Bus Crews.' July 12, 1973. *ATV Today,* http://www.macearchive.org/Archive/Title/atv-today-12071973-wolverhampton-corporation-bus-crews/MediaEntry/19563.html

12 Pin-Up Culture and Page 3 in the Popular Press

Adrian Bingham

INTRODUCTION

Giving evidence to the Leveson inquiry into the 'culture, practice and ethics of the press' in February 2012, Dominic Mohan, the editor of the *Sun*, argued that 'the Page 3 girl', forty-two years after its first appearance, had become 'an innocuous British institution, regarded with affection and tolerance by millions'. It was, indeed, a comforting reference point in an unstable world: 'It is as innocent today as it was in 1970. While social mores have changed over the years, Page 3 has not' (Leveson Inquiry, Second Witness statement, 1; Minutes of Evidence, Day 38, 117–18). The portrayal of the 'Page 3 girl' as part of the fabric of British culture has become a well-established rhetorical strategy for the paper and its supporters; rejecting Clare Short's criticism of its objectification of women in 2004, the *Sun* asked readers to sign a petition to ensure that 'one of Britain's great traditions remains', and quoted the observation of Julia Kirkbride MP, then shadow Culture Secretary, that '[i]t is a part of the British way of life' (*Sun* January 15, 2004, 4). Even in the 1980s, when the feature had far less of a history to draw upon, some feminists questioned the wisdom of taking on 'Page 3' because it appeared to be so firmly entrenched in popular culture: 'it seemed an institution', wrote Teresa Stratford, 'impossible to shift' (Stratford 1987, 58).

The familiarity and repetitiveness both of the feature itself, with its daily parade of topless women posing in one of a limited number of stock poses, and of the arguments surrounding it (ably restated for the Leveson inquiry in 2012 by representatives of a number of women's groups), has encouraged ahistorical readings of the 'Page 3 girl' as something that emerged fully formed and quickly became a fixed point of the journalistic landscape. This is a trap that should be avoided. The 'Page 3 girl' was a product of a specific historical context, and it cannot be accurately interpreted without understanding the particular social, cultural and commercial forces that shaped its emergence and contributed to its success. Despite several valuable pieces of scholarship on 'Page 3', including some discussion of its introduction and its evolution over time, aspects of its early history, in particular, are often misunderstood or misrepresented (Holland 1983, 84–102; Stratford 1987, 57–61; Chippindale and Horrie 1999, 27–30; Loncraine 2007, 96–111; Ross 2008, 123–132). It is important to address these gaps and misunderstandings because the *Sun*'s pin-up quickly became one of the most prominent and influential representations of femininity circulating in British popular culture; it developed a symbolic significance far beyond its original status as routine and ephemeral titillation for the heterosexual male audience. The content, presentation and reaction to 'Page 3' reveals much about feminism and femininity in this period. Popular newspapers provide a key arena for the contest between competing versions of different social identities, and the *Sun* made a distinctive contribution to the ongoing debate about gender, sexuality and the body. The 'modern', 'fun-loving', sexually assertive models smiling out from inside the newspaper posed a discursive challenge not only to the demure and restrained versions of femininity idealized in the first half of the twentieth century, but also to feminists gathering in increasing numbers to protest about the 'objectification' of women.

This chapter argues that it is possible to add new dimensions to our understanding of 'Page 3' by situating the feature in its proper historical contexts. More broadly, it also seeks to demonstrate the value of apparently trivial, static and stylised media genres to historians of women and gender. The chapter will consider three different contexts in turn. The first is that of the newspaper industry itself. The 'Page 3 girl' was part of a long tradition of newspaper pin-ups features, an evolution from previous practice rather than a revolutionary new development. 'Page 3' was also part of a very deliberate commercial strategy to locate the *Sun* in a specific place in the market: it was a symbol of the paper's identity as a brash and irreverent working-class publication, willing to challenge both middle-class respectability and flat-cap traditionalism. The second key context—far more commonly discussed—is the cultural liberalisation of the 1960s. The loosening of the censorship regime, and the increasing willingness of artists, directors, photographers and writers to explore sexual themes in their work, ensured that public nudity had become far more common—even fashionable—by the late 1960s (Aldgate 1995; Aldgate and Robertson 2005; Green 1999; Collins 2003, ch. 5). Despite the increasing sexual explicitness of its textual content in the 1950s and 1960s, the national press was rather slower than other media forms to test the boundaries of acceptability in its visual material (Bingham 2009). It was easier for a new entrant to the market, unburdened by the weight of readers' expectations about its offering, to take the plunge into regular semi-nudity. The apparent ubiquity of toplessness in British culture at the time, moreover, offered a valuable alibi and justification to the editors to defend 'Page 3'. Such a defence was necessary because of the emergence of a revitalised feminist movement in the late 1960s, with a preoccupation with media sexism and the objectification of the female body: this provides the third context. The first 'proper' 'Page 3 girl' appeared in November 1970, in the very same week that feminists famously flour-bombed Bob Hope on live television as he hosted the Miss World contest in London. Increasingly the criticisms of 'Page 3' were not grounded in morality, but in feminist arguments about women being demeaned and stereotyped—although the feminist movement itself would become seriously divided in its response to sexualized imagery (Segal and McIntosh 1992). The popular press was forced to develop a new language to defend their pin-ups, although, perhaps surprisingly, 'Page 3' did not become a target of concerted feminist campaigning until the mid-1980s. When placed in these contexts, it becomes clear that the novelty of 'Page 3 girl' was not so much in the routine and regular inclusion of semi-nudity in the press, as in the elevation of the feature into a key part of the *Sun*'s brand and self-identity, an expression of its consumerist embrace of sexual pleasure and a defiant rejection of moral traditionalism.

THE PIN-UP TRADITION

The novelty of the 'Page 3 girl' is often exaggerated—partly because historians have paid insufficient attention to the circulation of sexualized representations of the female body in British popular culture.[1] There was a long tradition of pin-up photography in the popular press, and bare breasts were by no means unprecedented either (Bingham 2009, ch. 6). Lord Northcliffe, the founder of the *Daily Mail* and the *Daily Mirror* and the most influential figure in the evolution of popular journalism in the early twentieth century, was a firm believer in the value of 'attractive ladies' for brightening up his newspapers. 'I have no use for a man who cannot appreciate a pretty ankle', he told Tom Clarke, his news editor (Clarke 1931, 246). He reminded his staff of the value of featuring eye-catching women so frequently that by 1920 he was 'almost weary of repeating this' (Northcliffe Bulletins August 6, 1920). As photography was gradually integrated throughout newspapers in the 1920s and 1930s, pictures of glamorous society hostesses in evening dress, and 'modern young women' wearing short skirts or figure-hugging beachwear, became standard features at the popular end of the market. As the research organisation Political and Economic Planning noted wryly in 1938, 'a popular newspaper, indeed, might almost be defined as one which features a photograph of the first bathing belles of the season on Easter Tuesday morning' (Political and Economic Planning 1938, 155).

Northcliffe was determined that his papers remain suitable for a mixed-sex middle-class audience, and he therefore sought 'tasteful' images that conveyed female beauty, glamour and elegance. His papers did not attempt to push at the boundaries of decency. It was only when one of his former papers, the *Daily Mirror*, reinvented itself for a working-class audience in the mid-1930s that newspaper photography became overtly sexualised.[2] There was a gradual shift into the pin-up genre, with photographs included in which more flesh was exposed, and curves were more obviously emphasized. Editors tested the limits of acceptability, and found ways of increasing the amount of nudity without alienating sections of the target readership. Photographs of bare-breasted black African women could be justified as imperial reportage of exotic and less 'civilised' societies; such pictures had been included in respectable magazines such as *National Geographic* since the 1920s (Loncraine 2007, 104).[3] In April 1938, the *Sunday Pictorial*, the *Mirror*'s sister paper, dared to publish what seems to have been the first photograph in a mainstream national newspaper of a topless white woman. This nude shot was a relatively tasteful picture of a 'spring nymph' reaching up to the blossom of an apple tree, but the model's exposed nipples were visible in the dappled sunlight (*Sunday Pictorial* April 17, 1938, 19). Hugh Cudlipp, the paper's young editor, was only allowed to publish this picture after personally obtaining the permission of the *Pictorial*'s chairman, John Cowley; the surprised Cowley seems to have been too embarrassed to refuse, to the amusement of Cudlipp and director Cecil King (Cudlipp 1962, 47–8; Cudlipp 1994, 17–19). This experiment was not repeated, but it did embolden the editorial team to continue their practice of including revealing and overtly sexualised shots. Perhaps the most productive strategy, though, was to render nudity safer by transposing it into cartoon form. The 'Jane' strip, drawn by Norman Pett, had been launched in December 1932 as a satire on a guileless 'bright young thing'; in the late-1930s it was transformed into a saucy feature in which the protagonist and her female companions contrived new ways of losing their clothing. During the Second World War, 'Jane' started brazenly displaying her breasts, and became one of the forces' most popular pin-ups (Daily Mirror Newspapers 1976; Saunders 2004). 'Jane' demonstrated, indeed, how a pin-up could become central to a paper's brand identity. When *Mirror* journalist Harry Procter joined the RAF, he was nicknamed 'the Jane-Man'—that was what the paper meant to his colleagues (Procter 1958, 74).

The editorial strategy of the *Mirror* and the *Pictorial* in the late-1930s clearly prefigured that of the *Sun* in the early-1970s—indeed, the *Sun*'s first editor, Larry Lamb, had worked at the *Mirror* and explicitly modelled the early *Sun* on the mid-century *Mirror* (Chippindale and Horrie 1999, 12–3, 25–6). The pin-up photographs and cartoons were designed to symbolise the character of the reinvented paper and to highlight that it had been editorially repositioned: Cudlipp's 'spring nymph' was conceived as 'one way of denoting to the readers that the old-fashioned Sunday sedative was positively under new management' (Cudlipp 1962, 47). This sexual content deliberately sought to provoke and polarise readers. It demonstrated the paper's credentials as an irreverent working-class voice unafraid to upset the sensibilities of the respectable middle-classes—the newspaper equivalent of the saucy seaside photograph. Criticism merely served to advertise its risqué content. The *Daily Sketch*, one of the *Mirror*'s main competitors, swallowed the bait and launched a 'Clean and Clever' campaign in 1938, denouncing the 'degradation' of journalism and pledging 'not to use the sensational, ribald and pornographic pictures which are making their appearance elsewhere' (*Daily Sketch* June 23, 1938, 2, 29; *Daily Telegraph* June 23, 1938, 21). The campaign seems to have done little more than advertise the illicit pleasures available elsewhere. A Mass-Observation survey of reading habits in December 1938 indicated the ways in which the market was becoming polarised around attitudes to sexual content. A female *Sketch* reader highlighted the disgust of those wedded to traditional morality, describing the *Daily Mirror* as 'the dirtiest little rag ever printed as a "daily" in this country', containing 'many photos of half-naked females' in its 'nefarious pages'. A male respondent, by contrast, admitted that the presence of daring 'sex photos' was one of his main reasons for taking the *Mirror*: 'I dislike the *Sketch*. It is not modern. I don't only want "All the news and pictures fit to print". I want the other side as well.' (Mass-Observation December 1938, 36). The former type of reader was already well catered for by the market; the latter, far less so. The triumph of the *Mirror* over the *Sketch* confirmed that there was, by the late 1930s, a substantial public appetite for unapologetically entertaining and titillating forms of sexual content. The reinvented *Mirror* appeared to many readers to be 'modern' and in tune with the times, unlike the moralistic and outdated *Sketch*.

During the 1950s and 1960s, the pin-up spread throughout the daily and Sunday popular press (Bingham 2009, ch. 6). After the acceptance of the wartime pin-up, film stars were marketed more explicitly than ever before as 'sex symbols': glamorous figures such as Marilyn Monroe, Jayne Mansfield, Sophia Loren and Brigitte Bardot obtained a global celebrity and were endlessly photographed and interviewed. Countless other models and actresses sought to emulate these icons and provided a steady supply of attractive images. Pin-up techniques were also used more insistently in advertising. In some respects, the genre became stale. The constraints on pin-up photography—that nipples and bottoms should not be exposed—generally remained in place and models recycled familiar poses. By the 1960s, the national newspaper market had lost some of its dynamism, and no editorial team consistently sought to generate controversy and push back the boundaries of acceptability, at least in terms of pin-up photography. The *Mirror* dominated the working class market—in 1967, it achieved the unprecedented circulation of 5.25 million copies per day—and its editors believed that the only way to expand was to move gently upmarket to meet the expectations of an increasingly educated and aspirational audience (Greenslade 2003, 156–8). There were no new entries to the daily newspaper market in this period, and the only substantial editorial reinvention was conducted by IPC (the owner of the *Mirror*), transforming the trade-union supporting *Daily Herald* into a more modern and consumerist left-of-centre paper. IPC did not want the *Sun* to encroach on the *Mirror*'s territory, and the new *Sun* remained respectable, and rather characterless (Greenslade 2003, 156–8).

The commercial complacency of the dominant and increasingly respectable *Mirror* opened up an opportunity for Rupert Murdoch, the Australian newspaper magnate who in 1968 bought the *News of the World* and the following year took the faltering *Sun* from IPC. Murdoch and Larry Lamb, poached from his job as the northern editor of the *Daily Mail*, agreed that there was a gap in the market for a brash and plain-speaking working-class tabloid aimed at the more 'permissive' younger generation that was receiving such publicity at this time (Osgerby 1998; Green 1999). They envisaged, in fact, the *Mirror* of the 1930s and 1940s updated for a new era (Chippindale and Horrie 1999, 12–14.) Provocative sexual content, and racy pin-ups in particular, would be used just as they had been by the *Mirror*: as a symbol of an irreverent, earthy, proletarian new paper seeking to disturb the market and willing to challenge notions of acceptability and propriety in the process. A naked woman appeared in the first issue of the relaunched *Sun*, albeit with her back turned to the camera, in a feature on the Rolling Stones (*Sun* November 17, 1969, 22, 27). The *Sun*'s boldness was more evident the following day with a centre spread including two topless shots of the Swedish model Uschi Obermeier (*Sun* November 18, 1969, 18, 23). Semi-nudity and exposed nipples soon became common, although such shots were not yet routinely located in one part of the paper. A key step towards the 'Page 3' phenomenon was taken on November 17, 1970, the first anniversary of the relaunch, when the German model Stephanie Rahn was displayed as a topless 'birthday suit girl' (*Sun* November 17, 1970, 3.) Rahn is usually regarded as the first 'proper' 'Page 3 girl' (Lamb 1989, 112, Chippindale and Horrie 1999, 28; Loncraine 2007, 98). Hers was a staged photograph, advertised on the front page, and insouciantly captioned: '*The Sun*, like most of its readers, likes pretty girls. And if they're as pretty as today's Birthday Suit girl, 20-year-old Stephanie Rahn of Munich, who cares whether they're dressed or not?' (*Sun* November 17, 1970, 3). Over the next few years, the 'Page 3 girl' became a regular, institutionalized feature that was central to the paper's brand identity. The paper unapologetically flaunted this aspect of its appeal—'The *Sun* is always best for nudes' was a frequently used tagline—and welcomed the associated controversy: 'The more the critics jumped up and down, the more popular the feature became', remembered Lamb in 1989. It also became a lucrative marketing opportunity as Page 3 calendars and playing cards rapidly sold out (Lamb 1989, 115).

THE 'PERMISSIVE SOCIETY'

The *Sun* consistently argued that it was doing no more than responding to changes in contemporary culture. 'The Permissive Society is a fact, not an opinion', the paper observed on its first anniversary, in an editorial piece directly opposite the topless Stephanie Rahn. 'We have reflected the fact where others have preferred to turn blind eyes' (*Sun* November 17, 1970, 2). It portrayed itself as a fun, cheeky, freewheeling publication in tune with the spirit of the time, 'Britain's brightest, most irreverent, most unpredictable paper' (*Sun* November 17, 1970, 1). If the commercial strategy behind the 'Page 3 girl' looked back to the 1930s, the feature was also very much part of the cultural liberalisation of the 1960s. Exposed flesh and simulated sex became much more common on television and cinema screens, and, after the abolition of the Lord Chamberlain in 1968, in theatres (Aldgate 1995; Aldgate and Robertson 2005, ch.7; Green 1999, ch. 6). A new wave of glossy pornographic magazines emerged to complement the expanding urban sex industry, and the 'underground' and countercultural publications that flourished in the second half of the decade, such as *Oz* and *IT*, used explicit pictures to challenge the norms of respectable society (Collins 2003, ch. 5; Fountain 1988). Nudity did not just enter the public realm through media outlets, though: topless women and men became regular sights on beaches and at music festivals and countercultural gatherings. 'It appears that people can't wait to take their clothes off these days', declared the *Sunday Times Magazine* in July 1969: 'The growing fad for nudity is everywhere' (Loncraine 2007, 97). So mainstream had nudity become, indeed, that in March 1971 Fisons, a venerable pharmaceutical company, advertising in Britain's most respectable paper, *The Times*, included a full-page photograph of topless model Vivian Neves (*The Times* March 17, 1971, 7).

During the 1960s, stories about contemporary permissiveness and public nudity provided a useful source of titillating images for newspapers not yet willing to cross the boundary into regular topless pin-up photography. The coverage of the Profumo scandal in 1963 was liberally sprinkled with provocative photography, including various versions of Lewis Morley's iconic shot of a naked Christine Keeler sitting astride a chair.[4] The following summer, the popular press was transfixed by a 'topless dress craze', prompted by the arrest for indecency in Chicago of an American bather wearing a topless swimsuit designed by Rudi Gemreich (Thesander 1997, 187). The *News of the World* printed a picture of a British woman wearing a 'topless' dress in 'a London high street' under the pretence that it wanted the opinions of readers on the new fashion (*News of the World* July 5, 1964, 11). It emerged the following week that 75 per cent of readers were not in favour of it, but that did not stop the stories or the photos (*News of the World* July 12, 1964, 6). By the time the *Sun* relaunched in November 1969, the 'permissive society' seemed to be at its height and there were countless opportunities for the paper to find 'news stories' that could be illustrated with risqué photographs.[5] A double-page spread reviewing 'a decade of sexual revolution in the arts', for example, was illustrated with a considerable amount of exposed flesh and several pairs of bare breasts (*Sun* November 12, 1970, 14–15). The *Sun* was by no means the only paper pursuing this strategy. The *Mirror* in July 1970, for example, printed an unusually explicit photograph of one of the 'sizzling sketches' from Kenneth Tynan's controversial revue *Oh! Calcutta!*, portraying several naked men and women dancing on stage, with breasts, buttocks and pubic hair unapologetically on show (*Daily Mirror* July 28, 1970, 3). Nor, indeed, was such nudity restricted to the popular press. When the *Sunday Times* attacked the *Sun* for 'baring their 17th nipple in nine days', Lamb pointed out that the *Sunday Times* had in fact displayed no fewer than 22 in its previous nine issues, and consoled *Sun* readers that although they were 'still fractionally under-privileged', the situation was 'not irretrievable' (Lamb 1989, 185).

Much of the nudity in the early *Sun*, therefore, was loosely based around news reporting or cultural coverage, and similar shots could be found in other newspapers; the staged 'Page 3'-style pin-up was only one part of a broader process of the exposure of the female body in the press and the wider media, and seemed less of a novelty when set against other sexualised images. But as 'Page 3' became a regular, heavily-marketed feature, central to the *Sun*'s brand, other papers were increasingly forced to define their policy on nudity. The leading mid-market newspapers, the *Express* and the *Mail*, maintained a clear distinction between the 'attractive ladies' that were part of Fleet Street tradition, and the crude and gratuitous modern 'pin-up'. Interviewed by the Longford Committee investigating pornography in 1971, the *Express*'s proprietor, Sir Max Aitken, declared that 'He saw no objection to pictures of pretty girls in the *Express*, but if the *Express* ever printed pictures of nudes or even bare breasts, he would be inundated with protests from readers'. The *Mail*'s owner, Vere Harmsworth, agreed that '*Daily Mail* readers would also dislike such material' (Longford Committee 1972, 325). For the *Daily Mirror*, the *Sun*'s main competitor, the decision was more difficult. Whereas the *Sun* had been born in the 'permissive age', and had integrated nudity unselfconsciously into its make-up from the start, the *Mirror*, despite its tradition of brashness, had an older readership, and had in recent years been seeking to move upmarket with more aspirational material. There was also considerable opposition to topless pin-ups from some senior journalists, notably the respected feature-writer and agony aunt Marje Proops (Patmore 1993, 189–90). Not to include nude photography was to risk being commercially outflanked by the *Sun*, however, and to appear dated in the modern, 'liberated' era. The outcome was an unconvincing compromise. The *Mirror*'s photography became more explicit, pin-ups became more provocative, and nipples were occasionally exposed, but there was no attempt to rival 'Page 3' until the appointment of Mike Molloy as editor in 1975. Molloy's experiment was not deemed a success and before long the policy was altered once again, with the paper settling on what Lamb felt was the hypocritical practice of printing 'naughty pin-up pictures—suspenders, wet t-shirts, phallic symbols, the lot', but without exposing nipples (Lamb 1989, 115). The *Sun* polarised the market around attitudes to 'permissiveness', and the *Mirror* was left uncertain in the disappearing middle ground.

THE FEMINIST CHALLENGE

'Permissiveness' was conceived by its proponents as freedom from the constraints of traditional (Christian) morality; according to this way of thinking sex was not shameful but a source of pleasure to celebrated, and public nudity was an act of glorious self-expression, a revelling in one's sensuality. Picture editors had conventionally appraised pin-ups with a finely-tuned sense of what was morally acceptable to their paper's audience. By embracing 'permissiveness' and modern notions of sexuality—'The *Sun* is on the side of youth', the paper declared in November 1969. 'It will never think that what is prim must be proper' (*Sun* November 22, 1969, 2)—Lamb and his team were able to justify nudity. Yet just as the moral opposition to nudity was crumbling, a powerful critique emerged from a different quarter: the resurgent feminist movement. In 1963, Betty Friedan's denunciation of the 'feminine mystique' constructed by women's magazines and consumer advertising had placed the media perpetuation of gender stereotypes firmly under the spotlight, and by the late 1960s the women's movement was pushing the objectification of the female body up the public agenda (Friedan 1963). The protests outside the Miss America contest in Atlantic City in 1968—in which campaigners dumped constricting underwear in a 'freedom trashcan', giving rise to the myth of 'bra-burning'—gained worldwide publicity and inspired similar protests, including the disruption of the Miss World contest in 1970 (Thesander 1997, 185). Women had been complaining about pin-ups for years, but now they were imbued with a fresh confidence that their feelings were shared, and offered a new intellectual framework within which to understand their feelings and formulate their complaints.

The 'Page 3 girl' itself did not become a major rallying point for feminist activity until the 1980s, when Clare Short raised the feature in the House of Commons (Stratford 1987, 58; Short 1991). Overtly sexualised images had become so widespread throughout the media that the women's movement campaigned on a broad front, and the *Sun*'s pin-ups were one offender among many. The organisations that emerged in the late 1970s, such as the Alliance for Fair Images and Representation in the Media (AFFIRM) and the Women's Media Action Group, tended to focus their efforts in areas where there seemed to be a chance of redress, such as by making representations about demeaning advertising to the Advertising Standards Authority (Davies, Dickey, and Stratford 1987, 203–222). Yet if the *Sun* did not have to fend off a targeted campaign against 'Page 3', its editorial team were aware that the *Sun* required not only a defence against the feminist critique, but also a language to address its female readers on this issue. A number of complementary strategies were used. The first was to highlight that the *Sun* was aimed at a broad readership of both sexes: the paper made a prominent effort to win over female readers with targeted material aimed at 'modern' women. The women's section was entitled 'Pacesetters' to underline the dynamism of its intended audience, and the introductory message from Joyce Hopkirk, the first women's editor, was headlined: ' We Enjoy Life and We Want You to Enjoy it With Us'. 'The new Pacesetters pages are for women who believe there is more to life than washing up, wrote Hopkirk': 'We plan to make your life more lively. The *Sun* will always remember that half its readers are women' (*Sun* November 17, 1969, 14). Women's pages had developed considerably since being established in the national daily press by Northcliffe; in the 1950s and 1960s Marje Proops at the *Mirror*, in particular, had updated the traditional formula of fashion and housewifery advice with celebrity interviews and more challenging articles on relationships and sexual welfare (Bingham 2004, chs. 1, 3; Bingham 2009, ch. 2). The Pacesetters pages continued this process of evolution and featured sex even more prominently; the writing was aimed at a liberated and consumerist audience, eager to find ways of enhancing their sexual pleasure. Early articles provided advice on 'Undies for Undressing', asked 'does beefcake turn you on?', and offered a quiz to 'Test Your Sex IQ' (*Sun* November 17, 1969, 33, December 30, 1969, 9, October 6, 1970, 12). Larry Lamb argued that these pages were in tune with a 'new mood of feminine feminism, as opposed to militant feminism', expressed by modern women who were in control of their lives but were suspicious of the women's movement (Lamb 1989, 56). Such a strategy became increasingly plausible as the divisions within the movement, particularly over issues of sexuality, became more evident and the press was able to highlight and caricature radical stances—such as 'political lesbianism'—adopted by a minority (Collins 2003, 180–204).

Modern newspapers have always functioned as a miscellany: a broad range of material is provided for different sections of a diverse mass audience, and it is assumed that few readers are interested in every part of the offering. The editorial team hoped that female readers who did not approve of the 'Page 3 girl' would still be enticed by the other material in the paper. The ultimate goal, though, was to attract women as well as men with 'Page 3'. As Patricia Holland has observed, 'there are important ways in which Page Three is addressed directly to women. It is part of the *Sun*'s discourse on female sexuality which invites sexual enjoyment, sexual freedom and active participation in heterosexual activity' (Holland 1983, 93). Attractive, 'liberated' and glorying in their sensuality, the 'Page 3 girls' were presented as aspirational figures; the paper missed few opportunities to emphasise how many young models sought to appear in its pages. Claims that the feature was a joyous celebration of the female body, and contrasted positively with the coy and hypocritical pin-ups of the past, had a certain credibility at a time when Germaine Greer was declaring that the '[r]ecent emphasis on the nipple, which was absent from the breast of popular pornography, is in women's favour, for the nipple is expressive and responsive' (Greer 1971, 34). Lamb also maintained a female perspective on the feature by seeking the advice of the Pacesetters team on the models used, and by using one of them, Patsy Chapman, to write the captions; he himself was adamant that 'they had to be nice girls' (Lamb 1989, 111).

Further balance was achieved by the regular inclusion of male pin-ups, complete with captions conducting a knowing dialogue with female readers (Loncraine 2007, 102). In January 1973, for example, the *Sun* printed a large photo of 'dishy Roger Moore' bearing his chest for 'two young ladies to feast their eyes on':

> The girls—calling themselves only Jane and Myra—wrote to us this week to say how much they've warmed to *The Sun* in the past year. And as a special favour they asked for a pin-up picture of 007 star Roger, who they'd just love to meet in the flesh (*Sun* January 11, 1973, 14–15).

By the mid-1970s a 'Daily Male' pin-up was frequently found in the *Sun*. Other papers followed suit, appropriating the language of equality to explain such features. The *Mirror* commemorated the Sex Discrimination and Equal Pay Acts becoming law in December 1975 with a front-page pin-up of 'hunky' singer Malcolm Roberts, and the headline 'Girls, it's your turn now' (*Daily Mirror* December 29, 1975, 1). When a female reader complained that the picture of Roberts was 'in no way equal to the girl on Page Five as she was virtually naked and he had his trousers on', and demanded instead 'a (nearly) nude every day', the *Mirror* responded with a more revealing image of actor Patrick Mower in briefs (*Daily Mirror* December 31, 1975, 12).

The *Sun*, then, used two different approaches in its defence of 'Page 3'. If the feature was openly criticized, the paper issued a robust response. Criticism from establishment figures on moral grounds was secretly welcomed, because it validated the *Sun*'s permissive and provocative credentials: when the *Sun* was banned by a local council in Yorkshire in 1970, the paper gleefully turned it into a news story about the 'Silly Burghers of Sowerby Bridge' (Loncraine 2007, 104). Feminist criticism, meanwhile, was met with accusations of joyless extremism, as Clare Short found in the 1980s. Behind the scenes, however, the *Sun* retained a certain amount of caution: it did not push back the boundaries of acceptability too far—in the early 1970s most 'Page 3' photographs fitted either into the naturist tradition, or sought to convey a saucy humour—it crafted a plausible form of words to justify the feature, and it worked hard to win over female readers in other ways. Over time, however, as the paper's circulation continued to rise and 'Page 3' became more well-established, some of this caution was gradually lost. The launch of the *Daily Star* in 1978 meant that the *Sun* for the first time faced a competitor unafraid to compete in the pin-up market. 'No newspaper in history lost sales by projecting beautiful birds', the *Star*'s editor, Derek Jameson, told his staff, as he introduced the first full-colour topless pin-ups, the 'Starbirds' (Chippindale and Horrie 1999, 83). Kelvin

Mackenzie, who became the *Sun*'s editor in 1981 with a remit to see off the *Star*'s challenge, was far more combative than Lamb, and combined a reinvigorated 'Page 3' with an unapologetically Thatcherite agenda. 'Page 3' photography increasingly borrowed the props and poses of soft-pornography, and popular models such as Samantha Fox and Linda Lusardi were transformed into national celebrities. By 1988, conscious that the formula he had developed was being increasingly disregarded, Larry Lamb was expressing his concern at the direction 'Page 3' had taken:

> I have come to the conclusion, over the years, that there is an element of sexploitation involved . . . [and] I do not like to feel that I was in any way responsible for the current fiercely competitive situation in which the girls in some of our national newspapers get younger and younger and more and more top-heavy and less and less like the girl next door (Lamb 1989, 110).

'Page 3' became so heavily promoted and so central to the *Sun*'s brand that it increasingly overwhelmed the other images of women in the paper. And with the paper showing considerable sympathy with Margaret Thatcher's call for a return to 'Victorian values', it was harder for the paper to pose as a champion of 'permissiveness'. 'Page 3's' function as a commercial tool was increasingly difficult to disguise.

CONCLUSIONS

The 'Page 3 girl' was the product of a market opportunity and a cultural moment. Rupert Murdoch and Larry Lamb spotted the *Daily Mirror*'s failure to keep pace with the social changes of the 1960s, and launched a paper that sought to ride the wave of sixties 'permissiveness'. They appropriated the discourses of sexual 'liberation' to revitalise the stale pin-up genre, and injected an emphasis on fun, individualism and consumerism. They presented the result as a celebration of sexual pleasure as well as a form of harmless titillation. 'Page 3' was not derailed by the challenge of a resurgent feminist movement because the pin-up tradition was firmly entrenched in the socially conservative and male-dominated Fleet Street; newspapers had enough cultural power to deflect the criticisms of protestors. Nevertheless, the feminist critique, even if not initially targeted directly at 'Page 3', did shape the evolution of the feature, and of the *Sun* more broadly, in its early years.

Understanding the context of the emergence of 'Page 3' underlines that it was by no means an unchanging 'institution'; as the commercial and cultural context shifted in the late 1970s and 1980s, so too did the feature evolve, becoming more eroticized and insistent. The significance of 'Page 3' is not so much in the nudity itself, but rather in the way that it has been made into a central part of the identity of Britain's best-selling national newspaper; as such, the *Sun* the normalized female toplessness as mainstream popular culture's primary symbol of sexual pleasure, and powerfully reinforced the idea that women's bodies should be available for public scrutiny and consumption. Once the symbol of permissive modernity, though, 'Page 3' now risks trapping the *Sun* in its past. In the era of easily accessible internet pornography, the 'Page 3 girl' looks increasingly dated, notwithstanding the introduction of 'page 3.com' and '360 degree' pin-up images.[6] So fundamental is the 'Page 3 girl' to the *Sun*'s brand, however, that dropping it would threaten the paper's identity in a declining market and risk leaving it without a point of difference from its rivals. It is significant that *Sun on Sunday*, launched in February 2012 and deliberately seeking to court female readers after the controversy of the phone-hacking scandal, has not included topless pin-ups on page 3. Here is the first overt sign of a lack of editorial confidence in 'Page 3', and a recognition that, despite protestations of its innocuousness, the feature alienates some women. 'Page 3' was born of commercial opportunism, and although it has withstood four decades of feminist campaigning, it will be dropped as unceremoniously as the *News of the World* if it appears to be damaging, rather than sustaining, the *Sun*'s brand.

NOTES

1. Joanne Meyerowitz has made a similar point with reference to mid-twentieth-century United States (Meyerowitz 1996, 9).
2. Northcliffe passed the *Mirror* to his brother, Lord Rothermere in 1914; Rothermere ceased to be owner in 1936. In the mid-1930s, under the guidance of a new editorial team led by Cecil King, Harry Bartholomew and Hugh Cudlipp, the *Mirror* was transformed from a picture paper largely read by middle-class women into the first modern tabloid, aimed squarely at a mixed-sex, working-class audience. On this, see Cudlipp 1953.
3. For example, *Daily Mirror* November 8, 1935, 19, November 11, 1935, 9.
4. For example, *Sunday Mirror* June 9, 1963, 36; *News of the World* June 9, 1963, 4–5, June 16, 1963, 2–4, June 23, 1963, 2–3; *People* June 23, 1963, 2–3.
5. For a similar trend in American publications, see Strub 2011, 148–9.
6. See http://www.page3.com/ (accessed 18 July).

BIBLIOGRAPHY / SOURCES

Aldgate, Anthony. 1995. *Censorship and the Permissive Society: British Cinema and Theatre 1955–1965*. Oxford University Press.

Aldgate, Anthony, and James Robertson. 2005. *Censorship in Theatre and Cinema*. Edinburgh University Press.

Bingham, Adrian. 2009. *Family Newspapers? Sex, Private Life, and the British Popular Press, 1918–78*. Oxford University Press.

Bingham, Adrian. 2004. *Gender, Modernity, and the Popular Press in Inter-War Britain*. Oxford University Press.

Chippindale, Peter, and Chris Horrie. 1999. *Stick It up Your Punter: The Uncut Story of the Sun Newspaper.* London: Simon & Schuster.

Clarke, Tom. 1931. *My Northcliffe Diary.* London: Victor Gollancz.

Collins, Marcus. 2003. *Modern Love: An Intimate History of Men and Women in Twentieth-Century Britain.* London: Atlantic Books.

Cudlipp, Hugh. 1962. *At Your Peril!* London: Weidenfeld and Nicolson.

Cudlipp, Hugh. 1994. 'Exclusive: The First Nude in Fleet Street.' *British Journalism Review* 5 (3).

Cudlipp, Hugh. 1953. *Publish and Be Damned! The Astonishing Story of the Daily Mirror.* London: Andrew Dakers.

Daily Mirror Newspapers. 1976. *Jane at War.* London: Wolfe.

Davies, Kath, Julienne Dickey, and Teresa Stratford. 1987. 'Conclusion: What Are We Doing about It?' In *Out of Focus: Writings on Women and the Media,* edited by Kath Davies, Julienne Dickey, and Teresa Stratford, 203–222. London: The Women's Press.

Fountain, Nigel. 1988. *Underground: The London Alternative Press 1966–74.* London: Routledge.

Friedan, Betty. 1963. *The Feminine Mystique.* London: Gollancz.

Green, Jonathon. 1999. *All Dressed Up: The Sixties and the Counterculture.* London: Pimlico.

Greenslade, Roy. 2003. *Press Gang: How Newspapers Make Profits from Propaganda.* London: Macmillan.

Greer, Germaine. 1971. *The Female Eunuch.* London: Paladin.

Holland, Patricia. 1983. 'The "Page Three Girl" Speaks to Women, Too.' *Screen* 24 (3): 84–102.

Holland, Patricia. 1988. 'The Politics of the Smile: "Soft News" and the Sexualisation of the Popular Press." In *News, Gender and Power,* edited by Cynthia Carter, Gill Branston, and Stuart Allan, 17–32. London: Routledge.

Lamb, Larry. 1989. *Sunrise: The Remarkable Rise of the Best-Selling Soaraway Sun.* London: Papermac.

Leveson Inquiry. February 7, 2012. Minutes of Evidence, Day 38—PM. Accessed July 18, 2012.

http://www.levesoninquiry.org.uk/.

Leveson Inquiry, February 5, 2012. 'Second Witness Statement of Dominic James Mohan.' Accessed July 18, 2012. http://www.levesoninquiry.org.uk/.

Loncraine, Rebecca. 2007. 'Bosom of the Nation: Page Three in the 1970s and 1980s.' In *Rude Britannia,* edited by Mina Gorji, 111. Abingdon, UK: Routledge.

Longford Committee. 1972. *Pornography: The Longford Report.* London: Coronet.

Mass-Observation. December 1938. File Report A11, 'Motives and Methods of Newspaper Reading.' Bodleian Library, Oxford (X. Films 200).

Meyerowitz, Joanne. 1996. 'Women, Cheesecake, and Borderline Material: Responses to Girlie Pictures in the Mid-Twentieth-Century US.' *Journal of Women's History* 8 (3): 9–35.

Northcliffe Bulletins. Bodleian Library, Oxford (MS Eng. hist d. 303–5).

Osgerby, Bill. 1998. *Youth in Britain since 1945.* Oxford: Blackwell.

Patmore, Angela. 1993. *Marge: The Guilt and the Gingerbread—The Authorized Biography.* London: Warner.

Political and Economic Planning. 1938. *Report on the British Press.* London: PEP.

Procter, Harry. 1958. *The Street of Disillusion.* London: Allan Wingate.

Ross, Karen. 2008. 'Post-Ironic Page 3: Porn for the Plebs.' In *Pulling Newspapers Apart: Analysing Print Journalism,* edited by Bob Franklin, 123–132. Abingdon, UK: Routledge.

Saunders, Andy. 2004. *Jane: A Pin-Up at War*. Barnsley, UK: Leo Cooper.

Segal, Lynne, and Mary McIntosh. 1992. *Sex Exposed: Sexuality and the Pornography Debate*. London: Virago.

Short, Clare, with Kiri Tunks and Diane Hutchinson. 1991. *Dear Clare. . . . . . this is what women feel about Page 3*. London: Radius.

Stratford, Teresa. 1987. 'Page 3—Dream or Nightmare?' In *Out of Focus: Writings on Women and the Media*, edited by Kath Davies, Julienne Dickey, and Teresa Stratford. London: The Women's Press.

Strub, Whitney. 2011. *Perversion for Profit: The Politics of Pornography and the Rise of the New Right*. New York: Columbia University Press.

Thesander, Marianne. 1997. *The Feminine Ideal*. London: Reaktion Books.

Part IV

80s and 90s

Thatcherism and Its Legacy

The election of Margaret Thatcher as Britain's first woman prime minister in 1979 has in retrospect turned out to be perhaps a rather greater victory for neo-liberalism than for feminism. Iconographically, she was an uncomfortable amalgam of femininity and feminism; her position of power at one level appeared to advance feminism, shifting perceptions of the roles women could fulfil in society; her handbags, pearls, hairstyle, ruffled necklines and most importantly her policies appeared to offer a continuity with traditional femininities of the past. Thatcherism's promotion of individual freedom, privatisation and significantly, an attempt to reduce at least the growth in government spending on the welfare state, left a strong legacy in Britain for many years after. It was particularly problematic for women who found themselves as victims of attempts to cut public spending.

Individualism and entrepreneurship were heralded and Paul Elliot's chapter argues that the prostitute can be interpreted as epitomising both these neo-liberalism traits. Indeed, individualism articulated via sexual promiscuity and greater instability in relationships could be seen as the logical conclusion of neo-liberalism. Cuts in welfare services, high unemployment and the struggles of single parenthood also contributed to an increase in prostitution during the Thatcher years, when the prostitute was also at times portrayed as a symbol of society's malaise in film. A number of those films which critiqued Thatcherism were produced by Channel 4 films, which alongside the introduction of Channel 4 Films in 1982 challenged the previous boundaries of censorship and taste. Neo-liberalism also facilitated an expediential increase in television and the proliferation of satellite and digital channels at the turn of the new millennium; the development of the internet; a proliferation of lifestyle magazines; and something of a revival in cinema attendance particularly after multiplexes began to appear in Britain from 1985 onwards. Magazines such as *The Face* (1980–2004), *Blitz* (1980–1991) and *i-D* (1980–) emphasised style, celebrated popular culture, and through their sometimes provocative photoshoots, challenged mainstream magazines' hegemonic sexuality. They also laid the path for the development of the men's magazine market and can be seen as precursors to the 'lad's mags' of the 1990s.

Thatcherism has been described as an uncomfortable and unstable coalition between neo-liberalism and neo-conservatism traditions (Hall and Jacques 1983). Although the choice of a woman as leader served to make the Conservative Party look young and modern, many of the Conservative government's values offered comfort to those who found the pace of change threatening. Whilst historians debated whether or not a Cultural Revolution occurred in the long 60s, Thatcherist rhetoric suggested it was a mistake and should be reversed. Instead, she articulated emotional discourses which promoted family values, scepticism about both Europe and immigration and a 'little-Englander' mentality. But then as Hall argues: 'Ideology works best by suturing together contradictory lines of argument and emotional investments' (2011, 717). Arguably, the marketization of public service and the rhetorical elevation of the consumer, given women's cultural associations with consumerism, offered a new confidence to consumer femininity. Andrews's chapter on the popular magazine *Marie Claire* (1937–) demonstrates how in the wake of Thatcherism readers were invited to navigate their way through a range of contradictory discourses when reading the magazine; able to flirt with fantasies of political engagement and feminism alongside the more usual focus of magazines on topics such as fashion and relationships. This mixing of consumer femininity and feminism had its precedent perhaps in the BBC series *Howards' Way* (1985–90) which featured a number of wealthy fashion-conscious but independent women who lived on the South Coast of England.

The 1990 and 2003 Broadcasting Acts encompassed the new free-market liberal agenda and the abundance of television channels led to a 'loosening of restraint and a greater desire to appeal directly to "popular" tastes, dispensing with normative values to address a culturally more diverse audience' (Arthurs 2004, 9). Popular tastes were, however, rather often more sexually explicit than traditional conservative family values condoned. Hence the instability and contradictory nature of Thatcherism and its legacy were ever present not only in the media texts themselves but also in the public debate that surrounded them. The need for the government to introduce policies to regulate the media industries was a reoccurring trope at the end of the twentieth and beginning of the twenty-first centuries. Anxiety about both capitalism and the horrors of the welfare state, however, was fiercest when what was perceived a 'traditional family' was seen as under attack (albeit that this was in many ways an invented tradition). Durham has documented a range of campaigns about sexuality during the Thatcherite era, for example, Victoria Gillick's campaign against teenagers being prescribed the pill without parental knowledge. He emphasised both the anxiety expressed about sexuality in some sections of society and that government was not necessarily leading the agenda on sexuality. Fan Carter's chapter, which explores the attempt to regulate teenage girls' magazines in

1996, documents a moral panic over teenage girls' sexuality which had both historical precedents and other manifestations. For example, Pat Thane has pointed to the growing scapegoating of single mothers at the end of the twentieth century (2013).

Another example of Thatcherism's attempt to hold together contradictory discourses can be identified in the growing fascination with history in media texts, leisure and tourism. Many of the Merchant Ivory Films and historical adaptions of literary classics on television have been critiqued for creating, as Raphael Samuel points out, a past which belongs in the imagination only. To Higson, they were ideologically aligned to Thatcherism (1996; 2007), however, Andrews's closing chapter again suggests that these texts are more contradictory than perhaps they first appear. She argues that they offer spaces for unlikely heroines to articulate feminist discourses. Perhaps, however, a note of caution is needed for as Hall points out, 'few strategies are so successful at winning consent as those which root themselves in the contradictory elements of common sense, popular life and consciousness' (Hall 2011, 717).

BIBLIOGRAPHY / SOURCES

Arthurs, Jane. 2004. *Television and Sexuality: Regulation and the Politics of Taste*. Maidenhead, UK: Open University Press.

Durham, Martin. 1991. *Sex and Politics: Family and Morality in the Thatcher Years*. Basingstoke, UK: Palgrave Macmillan.

Hall Stuart. 2011 'The Neo-Liberal Revolution' in *Cultural Studies* vol 25 Issue No 6 2011 pp 705–728.

Hall, Stuart and Jacques,Martin. 1983. *The Politics of Thatcherism*. London: Lawrence and Wishart.

Higson, Andrew. 2007. *Fires Were Started: British Cinema and Thatcherism*. New York, NY. Columbia University Press.

Samuel, Raphael. 1996. *Theatres of Memory: Past and Present in Contemporary Culture*. London: Verso.

Thane, Pat, and Tanya Evans. 2012. *Sinners? Scroungers? Saints? Unmarried Mothers in Twentieth Century England*. Oxford University Press.

Wheeler, Wendy. 1994. 'Nostalgia Isn't Nasty.' In *Altered States: Postmodernism, Politics and Culture*, edited by Mark Perryman, 94–112. London: Lawrence and Wishart.

13 The Iron Lady and the Working Girl
The Image of the Prostitute in 1980s British Cinema

Paul Elliott

INTRODUCTION

> Is the Prime Minister aware that since she has been in office two of the major growth industries within our inner city areas have been child prostitution and street crime? Is this what she meant by the restoration of Victorian values? (Tony Banks, May 12, 1987, Prime Minister's Question Time)

Images of prostitution are common in British cinema and depictions of prostitutes can be broadly historicised to conform to changing ethical opinion. These images, however, are always the product of more than one discourse as socioeconomics, morality, legislation and aesthetics shape both how prostitution is depicted and how such depictions are deployed in the popular media. This chapter looks at images of prostitution in British cinema of the 1980s and in particular how debates on public morality and macroeconomics linked to Thatcherism prompted sometimes complex renegotiations of the figure of the prostitute in film. It also suggests, through the use of Colin MacCabe's canonical essay on realism, that historical analyses of media and filmic texts should always be mindful of the political and social dimensions of aesthetic forms. The aesthetic practises of filmmakers, if their work is to be historicised, should then form part of our discussion.

In contrast to the common assumption that Thatcher's Britain represented a return to Victorian moral values, depictions of prostitution in 1980s British cinema were remarkably permissive, often overtly attempting to either de-objectify or de-demonise women engaged in the sex trade. Films like *Personal Services* (1987), *Hussy* (1980), and *Prostitute* (1980) successfully deconstructed the myth of the working girl and exposed the mundane quotidian nature of selling sex, whereas films like *Mona Lisa* (1986) and *Half Moon Street* (1986) managed (with varying degrees of success) to suggest that selling one's body can sometimes be a personal decision born out of rational and reasoned thought rather than desperation or penury. Of course these films are complex in terms of the ideologies they both construct and draw from. They often fall into the trap, like so many texts on prostitution, of descrying the objectification of women and yet, at the same time, revelling in that very act. As Russell Campbell points out, this position—of having one's ideological cake and eating it—is endemic to artistic and literary depictions of the sex trade *per se* (Campbell 2006, 6). Very few texts manage to successfully negotiate the delicate minefield of taking a critical stance on prostitution without turning the reader or viewer into a punter themselves.

Changes in the representation of prostitution in the cinema were both a reflection of, and a contributor to, changes in the wider debates surrounding sex workers and their clients. Several high profile and important public events fed into what was, as Roger Matthews (2008, 7) suggests, an increased willingness to subject prostitution to the public gaze and to openly discuss the issues that arose from it. In 1975 the English Collective of Prostitutes (ECP) not only advocated the decriminalisation of sex work but also stressed the importance of re-evaluating the stereotypes of women who engaged in it. 1975 was also the year in which Peter Sutcliffe, who would later be arrested as the Yorkshire Ripper, began his serial killings and although the case would highlight deep-seated antipathies toward prostitutes *per se* it would also eventually feed into debates surrounding the visibility and safety of those working on the streets. Such visibility was also a key aspect of increased agitation over the red light areas of Britain's large cities (Matthews 2008, 7) as prostitution ceased being a vague nationalised concept and began instead to be thought of as a series of more localised concerns.

The development of feminist discourse surrounding prostitution during the late 1970s and 1980s also opened up the workings of the sex industry to academic interrogation. As Teela Sanders, Maggie O'Neill and Jane Pitcher (2009, 1–12) outline, however, broadly speaking feminist theory engaged with prostitution in two main ways: firstly, highlighting the symptomatic place of the prostitute in an abusive patriarchy (Dworkin 1981; Barry 1979) and, secondly, asserting the position of sex workers as members of a profession and ipso facto in possession of both human and employment rights (McLeod 1982). As Lorna Ryan (1997, 42) details, these two basic positions were also augmented by a number of feminist engagements with legality and criminality in general. Contemporary discourse surrounding prostitution, then, in the 1980s was complex and heterogeneous and should not be confused with the cinematic representation which was, by comparison, remarkably unified. The prostitute films of the 1980s do not constitute a cycle in the usual sense of the word. They are not linked in terms of theme, approach or ideological stance but they do share a general sympathy with the figure of the working girl in whatever form that might take. The films themselves cover a wide range of genres, from the crime-inflected styling of *Mona Lisa* and *Tank Malling* (1989) to the social realism of *Prostitute*; from the overt farce of *Personal Services* to the thriller-based narrative of *Half Moon Street*. All in all there were around 15 mainstream generally released feature films produced in the UK that specifically dealt with prostitution or have a prostitute as their main character. This does not include images of male prostitution (such as those in Ron Peck's *Empire State* (1988) or the many films where the sex trade is used as background scenery to a crime narrative. Neither does it include pornography, but does include documentary films like Nick Broomfield's *Chicken Ranch* (1983).

One of the interesting (and perhaps telling) aspects of this corpus is that it featured many of the major female stars of the period. Although of course the willingness of female stars to play prostitutes has a long history and is certainly not specific to Britain in the 1980s, Sigourney Weaver, Helen Mirren, Cathy Tyson, Julie Walters and Amanda Donohoe all starred as working girls in the '80s and happily plied their trade in a range of popular films. Almost without exception images of prostitution in British cinema of the 1980s differed from either those of the 1960s or those of the 1990s. As previously stated, the reasons for this are manyfold, however, they can be read against the backdrop of Thatcherite socioeconomic policies that, on the one hand, valued capital acquisition above moral frameworks and, on the other, inspired anti-Conservative discourse to coalesce around micro-political concerns such as the inter-sections between crime and sexuality. It is no accident that Left wing or liberal directors such as Tony Garnett (*Prostitute*), David Leland (*Wish You Were Here* 1987) and Neil Jordan (*Mona Lisa*) all looked to prostitution in the '80s for a mirror to society and a way of discussing the decade's contradictions. The films of the 1980s are also noticeably reticent on many of the negative aspects of the sex trade such as AIDS, drug abuse, and illegal trafficking; areas that will become so prevalent in the 1990s and 2000s. Although it seems counter-intuitive, the 1980s can be thought of as a form of golden age for the prostitute in British film and Thatcherism provides a useful framework for understanding this.

THE IRON LADY—SOCIOECONOMICS

As Lester Freidman states in the Preface to the 2006 edition of *Fires Were Started: British Cinema and Thatcherism*, 'The most prominent component of Thatcherism remains its economic policies' (Friedman 2006, xii). The relationship between Thatcherist economic policy and 1980s cinema can be seen to rest in two main areas: the economic modes of cinema production and the representation of economics diegetically. As might be expected, 1980s British cinema is suffused with images of making money and explorations of greed. However, it was also a time when governmental policy directly affected how films were produced. In many ways the structure of the current British film industry (both good and bad) was shaped under Thatcher's term of office and her rejection of Keynesian protectionism. I am suggesting here that both of these areas can be explored using films dealing with prostitution.

Ever since the 1920s, British cinema had been protected from the onslaught of Hollywood by various quotas and levies. The infamous Eady Levy, instigated by Harold Wilson in 1950, for example, attempted to ensure that British film production was funded in part by returns from international (read: Hollywood) box office receipts. In reality of course the truth was far from that as Hollywood studios abused the system and cashed in on the ready money available, meaning that money could be made from a film even if it was a box office flop, as Julian Petley outlines:

> Unlike in France and Italy, the Levy was not used to encourage certain *kinds* of production, and indeed it may well have contributed to further influxes of American capital by encouraging American companies to form British subsidiaries to produce 'British' films that could qualify for Eady money. By 1984, the Levy was raising about £4.5m per year (Petley 1986, 38).

Recognising that such levies were the equivalent of subsidised production, the Thatcher government abolished them in 1985 with the *Films Bill*, effectively opening the film industry up to the free market (Quart 2006, 21).

The prostitute films reflected this new economic plurality and were funded by a variety of different means. Tony Garnett's *Prostitute* was made with a private gift of £400,000; *Mona Lisa* was jointly funded by Handmade films (George Harrison's film production company) and Channel 4; *Half Moon Street* was bank rolled by Hollywood studio RKO; Nick Broomfield's documentary *Chicken Ranch* was funded by Central Television; *Tank Malling* was funded by an independent production company, and so on. It is possible to see here how free-market Thatcherite economics directly affected the shape of British filmmaking and would provide an alternative to both the state-orientated model of the 1950s and the industrialised vertical integration of the 1920s and 30s. This model would come to dominate British film production until the setting up of the National Lottery in 1994, an event that would galvanise the industry and provide a successful substitute for the loss of state subsidisation.

In terms of representation, the 1980s prostitute films also reflected the political zeitgeist, as women were depicted as utilising the only tools that a patriarchal society allows them: their bodies. As Yvonne Tasker (1998, 126–127) details in relation to Hollywood texts like *Klute* (1971), the depiction of prostitution as merely an economic transaction rather than a moral black hole into which women fall was both shocking and innovative and highlighted the connections between sexuality and women's work *per se*. The sex industry was also shown as being highly stratified with a clear class distinction between those who control supply and those who were slaves to demand. In a literal rendering of the Thatcherite value of home ownership there is a clear moral demarcation between the prostitute on the street and the prostitute in the hotel or brothel. In films like *Personal Services*, *Half Moon Street* and

Hussy there is also an obvious class distinction that not only relativizes the moral position but negates much of the danger inherent in selling one's body. The prostitute in these scenarios was often depicted as the ultimate small business-woman, in charge of her product and able to cope with demand. This is contrasted, especially in a film like *Mona Lisa*, with the girl on the street, who is imagined as being marginalised, abused and in need of protection. The security of property denied her, the street walker (like her Victorian counterpart) was exposed to more than just the elements as class and socio-economic position made her vulnerable to abuse from clients and pimps.

THE IRON LADY—MORALITY

The 1980s added little in the way of concrete legislation to the area of prostitution. Then, as now, prostitution *per se* was legal but many of the behaviours that are associated with it were not: soliciting, keeping a brothel, kerb crawling, advertising sexual services in phone booths and so on were all punishable by fines and, sometimes, terms in prison. The major post-war statement on prostitution was the 1957 *Report of the Committee on Homosexual Offenses and Prostitution*, otherwise known as *The Wolfenden Report*. *Wolfenden* is, perhaps, better known for the impact it had on the de-criminalisation of homosexuality some years later, but it also set the moral tone for Britain's stance on the sex trade for the next 50 years. The main ideological position of *Wolfenden*, for both prostitution and homosexuality, was a belief in the separation of morality and politics. The mantra it repeated often was that "the law is not concerned with private morals or with ethical sanctions" (Wolfenden 1963, 133) and consequently its recommendations were often non-interventionist in character. However, *Wolfenden* did articulate many of the key concerns and prejudices surrounding prostitution in the post-war period, concerns that continue to be in the forefront of the debate even today. Whereas the selling of sex was seen as ultimately immoral and objectionable, it was also viewed as a matter for the private conscience and so allowed to exist unless it cause an annoyance to society at large. This of course included conspicuous loitering and soliciting, another manifestation of the abhorrence of the streetwalker and her place as an abject figure in the urban environment.

Ironically of course this position mirrored that of the early Thatcher Government whose statement in the 1983 election manifesto on public morality—that "It is not for the government to try to dictate how men and women should organise their lives" (Conservative Party 1983)—came close to that of Wolfenden 26 years earlier. Only in 1987 did the Thatcher government begin to employ rhetoric such as 'traditional values' and it was as late as 1997 (long after Thatcher vacated office) that the 'Back to Basics' philosophy manifested itself in Conservative party literature as it talked of the role schools have in the moral education of children.

As Elizabeth Wilson states (1987, 201) Thatcherism was never inflected with the religious far-right that characterised Reaganism in the United States. Although a tightening of law and order was always a major facet of Thatcherite social policy, this tended to be directed at the protection of property and the person rather than public morality. The term 'morality', sexual or otherwise, very rarely appears in Thatcherite discourse and less still in sources discussing it. When morals are mentioned, as Beatrix Campbell in *The Iron Ladies: Why Do Women Vote Tory*, suggests Margaret Thatcher herself is remarkably absent and the mantle of Tory morality taken up instead by figures such as Edwina Currie and Victoria Gillick (Campbell 1987, 182). The gap opened up by this lack of any distinct moral vision allowed filmmakers in the 1980s to increasingly engage with issues of sexuality in the popular arena. The prostitute films of the 1980s, for example, clearly reflected a growing interest in the sexuality of young working-class women whose liberal attitude towards their own bodies was held in comparison to an aged and repressive patriarchy.

As Justine King suggests, there was a discernible cycle of films produced in the '80s that, although tinged with a sense of desperation and longing, featured a specific brand of female sexual liberation (King 1996, 216–230). King looks at five films of the era: *Shirley Valentine* (1989); *Wish You Were Here*; *Letter to Brezhnev* (1985); *She'll Be Wearing Pink Pyjamas* (1985) and *Educating Rita* (1983) and interestingly, two of these—*Shirley Valentine* and *Wish You Were Here*—feature prostitutes in their narratives. This cycle extended into films where young female sexuality became the locus of class and socioeconomic experience: *Rita, Sue and Bob Too* (1987); *Sammy and Rosie Get Laid* (1987), and *Scandal* (1989) all depict young, largely working-class girls, who view sex as a way out of their mundane social positions.

In her essay from Stuart Hall and Martin Jacques's foundational text *The Politics of Thatcherism*, Jean Gardiner suggests that this position—of sex as cheap recreation—might be particularly pertinent to working-class women in the early 1980s (Gardiner 1983, 193). Women were particularly susceptible to the forms of under employment that came with a move from a Fordist to a post-Fordist society and were also less likely to register as unemployed, being denied the kinds of politicisation that we see explored in texts like *Boys from the Blackstuff* (1982) and films like Mike Leigh's *Meantime* (1984). In the Thatcherite era, then, male and female promiscuity was often depicted as less sexual liberation and more a way of filling in time and staving off the boredom of the dole queue. As Sue states, in Andrea Dunbar's script for *Rita, Sue and Bob Too*: 'There's nothing to do round here but have a jump'—a sentiment that is echoed in many films of the period. This not only inevitably personalises the political but also corporealizes it, reifying ideology through the awkward manifesto of sweaty flesh. The crucial element here is that this same moral sense can be detected in the prostitute films, which often depict sex from a female point of view as either fun, absurd or downright laughable. Many of these films evoke a bawdiness that is best thought of in terms of 18th century pornography; Gerry O'Hara's adaptation of *Fanny Hill* (1983) provides us with the most obvious example but there are also shades of this in the easy sexuality of *The Missionary* (1982), *Personal Services* and in American cinema films like *The Best Little Whorehouse in Texas* (1982). In the time of rising fears over the AIDS epidemic, cinema it seems nostalgically looked back to a time where sex could be enjoyed without fear and reprisals and where, in the words of Dolly Parton's character Mona Stangley, 'There's nothing dirty going on.'

THE WORKING GIRL—COUNTER-DISCURSIVE REALISM

One of the more striking aspects of British cinema in the 1980s was the sheer amount of anti-government feeling explored in its narratives. At no point in recent history has the popular media been used to such an extent to debate and critique party political issues. Such counter-discourse can be found in a wide variety of cinematic forms and genres; everything from the crime film (*Empire State*; *Stormy Monday* (1988); *The Long Good Friday* (1981)) to avant-garde art-house (*The Cook, The Thief, His Wife and Her Lover* (1989); *A Zed and Two Noughts* (1986); *The Last of England* (1988)) was used to critique all aspects of the Thatcher Government. Whether it was the costume drama or the thriller, genre was often merely another way of dealing with the political.

It was social realism, however, that provided the decade's longest lasting political statements and possibly the only genre that would maintain its ideological mandate after the resignation of Thatcher in 1991. Whereas the crime film would be transformed by postmodernity and post-feminism (*Lock, Stock and Two Smoking Barrels* (1998); *Snatch* (2000); *Love, Honour and Obey* (2000)) and art-house cinema would become inward looking and concerned with the personal and the literary (*Blue* (1993); *Prospero's Books* (1991); *Wittgenstein* (1993)), social realism would continue to produce politically motivated films throughout the 1990s and on into the new millennium. With this is mind, this last section takes a closer look at *the* most social realist prostitute film of the 1980s, Tony Garnett's *Prostitute*, and seeks to uncover some of the ways that the prostitute narrative provided a conduit for thematised dissent and political debate. A tacit assumption of this discussion is that the full political impact of Garnett's film can only be understood if it is viewed within the context of debates surrounding social realism coming out of the 1970s and feeding into the cinema of the Thatcherite period. I want to suggest here that historical debate around contentious and temporally specific texts like the prostitute films of the 1980s need to take into account the aesthetic as well as the narratological.

Garnett wrote and directed *Prostitute* after acting as producer on two high profile and controversial television projects for the BBC: 1975's *Days of Hope* and 1978's *Law and Order*. Both serials lent not only an ideological but also an aesthetic vision to what would be Garnett's directorial debut and, importantly, a project that he would have total control over. As Stephen Lacey states (2007, 98), *Days of Hope*, which detailed the precursors to and aftermath of the General Strike of 1926, was heavily rooted in the forms of social realism that Loach and Garnett had been fostering since *Cathy Come Home* (1966) and *Kes* (1969). Although it was, as John Hill says, 'a new turn in Loach's work' (2010, 134), representing, as it did, an historical drama, it was perhaps as noticeable for its ideological content as its deployment of a realist aesthetic; characters openly debated socialist principles and espoused philosophies in a narrative style that owes something to the Brechtian *Lehrstucke*.

Prostitute can also be read against two of the major debates occurring in British Media and Cultural Studies throughout the 1970s: the debate on naturalism and television drama instigated by Troy Kennedy Martin in his article 'Nats Go Home' (Kennedy Martin, 1964) and the debate between Colin MacCabe and Colin McArthur in the journal *Screen* (MacCabe 1974/1985; McArthur 1976/1985). Taken together these two discussions would shape the character of British realism throughout the 1980s and would provide a point of departure from the tropes and visual storytelling of the British New Wave. If the first great period of British social realism arose out of the theorising of Grierson and the Documentary Film Movement and the second out of Free Cinema, then a third major period can be seen to arise out of debates surrounding television and its place as a carrier of ideology.

Garnett's film declares its aesthetic intentions from its opening moments, as the director employs familiar social realist techniques: shots that establish space and place, details of the urban environment and editing that surveys a variety of possible narrative subjects. The opening shots, and the accompanying soundtrack, suggest that the narrative might consider the place of 'race' and immigration in contemporary Britain as the audience is presented with a series of images reflecting the range of Birmingham's diverse communities in the late 1970s. However, the film's true subject is soon revealed as the camera alights on Sandra (Eleanor Forsythe) leaving a punter's car and Jean (Kim Lockett) and Rose (Nancy Samuels) talking about their work by the steps of a dilapidated cinema.

Like other realist films of the period (*Letter to Brezhnev*; *Rita, Sue and Bob Too*; *Educating Rita*, etc.), *Prostitute* details the narratives of women who are left to pick up the pieces from the kinds of the masculine erosion that can be seen beginning in the films of the British New Wave. The heroines of the 1980s, however, are afforded none of the poetry of their 1960s male counterparts; the towns they inhabit offer none of the dreamy vistas studded with mineshafts, chimneys and 'That Long Shot of Our Town from that Hill' (Higson 1996, 134). Instead, Sandra, Jean and Rose are embedded within an urban cityscape that not only offers little in the way of escape but also allows them no magisterial view to look back from.

The camera-work in these opening scenes reflects the objectivity advocated by Kennedy Martin in his influential article of 1964. Kennedy Martin asserted that contemporary TV drama (that was, after all, still largely broadcast live) existed within the bounds of traditional theatre, making it heavily reliant on dialogue, staged performance and subjectivised (and therefore Bourgeois) camera work—the latter also being an element of Classical Hollywood production. Although Kennedy Martin is theorising about TV drama here, his points are still very much pertinent to *Prostitute*, schooled as Garnett was in the television of Ken Loach and Les Blair. For Kennedy Martin and for many other writers of the period (Garnett and Loach included), the 'new drama' of television (and by extension cinema inspired by television) should also avoid the usual processes of visual pleasure and audience identification that are endemic to Hollywood cinema, as Kennedy Martin writes:

> Since naturalism evolved from a theatre of dialogue, the director is forced into photographing faces talking and faces reacting. The director faced with a torrent of words can only retreat into the neutrality of the two- and three-shot where the camera, caged from seizing anything of significance, is emasculated and only allowed to gaze around the room following the conversation like an attentive stranger. This enslavement of the visual element is too binding. (Kennedy Martin 1964, 25)

It is precisely this aesthetic that underpins much of *Prostitute*'s cinematography, as the camera hangs back, burying itself in the crowd, viewing the central characters from a distance; not wanting to intrude. It is this documentary objectivity that allowed Garnett to avoid the kinds of voyeuristic pleasure usually associated with the prostitute narrative, as even scenes detailing sexual activity become clinical and removed. One notable scene in particular depicts a working girl manually pleasuring a client in a darkly lit brothel; however there is none of the erotic visual sense of the mainstream Hollywood film and none of the filmic mechanisms that attempt to suture us into the narrative through immersion and character identification. The prostitute's body is starkly photographed and her caesarean scar is clearly visible underlining what is a tacit assumption of the entire film: that prostitution is an occupation rather than state of being (a point that is the direct opposite of that taken by *Wolfenden*). This is the prostitute as small business-woman, an image that marks her instantly as one of Thatcher's children.

Perhaps *the* most important narrative strain in Garnett's film however concerns Jean's efforts to organise and unionise the girls on the street, a storyline that not only reflects Garnett's experience on *Days of Hope* but that also highlights the ways in which prostitute narratives, in the 1980s, were co-opted into a variety of different discursive practices. Organisation becomes a defence against the dangers of both punters and police, as the single, isolated prostitute is depicted as being both vulnerable and alone. In an era of increasing suspicion towards the unions, Jean's struggle against the apathy of her fellow co-workers takes on a metaphorical role as Garnett mirrors both the form and the pedagogic intent of his work with Loach. As Russell Campbell states:

> *Prostitute* goes beyond the social expose tradition in positing a response to the injustice in terms of collective political action. Working committee meetings are shown, distributing leaflets, visiting the local MP, handling publicity in the media. The hurdles met within such organizing are acknowledged: the reluctance of some streetwalkers to participate, fearing that they and their families may become more vulnerable (Campbell 2006, 308).

Prostitute narrativises dissent and uses sex as a way of challenging the dominant political ideology. By stressing Garnett's mandate in terms of prostitution, however, Campbell presents only part of the film's aims. When contextualised within its socio-political era and when read alongside *Days of Hope* it is possible to read *Prostitute* as a political as well as a moral film, and its depiction of Jean's struggle for unionisation an exploration of a more national concern; as already suggested this became especially important in an era that saw vast numbers of working-class women depoliticised and disenfranchised. As well as a study of the sex industry, Garnett's film is a political fable that encourages social change and reverses the trend highlighted by John Hill whereby British cinema of the '80s contained 'virtually no representation of "community" as such and very few images of collective action' (Hill 1999, 166).

Colin's MacCabe's influential essay 'Realism and the Cinema: Notes on Some Brechtian Theses' (1974/1985) originally suggested that the 'Classical Realist Text' can best be understood as consisting of a formal structure that organises various levels of discourse into a hierarchy with a totalising narrative equating to truth at its apex. Realism, asserts MacCabe, is a closed system, that denies the viewer agency and offers only predetermined moral and political choices. In order for a text to be truly revolutionary it should, suggested MacCabe, offer space for contradiction and multiple readings, as well as encouraging agency on the part of the audience.

MacCabe's overly formalist approach in this article has been criticised by a number of different writers since (Bordwell 1988; Caughie 2000, etc.) and may not be applicable to *all* realist texts as he claims, however, it does have a great deal to say about how *Prostitute* can be read as a text in both its narrative and its form and subsequently how this knowledge can be used to flesh out Realism's place as a counter-discourse in this period. For

MacCabe, the Classical realist text privileges the visual discourse above all others, encouraging an audience to believe what they see over what they are told by a voice-over. He uses the example of the Hollywood film *Klute* to illustrate this:

> In *Klute* the relationship of dominance between discourses is peculiarly accentuated by the fact that the film is interspersed with fragments of Bree talking to her psychiatrist. This subjective discourse can be exactly measured against the reality provided by the unfolding of the story. Thus all her talk of independence is portrayed as finally an illusion as we discover, to no great surprise but to our immense relief, what she really wants is to settle down in the Mid-West with John Klute (MacCabe 1985, 202).

The end of *Prostitute* has a similar split between audio and the visual; however, it is complicated by class and morality. In the final scenes we hear Louise (the middle-class social worker) talking to a BBC producer about her fears about the kinds of neat narrative closure that MacCabe suggests is endemic to the Classical realist text; she says for example:

> I have seen serious programmes before that have reinforced people's misconceptions . . . and with the best intentions, I have seen very well-meaning programmes on homosexuals for instance that showed two men making a bed, close up of ringed hands, and the men saying 'We have been accepted like any other couple'.

Against these fears the audience is presented with a series of images that close the film. Sandra is seen soliciting opposite an 'anglo-continental' grocer, Rose is seen against advertising hoardings reinforcing the connection between sex and business and June is depicted valiantly continuing her attempts to collectivise, walking the streets, chatting to girls and organising. The images serve to fully ground the prostitute in a world of competing discourses, as family, economics, the media, sex and small business act on the figure of the working girl.

Garnett's film is not the closed system that MacCabe's essay suggests it might be; the audience is left with a disquieting sense of contradiction—on the one hand Sandra (who has returned from a disastrous stint in London) is back home but, on the other, she is back in the game. Louise voices her concerns about stereotypical images of prostitutes in the media and yet visually we are presented with a series of tableaus that are recognisably drawn from the collective cultural store and the final figure we see is an unnamed girl, isolated, standing next to a sign that says 'On Sale'. The text cannot resolve the tension between the voice-over and the images in the neat way that MacCabe does with *Klute*; there is no objective truth here, just the hint of a debate in progress, a debate that was noticeably played out in 1980s British cinema. As the previous two sections of this chapter have suggested, these contradictions mirror those of the wider society and, more importantly, the Thatcherite socio-economic policy that helped to shape it.

CONCLUSION

In contrast to the figure of the Iron Lady, the working girl presented a picture of much needed plenitude in the 1980s, an ebullient sexuality that was often held in contrast with the stuffiness of middle class propriety. The girls in Richard Loncraine's *The Missionary* serve to undercut the staid conservatism of The Reverend Charles Fortescue with their buxom sexual liberation; the young Cynthia Payne does the same in Leland's *Wish You Were Here*. Like *Sammy and Rosy Get Laid*, *Rita, Sue and Bob Too* or characters in John Goldschmidt's *She'll Be Wearing Pink Pyjamas*, working-class sexuality in the prostitute films is often depicted as an antidote to the austerity of Conservative Party politics, a way of surviving the decade of have and have nots. With films like *Stella Does Tricks* (1996), *Everything* (2004) and *London to Brighton* (2006) the 1990s and 2000s would take a noticeably different stance on prostitution and see it as a problem for both society and women. It would be allied to discourses of disease, child abuse, drugs, and human trafficking and very rarely would films offer the images of female agency that were seen in the 1980s. The fact that men produced, wrote and directed all of the prostitute films of 1980s of course problematizes, if not negates entirely, any claim that the 1980s prostitute films could be thought of as feminist texts—they are not. No matter how much they renegotiate the traditional view of the working girl as either inherently without any agency or morally problematic, these films are still viewed through male gaze as some of the semiotic signifiers of the advertising posters attest to.

I have tried to suggest here that texts like the prostitute films of the 1980s should not only be examined for their narratives but for their form as well. If the generic properties of a film like *Prostitute*, for example, are ignored, so is much of the cultural specificity of film's textual presence and moreover much of its subversive, counter-discursive impact. This is of course especially important in Realist texts that tend to be framed as mimesis rather than representation. This inevitably involves cross-disciplinary methodology, drawing from both history and areas like film and media studies.

BIBLIOGRAPHY / SOURCES

Barry, Kathleen. 1979. *Female Sexual Slavery*. New York University Press.
Bordwell, David. 1988. *Narration in the Fiction Film*. London: Routledge.

Cameron, Deborah, and Elizabeth Frazer. 1987. *The Lust to Kill*. London: Polity Press.

Campbell, Beatrix. 1987. *The Iron Ladies: Why Do Women Vote Tory?* London: Virago.

Campbell, Russell. 2006. *Marked Women: Prostitutes and Prostitution in the Cinema*. Madison: University of Wisconsin Press.

Caughie, John. 2000. *Television Drama: Realism, Modernism and British Culture*. Oxford University Press.

Dworkin, Andrea. 1981. *Pornography: Men Possessing Women?* London: Women's Press.

Friedman, Lester D. 2006. 'The Empire Strikes Out: An American Perspective on the British Film Industry.' In *Fires Were Started: British Cinema and Thatcherism*, edited by Lester D. Friedman, 1–14. London: Wallflower Press.

Gardiner, Jean. 1983. 'Women, Recession and the Tories.' In *The Politics of Thatcherism*, edited by Stuart Hall and Jacques Martin, 188–206. . London: Lawrence and Wishart.

Higson, Andrew. 1996. 'Space, Place, Spectacle: Landscape and Townscape in the Kitchen Sink Film.' In *Dissolving Views: Key Writings on British Cinema*, edited by Andrew Higson, 133–156. . London: Cassell.

Hill, John. 1999. *British Cinema in the 1980s*. Oxford University Press.

Hill, John. 2011. *Ken Loach: The Politics of Film and Television*. London: BFI.

Kennedy Martin, Troy. 1964. 'Nats Go Home: First Statement of a New Drama for Television.' *Encore*, March-April, 21–33.

King, Justine. 1996. 'Crossing Thresholds: The Contemporary British Woman's Film.' In *Dissolving Views: Key Writings on British Cinema*, edited by Andrew Higson, 216–231. London: Cassell.

Lacey, Stephen. 2007. *Tony Garnett*. Manchester University Press.

Matthews, Roger. 2008. *Prostitution, Politics and Policy*. London: Routledge.

MacCabe, Colin. (1975) 1985. 'Days of Hope: A Response to Colin McArthur.' In *Popular Television and Film*, edited by Tony Bennett, Susan Boyd-Bowman, Colin Mercer, and Janet Woollacott, 310–313. London: BFI.

MacCabe, Colin. (1974) 1985. 'Realism and the Cinema: Notes on Brechtian Theses.' In *Popular Television and Film*, edited by Tony Bennett, Susan Boyd-Bowman, Colin Mercer, and Janet Woollacott, 216–235. London: BFI.

McArthur, Colin. (1976) 1985. 'Days of Hope.' In *Popular Television and Film*, edited by Tony Bennett, Susan Boyd-Bowman, Colin Mercer, and Janet Woollacott, 305–309. London: BFI. McLeod, Eileen. 1982. *Women Working: Prostitution Now*. London: Croom Helm.

McSmith, Andy. 2011. *No Such Things as Society: A History of Britain in the 1980s*. London: Constable.

Petley, Julian. 1986. 'Cinema and the State.' In *All Our Yesterdays: 90 Years of British Cinema*, edited by Charles Barr. London: BFI.

Quart, Leonard. 2006. 'The Religion of the Market: Thatcherite Politics and the British Film of the 1980s.' In *Fires Were Started: British Cinema and Thatcherism*, edited by Lester D. Friedman, 15–29. London: Wallflower Press.

Sanders, Teela, Maggie O'Neill, and Jane Pitcher. 2009. *Prostitution: Sex Work, Policy and Politics*. London: Sage.

Tasker, Yvonne. 1998. *Working Girls: Gender and Sexuality in Popular Cinema*. London: Routledge.

Wilson, Elizabeth. 1987. 'Thatcherism and Women: After Seven Years.' *Socialist Register* 23. Accessed July 14, 2012. http://socialistregister.com/index.php/srv/article/view/5546.

The Wolfenden Report: Report of the Committee on Homosexual Offenses and Prostitution. (1957) 1963. New York: Stein and Day.

FILMOGRAPHY AND TELEVISION PROGRAMMES

A Zed and Two Noughts (1986)
Blue (1993)
Boys from the Blackstuff (1982)
Cathy Come Home (1966)
Chicken Ranch (1983)
Educating Rita (1983)
Empire State (1988)
Everything (2004)
Half Moon Street (1986)
Hussy (1980)
Kes (1969)
Klute (1971)
Letter to Brezhnev (1985)
Lock, Stock and Two Smoking Barrels (1998)
London to Brighton (2006)
Love, Honour and Obey (2000)
Meantime (1984)
Mona Lisa (1986)
Personal Services (1987)
Prospero's Books (1991)
Prostitute (1980)
Rita, Sue and Bob Too (1987)
Sammy and Rosie Get Laid (1987)
She'll Be Wearing Pink Pyjamas (1985)
Scandal (1989)
Shirley Valentine (1989)
Snatch (2000)
Stella Does Tricks (1996)
Stormy Monday (1988)
Tank Malling (1989)
The Best Little Whorehouse in Texas (1982)
The Cook, The Thief, His Wife and Her Lover (1989)
The Last of England (1988)
The Long Good Friday (1981)
The Missionary (1982)
Wish You Were Here (1987)
Wittgenstein (1993)

14 Feminism and Femininity

The Potential Politics of Consuming Popular Culture: A Case Study of *Marie Claire*'s Reportage of Global Humanitarian Politics

Maggie Andrews

INTRODUCTION: CONTEXTUALISING *MARIE CLAIRE*, CONSUMER FEMININITY AND POST-FEMINISM

The popular women's magazine *Marie Claire* was launched in Britain in 1988 and offered readers a web of contradictory discourses to navigate their way through. Unlike many women's magazines of the era these discourses portrayed not only consumer femininity but also invited readers to flirt with fantasies of political engagement and feminism commensurate with the new visibility for women in positions of power. Britain's first woman prime minister, Margaret Thatcher, had been elected in 1979, while 1997 saw the election of 101 women Labour MPs, known as 'Blair's Babes', after their party leader Tony Blair achieved a landslide election victory. A range of features in *Marie Claire* explored global political issues such as world debt and motherhood in repressive regimes, or discussed women as victims of war in Sierra Leone or footbinding in China. Drawing upon textual analysis of such articles and readers' responses to them gleaned from: their published letters, website entries and informal interviews, it will be suggested that these representations were certainly problematic, often portraying non-white women as spectacles of otherness (Hall 1998) or the objects of the voyeuristic gaze (Mulvey 1975). This was, however, perhaps preferable to the more repressive regimes of silence that surrounded non-white women within the apolitical consumer femininity of the majority of women's magazines of the era.

Marie Claire was launched in the wake of second wave feminism of the 1970s which had been wary and critical of both consumer culture and women's magazines, and established alternative publications such as *Spare Rib* (1972–1993) which by 1988 already had a dwindling circulation. Nevertheless, in the late 1980s and 1990s academic work by feminist scholars (such as Nava 1992 and Carter 1997) had stimulated debate around the relationship of women to consumption and introduced the thesis that consumption was for many women a potential space in which to develop expertise, and to a certain extent power (Andrews and Talbot 2000).

Indeed in the twentieth century the media, whether via the *Daily Mail* Ideal Home Exhibition (Ryan 2000) or women's magazines, was a key area in which the potential creativity and constraints of consumer culture and the contradictory pleasures of acceptable envy were beginning to be explored. The Thatcherite 80s and the emergence of 'post-modern society' placed consumerism in a culturally central position by the new millennium. This was affirmed by the British film comedy *About a Boy* (2002) starring Hugh Grant, in which single mother Fiona Brewer's successful transition from 'suicidal self-obsession' to 'proper self-effacing motherhood', and the establishment of an understanding connection with her son, was signalled when she abandoned her anti-globalisation political principles and offered to take him to McDonalds. Here 'normality' is defined by a willingness to participate in consumer culture, an indication of the degree of slippage that operated between notions of 'consumer' and that of 'citizen', which Anne Cronin has remarked upon (2000). Any apparent tension between political engagement and consumerism was not so starkly presented in many of the female cultural spaces where feminism operated as a structuring absence, a feminism that Probyn suggested was 'bound up with the discourse of choice' (1993, 284). Life choices between, for example, motherhood and childlessness, or paid and domestic labour, were in the 80s and 90s increasingly articulated in terms of lifestyle and consumer culture. A number of women's magazines, for example *Cosmopolitan* under Julie D'Acci's editorship, built their success on allowing women to play with fantasies of a range of subject positions, defined by consumption choices, the first of which was the purchase of the magazine itself. This strikes a chord with Hilary Radner's perception of women's consumption of glossy magazines as providing their readers with 'a position of circumscribed autonomy' whereby 'the reader is recognised as complicit in the system of consumerism that constitutes her as subject. But she is actively rather than passively engaged in a process of her own constitution as subject' (1995, 78). Discourses of choice became increasingly pervasive and as Angela McRobbie has argued, by the turn of the new millennium ideas of post-feminism could be identified in a range of popular media texts, with films such as *Bridget Jones's Diary* (2001) and magazines like *Cosmopolitan* (2004) suggesting many of the goals of feminism had been achieved. At first glance *Marie Claire*, the magazine, which is the focus of this case study, seems no different; its 300–400 sumptuous glossy pages were packed with all the usual elements of an up-market women's monthly. Its advertising brief in 2000 explained: '*Marie Claire* regularly featured fashion, beauty, health, interior design and entertaining, in a style designed to appeal to the readers' own chic and sophisticated tastes'. All these things ensured that, for women in social groups A, B and C-1, aged approximately 30 (the magazine's target audience), *Marie Claire* provided a 'mental chocolate' (Winship 1987, 160). It did this so successfully that in May 2002 it was the third best-selling women's magazine in the UK after *Cosmopolitan* and

Glamour. What distinguished *Marie Claire* from its rivals was, according to the magazine's own publicity material at the turn of the millennium, 'regular, thought provoking articles on a diverse range of topics aimed at those with an intelligent outlook on life' (*Marie Claire* media pack 1996). Some of these articles give a less than conventional, even a quirky take on sex or relationships—for example, 'Why I prefer sex with married men' (August 1999). However the middle-class and middle-aged women whose opinions graced readers' websites and *Marie Claire* letters pages were just as likely to refer to the inclusion of the political features which contributed to its reputation as 'the only glossy with brains', to quote the magazine cover's strap line. *Marie Claire* therefore offered its readers politically engaged subject positions, including a feminist sensibility (Gill 2007). Celebrity features focused on women in the news such as Monica Lewinsky, the intern who had a sexual relationship with President Bill Clinton (April 1999), and Louise Woodward, the British nanny accused of shaking a baby to death in the U.S. (August 1999). Features included political or social issues such as 'How Racist is Britain?' (March 1999) and 'Women who Kill Their Plastic Surgeons', which suggested independent thoughtful subject positions were on offer to readers who through the magazine were invited to participate in critical political engagement.

Many of the articles and campaigns that *Marie Claire* featured during the late 1990s and at the turn of the millennium could be categorised as specifically women's, even feminist, issues—for example, the Breast Cancer Awareness campaign in October 1999 and the campaign to highlight violence against women linked to V-Day in 2002. As Joanne Hollows suggests, 'many modes of femininity are articulated in relation to feminism' (2008, 203), something which can be clearly seen in the 32-page special supplement on British fashion *Marie Claire* produced in October 1993 for the celebration of 75 years of women's enfranchisement in Britain. The inter-twining of the pleasures of consumer femininity and political awareness were on offer to the reader through eight sepia-coloured pages revealing long-length skirts and numerous layers of tweedy clothing on willowy and shorthaired models. The women were all photographed in traditional London settings—such as by the Thames. It is the prefix to the images which attempts to anchor the meaning of the supplement: 'In keeping with the turn of the century campaigners, traditional British fabrics have made a return. Flannel and herringbone, long skirts and layers are teamed with lace-up boots and crisp shirts and trimmed with lace and velvet. These are clothes for women of action'. Furthermore, the women carry banners, badges or symbols of more recent post-sixties feminism—'a woman's right to choose' or 'reclaim the night' for example. The polysemia of these images was almost boundless; the reader had the possibility of playing through lifestyle or dress with a fleeting affiliation to a subject position which is identifiably feminist, but they do, I would suggest, offer a displacement of the political concerns of feminism onto a somewhat ambivalent sense of the past, albeit a past which is confused between two different historical periods. By comparison, *Cosmopolitan* in the same month devoted thirty pages to an attempt to portray feminism as sexy and fun under the heading 'Feminism Now'.

Marie Claire invited their readership to flirt with the subject position of politically engaged femininity, and embrace at least a passing involvement with gender politics. That this was core to the magazine's identity is endorsed by a letter published in 2000 under the heading 'Taking Women Seriously' which explained: 'What a relief—a magazine that recognises that 'female' doesn't mean feeble-minded, feather brained, fashion fanatic. Women can, and do, think, observe, and participate politically. It is refreshing to find a mainstream women's publication that caters for reader's interest in global humanitarian affairs' (November 2000, 84). The focus of this letter, the coverage of 'global humanitarian affairs' was presented within the magazine as either 'reportage' or under the headings of international or global affairs, which included titles such as: 'The Girls from Ipanema' (July 2000), 'Where Women Are Tortured for Being Single' (February 2000) and 'Glimpses of Hope from Behind the Veil' (August 2001). Analysing the significance and meanings of such material is problematic; they were open to varied interpretations at the point of consumption. For as Jokes Hermes has suggested, readers may have consumed the magazine mindlessly, as a form of relaxation, vegging out on the fantasy world it offered and rarely reading the more 'earnest' articles (1995, 8). However, the letter above suggests that for some readers the selection of *Marie Claire*, rather than numerous other magazines on sale, rested upon the features which focussed upon global and political issues. The 'what if' element that is part of the experience of reading all magazines that is usually completed by 'I buy' such and such an item becomes instead in these articles 'what if . . . I were a woman whose life was framed by a very different cultural framework'. This therefore was a version of post-feminism with the capacity to looking beyond the concerns of white western women.

MARIE CLAIRE'S UNIQUENESS: REPORTAGE OF GLOBAL HUMANITARIAN POLITICS

Arguably *Marie Claire*'s reportage of global humanitarian politics offered readers scope to construct a post-feminist identity predicated on a displacement of gender oppression onto non-western 'other' women, but this displacement was not straightforward. The articles simultaneously stress points of sameness and difference between readers and the 'subjects', although these fragmented and ambiguous texts incorporated 'danger points' where discourses might begin to unravel and be questioned.

Arguably the appeal of the articles, and perhaps the magazine as a whole, lay in its ambivalence. One feature entitled 'Chinese Footbinding: The Last

Survivors Tortured for Men's Pleasure in an Isolated Village in South West China' and went on to explain that is was about women 'whose feet have been crushed to the size of a child's' (March 1999, 192) displaced gender oppression onto non-western women but also suggested complex contradictory discourses of femininity and feminism were at work. The reader was informed the Liuyu women were remnants 'of a mutilating tradition that lasted a thousand years' (March 1999, 193). An implied narrative of historical progression and development operated alongside one that refused a sense of victimhood. Footbinding, the reader was re-assured, no longer occurred in China. A liberal history of women's developing independence was suggested, which if not exactly mirroring that of Western women readers' perceived progress to post-feminism, at least legitimating it. The determination of the Chinese women that their daughters should have a better life echoes one of the discourses of second wave western feminism. It could be argued the article perpetrated a notion of the irredeemable difference and inherent inferiority implicit in the discourse of orientalism which Edward Said argues 'came to define the nature of the Orient and the oriental as irredeemably different and always inferior to the West. Thus orientalism establishes a set of polarities in which the orient is characterised as irrational, exotic, erotic, despotic, and heathen, thereby securing the West in contrast as rational, familiar, moral and Christian' (1996, 16). The binary opposition between the West and the Orient can be identified in the discourses at play which suggest the Liuyu women were 'victims' struggling towards self-determination and *Marie Claire* readers were confident, discerning, sophisticated and aware of the world around them, women who perceived discussions about equality to be irrelevant. Arguably, the post-feminist consumer femininity of this magazine was predicated upon the disempowerment of 'the other' women.

The women interviewed were not, however, represented as passive victims, but as resourceful and resilient. It was explained:

> most of Liuyi's bound-foot women were not content to remain help-less daughters or erotic wives, despite their immobilising condition. Luo Lin, for one, managed a passable hobble only two years after her feet were bound . . . These women who for so many years could barely even stand upright, now do t'ai chi, sword dancing, fencing, even disco dancing. They are fierce lawn bowlers and have won several provincial competitions (March 1999, 194).

If one of the tropes of second wave feminism was 'communality through shared victimhood' then one of the tropes of post-feminism was of the multiplicity of women's capabilities, their ability if not to 'have it all' then at least to 'do it all' which these women conform to. Moreover, if the representations of women who bind their feet enabled the readership of *Marie Claire* to construct an identity as rational and independent, no longer in need of feminism, then any oppression the reader might experience in relationships or the workplace consequently lacked the iconography of 'real oppression' offered within the pages of the magazine just as in the 1980s the rediscovery of poverty had 'been ideologically blocked by a corresponding re-discovery of real poverty at a time when it was nobody's fault' (Bromley 1988, 8).

The representation of women as 'othered' in the 'reportage' and global and international affairs features, which included Amnesty International award-winning articles entitled 'Where girls are killed for going to school' (June 1996) and 'Where Pregnancy is a crime' (November 1997), were by no means limited to discourses of the orient. Significantly, when the reportage features examined 'othered' women in the West, there was greater linguistic emphasis on similarity and commonality. A feature entitled 'Why I Swapped the High Life for a High Rise, by IT Girl Tamara Beckwith' (July 1999) described her two-day stay with a single mother on an urban council estate in Bristol. As Pat Thane and Tanya Evans have argued: 'the 1980s and early 1990s saw the most outspoken and persistent attack on lone mothers by representatives of any government of the century' (2013, 169) and this rhetoric remained widespread in the late 1990s. Yet although the single mother was objectified in the text, the frequent use of the first person plural—for example 'we shop at the mini-market'—emphasised an approach based on participant observation rather than voyeurism. Rather than merely attempt to construct and convey 'knowledge' about a single mother living on social security, a dialogue of understanding was suggested instead. Interestingly, the last two or three paragraphs of the article focussed on how the experience had changed the life of Tamara Beckwith herself. What linked the reportage features of both 'disadvantaged' Western and non-Western women was an underlying assumption that a key element of their victimhood was the absence of choice, particularly the choices that consumer culture offered. This was demonstrated more overtly in an article entitled 'Journey into No Man's Land' in the September 1999 issue. The reportage was contextualised in the following way: 'In the isolated mountain villages of Ecuador, thousands of women have been abandoned. They are left to work the lands alone, while their husbands seek jobs in the cities. Bridget Freer visits the women learning to live without men' (September 1999, 21) and discovered that their hardship and oppression is not merely the lack of a man to 'keep you warm in the middle of the night' (Shania Twain lyrics 1997) although I would suggest that the Western ideal of a caring, sharing new-man-type-partner often operated as a structuring absence within such features. Indeed in an implied validation of this ideal, one woman of the village is quoted saying: 'It's not right the men have to go away. We should be working together, supporting each other on our land' (September 1999, 22). Nevertheless, it was their solitary undertaking of 'primitive' subsistence farming unaided even when heavily pregnant which really appalled Freer. She wrote:

After being tear-gassed, pelted with rocks, bribing my way through barricades of burning tyres, and heaving tree trunks out of the way of my car, I thought I knew what trouble was. Now, in the villages of Pungalo and Alao, I realise I don't know the meaning of the word—up here trouble is a way of life. My preoccupations . . . were as nothing compared to theirs: scratching out a living against mounting odds'. (1999, 22)

And of course by implication—the readers' troubles were likewise nothing compared to this 'real poverty and oppression', poverty and oppression which was signified by an iconography of physical labour, multiple childbirth and powerlessness at the very least. The representation of the horror of these women's conditions and its polarity to the magazine's readers' experience was emphasised by reference to the women spreading manure with their feet and 'looking old before their time'. These examples set within the context of a magazine with a discourse of body beautiful and instructions on exfoliating, defuzzing and the horror of oily outbreaks (1999, 306–8) emphasised the polarity of western and non-western women's experiences and identity positions.

Many of the reportages or features on 'women from other countries' had a sumptuousness akin to a fashion spread; they utilised strong colour, exuberantly signifying a fantasy of 'ethnic', exotic 'otherness'. Possibly the pleasure in such fantasy relied upon saying 'the unsaid and the unseen in culture, that which is repressed' (Jackson 1981, 3). A repression in terms of the 'spectacle of the other' (see Hall 1997) which may be both fetishized and seen as desirable is a feature entitled 'Killer Catfights: Where Wives and Mistresses Get Their Claws Out'. The heading further explains: 'When two women in the Paraguayan village of Obrerso set their sights on one man, it's war. Fingernails are sharpened, fists fly, blood is spilled and winner takes all' (July 1999, 5). The fights were represented as a public spectacle akin to an early *Jerry Springer Show*, but also contained the twin fantasy of unrestrained physical expressions of jealousy and of myths of female amazons who dominated their villages. A quote from the article illuminates this:

Anthropologist Chase Sardi explains the fights are all that remains of the Nivacle women's traditionally proud and dominant place within society . . . The women traditionally had greater prestige in society than men did. The women owned the hut and the cattle and she could leave her husband whenever she wanted (July 1999, 7).

Knowledge about the Nivacle is presented for the reader through the prism of the expert anthropologist. However, arguably *Marie Claire* does not merely make women the subjects of the discourse, passively represented by the writer; the women's own words are given space providing authenticity

particularly when combined with photo-stories of non-western women utilising grainy black and white images to signify 'gritty' realism.

Discussing the use of colour or black and white heightens the inevitable
problem of representation which is never neutral but rather part of culturally
shared signification system, and intrinsically tied up with ever shifting relations of power. How then can these words and narratives of 'othered' women
be interpreted within the magazine articles? One condemnatory response
would be to follow the interpretations of Gareth Griffiths who argues:

> Authentic speech, where it is conceived not merely as a political strat-
> egy within a specific political discursive formation but as a fetishized
> cultural commodity . . . is employed to enact a discourse of 'liberal
> violence', re-enacting its own oppressions on the subjects it purports to
> represent' (1995, 86).

Indeed support for Griffiths' argument came in a letter published in April
2000 with the name and address withheld under the title 'Some Enlightenment' which argued, with reference to an article on mourning rituals:

> As a Nigerian woman who has lived in Nigeria, I have never heard of
> the mourning rituals mentioned in February's reportage, 'A Year in
> Darkness', or met anyone who has gone through them. I am not saying
> these things never occur, as each area in Nigeria has distinct tribes and
> customs, but I am saddened to think that readers will see this article
> and assume it is just another example of Nigerians/Africans behaving
> ignorantly' (July 2000, 93).

SCOPE TO CONTEST POPULAR POLITICAL
DISCOURSES IN THE PAGES OF *MARIE CLAIRE*

Marie Claire's reportage of global humanitarian politics often make
uncomfortable reading and are open to critique but it must be remembered
that women have had a problematic relationship with the discourses of
imperialism and its critiques including Said's work on orientalism. Indeed,
Jane Miller has noted:

> In accepting the power and usefulness of an analysis like Said's there is
> an essential proviso . . . to be made. If women are ambiguously present
> within the discourses of orientalism, they are just as ambiguously pres-
> ent within the discourse developed to expose and oppose orientalism
> (1990, 18).

Consequently, it may be useful to focus on the potential for popular culture
to become a site of political contestation (Hall 1981); perhaps *Marie Claire*

should be seen as having offered women access to the public domain and the discursive struggle that Fiske points out are significant in any political and cultural campaign (1996, 8). Furthermore, following Fiske's approach to the consumption of popular culture (1991) it can be suggested that a representational text does not carry its meaning uncontested or unproblematically, rather its meanings are read in a variety of ways as different individuals, belonging to a range of different identity groups, consume the text. If *Marie Claire* at the end of the millennium could be seen as having offered western readers an identity position defined through binary opposition and difference, it also lay itself open for the reader to identify points of sameness, which potentially could become starting points for political affiliations and allegiances. This sameness was given a biological foundation in a predominantly visual reportage entitled 'Dear Mother'. The caption under the title explained:

> Whether they are living in a war zone or western luxury, women across the globe share a common bond—the overpowering love they feel for their children and a fierce need to protect them; *Marie Claire* celebrates Mother's Day with a global view of the role of the mother (April 2002, 12–17).

The five pages of pictures all conveyed women mothering, in a range of non-European countries including the U.S., in conditions of hardship (whether as a result of war, disease, poverty or medical mishap) and drew upon one of the underlying tropes of second wave feminism that biological femininity and motherhood created gender communality. This mixture of sameness and difference offered a 'diasporic' political identity; maybe the only one open to women given their tortuous relationship with imperialist power or opposition to it, mentioned above. This simultaneous sameness and difference can also be identified in a reportage entitled 'Mothers Who Raise Animals as Their Own Children' on the Bishnoi tribe in the Indian Desert (June 1999). The women's commitment to nurturing animals was presented in terms of an early version of the green movement of the West. 'Centuries before the West were aware of environmental issues, the young Bishnoi mother gave up her life to protect her land' (June 1999, 23). Furthermore, their 'strict vegetarianism' is emphasised at a time when vegetarianism was growing in popularity amongst white middle-class young women.

One way of reading the 'sameness' and links between the readers of articles in *Marie Claire* is as consistent with Gayatri Spivak's analysis that: 'The project of imperialism has always historically refracted what might have been absolute other into a domesticated other that consolidated an imperialist self' (1985, 253). At one level the placement of the reportage articles within the overall context of the magazine, and the fluidity of themes between different areas of the magazine, seems to support this argument. For example, the focus on clothes in 'Queens of the Desert' (July 1999,

154–161), explored the different costumes worn by two communities in Namibia in South-West Africa. The women of the Herero wearing colourful, full-skirted, ornate Victorian style dresses, with as many as seven layers of petticoats, were contrasted with the Himba who were bare breasted and wearing goatskin 'mini-skirts and jewellery'. Knowledge of these two groups of women is conveyed initially in terms of a narrative of the Herero's irrational assimilation of the westernised culture of nineteenth-century German settlers. The Himba are apparently 'a constant reminder to the Herero of how their great-great grandmothers once lived and dressed' (July 1999, 158). Yet this exploration of the Himba and Herero dress could also be seen as an invitation to the readers to engage with the degree to which consumption practices are always framed by individual creativity operating within a range of cultural constraints (McKay 1998). The multiple layers of the Herero costume were both revered for the indulgent sensual consumer pleasures they offered and described as impractical when undertaking mundane domestic tasks. The Herero were represented as making the Victorian fashions their own: 'A Herero woman explains "but for us it is not a German thing—we've taken it over and added colour, life and meaning to the dresses. They are no longer European but African' (July 1999, 22). The photographic images of the Herero and Himba women were arranged to emphasize the difference between the two communities, which was all to do with style (an interestingly post-modern perspective), whilst the way of life of both groups was portrayed as 'endangered'. The lighting stressed the Herero's choice of bold bright colours, a theme that was taken up in other parts of the magazine; one fashion feature entitled 'Dress Line' instructs the reader 'Long and Sexy or Short and Strappy or simply utility whatever dress you choose make sure it is in the boldest colours' (July 1999, 177). The discourse of rationality exercised in the choice of fashion and clothes as counterpoint to irrational choices was undermined by the shared appeal of bold colours. Bold colours were also encouraged in the shopping section, which enthused on the simple life of camping, providing, of course, the reader-selected 'brightest, and boldest colour separates' to enjoy at the same time (July 1999, 225). Similarly, a fashion feature on 'holiday season buys' incorporated 'cheesecloth skirts and peasant-style camisoles' and explained: 'The key is to relax into the look and the rest will fall into place' (June 1995, 226). Further examples of the domestication of 'otherness' can perhaps be seen in a travel feature in the same edition of the magazine which focuses on Africa under the headline '3 Faces of Africa: When you're offered the diversity of Egypt's vitality, Morocco's sensuality and South Africa's sheer scale—what's a traveller to choose?' (June 1995, 248). In this feature African 'otherness' could be seen as domesticated tourism and fantasies of holidays; the reader was informed that Marrakech has a familiarity based upon its role as a backdrop for films and fashion shoots. Certainly there were elements within 'Queens of the Desert' that can be read as offering a binary opposition between post-feminist consumer femininity and 'othered' victimhood, but alternatively they could be read as presenting a domesticated 'other' that may be picked up and put down like any other element of objectified consumption. But, and perhaps this is the key point, discourses of otherness are both unstable and varied. They may be disrupted, rubbed away, and laid bare within the magazine that is itself fragmented and ambivalent. Indeed *Marie Claire*, like all such magazines, is not designed to be read methodically cover-to-cover but to be flicked through, dipped into—so that readers create their own bricolage of meaning. Furthermore, Spivak's arguments about domestication of 'otherness' perhaps problematically rely upon a notion of consolidating the imperialist self, and thereby assume a stability of identity and circumstances. Alternatively, the discursive approach to identity, utilised by Stuart Hall and Paul du Gay, drawing upon Foucault, sees identity not as fixed, static or uniform but always in process, 'conditional lodged in contingency' (1996, 3).

FROM FRAGMENTED IDENTITY POSITIONS TO POLITICAL ACTIVISM

Marie Claire appealed to the fragmented identities of the turn of the millennium women, inviting them, as they read the magazine, to fantasize about assuming a multiplicity of subject positions. Arguably the magazine's ability to hold within its covers many diverse and perhaps contradictory facets of global womanhood in a momentary stability of the printed physical text contributed to the pleasure it offered women readers whose own identity was unstable, always in the making. The magazine, sometimes, enabled women to do more than play with subject positions; one letter writer explained how an article inspired her to undertake aid work and simultaneously thanked the magazine for including, in the same issue, an article on the American sitcom *Friends* (Warner Bros. and Channel 4 1994–2004) (April 2000, 89). Her pleasure in the text, I would suggest, was gained from its legitimation of her multiple and fragmented subject positions both as politically and morally motivated aid-worker in the developing world, and as the twenty-something carefree singleton of the very white world of *Friends*. Only a couple of months later *Marie Claire* announced in a summary of its post-bag that fifty-three of their readers thought women should fight for their country and twenty-seven believed that pornography empowered women. The majority of these letters had simultaneously expressed other concerns with the celebrity and beauty elements of the magazine. Such responses indicated that the magazine played a tortuous balancing act between a range of different feminine subject positions which readers found alluring, and in so doing prevented any fixity of meaning or identity. Finally, the readers may have been attracted to the way in which *Marie Claire* alongside many fictional fantasies offered 'a private unrestrained space in which socially impossible or unacceptable subject positions, or those which are in some way too dangerous or too risky, to be acted out in real life, may be adopted' (Ang 1990, 86).

Readers were not only invited to flirt with fantasies on a range of subject positions, they were also encouraged, through a range of strategies, to participate in political activism and to enthusiastically become involved with and respond to the topics of the magazine's 'thought provoking articles'. Rather than passive consumption, readers were coaxed into participation in campaigns such as 'Drop the Debt' (November 2000) and 'Women in Black' (March 2002). They were encouraged to write letters or donate money, and the letters pages often carried testimonies of readers who claimed they had been moved by the magazine to take part in campaigns or donate to charities. This was underlined by articles on global affairs which included a spotlight upon women actively trying to change the problems being discussed. 'Heroes for a Living' (January 2002) examined 'women around the world who quietly and determinedly devoted their lives to taking on terrorists' and included an Afghan revolutionary and an Irish peace activist. 'Calcutta Calling' (November 2001) focused on women doing volunteer work in this part of India. Such articles offered the reader a more tangible subject position to play with in relation to fantasies of 'becoming' politically active; fantasies which may have seemed tantalisingly closer when readers were invited to enter a competition to undertake their own 'reportage' feature for the magazine. In December 2000, one reader's winning entry enabled her to visit the women of Pakistan who made the hand-spun fabrics gracing catwalks as part of the Dai Rees collection. Interestingly, this reader-written article entitled 'Material Girls' (December 2000) overtly raised questions about the conditions under which all clothes women wore were made. Similarly, 'Causalities of War', which discussed victims of the war in Sierra Leone, pointed out: 'The conflict arose from a battle for the mines that supply diamonds to women all over the world' (August 2000, 134). These are two examples of chinks in discourses that, if scrutinised closely, laid themselves, and their consumers, open to an engagement with a colonial past and racist present upon which the rest of the text, and significant elements of consumer culture, were predicated. However, how many of *Marie Claire*'s 1,724,000 readership, as opposed to the less than half a million women who bought the magazine, participated in such an engagement is uncertain. Arguably, the reader was just as likely to have chosen to avoid the difficult questions the magazine raised and to leave the danger points lurking underneath the surface.

CONCLUSION

Marie Claire at the turn of the millennium was like all popular culture texts a web of contradictory discourses through which readers navigated, clashing against regimes of representation with armour of cultural baggage to protect them and assist them in any confrontations that such encounters involved. It offered women the chance to construct an identity as an independent and perhaps post-feminist woman. Indeed the magazine's specific offering was according to their website at the time intended to appeal to women who were: 'confident, discerning, sophisticated and aware of the world around them'. The articles I have looked at may have served merely to register their awareness of 'the world around' to the readers, and to reassure them that they were not totally Eurocentric or American focused. Their consumption may have offered an identity position without any pretensions of 'knowing' in any sense the subjects of these articles. Alternatively, readers may have engaged thoughtfully with the danger points, enjoying a post-feminist consumerism based upon a binary opposition or the 'othering' of non-western women. Readers may even have taken pleasure in the text's ability to articulate both feminism and femininity or perhaps swung between all these positions and many more possible readings of the text I have not engaged with. That *Marie Claire* offered these possibilities, when most women's magazines maintained a more repressive post-colonialism regime of silence, suggests that perhaps feminism and political engagement was not entirely over as the twentieth century ended and women looked towards the start of a new millennium.

ACKNOWLEDGMENTS

This is an expanded version of Andrews, Maggie (2004), 'Feminism, Femininity and the Potential Politics of Consuming Popular Culture: A Case Study of *Marie Claire*'s Reportage of "Global Humanitarian Politics"', *Imperium* 4 (online journal).

BIBLIOGRAPHY / SOURCES

Andrews, Maggie and Talbot, Mary. 2000 (eds). *All the World and Her Husband: Women in Twentieth Century Consumer Culture* London: Cassell.

Ang, Ien. 1990. 'Melodramatic Identifications: Television Fiction and Women's fantasy.' In *Television and Women's Culture*, edited by Mary Ellen Brown. London: Sage.

Bromley, Roger. 1988. *Lost Narratives*. London: Verso.

Carter, Erica. 1997. *How German Is She? Post War German Reconstruction and the Consuming Woman*. University of Michigan Press.

Cronin, Anne. 2000. 'Advertising Difference: women, Western Europe and consumer citzenship' ' in Andrews, Maggie and Talbot, Mary. 2000 (eds*). All the World and Her Husband: Women in Twentieth Century Consumer Culture London*: Cassell. pp162–176.

Fiske John. 1996. *Media Matters*. Minneapolis, London: University of Minnesota Press.

Fiske, John. 1991. *Reading Popular Culture*. London: Routledge.

Gill, Rosalind. 2007. 'Postfeminist Media Culture: Elements of a Sensibility.' *European Journal of Cultural Studies* 10 (2): 147–166. doi:10.1177/1367549407075898.

Griffiths, Gareth. 1995. 'The Myth of Authenticity.' In *The Post-Colonial Studies Reader*, edited by Bill Ashcroft, Gareth Griffiths, and Helen Tiffin. London: Routledge.

Hall, Stuart. 1981. 'Notes Towards Deconstructing the Popular.' In *People's History and Socialist Theory*, edited by Ralph Samuel, 88–101. London: Routledge.

Hall, Stuart, and Paul du Gay. 1996. *Questions of Cultural Identity*. London: Sage.

Hall, Stuart. 1997. *Representation and Signifying Practice*. London: Sage.

Hermes, Jokes. 1995. *Reading Women's Magazines*. Cambridge: Polity.

Hollows, Joanne. 2008. *Domestic Cultures*. Maidenhead:Open University Press.

Jackson, Rosemary. 1981. *Fantasy: Literature of Subversion*. London: Methuen.

Lewis, Reina. 1996. *Gendering Orientalism*. London: Routledge.

McKay, Hugh. 1998. *Consumption and Everyday Practices*. London: Sage.

McRobbie, Angela. 2004. 'Post-Feminism and Popular Culture.' *Feminist Media Studies* 4 (3): 255–264.

Miller, Jane. 1990. *Seductions: Studies in Reading and Culture*. London: Virago.

Mulvey, Laura. 1975. 'Visual Pleasure and Narrative Cinema.' *Screen* 16 (3): 6–18.

Nava, Mica. 1992. *Changing Cultures: Feminism, Youth and Consumerism*. London: Sage.

Probyn, Elspeth. 1993. 'Choosing Choice: Working Images of Sexuality in Popular Culture.' In *Negotiating at the Margins: Gendered Discourses of Resistance*, edited by Sue Fisher and Kathy Davis. New Brunswick, NJ: Rutgers University Press.

Radner, Hilary. 1995 *Shopping Around*. London: Routledge.

Ryan, Deborah. 2000. 'All the World and Her Husband: the *Daily Mail* Ideal Home Exhibition 1908–1939' in Andrews, Maggie and Talbot, Mary. 2000 (eds). *All the World and Her Husband: Women in Twentieth Century Consumer Culture*. London: Cassell. pp10–22.

Said, Edward, 1996. *Representations of the Intellectual* USA: Vintage Books.

Spivak, Gayatri Chakravorty. 1985. 'Three Women's Texts and a Critique of Imperialism.' *Critical Inquiry* 12 (1).

Thane, Pat, and Tanya Evans. 2013. *Sinners? Scroungers? Saints? Unmarried Motherhood in Twentieth-Century England*. Oxford University Press.

Twain, Shania. 1997. 'That Don't Impress Me Much.' Song lyrics. http://www.elyrics.net/read/s/shania-twain-lyrics/that-don_t-impress-me-much-lyrics.html. 15/5/2003

Winship, Janice. 1987. *Inside Women's Magazines*. London: Pandora.

15 What's Luff Got to Do with It?

Teenage Magazines, Sexuality and Regulation (Too much, too young? Teenage Magazines, Sexuality and Regulation)

Fan Carter

INTRODUCTION

This chapter focuses attention on the 1990s when teenage girls' magazines were at the centre of popular and political debates about media regulation and sexual morality. For a brief period, these magazines became the focus of intense scrutiny from politicians, moral campaigners and large sections of the British press, all keen to expose and condemn magazines for their allegedly powerful and negative influence on teenage girls' sexual knowledge and behaviour. The supposedly graphic contents of magazines like *Bliss* (1995–) and *Just Seventeen* (1983–2004) were criticised for promoting underage sexual activity, contributing to the rise in teenage pregnancies and taken as general evidence of the increasing moral decline of the nation.

An examination of the morally charged furore which surrounded the campaigns to regulate the contents of magazines for teenage girls in the 1990s offers a salutary example through which to explore the dynamics of what Kirsten Drotner (1992) has termed a media panic. In this instance, the panic took on a particularly gendered and sexualised inflection. The efforts of the then back-bench MP Peter Luff to introduce his *Periodicals (Protection of Children) Bill* in 1996, whereby magazine titles marketed to teenage girls were to be sold with age limit specifications, captured the imaginations of the right-wing popular press and moral campaigning groups alike. Together they capitalised on the situation, producing a storm of media coverage, studded with graphic details and personal testimony. Across these a particular image of the teenage girl was drawn as simultaneously vulnerable and dangerous, innocent and uncomfortably knowing. While Drotner identifies the child as the central figure in these debates, her analysis does not draw attention to the particularly gendered forms these configurations often take. By focusing on the ways that the figure of the girl enters into popular discussions of media regulation and sexual moralism, this chapter explores the significance of both gender and generation in relation to the category of the youthful media consumer and the operations of media panic.

NEW FEMININITIES:
FEMINIST SENTIMENTS AND MARKETABILITY

At first glance it might seem a surprise that the editorial content of teenage magazines should have become the focus for such intense scrutiny given the broader changes and developments within popular culture of the period. The 1980s had seen considerable changes in the representation of women in the media and the formats and products addressing them as consumers. Across advertising, television drama, popular fiction and magazine publishing new femininities which were bold, assertive, financially independent and sexually confident were increasingly making their mark (Gamman and Marshment 1988; Gough-Yates, 2000, 2003; Hollows 2000). These popular feminist sensibilities were readily incorporated into broader ideals of sovereign consumption and individualism which celebrated the neo-liberal economics of the period (Andrews and Talbot 2000). The impact of these shifting representations of femininity was also evident in the teenage magazine market which underwent considerable expansion and transformation in the 1980s and 1990s.

Teenage magazines had been a feature of the publishing landscape since the 1960s (White 1970). They were traditionally characterised by titles such as *Jackie*, a weekly publication, from the family-run company DC Thompson which focussed on picture, and later photo, stories of romance, line-drawn fashion pages, pop trivia and the problem page. Long criticised by feminist scholars (McRobbie 1982) and mocked within the industry for its staid approach, *Jackie* was challenged in the mid-1980s by the launch of a new type of teenage magazine in the form of *Just Seventeen* which promised 'glory without the schmaltz' (Campaign 1984, 33). These new magazines opted for a vibrant visual layout, irreverent and ironic style and importantly spoke to their readers in a new way, one that was upbeat and fun. This development was underpinned by the increasing confidence of advertisers and the sustained growth of, and increased diversification within, consumer markets in pop, fashion and beauty products. This first wave of change in the teenage market was followed 10 years later by the launch of *Sugar* (1994–2011) a monthly publication with a glossy look and a bound spine. Magazines like *Sugar*, its competitors *It's Bliss* and later *Cosmo Girl* brought about increased segmentation within this niche market. The marketing pitches for teenage magazines positioned themselves as natural counterparts to the different specific stages of adolescence and as expert guides to the increasingly busy world of teenage consumer culture (Carter 2005).

Feminist media scholars commented on the shifting representations and discourses of femininity circulating in these new titles, noting the traces of feminist politics in their editorial approaches. Janice Winship argued that magazines of this period reworked traditional codes of fashion and femininity, and as so drew on a 'feminist culture, if not a feminist politics' (Winship 1987, 129). Angela McRobbie, meanwhile, revised her earlier critical assessment of traditional teenage magazines as pedlars of romantic ideology, noting that these new titles had replaced romance with 'the logics of consumerism' (McRobbie 1991, 136) and sexuality (McRobbie 1996, 184). However, while the figure of the sexually knowledgeable, confident and assertive young woman flourished within the schedules of Channel 4 and the pages of grown-up glossies, she cut a more awkward figure within the confines of teenage magazines, an issue which moral campaigners and right-wing journalists became increasingly keen to contest across the period.

POPULAR CULTURE AND MEDIA PANICS

Children and young people have been targeted as consumers of popular media since the nineteenth century. Facilitated by the combination of new print technologies, burgeoning consumer capitalism and rising literacy rates young people of all classes were constituted as a distinct generational market—especially for print media (Drotner 1988; Denisoff 2008). At various points, children's consumption of popular culture has met with concern on the part of moral guardians who have raised anxious complaints about the potential impact and influence of popular media on the young and vulnerable. Print media has featured strongly in such campaigns for regulation: the 'penny dreadfuls' of the 1890s were reviled for their bloodthirsty violence and unchristian values, leading the Christian publisher, *The Religious Tract Society*, to set up alternative publications with more appropriate moral codes (Dunae 1980; Springhall 1999). The U.S.-imported horror comics of the 1950s were similarly criticised for their potential to incite young readers to delinquency (Barker 1989; Springhall 1999). Kirsten Drotner (1992) characterises such campaigns as examples of 'media panic' and argues that across different European countries, the emergence of new media forms addressing youthful consumers have periodically given rise to concerns over the moral welfare of children at risk to various pernicious media effects. Drawing on the seminal work of Cohen and his study of folk devils and moral panics (Cohen 1972), Drotner argues that media panics work to galvanise political and public opinion in support of media regulation. While each panic has its individual details, they share a taxonomy whereby various public concerns over the impact of new media forms and practices are harnessed by sets of proclaimed experts who publically pronounce the specific media form to be a moral threat to the nation and so legitimise appeals for its regulation.

According to Drotner, this cycle of media panic is completed when the newly regulated media form is then reassessed in terms of its potential pedagogic value, rather than a dangerous social ill. In this way, new media threats are symbolically neutralised, redeemed and co-opted into political and social projects of management and governance. Drotner draws attention to the ways in which media panics operate as symbolic flashpoints where competing discourses of childhood, youth and progress collide.

The values of self-discipline, improvement and the Protestant work ethic, which characterise narratives of education and employment, clash with the hedonistic pleasures offered by leisure and consumer capitalism. Media panics then operate as 'safety valves' through which potential disruptions to social order can be identified, challenged and defused (Drotner 1992, 43–56). Drotner identifies the ways in which media panics channel fears around class difference and perceived deviance; however, her account pays little attention to the gendered dimensions of these debates. By focussing on the ways that the figure of the teenage girl enters into popular discussions of media regulation and sexual moralism, this chapter explores the significance of both gender and generation in relation to the category of the youthful media consumer and the operations of media panic.

Historically, the relationship between girls and popular media is one that has been framed by discourses of sexuality, desire and corruption. As far back as the nineteenth century, stories of the sexual exploitation of girls and young women have made headlines and sold newspapers as W. T. Stead's famous campaign in the *Pall Mall Gazette*, 'The maiden tribute to modern Babylon' of 1885 exemplifies. This series of reports was based on the editor's own undercover investigations of the trade in young girls for prostitution on the streets of London. It made for scandalous reading and trod a fine line between titillation and moral outrage. While Stead's investigative methods resulted in his own criminal conviction, the paper's campaigning efforts were also recognised as contributing to the success of the Criminal Law Amendment Act of 1885 which raised the age of consent from 13 to 16 years (Walkowitz 1992). Stories about women and girls as sexual victims within popular print ran alongside fears for their moral virtue as consumers of popular print. As women became targeted markets for cheap, popular fiction and the 'new journalism', of which Stead's *Pall Mall Gazette* was an example, concerns were raised over the dangers such sensational content posed to impressionable readers (Beetham 1996, 119–121). The furore over teenage magazines in the 1990s bears the traces of these older concerns over the suitability of popular media products for girls and fears that reading such material will have a detrimental effect on girls' virtue. Within these parameters, girls are constructed as sexually passive and innocent, devoid of sexual desire. This view comes into conflict with the more progressive and permissive construction of female sexuality articulated in the pages of teenage magazines of the period.

THE MEDIA AND MORAL CONSERVATISM: MIXED MESSAGES AND COMPETING AGENDAS

The concern surrounding teenage girls' magazines that erupted in the mid-1990s was set amid a wider context of moral conservatism which characterised the Conservative governments of the 1980s and 1990s. As noted by commentators such as Hall (1988), Durham (1991) and Pilcher and Wagg (1996) the successive Conservative governments operated a particular ideological agenda which combined a commitment to free market economics with a conservative moral stance with respect to the regulation and management of private and family life. Such a combination was not easily maintained and produced particular tensions and inconsistencies with regard to the regulation of media. For example, Robert Bocock (1997) notes that the BBC in particular was viewed with mistrust as a harbinger of permissive values and so singled out for scrutiny, while at the same time commercial broadcast companies enjoyed a loosening of regulatory mechanisms which saw the launch of satellite television in Britain in the mid-1980s. Similarly, Lesley A. Hall records that while the deregulation of telecommunications in the 1980s enabled premium rate sex chat lines to flourish, measures were taken to ensure that satellite television decoders blocked European adult sex channels from the UK (Hall 2000, 190). Hall notes that children and young people were singled out as targets for moral campaigns and interventions by reformers, with sex education provision taking centre stage in the then government's agenda to turn back the tide of 1960s permissiveness. The overhaul of sex education provision by the then Conservative government is examined in detail by Rachel Thompson (1993) who maps out the raft of legislation and policy documents which not only placed responsibility for sex education in the hands of parents and governors rather than teachers and Local Education Authorities, but also prescribed a clear moral agenda for the curriculum. Sex education was required to emphasise 'moral dimensions and the value of family life' (1986, Education (No.2) Act, cited in Thomson 1993, 227) while later amendments to the Bill gave parents the right to remove their children from classes altogether. While educational policies operated with a high degree of moral certainty with regard to sex education their focus was limited. In contrast, the Department of Health began to expand its horizons to include areas of commercial popular culture and specifically teenage girls' magazines within its remit. Although operating from a seemingly more pragmatic health framework, the public education initiatives around young people's sexual health displayed an increasingly obvious moral agenda in the period.

In response to government targets to reduce teenage pregnancies and rates of sexually transmitted diseases and HIV, a number of promotional initiatives were developed to target young people which built alliances between the publically funded but semi-autonomous organisation, Health Education Authority (HEA), and sections of commercial media. The 1994 joint initiative with BBC Radio 1 to produce and market a glossy magazine for post-sixteen readers entitled *The Best Sex Guide* met with considerable criticism from MPs who raised concerns that such explicit material might get into the hands of under-age readers (*Hansard* March 11, 1994, cl. 483). While these criticisms were successfully rebuffed on this occasion, the planned publication of *The Pocket Guide to Sex* in the same year fared less well. Nick Fisher, an agony uncle from *Just Seventeen*, had been commissioned by the HEA to write the book. Selected for his popular appeal and approachable writing style (Moir 1994, 8), Fisher was a well-known figure among the target readership. This effort by the HEA to capitalise on the credibility of Fisher and *Just Seventeen* and work collaboratively with commercial media was thwarted by a flurry of complaints from MPs and sympathetic news coverage. The publication was dropped and branded 'inappropriate, distasteful and smutty' by the Minister for Public Health, Dr Brian Mawhinney (Moir 1994, 8; Norman 1994, 16). In the ensuing media coverage, Fisher was recast by Michael Fallon, a former School's Minister, as a permissive campaigner profiting from 'ramming sex down young people's throats' (quoted in Connolly 199, 3) while Victoria Gillick, a prominent moral campaigner, branded the HEA a subversive organisation peddling 'state funded official pornography' (Connolly 1994, 3).

This brief episode represents an attempt to extend a disciplinary gaze of governance over the area of commercial popular media in which both teenage magazines and their journalists emerge as objects of concern and at the same time are imagined as potential. In drawing together popular magazines, sexuality and adolescent readers, it anticipates the anxiety and commotion which came two years later in 1996 with the introduction of the *Periodicals (Protection of Children) Bill*, by the back-bench Conservative MP, Peter Luff. It is important to note that these calls for the regulation of magazines did not erupt unexpectedly and without precedent in February 1996. They can be seen to fit into a wider discursive framework of moral regulation operating within the Conservative governments of the period and their efforts to exact a firmer regulatory hold over the production of knowledges around adolescent sexuality.

TEENAGE MAGAZINES: A MEDIA PANIC

On February 6, 1996, the Conservative MP, Peter Luff, introduced a Private Member's Bill to the House of Commons. His *Periodicals (Protection of Children) Bill* called for magazines marketed at teenage girls to display an advisory notice of age restrictions on their front covers which, in his speech to the Commons, Luff likened to the film classificatory system currently used in Britain (*Hansard* February 6, 1996, cl. 146). These proposals developed as a response to Luff's concern over what he perceived to be the increasingly explicit coverage of sexuality in teenage girls' magazines. Luff's Bill sought to limit access to this material by ensuring that both parents and retailers could better monitor the consumption patterns of young female consumers. While the Private Member's Bill was unsuccessful (it failed to receive ministerial backing and was withdrawn in July 1996), initially it received a degree of cross-party support in the Commons and garnered considerable coverage in sections of the national press. It also importantly resulted in the formation of the Teenage Magazines Arbitration Panel (TMAP), a voluntary body organised by the Periodical Publishers' Association which has responsibility for adjudicating on complaints made on the contents of magazines under their regulatory remit (TMAP 1996). Together with Luff's Bill, which proposed regulatory restrictions to magazines at the point of sale, the ensuing media coverage in the popular press and the following industry-backed resolution exemplify Drotner's characteristics and stages of a media panic.

In his speech to the Commons, Luff invoked a particular image of the teenage girl, which worked with an implicit model of development in which adolescence is construed as a problematic period for girls leaving them sexually vulnerable. While Luff spoke in general terms of the dangers to children, his argument had a gendered inflection in which teenage girls were positioned as especially vulnerable. It was girls' access to information on sex which he identified as the problem. Teenage girls' magazines posed a particular threat, not simply because they carried increasing amounts of sexual contents, but also because of the attractive and inviting style in which this was done. In Luff's formulation, information on sex should serve to 'warn children of dangers' and must not 'go further than is absolutely necessary to protect them' (*Hansard*, February 6, 1996, cl. 146). Such a perspective positioned sex as an inherently problematic, indeed dangerous, area for girls.

Luff juxtaposed a nostalgic and idealised invocation of children's 'comics' with an image of 'salaciousness and smut' which characterised his vision of contemporary teenage girls' magazines. Offering a sample of especially dramatic tag lines from magazines, '"Men Unzipped—An Intimate Guide to Men's Minds (and Bodies!)", "Seven Steps to Sexual Heaven—Bedtime Bliss Starts Here", "Your Sex Secrets—I've Slept with over 100 Boys"' (*Hansard* February 6, 1996, cl. 146), Luff contrasted this sensationalist approach with a model of appropriate and responsible advice, which he felt magazines should offer. Significantly, this model is one that is couched firmly within the Christian tradition, as Luff stated: 'I believe that sex is not a mechanical activity performed for immediate gratification, but a God-given gift that, in a loving relationship, is one of the best things about being a human being. Those magazines undermine the importance and value of sex' (*Hansard* February 6, 1996, cl. 147). Such rhetoric, with its critique of immediate consumerist pleasures, positions Luff's argument within an anti-hedonistic, puritanical standpoint. In this it can be readily seen as part of a tradition of Christian moralism which is suspicious of bodily pleasures (Bocock 1997).

Together with his negative view of the onset of sexual knowledge for girls, Luff's model of mature sexuality invoked a particular discourse of sexuality, that of responsible heterosexual romance with a reproductive imperative. For Luff, the effects on girls of reading such material was clear, it led to promiscuity and the concomitant loss of childhood innocence.

The magazines, in his view, were little more than incitements to sex. Interestingly, Luff also drew on the discourse of liberal feminism in order to strengthen his claims on the deleterious effects of teenage magazines:

> The only impression any girl reading such magazines could be left with is that her personal fulfilment will come only from looking good, wearing the right clothes and getting a better sex life. That is deeply sexist. Girls should be encouraged to believe that there are other ways of leading a meaningful life. Sexual stereotyping of that sort is wrong. (*Hansard*, February 6, 1996, cl. 147)

The appropriation of feminism as an alternative discourse attempted to build a broad base of support for the issue while appeasing potential criticisms. This supposed feminist critique of magazine culture was also one which emerged in the popular representations of the Bill in the press and will be discussed below. In keeping with the tenor of Conservative family values, Luff also made specific reference to parents, who he positioned as a significant lobbying group in his speech. As with the experience of the Education Act (Wagg 1996), the rights of parents were foregrounded over those of teenage girls and children more generally.

While Luff attempted to offer a stringent critique of teenage magazines, his speech also betrayed a miscomprehension of the magazine as a cultural form. Luff was unable to distinguish the different niches of the teenage magazine market and instead drew across diverse titles, aimed at different age groups, in his efforts to criticise the genre. Furthermore, his insistence that the informational function of magazines could be contained within appropriate formats and that issues such as sexuality should be dealt with in a serious way suggested that he misunderstood the ways in which magazines operate as texts. The informational and entertaining functions of magazine formats cannot be so easily separated, which may well be linked to their success and appeal. Indeed, magazine editors contested his account, arguing that Luff's ideal model of teenage magazine would not sell and so would have even less chance of fulfilling his specific pedagogic and political aims (Baker 1997). Moreover, Luff worked with an understanding of the relationship between magazines and readerships which assumed the readers' passivity and vulnerability. In so doing he overemphasised the significance of the magazine as an expert text within teenage girls' lives rather than as one source among many to which girls might turn.

Luff's proposals received immediate coverage in the national press, assisted in part by his adroit use of the sympathetic Tory press to build his campaign prior to the reading of his Bill. Debates around media representations of femininity were widespread that year with many column inches devoted to discussion of Channel 4's *The Girlie Show* and the launch of *Minx* magazine. Both of these were considered to signal a shift in representations of femininity, heralding the arrival of the 'ladette' (Gough-Yates

2003, 140), who challenged gender expectations with her brash and assertive approach to sexuality. Within such a context, a parliamentary bill to limit the sale of teenage magazines on the grounds of their inappropriate content had a high degree of 'consonance' with existing news agendas and cultural debates.

Papers sympathetic to the cause condemned the contents of teenage girls' magazines while repeating the explicit examples from the magazines Luff cited in his speech. The coverage of *The Mail on Sunday*, which labelled teenage magazines 'pornographic', was illustrative of a more general sentiment among right-of-centre publications. Jessica Davies decried magazines for representing 'a victory of lust over love, and a sense when you open the pages that you have strayed into a moral wasteland' (Davies 1996, 8). In contrast, *The Guardian* took pains to distance itself from the more censorious coverage of the Tory press. Rather than simply appeal to readers as parents, the extensive coverage drew on the voices of professionals such as magazine advice writers, experts in the form of publishers and sex educationalists and even young people themselves (Weale 1996, 1996; Heeks 1996).

In the case of the media panic around teenage girls' magazines, print journalism played a significant part in representing and giving shape to the debate. The coverage of Luff's campaign in newspapers afforded opportunities for papers to engage in the contradictory and unstable practices of what John Hartley has referred to as 'juvenation': 'the creative practice of communicating with a readership via the *medium* of youthfulness' (Hartley 1998, 52, emphasis in original). While images and stories of youth offer attractive ways of addressing readerships and framing stories, they are not without their tensions especially when those stories concern the pernicious effects of popular media themselves. As David Buckingham notes, popular discourses around children and young people are increasingly marked by ambiguity in which children are produced as objects of concern both in terms of their vulnerability to harm and also as threats to social and sexual order themselves (Buckingham 2000, 4). News journalism has provided spaces for such discourses to circulate, but at the same time media formats themselves are often implicated as the cause of unease and potential corruption. The challenges and contradictions surrounding practices of 'juvenation' involve marshalling the tensions between the different categories of youth and media. Newspaper columns were able to reflect at length, and in detail, on contemporary trends towards sexualisation in teenage magazines while maintaining a critical and censorious position on the topic. This was achieved through appealing to a hierarchy of media forms in which newspapers positioned themselves as highbrow, distancing themselves from the low form of magazines. By utilising the established codes and conventions of 'news' journalism—balance of sources, claims to objectivity—newspapers appealed to their readerships as informed citizens. This worked to further distance the papers from the conventions of magazine journalism and the associated modes of readership. Rather than the heightened emotional and pleasurable mode of consumption associated with popular media, the papers constructed a mode of engagement in terms of rational debate and reasoned reflection.

While newspapers continued to produce related stories for some months to come, keeping the discourse of panic in circulation, a regulatory solution to the episode was found relatively swiftly. This came in the form of the *Teenage Magazine Arbitration Panel* (TMAP), a self-regulatory board affiliated with the Periodical Publishers Association with membership drawn from the industry and medical experts. The Panel's initial briefing document, while broadly sympathetic to Luff's argument, shifted the terms of the debate from the castigation of magazines to outlining a proposal for their rehabilitation. Drawing on feminist work within the field it argued that magazines had a part to play in 'filling the knowledge gap' for teenage girls (Wellings 1996, 12) and commended magazines for their empowering approach to sexuality which enabled 'young people to adopt routine safer sex behaviours and exercise healthy choices in their personal lives' (Welling 1996, 17).

The guidelines formulated by the Panel established a code of conduct relating to retail display of magazines, editorial guidance for features on sex as well as points relating to the implementation of the code by journalists and publishers which are still in place today. The moral rhetoric found in the campaigners' criticisms of magazines was largely absent from the language employed in the guidelines. Instead, a professional and expert discourse was utilised which appeared to neutralise those criticisms and attempted instead to produce a consensus around the debate. The establishment of TMAP fulfilled the final stage of Drotner's taxonomy of a media panic. Speaking at the Periodical Press Association in 1998, the newly appointed Labour Minister for Health, Tessa Jowell, reminded publishers that readers placed great trust in their magazines as sources of reliable and authoritative health information, imploring them to 'exercise this power responsibly, in the same way Government does' (Department of Health 1998). Teenage magazines had been successfully repositioned as potential pedagogic devices, instruments of governance and deployed in the 'management of populations' (Foucault 1984, 145).

CONCLUSIONS AND CONTINUITIES: GIRLS, MEDIA AND SEXUALITY

This chapter has considered the ways in which the relationship between teenage magazines and their readers was constructed as a site of concern within moral campaigns for media regulation in the 1990s. It has argued that the campaign to regulate teenage magazines can be seen as an example of a media panic wherein a specific media form was singled out as a potential moral threat to the nation's youth. The pattern of parliamentary debate, media coverage and regulatory solution that the campaign followed fits within Drotner's (1992) conceptual model. While Drotner's analysis draws attention to the significance of the child in discourses of modernity and media panic, this chapter has attempted to revise this argument by exploring the particular significance of gender as well as generation. Within this example of media panic girls emerge as especially vulnerable to the seductions of popular media and in need of vigilant protection from the dangers associated with inappropriate sexual knowledge.

This case study has identified tensions and shifts between government bodies and their approach to popular media in this period. Teenage magazines appear as objects of concern and potential regulation while simultaneously offering potential instruments of governance to successive governments and their attempts to manage the population's sexual health. These contradictory framings of magazines as both dangerous and potentially beneficial illustrate the ways in which media panics attempt to seek regulatory solutions by appropriating the source of panic within official discourse. They are also characteristic of the tensions operating within the then current Conservative government and shifting priorities between moral conservatism and pragmatism which characterised its approach to sexual regulation and moral reform (Hall 2000).

A distinctive feature of any media panic is that of 'historical amnesia' (Drotner 1992) whereby current concerns are imagined to be both original and unparalleled in their urgent demands for regulatory attention. By locating the 1996 media panic within an historical framework it has been possible to chart a number of continuities and similarities between this episode and earlier moments of gendered media panic. Stories highlighting the dangers of sexuality for girls and women have been popular ways for newspapers to build circulations and position themselves as moral guardians since the late nineteenth century. These stories themselves and their stylistic forms have been subject to moral and aesthetic censure. In much the same way that Luff complained about the pages of *Sugar* magazine offering readers 'sensational smut' so too the reputed literary critic Matthew Arnold criticised the journalism of *The Pall Mall Gazette* as 'featherbrained', appealing to sensation rather than reason (Arnold 1887 cited in Beetham 1996, 115).

The discursive rhetoric circulating in Luff's attack on teenage magazines is informed by a much older model of female sexuality which operates an uncomfortable dualism between innocence and culpability, vulnerability and danger. This is an image that has long haunted debates on female sexuality, knowledge and regulation. Historically, these debates have focussed on issues of class, and have been concerned with the management and control of working-class femininities (Bland and Mort 1983; Walkerdine 1997). More recently, as has been shown, these have taken on a generational inflection as youthful femininities increasingly meet with moral scrutiny and criticism.

BIBLIOGRAPHY / SOURCES

Andrews, Maggie, and Mary Talbot, eds. 2000. *All the World and Her Husband: Women in Twentieth-Century Consumer Culture*. London: Contiuum.

Baker, Sam. 1997. Author's interview with editor of *J-17*, April.

Barker, Martin. 1989. *Comics, Ideology, Power and the Critics*. Manchester University Press.

Beetham, Margaret. 1996. *A Magazine of Her Own? Domesticity and Desire in the Woman's Magazine, 1800–1914*. London: Routledge.

Bland, Lucy, and Frank Mort. 1983. 'Look out for the "Good-Time Girl": Dangerous Sexualities as a Threat to National Health.' In *Formations of Nation and People*, edited by James Donald, 131–151. London: Routledge.

Bocock, Robert. 1997. 'Choice and Regulation: Sexual Moralities.' In *Media and Cultural Regulation*, edited by Kenneth Thompson, 69–116. London: Sage.

Buckingham, David. 2000. *After the Death of Childhood: Growing Up in the Age of Electronic Media*. Cambridge: Polity.

Campaign. 1984. '*Just Seventeen*: Glory without the Schmaltz.' *Campaign*, June 11, 32–33.

Carter, Fan. 'It's A Girl Thing: Teenage Magazines: Lifestyle and Consumer Culture.' In *Ordinary Lifestyles: Popular Media, Consumption and Taste*, edited by David Bell and Joanne Hollows, 173–186. Maidenhead, UK: Open University Press.

Cohen, Stanley. 1972. *Folk Devils and Moral Panics: The Creation of Mods and Rockers*. London: MacGibbon & Kee.

Connolly, Matthew. 1994. 'Parents Win Apology over Sex Act Words.' *The Guardian*, March 25, 3.

Davies, Jessica. 'How Can This Porn Be Sold to a Girl of 11?' *The Mail on Sunday*, February 11, 8.

Denisoff, Dennis. 2008. *The Nineteenth-Century Child and Consumer Culture*. London: Ashgate.

Department of Health. 1998. 'Tessa Jowell Calls on Teen Magazines to Work in Partnership with Government.' Press Release no: 98/194.

Drotner, Kirsten. 1988. *English Children and Their Magazines, 1751–1945*. New Haven: Yale University Press.

Drotner, Kirsten. 1992. 'Modernity and Media Panics.' In *Media Cultures: Reappraising Transnational Media*, edited by Michael Skovmand and Kim Christian Schroder, 42–62. London: Routledge.

Dunae, Patrick. 1980. 'Boys' Literature and the Idea of Empire, 1870–1914.' *Victorian Studies* 24: 105–121.

Durham, Martin. 1991. *Sex and Politics: The Family and Morality in the Thatcher Years*. Basingstoke, UK: Macmillan.

Foucault, Michel. 1984. *The History of Sexuality: An Introduction*. Translated by Robert Hurley. London: Penguin.

Gamman, Lorraine, and Margaret Marshment. 1988. *The Female Gaze: Women as Viewers of Popular Culture*. London: The Women's Press.

Gough-Yates, Anna. 2000. '"Sweet Sell of Sexcess": The Production of Young Women's Magazines and Readerships in the 1990s.' In *Ethics and Media Culture: Practices and Representations*, edited by David Berry, 225–247. Oxford: Focal Press.

Gough-Yates, Anna. 2003. *Understanding Women's Magazines: Publishing, Markets and Readerships*. London: Routledge.

Hartley, John. 1998. 'Juvenation: News, Girls and Power.' In *News, Gender and Power*, edited by Cynthia Carter, Gill Branston, and Stuart Allan, 47–70. London: Routledge.

Hansard. HC. 1994. March 11. Cl. 437–438. London: HMSO.

Hansard. HC. 1996. February 6. Cl. 146–147. London: HMSO.

Hall, Stuart. 1988. *The Hard Road to Renewal.* London: Verso.

Hall, Lesley A. 2000. *Sex, Gender and Change in Britain since 1800.* Basingstoke, UK: Macmillan.

Heeks, Laura. 1996. 'Safety in Knowledge.' Letters to the Editor. *The Guardian,* April 2, 8.

Hollows, Joanne. 2000. *Feminism, Femininity and Popular Culture.* Manchester University Press.

McRobbie, Angela. 1991. *Feminism and Youth Culture.* Basingstoke, UK: Macmillan.

McRobbie, Angela. 1982. '*Jackie:* An Ideology of Adolescent Femininity.' In *Popular Culture: Past and Present: A Reader,* edited by Tony Bennett, Graham Martin, and Bernard Waites, 263–83. London: Croom Helm.

McRobbie, Angela. 1996. '*More!* New Sexualities in Girls' and Women's Magazines.' In *Cultural Studies and Communications,* edited by James Curran, David Morley, and Valerie Walkerdine, 172–194. London: Arnold.

Moir, Jan. 1994. 'Bike Sheds Revisited.' *The Guardian,* March 30, 8.

Norman, Margot. 1994. 'Too Sexy for a Minister.' *The Times,* March 25, 16.

Pilcher, Jane, and Stephen Wagg, eds. 1996. *Thatcher's Children? Politics, Childhood and Society in the 1980s and 1990s.* London: Falmer Press.

Springhall, John. 1999. *Youth, Popular Culture and Moral Panics: Penny Gaffs to Gangsta Rap 1830–1996,* Basingstoke, UK: Palgrave Macmillan.

Thompson, Rachel. 1993. 'Unholy Alliances: The Recent Politics of Sex Education.' In *Activating Theory: Lesbian, Gay, Bisexual Politics,* edited by Joseph Bristow and Angie Wilson, 219–244. London: Lawrence & Wishart.

TMAP. 1996. *Guidelines on Sexual Content of Teenage Girls' Magazines.* London: Periodical Press Association.

Wagg, Stephen. 1996. '"Don't Try to Understand Them": Politics, Education and the New Education Market.' In *Thatcher's Children? Politics, Childhood and Society in the 1980s and 1990s,* edited by John Piltcher and Stephen Wagg, 8–28. London: Falmer Press.

Walkerdine, Valerie. 1997. *Daddy's Girl: Young Girls and Popular Culture.* Basingstoke, UK: Macmillan.

Walkowitz, Judith R. 1992. *City of Dreadful Delight: Narratives of Sexual Danger in Late-Victorian London.* London: Virago.

Weale, Sally. 1996. 'Publishers Fight Curb in "Explicit Sex" in Teenagers' Magazines.' *The Guardian,* February 6, 2.

Wellings, Kaye. 1996. *The Role of Teenage Magazines in the Sexual Health of Young People.* Department of Public Health and Policy, for TMAP. London: Periodical Press Association.

White, Cynthia. 1970. *Women's Magazines, 1693–1968.* London: Michael Joseph.

Winship, Janice. 1987. 'A Girl Needs to Get Street Wise: Magazines for the 1980s.' In *Looking On: Images of Femininity in the Visual Arts and Media,* edited by Rosemary Betterton, 25–39. London: Pandora.

16 Fantasies, Factions and Unlikely Feminist Heroines in Contemporary Heritage Films

Maggie Andrews

INTRODUCTION: ROYAL AND ARISTOCRATIC FANTASIES AND FACTIONS IN THE WAKE OF PRINCESS DIANA

Since the 1980s, and especially in the last twenty years, women's history, in popular culture if not necessarily in the academy, has become increasingly mainstream, no longer 'hidden from history' (Rowbotham 1977). There are now a range of pleasurably consumable pasts offered to multifarious viewing publics, as women's history can be identified in: museums, popular fictions, films, television drama and documentaries, websites, popular newspapers and magazines. Women's history in Britain has a significant tradition outside the academy, and organizations such as the Women's History Network bring together amateur and professional historians. It should therefore be of no surprise that the boundaries between popular and academic history have become blurred in television programmes such as Lucy Worsley's *If Walls Could Talk* (BBC 2012) and Amanda Vickery's *At Home with the Georgians* (BBC 2011) or in biographies such as Linda Colley's *The Ordeal of Elizabeth Marsh: How a Woman Crossed the Seas and Empires to Become Part of World History* (Harper Perennial 2008) and Ffion Hague's *The Pain and Privilege: The Women in Lloyd George's Life* (2009). The popularity in recent years of biographies and autobiographies in libraries and bookshops, and television and film biopics which focus upon the personalization of the past are all manifestations of the phenomenon of women's history as leisure and pastime, a phenomenon which can be identified in television series such as *The Women We Loved* series (BBC 2009), with episodes on the lives of Gracie Fields and Enid Blyton, and in the recent film *Iron Lady* (2012) which explored Margaret Thatcher's life.

Each of the three royal (or at least aristocratic) heritage films which this chapter focuses upon, *The Duchess* (2008), *The Other Boleyn Girl* (2008) and *Young Victoria* (2009), use individual and privileged lives as prisms for the exploration of women's history. The need for films to appeal to a wider audience than academic history necessitates both compromise and challenge, for to get into bed with the media is to embrace the pressures and restraints of their institutional practices, competitive market forces and the pressure for profit. Thus the tendency, as Sanello (2003) points out, is that: 'Complex economic and social issues are pureed into easily digestible bits of information intended for consumption by Hollywood's most sought after demographic: the lowest common denominator' (quoted in Hughes-Warrington 2007, xi–xii), although it could be argued that selectivity and simplification is in the nature of all history and life writing and the question is one of degree. Indeed, these three films also suggest that there is scope for some optimism about the relationship between film and history. In the pursuit of popular audiences these texts were necessarily polysemic, open to a range of interpretations and readings which encouraged ethical debate and engagement on issues of both power and gender alongside the inter-relationship of past and present.

The Duchess (2008) was based upon Amanda Foreman's 1998 award-winning biography of Georgiana, Duchess of Devonshire, and focussed upon her celebrity status, her position as a fashion icon, her affair with Charles Grey and centrally her and her husband's relationship with Bess, Lady Foster. *The Other Boleyn Girl* (2008) is an adaptation of Philippa Gregory's faction novel loosely based on the relationships between Anne Boleyn, her sister Mary and Henry VIII. Finally *Young Victoria* (2009), which was an idea pitched by the Duchess of York and produced by Martin Scorsese, narrated Queen Victoria's teenage years, early reign and romance with Prince Albert. Geared to a youth market, it portrayed Victoria as sassy, both an ordinary and extraordinary teenager (a portrayal familiar to many from *Buffy the Vampire Slayer* (Twentieth Century Fox 1997–2003)). This representational practice, a merging of the ordinary and the extraordi-nary, can also be identified in the portrayal of celebrities within magazines and is thus familiar to the target audience.

The interest in these films, most particularly *The Duchess*, must be seen as linked to the extensive media coverage of Princess Diana in the 80s and 90s when as Paglia suggests Princess Diana was 'possibly the most powerful image in the world of popular culture today' (1994, 318). The coverage of not only her public engagements and charity work but also her private life, established the royal family's personal lives as a national soap opera. As the royals were interpellated by the general public as celebrities, the celeb-rity status of past royals were used to sell films which starred wealthy and equally privileged contemporary celebrities such as Keira Knightley and Scarlett Johansson. In considering the celebrity status of the 'historical' figures portrayed in these films it is useful to draw upon a constructionist view of celebrity (see Alasuutari 1999; Evans and Hesmondhalgh 2005), which suggests audiences may take up shifting, unstable and fleeting posi-tions with respect to celebrity. Arguably these three unlikely feminist hero-ines, a queen, an aristocrat's wife and a Tudor king's lover do not elicit a position of resistance or identification in the audience; rather they served as catalysts for audiences to engage with ideas about relations of power and gender politics.

All three films' construction of their historical characters rests upon their utilization of narrative tropes which, like the discursive formations around Princess Diana, as Jude Davies argues, borrowed from second wave feminism and include: victimisation, life story as empowerment and the 'emergence of femininity from private and domestic life into the public sphere' (2001, 94). Arguably, however, *The Young Victoria*, perhaps mindful of appealing to a younger audience, abandoned the trope of victimhood and replaced it with the trope of girl power. As Orbach has suggested, Princess Diana's celebrity status and the tropes of feminism meant she feminized the public sphere, although it is worth pointing out that the private and public divide established so firmly in nineteenth century bourgeois culture (Davidoff and Hall 1987) was not so neatly divided for the hereditary monarchy and aristocracy—where fortune and thrones rest upon, to put it bluntly, 'who fucks who'. As Hartley points out—'their continuing legitimacy depends on the sleeping arrangements of one man and one woman' and thus 'the sexual comportment of the heirs to the throne is not at all a matter of their private sexual preferences, but is something that cuts to the core of the constitution' (1996, 11). Indeed, the significance of women's private/public role as a breeder of children was a preoccupation in each of the three films, hence as the Duke of Norfolk explains to Mary Boleyn in *The Other Boleyn Girl* 'If you sleep with the king you'd better get used to talking about it'.

Arguably this fluidity between public and private in the royal/aristocratic drama is appealing in the era of confessional and therapeutic culture in which public and private are merged in the media spheres of *The Jeremy Kyle Show*, tabloid newspapers, Facebook, *OK!* magazine, the tabloids and victimographies. In what has been described as the 'Genderquake' of the 1997 election (Wilkinson 1994), the New Labour Politics of Blair's government was not seen to 'respect the polarity between public and private'; rather, it was perceived to appropriate 'the language of affection, emotion, intimacy'. As Orbach suggested: 'New Labour certainly presents itself as female, it uses the language of compassion, forgiveness, apology, understanding and nurturing . . . It wants to be loved' (1998 in Harper 2009). Indeed, the desire to be loved at private and public levels—to become the 'Queen of Hearts' or 'People's Princess', to be a celebrity, seeps through all three of these texts. The young Queen's shaky public approval is a cause for concern amongst her ministers in a period of social turmoil in *Young Victoria*, whilst Georgiana in *The Duchess* craves public and private admiration. The most overt use of the Diana narrative is *The Duchess*; its publicity and script borrowed mercilessly from the mythologies and catchphrases that surrounded Diana, the comment in the film 'everyone in England is in love with the duchess except her husband' surrounded Princess Diana and the publicity tagline for *The Duchess* trailers. 'There were three people in this marriage' comes straight from Diana's famous *Panorama* interview (November 20, 1995), which Campbell suggests alongside the

Andrew Morton book (1992) were pivotal moments in calling the monarch to account by making their private lives very public (1999). The exaggeration of the age gap between the Duke and Duchess—not 8 years but closer to the 17 years between Charles and Diana, the Duke's staid conventionality and extra-marital relationships serve to merge the characters of the Duchess and Princess Diana and beg the question: whose life story is the audience consuming? Thus films such as *The Duchess* serve to emphasize the multiplicity of lives that emerge in reading, writing and representing life stories (Eakin 1999).

IN DEFENSE OF HERITAGE FILMS AND THEIR SCOPE TO CREATE 'GENDER TROUBLE'

It is important to consider, briefly, the specificity of the film as a medium for presenting the past and portraying private life for public consumption. Film viewing involves sitting with strangers in a public place voyeuristically gazing at what purports to be an individual's private intimate activities; it emphasizes the personal, the melodramatic and the intimate, otherwise usually reserved not only for the private sphere, but often behind the closed doors of the bedroom. Whilst broadcast media and print media also promise intimate, supposedly hidden, and spontaneous insights into their subjects' personal lives for public consumption, these mediums belong to and primarily focus on the mundane and every day of life stories. Alternatively the cinema, as Christian Metz pointed out, is a dreamlike experience; the viewer's relative size towards, and powerlessness over, the images on the screen places them in a childlike world in which fantasy and the extraordinary play a constitutive role (1990). Hence the appeal of aristocratic and royal heroines; the 'past' or rather a range of pasts (not necessarily recognizable to academic historians) contribute a repertoire of settings for fantasies, from which cinematic dreamscapes have been structured since the early 1900s. These operate alongside or even overlap with, for example, the gothic in Dracula films or the supernatural, science fiction and the geographically exotic.

Critics such as Andrew Higson (1995) have singled out heritage versions of the past in costume dramas, such as the Merchant Ivory Films of the 1980s, for particular criticism, suggesting they offer a commodification of the past, providing the audience with a prettified and politically conservative predictable package to accompany their popcorn and Coke. Certainly the heritage dreamscape is a prettified past, a fantasy with, for example, perfect teeth, few if any physical disfigurements or facial blemishes and elaborate costumes, but this should be seen perhaps more as a critique of contemporary social and cultural conditions rather than a commentary on the past (Wheeler 1994). The visual style of heritage texts has to be constructed to be recognizable and appear sufficiently authentic to the viewing public. In other words, in the post-modern world of popular history, the past's authenticity is established first and foremost in relation to other representations of the past on television or in films (Noakes 1998, 12). Furthermore, these representations are framed by the marketing role that films play for tourist sites and stately homes which provide the locations; Keddleston Hall, Hardwick Hall, Blenheim, Arundel Castle, Chatsworth House and the Royal Crescent at Bath make frequent appearances in the three films under discussion and provide these visitor attractions with useful and well-used publicity hooks in the months after their release.

Whilst Jeremy de Groot argues the past of heritage texts are 'homogenous, class ridden, visually rich and viewed through the twin lenses of quality and authenticity' (2009, 212) Samuel has noted the critical disdain heritage productions often receive may say something about the status of their predominantly female and queer audiences in contemporary culture (1996). It may therefore be useful to heed Claire Monk and Amy Sargeant's (2002) challenge to the all-too-easy dismissal of heritage films and instead argue there is a need for a more complex engagement with heritage texts and their audience appeal. Arguably, although set in a period of time when women were economically and politically more powerless than now, their appeal to female and queer audiences lies in part at least in drawing attention to the construction and performance of gender and to challenges and deconstructions of gendered power relationships that these texts prompt through their visual style. The display and pageantry of historical representations of royalty and the aristocracy and the camera's fetishisation of costume, hair and dress all lead to a slippage towards exaggerated, disruptive, tongue-in-cheek representations of gender. In so doing they draw attention to the constructedness of gender, its unnaturalness and the performance of gender scripts to produce what Butler describes as 'Gender Trouble' (1999). Some scenes in these films portray protagonists actually learning their scripts; for example, in *The Other Boleyn Girl*, the sisters are schooled for their parts in the public and private worlds of the Tudor court, while in *Young Victoria* a role reversal in gender scripts occurred. Albert is portrayed being instructed by his tutor in the British political system, dancing the waltz and learning Victoria's favorite operas and books in order to make him a desirable suitor for Victoria. This further serves to emphasize the unnaturalness and constructedness of gender as the visual spectacle of costume and clothing does.

Exaggeratedly pinched-in waists and heaving breasts in *The Other Boleyn Girl*, the corseted and bustled silhouettes of women in *The Young Victoria* and excessive hair with tall feathers worn by Georgiana in *The Duchess* all draw attention to how gender is a construction, rather than 'natural'. Furthermore, 'Royalty', like celebrity, is often seen as a public performance juxtapositioned against a private authentic self which film, like autobiography and biography, suggest the audience or reader is being given privileged access to. However, because of the public significance of royal childbearing and the symbolic maternal roles in terms of nationhood assigned to royal women, the private and public are made fluid—suggesting there is a performativity involved in all gender scripts. Indeed, Wilson suggests fashion 'creates a space in which the normative nature of social practices, always so intensely encoded in dress, may be questioned' (1990, 211). In *The Duchess*, an exchange takes place between the Duke and Duchess of Devonshire on their wedding night, when he literally cuts her out of her garments saying: 'For the life of me I can never understand why women's clothes must be so damned complicated', to which the Duchess replies: 'It's just our way of expressing ourselves I suppose. You have so many ways of expressing yourselves where we make do with our hats and our dresses'. The scene serves both to emphasize the performance and the politics of clothing, the link between Georgiana and Princess Diana as the fashion icon of their eras and that consumption and costume are areas of deliberate female identity construction.

HISTORICAL 'GENDER TROUBLE' CREATES UNLIKELY FEMINIST HEROINES

Narratively, all three films suggest that an acceptance of the limitations of historically and culturally specific gender scripts is the safest course of action. However, cinematically (in the camera work, lighting, screen composition, costume, etc.) they celebrate women who were ambitious, clever, actually or nearly out of control, reckless, difficult, spirited and pleasure seeking. For it is such women, these unlikely feminist heroines like Princess Diana, who were and remain a source of fascination and pleasure for the viewing public. It is when the heroines were rejecting, redefining, renegotiating and rallying against their ascribed roles that they offer the scope for cultural citizenship, 'the process of bonding and community building, and reflection on that building, that is implied in partaking of the text related practices of reading, consuming, celebrating and criticizing offered in the realm of (popular) culture' (Hermes 2005, 10). One of the communities that the audience, perhaps particularly the older audience, could bond with in consuming these heritage texts is second wave feminism. There are points in all the films where the audience is offered nostalgic images and fragments of a feminism that although culturally familiar had by the new millennium become marginalized, perhaps seen as belonging to the past, no longer needed in what was apparently a post-feminist era. Nevertheless, daring and courageous acts of 'feminist heroism' occur when, for example, Georgiana in *The Duchess*, however briefly, refuses, even for the sake of her children, to bend to her husband's demand that she end her affair with Grey and return to him. A similar moment occurs when Mary Boleyn defies the King's injunction and marches into the Tudor Court and scoops up her niece, the future Elizabeth the first, in *The Other Boleyn Girl*. As

Harper points out, film culture contains fossils from the past which, utilizing Gramsci, she suggests enable viewers to recognize themselves as the product of 'the historical processes' and which leave 'an infinity of traces' (Harper 1997, 164). For some of the audience to these films, fossils of feminism offered the pleasures of recognition. There was also scope for the audience to reflect on other communities linked to different femininities circulating in the new millennium; the teenage girl in *Young Victoria*, the wronged wife in *The Duchess* or the jilted lover and desperate mother in *The Other Boleyn Girl*.

Like many heritage texts, these films explored ethical debates about power, its basis, its use and abuse and its relationship to issues of gender, sexuality and ideals of freedom as seen when Georgiana in *The Duchess* debates freedom with Fox, a fellow Whig.

Georgiana: I have great sympathy with your sentiments in general but I fail to fully comprehend how far we—the Whig party that is—are fully committed to the concept of freedom.

Fox: We intend to extend the vote.

Georgiana: To all men?

Fox: Oh Heavens no but certainly to more men, freedom in moderation.

Georgiana: Freedom in moderation?

Fox: Precisely.

Georgiana: I am sure you are full of the best of intentions but I dare say I would not spend my vote, if I had it of course, on so vague a statement. One is either free or one is not. The concept of freedom is an absolute. After all one cannot be moderately dead or moderately loved or moderately free it must always remain a matter of either/or.

Here the Duchess champions the ideals of freedom, romantic love and universal suffrage whilst drawing attention to women's disenfranchisement in the eighteenth century, and by association providing a fragmentary reference to women's suffrage campaigns and their place in twentieth century feminism. In *Young Victoria*, with its intended appeal to a younger demographic, freedom was perceived in terms of escape from Victoria's mother and her pseudo step-father, her mother's advisor, Jon Conroy. However, in an exchange Victoria has with her deceased Uncle's wife, Princess Adelaide, it is suggested that freedom, even for those who appear to have the power of wealth and status, has its limitations:

Victoria: Can't I be my own mistress for a while? Haven't I earned it?

Adelaide: You may dream of independence but you won't get it. From now on everyone will push you and pull you for their own advantage.

The ideal of freedom is compromised for Victoria by political maneuverings, and the text portrays her attempt to negotiate, with varying degrees of success, her way through these compromises. A more contemporary debate about freedom, the degree to which the needs, demands and obligations of family, children and relationships should curtail women's self–expression and self-determination, is raised by all texts. Importantly, as Jokes Hermes suggests, each of the films 'allows political issues to be raised' but serves to facilitate debate as 'the very strength of popular culture is that it is not a manifesto (2005, 11). Ethical debate about compromising individual freedom for relationships is achieved through the structural device of pairings in each text, in *The Other Boleyn Girl* between Anne and her sister Mary, in *The Duchess* between Georgiana and Bess and in *The Young Victoria* between Victoria and Albert. Narrative comparisons and dialogue between the characters explore different ethical positions in relation to choices and dilemmas. Thus Mary and Anne Boleyn are portrayed as pawns in their family's power games, and as competitors for Henry VIII's attentions. Mary is represented as having put family before herself, while by comparison Anne is more ambitious and selfish, accused by Mary of 'aiming too high'. Alternatively, in *The Duchess*, Bess explains to Georgiana that she is sleeping with the Duke because, as the most powerful and rich aristocrat in the land, he can help her get access to her children. Although Georgiana argues: 'There are limits to the sacrifices one makes for one's children' and Bess replies: 'No, there are no limits whatsoever', later in the film when threatened with losing access to her own children Georgiana gives up Charles Grey with the words' I cannot abandon my children'.

The ethical debates about power are brought into relief within the texts by the very scale of power which the aristocratic and royal protagonists are portrayed as possessing. In the face of such power even the questioning of its excess seems heroic. The Boleyn girls and Georgiana, Duchess of Devonshire are perhaps strangely similar to Princess Diana in being interpreted as conditional, marginal, even ambivalent in their identification with royal and aristocratic political power. Their marginality also ensured they were able to be removed, replaced or further marginalized for transgressions; Georgiana was threatened with social ostracism, Mary Boleyn banished from Court and Anne Boleyn beheaded.

Tensions over the containment of women within the private sphere are also a recurring theme; Mary Boleyn's fate is sealed by an early and long confinement for childbirth in *The Other Boleyn Girl*, Victoria is confined by her mother as a teenager in *The Young Victoria* while Georgina in *The Duchess* was confined to the domestic sphere until she bore a son. Georgiana on returning home after her affair with Grey describes her home as a prison. The term is also used in *The Young Victoria* to refer to the palace of her childhood. The royal or aristocratic 'home' was historically simultaneously a private and public place, a palace where the business of government was enacted or a site of political intrigue and planning for the Whig party in *The Duchess*. The exploration of constraints of home, the family and romance in film has been a particular preoccupation of melodrama within which, as Giddens suggests, romantic love was 'allied to women's subordination in the home and her relative separation from the outside world'. However, 'the development of such ideas was also an expression of women's power, a contradictory assertion of autonomy in the face of deprivation' (1992, 43).

The Duchess and *The Other Boleyn Girl* in particular draw upon melodramatic conventions. Their visual style, camera work, use of close-ups and music interweave to produce narratives of emotional intensity. In line with melodramatic narrative tropes, protagonists are victims of forces outside their control and romantic love is thwarted. Mary Boleyn's love for Henry VIII in *The Other Boleyn Girl* and Georgina's love for Grey in *The Duchess* end abruptly, while in *The Young Victoria* the structuring absence is Albert's early death at the age of 42 from typhus with the audiences very aware of the iconic image of Queen Victoria as a grieving widow. Romance within film often offers escapism from constraints, and romantic comedy in particular involves the retraining of masculinity when 'the heroine tames, softens and alters the seemingly intractable masculinity of her love object, making it possible for mutual affection to become the guideline for their lives together' (Giddens 1992, 46). Mutual affection is illusive in these more melodramatic texts. In *The Other Boleyn Girl* and *The Duchess* men were un-trainable—as the Duke of Devonshire exclaimed: 'I don't do deals. Why would I—I've got all the power.' In the gender reversal of *The Young Victoria* it was Victoria who was retrained: in one argument Albert withdrew from the room as Victoria impotently shouted after him: 'I am your queen and I am telling you to stay, you may not go, I order you to stay in this room.' The emotional, financial and at times violent power struggles that operated across public and private spaces at various points in the past rumble through all these texts but occasionally are brought into sharp relief, making it difficult for a contemporary audience to avoid issues of gendered power relations. The young Princess Victoria is manhandled by Fitzroy, both Anne Boleyn and Georgiana are raped. The rape scene in *The Duchess* is used to convey the underlying violence of a loveless marriage and the strong imperative to produce a male heir, but it raises issues of the historical authenticity of such texts. The very areas they are exploring—the gendered power battles of personal life and relationships—are not likely to be well documented.

AUTHENTICITY AND AUDIENCE

The Young Victoria slipped towards the realm of fantasy when Albert was injured saving Victoria from a gunman. The accepted historical narrative of this incident in which an eighteen-year-old youth with pistols in both hands unsuccessfully fired two shots at the Royal Carriage was abandoned. The filmic version firmly established Albert as Victoria's protector and was portrayed as pivotal in the negotiation of power within their relationship. It was soon followed by his role as her advisor being affirmed in a subsequent scene when their desks were placed together. This tendency to rewrite history for dramatic effect, concentrating subtle shifts in relationships into inauthentic events or dialogue is consistent with Sanello's suggestion that Hollywood cinema '[n]ever . . . lets historical truth get in the way of a good, two hour blockbuster that earns $200 million'; similarly, his argument that '[c]ommercial imperatives most often fuel cinematic rewrites of history' cannot be entirely dismissed (2003 xi–xii). Indeed even the Public Service Broadcaster, the BBC, adapting Kathryn Hughes's *The Short Life and Times of Mrs Beeton* (2006), had no qualms shifting from the suggestion that Mrs Beeton may have had a Venereal Disease to making this disease, rather than consumption, the cause of her death.

In critiquing authenticity, the degree to which it is the constructedness of text which engages the audience needs to be considered. While some of the more flagrant abandonment of historically verifiable 'facts' is sometimes perceived to be breaking faith with the audience, a complex process is at play. In the historical life story the narrative is predictable, the audience is aware of the fate of Anne Boleyn, and of Victoria and Albert's courtship, although they were perhaps not aware of the complexity of the fifth Duke and Duchess of Devonshire's domestic arrangements. A significant element of the audience's pleasure and engagement lies in seeing how the past is reconstructed. This fascination with the 'how' of reconstruction is fed by documentaries and museum and heritage site exhibitions on the making of heritage films including the exhibition which accompanied the release of *The Duchess* at the Duke of Devonshire's country house—Chatsworth in Derbyshire. Arguably, the representation of a historical life in each of these three films rests upon offering interpretations, engaging in debate about causation, suggesting a number of 'what ifs' for the audiences to engage with. The faction that such texts become is in part because of the focus on dialogue. The films recreate history that can rarely be written as it is located in imagining the unknowable—personal emotional responses and discussions. Historians can only offer conjectures as to how the conversation between the Duchess of Devonshire and her mother went when they first discussed the ménage à trois that Georgiana was living in with her best friend, and possibly lover, who also slept with the Duke. This approach grows naturally from the emphasis on 'empathy' which came to the fore in history teaching in schools around the 1980s, yet biographer Amanda Foreman describes *The Duchess* as having 'dramatic truth' and 'emotional authenticity', whilst the film makers talk about the film being 'based upon' Amanda Foreman's biography. Such films are episodic, as memory and dreams often are, and *The Duchess* was selective in its use of Foreman's research. Although Georgiana was frequently seen gambling, her crippling gambling debts are never referred to, nor are Bess's two illegitimate children fathered by the Duke. These omissions ensured both women were more sympathetic characters, and helped turn them into contemporary heroines and celebrities.

Philippa Gregory in discussing her Tudor novels, including *The Other Boleyn Girl*, argues:

> I am experimenting with a new way of approaching historical fiction. . . . It is based on rigorous historical research which forms the basis of the story, and then written in the first person, often in the present tense, in an attempt to take the reader into the real world of the Tudor court in an immediate and engaging way. Readers know the books are fiction: we cannot know what someone, dead five centuries ago was thinking and feeling (2009).

Her approach is problematic, given the books and films do by implication make truth claims (but it does point to one of the issues raised by these popular texts—the impossibility of writing the past in a way which is not discursively articulated through, by and in the twenty-first century. What is involved in the production of heritage film is a form of translation, initially linguistically, as audiences do not pay to go to a cinema for a lesson on fifteenth, eighteenth of nineteenth century language. However jarring some of the audience no doubt found Princess Victoria's use of 'Hello' to greet Prince Albert, it was an appropriate translation. More problematic is the translation of what Raymond Williams terms 'the structure of feeling' and 'the common sense' (1977) from one era to another so that the text operates within a discursive framework the audience can relate to. This requires elements of sameness with the audience's era—and some clear signifiers of difference confirming the historical past in which the film is set. Thus heritage films engage in a complex oscillation between the past and present, as historians do when undertaking research. However, films and academic historians work under different economic and institutional pressures and restraints and arguably a film's process of translation may have a democratising potential, providing audiences with 'languages' to construct and interrogate their own pasts consistent with Giddens' suggestion that at the end of the twentieth century 'the self today is a reflexive project—a more or less continuous interrogation of past, present and future' (1992, 30). Furthermore, Andre Bazin pointed out 'reality' or 'truth' in cinema cannot be separated from viewer engagement, something that relies upon the imagination (1967). In viewing historical films arguably the audience's imagination rests upon an engagement with the possibilities of difference from the present, imagining a life without modern technology or with very different assumptions to the contemporary culture in which they live. All three films frequently draw attention to historical difference, or spell out such differences. Cameras dwell on pre-car modes of transport, horses and carriages, or on the mechanics of writing with a quill and ink. Difference is frequently articulated by the attitudes towards, or the treatment of, women. The desirability of male as opposed to female children is at the heart of *The Other Boleyn Girl* and *The Duchess* in which Bess explained to Georgiana (and the audience): 'It is not illegal for a man to beat his wife with a stick unless the stick is thicker than his thumb.' Foreman's historical works did not portray Bess as an abused wife, so this is an interesting interjection that operates purely, I would suggest, to draw attention to the difference between women's social, cultural and legal position in the late eighteenth century and the present. These differences were entwined with patriarchal power as Ann Boleyn's mother points out in one of her many discursive critiques stating: 'women are traded like cattle for the advancement and amusement of men.' The audience was steered through their comparison of past and present by positively coded characters who shared contemporary values and 'common sense' assumptions, bridging the gap between past and present. In *The Duchess* Georgiana decided to breastfeed her first baby rather than have a wet nurse. When she explained, 'I will feed her. I am after all her mother', she both revealed the film's presentcentredness and courted audience identification.

CONCLUSION

It has been argued that *The Duchess*, *The Other Boleyn Girl* and *Young Victoria* present popular and pleasurable women's history in films which have both fragments of feminism and spaces in which audiences are encouraged to challenge and question gendered power relations and scripts. The films' success and the public support for Kate Middleton on her marriage to Prince William in 2011 and for the Queen in her subsequent diamond jubilee year suggest that women in the middle of a period of significant economic crisis can select the most unlikely heroines. The significance of the popularity of past and present royal or aristocratic women when taken together is that they all lean towards a perception, however inauthentic, of the past. It is no coincidence that these phenomena occurred as the New Labour project ended and the new predominantly male Conservative and Liberal Democrat Coalition government, led by David Cameron, moved British politics significantly further to the political right in 2010. These fragments of feminism, the ethical debates raised by heritage films, are one of the few discursive spaces open to women who want to question the exercise of power.

BIBLIOGRAPHY / SOURCES

Alasuutari, Pertti. 1999. *Rethinking the Media Audience*. London: Sage.
Bazin, Andre. 1967. *What Is Cinema?* Vol 2. Berkley: University of California Press.
Butler, Judith. 1999. *Gender Trouble*. Oxford: Routledge

Campbell, Bea. 1999. *Diana: How Sexual Politics Shook the World*. London: Women's Press.

Colley, Linda. 2008. *The Ordeal of Elizabeth Marsh: How a Woman Crossed the Seas and Empires to Become Part of World History*. London: Harper Perennial.

Davidoff, Leonora, and Catherine Hall. 1987. *Family Fortunes*. Oxford: Routledge.

Davies, Jude. 2001. *Diana, A Cultural History: Gender, Race, Nation and the People's Princess*. Basingstoke, UK: Palgrave Macmillan.

de Groot, Jeremy. 2009. *Consuming History*. Oxford: Routledge.

Eakin, Paul John. 1999. *How Our Lives Become Stories: Making Selves*. Ithaca, NY: Cornell University Press.

Evans, Jessica, and David Hesmondhalgh. 2005. *Understanding Media: Inside Celebrity*. Maidenhead, UK: Open University.

Foreman, Amanda. 1998. *Georgiana: Duchess of Devonshire*. London: Harper Collins.

Giddens, Anthony. 1992. *The Transformation of Intimacy: Sexuality, Love and Eroticism*. Cambridge: Polity Press.

Gregory, Philippa. 2009. Accessed May 7. http://www.philippagregory.com/.

Hague, Ffion. 2009. *The Pain and Privilege: The Women in Lloyd George's Life*. London: Harper Perennial.

Harper, Stephen. 2009. *Madness, Power and the Media: Class, Gender and Race in Popular Representations of Mental Distress*. Basingstoke, UK: Palgrave Macmillan.

Harper, Sue. 1997. 'Popular Film and Popular Memory: The Case of the Second World War' In *War and Memory in the Twentieth Century*, edited by Martin Evans and Ken Lunn. Michigan: Berg. pp163–174.

Hartley, John. 1996. *Popular Reality: Journalism, Modernism, Popular Culture*. London: Arnold.

Hermes, Jokes. 2005. *Re-Reading Popular Culture*. Oxford: Blackwell.

Higson, Andrew. 2003. *Waving the Flag: Constructing a National Cinema*. Oxford: Clarendon Press.

Hughes, Kathryn. 2006. *The Short Life and Times of Mrs Beaton*. London: Harper Perennial.

Hughes–Warrington, Marnie. 2007. *History Goes to the Movies: Studying History on Film*. Oxford: Routledge.

Metz, Christian. 1990. *Film Language: A Semiotics of the Cinema*. University of Chicago Press.

Monk, Claire, and Amy Sargeant. 2002. *British Historical Cinema*. Oxford: Routledge.

Morton, Andrew. (1992) 2003. *Diana: Her True Story*. London: Michael O' Mara Books.

Noakes, Lucy. 1998. *War and the British: Gender, Memory and National Identity*. London: I. B. Tauris.

Orbach, Susie. 1998. 'A Crying Shame.' *Marxism Today*, November 1998, 61–63.

Paglia, Camille. 1994. 'Diana Regina.' In *Vamps and Tramps: new essays by Camille Paglia*. USA New York : Vintage Books pp 163–172

Rowbotham, Sheilia. 1977. *Hidden from History: 300 Years of Women's Oppression and the Fight against It*. London: Pluto Press.

Samuel, Raphael. 1996. *Theatres of Memory: Past and Present in Contemporary Culture*. Vol. 1. Cambridge: Verso Books.

Sanello, Frank. 2003. *Reel v. Real: How Hollywood Turns Fact into Fiction*. Chicago: Taylor Publications. Quoted in Marnie Hughes-Warrington. 2007. *History Goes to the Movies*. Oxford: Routledge.

Wheeler, Wendy. 1994. 'Nostalgia Isn't Nasty—The Postmodernising of Parliamentary Democracy.' In *Altered States: Postmodernism, Politics and Culture*, edited by Mark Perryman, 64–78. London: Lawrence and Wishart.
Wilkinson, Helen. 1994. *No Turning Back: Generations and the Genderquake*. London: Demos.
Williams, Raymond. 1977. *Marxism and Literature*. Oxford Paperbacks.
Wilson, Elizabeth. 1990. 'These New Components of the Spectacle: Fashion and Postmodernism.' In *Postmodernism and Society*, edited by Roy Boyne and Ali Rattasi, 209–236. London: Macmillan.

FILMOGRAPHY AND TELEVISION PROGRAMMES

At Home with the Georgians. 2011. BBC.
Buffy the Vampire Slayer. 1997–2003. Twentieth Century Fox.
If Walls Could Talk. 2012. BBC.
Iron Lady. 2012. Pathé, Film4.
Panorama interview of Princess Diana. November 20, 1995. BBC.
The Duchess. 2008. Paramount Vantage, Pathé, BBC Films.
The Other Boleyn Girl. 2008. Columbia Pictures, Focus Features, BBC Films.
Young Victoria. 2009. GK Films.
Women We Loved. 2009. BBC.

Contributors

Professor Maggie Andrews, University of Worcester

Maggie Andrews is Professor of Cultural History and in the Institute of Humanities and Creative Arts at the University of Worcester. Her research covers the social and cultural history of twentieth century Britain and representations of the past and remembrance within popular culture. She has particularly focussed on the relationship between popular culture, domesticity and femininity and is the author of a feminist history of the Women's Institute movement, *The Acceptable Face of Feminism* (Lawrence and Wichart 1998), and more recently, *Domesticating the Airwaves: Broadcasting, Domesticity and Femininity* (Continuum 2012). She has co-edited a collection of essays exploring women's relationship with consumer culture in the twentieth century—*All the World and Her Husband* (Continuum 2000) with Mary Talbot –and *Lest We Forget: Remembrance and Commemoration* (History Press 2011) with Nigel Hunt and Charlie Bagot- Jewitt.

Dr Adrian Bingham, University of Sheffield

Adrian Bingham is a Senior Lecturer in Modern History at the University of Sheffield. His research has focused on the national popular press in the decades after 1918, examining the ways in which newspapers both reflected and shaped attitudes to gender, sexuality and class. His first monograph, *Gender, Modernity and the Popular Press in Inter-War Britain* (Oxford University Press 2004) explored press debates about femininity and masculinity in the inter-war period. His second book, *Family Newspapers? Sex, Private Life and the British Popular Press 1918–1978* (Oxford University Press 2009) discussed the role of the press as a source of information and imagery about sex, morality and personal relationships. He is co-director of the University of Sheffield's Centre for the Study of Journalism and History.

Dr Fan Carter, Kingston University

Fan Carter is a Principal Lecturer in Media and Cultural Studies at Kingston University. Her research focusses on the intersections between commercial constructions of femininity and lifestyle media. She is currently working on a study of 1960s magazines and the construction of 'new' femininities.

Dr Paul Elliott, University of Worcester

Dr Paul Elliott holds a PhD from the University of Essex and is subject leader for Film at the University of Worcester. He is the author of *Hitchcock and the Cinema of Sensations* (I. B. Tauris 2012), an introductory guide to the French psychoanalyst and activist Felix Guattari (I. B. Tauris 2012) and a forthcoming monograph on the British crime film (Auteur 2013). He has also published articles on film theory, philosophy and British cinema.

Janet Harrison, University of Worcester

Janet Harrison is Senior Lecturer in Art History and Theory at the University of Worcester. Her research is centred around women's art practices and feminist aesthetics specializing in early 20th century and modernist women, artists, writers and photographers. Currently, the Second World War photojournalism of Lee Miller and other women photographers engaged in this field has been the subject of research and reappraisal in the light of shifting theories around the issues of feminine optics, aesthetics, subjectivity and history.

Dr Mary Irwin, University of Warwick

Mary Irwin is currently the postdoctoral research fellow on a three-year AHRC research project, 'A History of Television for Women in Britain 1947–89', run jointly by Warwick and De Montfort Universities. She has written and published on early women's television and is currently researching women's relationships with television romantic situation comedy. Mary also has research interests in television documentary and television drama. Most recently, she has contributed to the first extended account of the BBC series *Life on Mars*—*Life on Mars: From Manchester to New York* (University of Wales Press 2012).

Dr Sallie McNamara, Southampton Solent University

Dr Sallie McNamara is a Senior Lecturer in Cultural and Media Theory at Southampton Solent University. Research interests are varied but focus on gender, class and the body, with projects looking at fashion and *Downton Abbey*, erotic fiction, and the glossy magazine. She is editor of collection, *(Re)Possessing Beauty: Politics, Poetics, Change* (Fisher Imprints 2014), which explores the performance of beauty and its transient nature.

Dr Kate Murphy, Bournemouth University

Kate Murphy is Senior Lecturer, Radio Production at Bournemouth University and a former radio practitioner who has a long association with women's history. She worked at the BBC for 24 years, predominantly as a senior producer on Radio Four Woman's Hour. In 2011, she completed her PhD thesis 'On an Equal Footing with Men? Women and Work at the BBC 1923–1939.' Now an academic at Bournemouth University, her research interests are women in inter-war Britain, the development of radio broadcasting, in particular programming for women, and the lives and careers of women who worked at the early BBC.

Gillian Murray

Gillian Murray is an early career researcher based at the Centre for Urban History at the University of Leicester and part-time lecturer at the University of Worcester. Her research interests include the development of visual technologies in the twentieth century, especially film and television, and the potential for moving images to provide historical evidence of the process of social and cultural change over time. Her doctoral thesis 'Women and the Work of Cultural Production in ATV's Regional Television News, 1956–1968' examined the parallel histories of the establishment of regional television news and the changing patterns of women's employment in the English Midlands. Analysing the points of intersection between these two historical processes provided new historical insight into the cultural production of 'ordinary' women and the pace of social change in women's lives in this era. She has also published on the employment of women at ATV in the *Journal of British Cinema and Television* in July 2013.

Dr Rachel Ritchie, Brunel University

Rachel Ritchie received her PhD in History from the University of Manchester in 2011. She is interested in the social and cultural history of Britain in the 1950s and 1960s, particularly how those usually excluded from conceptualisations of modernity (such as older women or those in rural areas) understood themselves as modern subjects. Her research focuses on women's organisations (the Women's Institute and Women's Co-operative Guild) and women's magazines, especially depictions of personal appearance (fashion, beauty, home-dressmaking) and the home (domestic consumption, interior design and decor). In 2012, she received the Clare Evans Prize for best new essay in the field of gender and history for an article on glamour and beauty in 1950s women's magazines. This will appear in *Women's History Review* in 2014.

Dr Kristin Skoog, Bournemouth University

Kristin Skoog is currently working as a Lecturer in Media (Broadcasting History) in the Media School at Bournemouth University where she is the Assistant Director of the Centre for Media History. She has an interest in the social and cultural impact of broadcasting, and a further interest in media history and popular culture. Her research is currently focused on radio and re-construction in post-war Britain, and in the history of women's radio in Europe. She completed her PhD thesis in 2010 at the University of Westminster (Communications and Media Research Institute), which focused on women's radio at the BBC 1945–1955.

Glenda Strong, Southampton Solent University

Glenda Strong is a Senior Lecturer in Interior Design Decoration at Southampton Solent University. After graduating in Architecture from the University of Natal in South Africa in 1993, Glenda worked for six years on a variety of high-end tourism projects in Namibia. During this time she developed an interest in Interior Design which she was able to take further on moving to southern California, between 1997 and 1999. In 2000, Glenda switched continents again, this time to Australia where she began working on small-scale boutique residential projects in Brisbane and lecturing and tutoring in Architecture and Interior Design at Queensland University of Technology. During thirteen years of practical experience in Architecture and Interior Design, combined with six years of lecturing, Glenda has cultivated an interest in the role of the architect, interior designer and the rehabilitation of the term 'decoration'.

Rosey Whorlow, University of Chichester

Rosey Whorlow is a Senior Lecturer in the Department of Media and Music at the University of Chichester. Her research interests include representations of women's motorcycling and motorcycle sub-cultures in the press and on film. Her current research projects include the pedagogical challenges of embedding employability into the Media Studies undergraduate curriculum. Rosey is also researching a biography of one of her motorcycling heroines, Muriel Hind.

Index